Sex Discrimination in Uncertain Times

Sex Discrimination in Uncertain Times

Edited by Margaret Thornton

ANU

THE AUSTRALIAN NATIONAL UNIVERSITY

E PRESS

ANU

E PRESS

Published by ANU E Press
The Australian National University
Canberra ACT 0200, Australia
Email: anuepress@anu.edu.au
This title is also available online at: http://epress.anu.edu.au/discrimination_citation.html

---

National Library of Australia
Cataloguing-in-Publication entry

Title: Sex discrimination in uncertain times / edited by Margaret Thornton.

ISBN: 9781921666766 (pbk.) 9781921666773 (eBook)

Notes: Includes bibliographical references.

Subjects: Sex discrimination against women--Australia
              Sex discrimination--Law and legislation--Australia.
              Sex discrimination in employment--Australia.

Other Authors/Contributors:
              Thornton, Margaret.

Dewey Number: 305.420994

Cover design and layout by ANU E Press

Cover image: Judy Horacek

Contents

Part I: A Silver Anniversary

Part II: Then and Now

Part III: Critiquing the *SDA*

Part IV: Equivocations of Equality

Part V: Women's Rights as Human Rights

Acknowledgments

The initiative for this collection arose from a conference held in Canberra in 2009 to celebrate the twenty-fifth anniversary of the federal *Sex Discrimination Act 1984* (*SDA*) and to take stock of the Act in light of contemporary developments. I thank the ANU College of Law for financial support to facilitate the Silver Anniversary Conference. Special thanks are extended to the College Outreach and Administrative Support Team (COAST)—Christine, Wendy, Kristian and Sarah—for administration of the conference, Bea Hogan of the College Research Support Team (CReST) for assistance with assembling the papers for publication, Vidhi Mahajan for research assistance, Jan Borrie for editorial work and the anonymous referees for their helpful comments.

I thank Old Parliament House, Canberra (now the Museum of Australian Democracy), for allowing me to use the House of Representatives Chamber for a dramaturgical performance of the *SDA* debates, 'The *SDA* and its Rocky Rite of Passage', at the opening of the conference. Warm thanks to my thespian colleagues, who played the historic roles, and to my former research associate, Dr Trish Luker, for assistance with the performance and the script. (A video of the performance can be viewed online at <http://law.anu.edu.au/coast/events/Sex_Discrim/conference.htm>.

I acknowledge the support of the Australian Research Council in funding a fellowship, which enabled me to organise the conference and prepare the papers for publication.[1]

I am particularly grateful to the Dean of the ANU College of Law, Professor Michael Coper, for his support and for providing me with a congenial environment in which to work.

I am also grateful to Judy Horacek for granting permission to reproduce the cartoon on the cover and to the ANU E Press for agreeing to publish the collection.

Last, but not least, I thank the contributors for their scholarly contributions and for their collegiality over the years in traversing the rocky road of the *SDA*.

Australian Government
Australian Research Council   ARC Discovery Project DP0664177

---

1   M. Thornton, EEO in a Culture of Uncertainty, (DP0664177).

Contributors

Sara Charlesworth

Sara Charlesworth is a Principal Research Fellow at the Centre of Applied Social Research at RMIT University. Her research focuses on gender inequality in employment at both the labour market and the organisational levels and she has undertaken research on pay equity, job quality, sex discrimination and working-time regulation. Sara is currently working on Australian Research Council-funded projects on sexual harassment and the impact of changing employment regulation on employee work/life balance as well as a Canadian Social Sciences and Humanities Research Council-funded project on cross-national comparisons of paid caring work in non-profit community services.

Beth Gaze

Beth Gaze is an Associate Professor at the University of Melbourne Law School, where she teaches and researches in anti-discrimination law, with a focus on feminist legal thought and women's rights. In 2008, she was a member of the Advisory Committee to the Gardner Review of Victoria's *Equal Opportunity Act*, and in 2009 she was a consultant to the Victorian Parliament's Scrutiny of Acts and Regulations Committee in its Review of the Exceptions and Exemptions in the *Equal Opportunity Act 1995*.

Ann Genovese

Ann Genovese is a legal historian who teaches at the Melbourne Law School. She works on the history and theory of the relationship between Australian law, the state and political culture. Her major projects focus on histories of Australian Indigenous peoples' engagement with law and histories of Australian feminism. Her most recent representative publications include (with Ann Curthoys and Alexander Reilly) *Rights and Redemption: Law, History, Indigenous Peoples* (UNSW Press, 2008) and, as contributing editor, Issue 95 of *Feminist Review: Transforming academies* (2010).

Reg Graycar and Jenny Morgan

Reg Graycar is a Professor of Law at the University of Sydney and a practising barrister. Jenny Morgan is a Professor of Law at the University of Melbourne and was Deputy Dean of the Law School from 2003 to 2007. Together (and separately) they have been involved in a number of law-reform activities. Both were part-time members of the Australian Law Reform Commission on its Equality Before the Law reference in the early 1990s; Jenny has been a consultant to the Victorian Law Reform Commission and is currently a member of the Victorian Sentencing Advisory Council and Reg was full-time Commissioner with the NSW Law Reform Commission in the latter part of last century. They are the authors of *The Hidden Gender of Law* (First edition, 1990; second edition, 2002) and of a number of articles/chapters on a range of topics, the central themes of which are equality and law reform. They have also been engaged recently with an Australian Research Council-funded research project entitled 'Changing Law/s, Changing Communities: A Study of Law Reform and its responses to rapid social and community change'.

Susan Harris Rimmer

Susan Harris Rimmer (BA[Hons]/LLB[Hons] UQ, SJD ANU) is a Visiting Fellow at the Centre for International Governance and Justice, Regulatory Institutions Network, The Australian National University. She is the Manager of Advocacy and Development Practice at the Australian Council for International Development (ACFID), the peak body for Australian development non-governmental organisations. She has previously worked for the UN High Commissioner for Refugees and the Parliamentary Library. She is a board member of UNIFEM Australia and has previously been president of the voluntary non-governmental organisation Australian Lawyers for Human Rights. Susan is the author of *Gender and Transitional Justice: The Women of Timor Leste* (Routledge, 2010).

Caroline Lambert

Caroline Lambert PhD is the Executive Director of YWCA Australia. She has published on women and human rights, particularly in the context of the Convention on the Elimination of All Forms of Discrimination Against Women. She is interested in the use of international human rights standards in domestic policy advocacy for women's equality.

Trish Luker

Trish Luker is an early career researcher working at the intersection of law, social sciences and the humanities. After completing her PhD at La Trobe University, she worked as a research associate for Margaret Thornton on the EEO in a Culture of Uncertainty project at The Australian National University.

In 2010, she took up a postdoctoral research fellowship at the University of Queensland. Her work draws on critical theory to investigate the reception of evidence in human rights claims.

Susan Magarey

Susan Magarey AM, FASSA, PhD is the founder of the Magarey Medal for Biography and Adjunct-Professor in History at Adelaide University. Her prize-winning biography of Catherine Helen Spence, *Unbridling the Tongues of Women*, is to be republished in 2010; her biography of Dame Roma Mitchell, *Roma the First*, which she wrote with Kerrie Round, is in its second imprint.

Archana Parashar

Archana Parashar is Associate Professor in Law at Macquarie University, Sydney. Her research interests focus on the potential of law to achieve social justice. She has written in the areas of critical legal theory, feminist legal theory, family laws and anti-discrimination laws. In her research, she relies on interdisciplinary approaches to critique legal theory. Her latest book is a co-edited volume, *Decolonisation of LegalKnowledge* (Routledge, 2009).

Simon Rice

Simon Rice is an Associate Professor and Director of Law Reform and Social Justice at the College of Law, The Australian National University, Canberra. He is a part-time judicial member of the NSW Administrative Decision Tribunal in the Equal Opportunity Division, and Chair of the ACT Law Reform Advisory Council. With Neil Rees and Kate Lindsay, he wrote *Australian Anti-Discrimination Law* (Federation Press, 2008).

Chris Ronalds

Chris Ronalds AM, SC is a Sydney barrister specialising in discrimination and employment law. She was closely involved with the development of the Sex Discrimination Bill and its subsequent passage through the Commonwealth Parliament. She has run various sex discrimination test cases exploring a myriad issues, including returning to work after maternity leave and working part-time.

Susan Ryan

Hon. Susan Ryan AO was responsible for the landmark *Sex Discrimination Act 1984* and the *Affirmative Action Act 1986*. From 1975 to 1988, she was Senator for the Australian Capital Territory and the first woman to hold a cabinet post in a federal Labor Government, serving as Minister for Education 1983–87 and Minister Assisting the Prime Minister on the Status of Women 1983–88. She is a Pro-Chancellor and council member of the University of New South Wales, chair of a major superannuation plan and chair of the Australian Human Rights Group, an organisation committed to a human rights act.

Marian Sawer

Marian Sawer AO is an Emeritus Professor in the School of Political Science and International Relations, The Australian National University, and Vice-President of the International Political Science Association. Her most recent book is the co-edited *Federalism, Feminism and Multilevel Governance* (2010). She has had a long association with the *Sex Discrimination Act*, since before it was born.

Belinda Smith

Dr Belinda Smith holds a Senior Lectureship in the Faculty of Law, University of Sydney. Her main field of research is anti-discrimination laws, with a focus on gender equity and workers with family responsibilities. In articles and chapters published in Australia, the United States and Japan, she has explored alternative regulatory tools and frameworks for promoting equality.

Margaret Thornton

Margaret Thornton is Professor of Law and Australian Research Council Professorial Fellow at The Australian National University. She has a longstanding interest in discrimination law, having taught and published extensively in the area since the late 1970s. She is a Fellow of the Academy of Social Sciences in Australia and a Foundation Fellow of the Australian Academy of Law.

Sharon H. Venne

Sharon H. Venne worked at the United Nations before the establishment of the Working Group on Indigenous Peoples in 1982. The background research to the many clauses in the Declaration on the Rights of Indigenous Peoples is included in her book *Our Elders Understand Our Rights: Evolving International Law regarding Indigenous Peoples*, (Theytus Books, Penticton, BC, 1999).

Helen Watchirs

Dr Helen Watchirs OAM was appointed the ACT Human Rights and Discrimination Commissioner in 2004. She is a member of the Federal Ministerial Advisory Council on Blood Borne Viruses and STIs. Dr Watchirs has worked for 28 years as a human rights lawyer and/or consultant including with the Federal Government and UN agencies, such as UNAIDS, the World Health Organisation (WHO), the International Labour Organisation (ILO), United Nations Development Programme (UNDP) and the Office of the High Commissioner for Human Rights. Her PhD in human rights and master's in public law from The Australian National University focus on HIV/AIDS issues.

Irene Watson

Irene Watson is an Associate Professor at the University of South Australia and is the author of a number of articles and books on Aboriginal peoples and the law. She is currently completing a manuscript, 'Raw Law', for publication.

Preface

A Silver Anniversary

Anti-discrimination legislation in Australia has had a chequered history since its inception 40 years ago. Discrimination on the ground of sex, race, sexuality, disability, age or other characteristic of identity was not recognised by the common law. Its proscription was entirely a statutory creation and the legislation has been beset with uncertainty and timorousness, which have contributed to its volatility. This is clearly apparent in regard to sex discrimination, as differential treatment between the sexes was historically and philosophically viewed as 'natural'. The anxiety underpinning the legal proscription of discrimination is in evidence in the parliamentary debates on the *Sex Discrimination Act 1984* (Cth) (*SDA*). While some of the views of the opponents can appear quaint in the twenty-first century—albeit only 25 years after they were articulated—the commitment by the state to anything other than formal equality continues to be contentious.

Indeed, the years since the enactment of the *SDA* have been marked by struggles for substantive equality (equality of outcome) for women and for members of minority groups still consigned to otherness within the polity. Such struggles have sometimes succeeded in eliciting official responses, usually in the form of inquiries and reports rather than legislative change, and the small gains attained have all too often resulted in a backlash.

Recent government activity includes a review of the *SDA* in 2008,[1] the *National Human Rights Consultation Report* in 2009[2] and the workplace reforms incorporated in the *Fair Work Act 2009* (Cth). The review of the *SDA* raised the possibility of an Equality Act—an avenue that has been followed in the United Kingdom[3]—which poses complex questions regarding the interaction between the *SDA* and other federal anti-discrimination legislation, as well as State and Territory legislation. In 2010, the federal government announced that the Commonwealth anti-discrimination laws, including the *SDA*,[4] would be

---

1 Australian Senate Committee on Legal and Constitutional Affairs, *Effectiveness of the* Sex Discrimination Act 1984 *in Eliminating Discrimination and Promoting Gender Equality*, Commonwealth of Australia, Canberra, 2008.

2 Commonwealth of Australia, *National Human Rights Consultation Report*, Attorney-General's Department, Canberra, 2009 [*Brennan Report*] .

3 *Equality Act 2010* (UK).

4 The other Acts are the *Racial Discrimination Act 1975* (Cth) (*RDA*), the *Disability Discrimination Act 1992* (Cth) (*DDA*) and the *Age Discrimination Act 2004* (Cth) (*ADA*).

incorporated into 'one single comprehensive law'.[5] The prospect of a federal Human Rights Act was also temporarily on the agenda, although the Attorney-General announced in 2010 that the idea of a national charter of human rights had been shelved.[6]

This collection of essays traces the life of the *SDA*, paying particular attention to the socio-political context in which the *SDA* was conceived and debated. While South Australia, Victoria and New South Wales all proscribed sex discrimination earlier than the Commonwealth through the enactment of omnibus anti-discrimination Acts in the 1970s, with other States and Territories following in the 1990s, the special status attaching to national legislation within a federal compact inevitably becomes the primary focus of attention. Nevertheless, many of the observations made about the *SDA* apply also to State and Territory legislation. While there is an absence of harmonisation between jurisdictions, the same compensatory model is utilised, together with a similar ambit of operation and procedure. The individual complaint-based model of anti-discrimination is now showing signs of stress.[7] This is due partly to age but, more specifically, to contextual factors, including changes in the political climate, which have induced a move away from workers' rights to employer prerogative. Anti-discrimination legislation is extraordinarily sensitive to the political pulse of the time, a proposition I illustrate by reference to the area of employment from where the overwhelming preponderance of complaints under the *SDA*—91 per cent in 2008–09—emanate.[8]

The Market as the Measure of all Things

Neo-liberalism, which has become the dominant political philosophy of our time, has exerted a profound effect on the culture and practice of anti-discrimination law. Social liberalism, in which the legislation had its genesis and which reached its high point in Australia in the 1970s, evinced a concern for collective good, distributive justice and other egalitarian values associated with the welfare state. While this incarnation of liberalism was not opposed to the operation of the free market, its excesses were tempered by state regulation in the interests of the greater good.

---

5   Attorney-General Hon. Robert McClelland MP and Minister for Finance and Deregulation Hon. Lindsay Tanner MP, Reform of anti-discrimination legislation, Media release, 21 April 2010, Parliament House, Canberra. The Government Response to the Senate Report was tabled on 4 May 2010: < http://www.ag.gov. au >

6   Chris Merrit, 'A-G pulls plug on charter of rights', *The Australian*, 21 April 2010, p. 7.

7   It is notable that updated legislation was enacted in Victoria in 2010. See *Equal Opportunity Act 2010* (Vic.).

8   Australian Human Rights Commission, *Annual Report 2008–09*, s4.4.5, Australian Human Rights Commission, Sydney, 2009, <*http://www.humanrights.gov.au/about/publications/annual_reports/2008_2009/chap4.html#s4_4*>

The state is therefore central to the realisation of equality for women despite its fickleness, which is clearly evident when the political pendulum swings rightwards. The neo-liberal state is not in fact concerned with equality at all, but with its liberal twin—freedom—particularly the 'free' market and the freedom to maximise wealth. The inevitable result of untrammelled freedom and competition within the market is *inequality*, not equality.

Despite all the talk of deregulation and the privatisation of public goods associated with neo-liberalism, the state has not resiled altogether from its regulatory role but has transformed and adapted it. Instead of sustaining and promoting the common good associated with civil society, it has formed an intimate association with the market. Productivity and the maximisation of wealth, not just nationally, but globally, have become the primary aims of the neo-liberal state. Government has therefore been busy removing obstacles to facilitate the untrammelled operation of the market—such as centralised wage fixing and worker protections. Work intensification, casualisation and flexibility became the new norms during the period of the Howard Government in the 1990s. In contradistinction, egalitarianism, social justice and equity—the hallmarks of social liberalism—were treated as dispensable.

While neo-liberalism is thought of primarily in terms of the economy and the market, it has also exercised a profound effect on the social fabric of our society, to the extent that it has entered the very soul of the citizen.[9] Neo-liberal subjects are expected to promote themselves and take responsibility for their own lives. If they do not succeed, it is deemed to be their fault. This individualised focus deflects attention away from the collective harms of sexism, as well as racism, homophobia, ageism and ableism. As rational choice is the leitmotif of neo-liberalism and the social has been whittled away, there is an ever-contracting space within public discourses to accommodate critiques of discrimination. The history of inequality and the abuse of power are not only discomfiting within a neo-liberal milieu; critique has no use value in the market. The assumption is that it should be sloughed off in favour of applied knowledge. Indeed, feminism—with its critical eye always directed to the way things might be— was conveniently described by former Prime Minister John Howard as passé.[10] The social-liberal concern with anti-discrimination and equal employment opportunity (EEO) has also been depicted as cumbrous and old-fashioned. As a result, discourses involving the 'woman question' became de-gendered, desexualised and depoliticised.

---

9   Wendy Brown, *Edgework: Critical Essays on Knowledge and Politics*, Princeton University Press, NJ, 2005, p. 39.
10   Anne Summers, *The End of Equality: Work, Babies and Women's Choices in 21st Century Australia*, Random House, Sydney, 2003, p. 21.

While the Rudd Labor Government replaced the Howard Coalition Government at the end of 2007 and promised an end to the hardline policies of the Howard years, the political pendulum did not swing back to the social-liberal position, although a softening of some of neo-liberalism's more egregious manifestations could be detected. Even the global financial crisis of 2008–09 did not seriously challenge the love affair of the Australian state with the values of neo-liberalism. One must therefore ask what space is there within a neo-liberal climate for a critical sex discrimination discourse committed to equality and egalitarianism?

As testament to neo-liberalism's cynicism for anti-discrimination legislation, it is notable that a decline in the lodgment of complaints occurred during the Howard years. While the percentage of formal hearings was always low, the figure dropped to approximately 1 per cent of complaints, with a minuscule number of appeals having little chance of success for complainants, as Beth Gaze shows in her chapter. The High Court picture regarding sex discrimination is also dispiriting. After the initial trailblazing successes of *Wardley v Ansett*[11] and *Australian Iron & Steel*,[12] every anti-discrimination decision since Wik[13] has favoured the corporate respondent, supported by a narrow legalism.[14]*Amery*,[15] a representative complaint based on indirect sex discrimination, is a case in point. The shift away from the beneficent aims of anti-discrimination legislation has affected all grounds.[16]

The interpretative role of the courts during these years is a salutary reminder of the fact that all three branches of government—the legislature, the executive and the judiciary—are important sites for the constitution and reconstitution of sex discrimination. Hence, as I argued on the twentieth anniversary of the *SDA*,[17] we are not dealing with a finite variable that can be *eliminated* over time, as suggested by the wording of the Convention on the Elimination of All Forms of Discrimination Against Women (CEDAW). Sex discrimination is a slippery concept, tolerance for which depends on the socio-political mood of the moment. As long as 'the good of the economy' is permitted to trump the idea of gender justice, change will not occur. These essays seek to challenge what has become the prevailing orthodoxy.

---

11   *Ansett Transport Industries (Operations) Pty Ltd v Wardley* (1980) 142 CLR 237.

12   *Australian Iron & Steel Pty Ltd v Banovic* (1989) 168 CLR 165.

13   *Wik Peoples & Thayorre People v Queensland* (1996) 141 ALR 129.

14   Margaret Thornton, 'Sex Discrimination, Courts and Corporate Power' (2008) 36(1) *Federal Law Review* 31.

15   *New South Wales v Amery* (2006) 226 ALR 196.

16   For example: *IW v City of Perth* (1997) 191 CLR 1; *Qantas Airways Limited v Christie* (1998) 193 CLR 280; *X v Commonwealth* (1999) 200 CLR 177; *Purvis v New South Wales (Department of Education and Training)* (2003) 217 CLR 92.

17   Margaret Thornton, 'Auditing the *Sex Discrimination Act*' in Marius Smith (ed.), *Human Rights 2004: The Year in Review*, Castan Centre for Human Rights Law, Monash University, Melbourne, 2005.

The Collection

Part One: A Silver Anniversary

The addresses by Watchirs, Ryan and Ronalds at the launch of the conference throw light on the genesis of the *SDA* and subsequent chapters. They also give voice to all those (mainly women) who played a prominent role in the struggle for gender equality, ensuring that their voices are not entombed in silence.

Dr Helen Watchirs, ACT Human Rights and Discrimination Commissioner, pays tribute to the contribution of a line of federal sex discrimination commissioners over 25 years, as well as presenting an overview of the state of play in regard to sex discrimination. In addition to summarising the main points of the Senate Report on the *SDA*, she draws attention to the roller-coaster ride of gender equality, for just as one issue is addressed, another problem emerges on the scene.

The Hon. Susan Ryan was the major political force behind the *SDA*. As a senator in 1981, she introduced the first Private Member's Bill, which lapsed. When Labor came into power in 1983, she was able to introduce a revised bill. While the *SDA* has often been criticised for being weak and wimpish, Susan Ryan's comment succinctly exemplifies the adage that 'politics is the art of the possible'. Her view—a salutary one in difficult times—is that law reform should not be deferred indefinitely until the ideal legislative instrument has been attained.

Chris Ronalds SC, who drafted the Sex Discrimination Bill, echoes Ryan's view that a pragmatic incremental approach to legislation is the appropriate way to proceed. Ronalds also acknowledges the contribution of another distinct group of women pioneers within the annals of the *SDA*—namely, those who gave their names to the landmark test cases that validated the passage of the Act.

Margaret Thornton and Trish Luker's chapter focuses on the rhetoric of the parliamentary debates of 1983–84, which highlights the deep anxiety concerning sex roles and the patriarchal family that surrounded the passage of the *SDA*. They suggest that the progressive legislative initiative induced a backlash or sense of *ressentiment* (to use Nietzsche's term) on the part of conservatives, which manifested itself in the neo-liberal swing in favour of conservatism that occurred soon afterwards.

Part Two: Then and Now

Ann Genovese presents a prehistory of the *SDA* through an examination of the genesis of gendered law reform. She argues that early 1970s feminism, in the main, was not intellectually or politically centred on questions of the law and legislative reform but on praxis. She shows how feminist engagement with the state evolved from practical movements and New Left politics, such as Women Behind Bars. The chapter raises questions about the way contemporary feminist legal thinking could have become overly concerned with the lego-centric at the expense of the grassroots.

Marian Sawer shows that women's struggle for equality did not end with the passage of the *SDA*. Rather, the Act presaged a continuing struggle to retain the status quo, despite the appearance of progress. Sawer shows how political shifts, including budget cuts and changes in industrial relations, have effected new manifestations of inequality, which are salutary reminders of the fact that any semblance of equality for women is tentative and contingent. Her text is illuminated by graphic images.

Susan Magarey similarly stands back to take a bird's-eye view of the trajectory of the *SDA*. In highlighting the significance of context, she alludes to the feminist discourses of the 1980s—women's liberation, the women's peace movement, women's studies and Indigeneity—to highlight the way the notion of the collective good has been eviscerated and replaced by individualism. The economic and environmental disasters of today are salutary reminders of the continuing relevance of the women's movement, not just as a question of justice for women, but for society as a whole.

Part Three: Critiquing the *SDA*

Beth Gaze overviews the experience of sex discrimination in the courts, where judges have tended to undervalue discriminatory harms. Drawing on the insights of social psychology, she argues that litigation is a limited mechanism for dealing with pervasive discrimination. She recommends that we move beyond the remedial model to pay attention to proactive measures, although she acknowledges that monitoring such schemes could prove difficult and expensive.

Sara Charlesworth identifies three distinct regulatory frameworks for dealing with sex discrimination at the federal level—the *SDA*, affirmative action and industrial relations—drawing attention to their weaknesses and limitations. She recommends, as an alternative to these modes, the decent work agenda proposed by the International Labour Organisation (ILO) as the basis of an integrated legislative framework. While gender equality necessarily lies at the heart of decent work for women, it has not received the attention it deserves. She argues that it be brought into the mainstream work agenda rather than being allowed to languish at the margins.

Caroline Lambert shows how the figures of the 'ideal worker' and the 'domestic care giver' are inscribed and reinscribed in gendered ways on the bodies of workers by virtue of the limitations of the *SDA* in addressing caring work. She focuses on the notion of the comparator, indirect discrimination and the concept of reasonableness to highlight the way a formalistic rather than a substantive approach to equality is perennially favoured, despite CEDAW's recognition of the importance of reproductive labour.

Part Four: Equivocations of Equality

Reg Graycar and Jenny Morgan examine a recent suggestion by the Senate Standing Committee on Legal and Constitutional Affairs that it might be timely to consider an Equality Act. They consider a number of questions: whether this proposal has any potential to enhance women's equality in Australia; whether it more readily addresses problems of intersectionality—the fact that women have a race, a sexuality or a multiplicity of identities that operate differently at different times and in different contexts; and whether such an approach would encourage a move beyond the complaint-based focus of traditional discrimination laws. They conclude by raising questions about the processes, the fora and the identity of the personnel engaged in the debate of these issues.

Simon Rice also considers the idea of an Equality Act, which was first raised by the Australian Law Reform Commission in its report that coincided with the tenth anniversary of the *SDA* and, again, in the Senate Committee Report on the *SDA* in 2008. Rice examines the law reform process underpinning the *Equality Act 2010* (UK) to consider what lessons Australia might learn from it. While there is much to be said for the positive duty in the UK Act, Rice emphasises that the enactment of an Equality Act ultimately depends on political will.

Belinda Smith turns to the Canadian equality jurisprudence to consider why the judicial approaches appear to be more robust than those favoured by Australian courts. Through a comparative analysis, she argues that the prescriptive wording of the Australian statutes has induced a technical and formalistic approach towards equality and discrimination. Leaving aside the fact that there is a constitutional guarantee of equality in Canada, Smith suggests that Australian reformist bodies could learn much from the Canadian approach.

Archana Parashar also focuses on the judicial role but her approach contrasts with that of Smith. Parashar is most concerned with the interpretative dilemmas that beset equality jurisprudence. She takes her cue from the post-structural insight that knowledge is always historically contingent. She argues that the attribution of meaning is not dependent on the words of the text alone but is informed by context, judicial subjectivity and responsibility, which involve choice. Parashar concludes by arguing that the interpretative role of judges should be linked to the critical and ethical education of law students.

Part Five: Women's Rights as Human Rights

The springboard for Susan Harris Rimmer's chapter is a speech made by Elizabeth Evatt on the twentieth anniversary of the *SDA*. Evatt argued that Australian law falls short of its obligations under CEDAW and other international instruments to provide equality rights and non-discrimination in regard to women. Harris Rimmer reviews progress in Australia in the past five years according to Evatt's criteria. She also celebrates the role of key figures—Evatt, Jane Connors, Andrew Byrnes and Helen L'Orange—who contributed to the creation of multilevel strategies to raise up Australian women and realise their rights.

Margaret Thornton considers whether a domestic human rights charter might assist in the realisation of substantive gender equality despite the fact that the discourse of human rights poses both a political and an epistemological dilemma for women. Although there has been a rhetorical shift from discrimination to human rights, it is apparent that there is still timidity about human rights at the domestic level. This does not bode well for the prospects of a charter addressing intersectionality challenges, such as sex plus race or sex plus sexuality. Thornton considers the Australian initiatives of the twenty-first century and illustrates her concerns with some examples from the United Kingdom.

Irene Watson and Sharon Venne acknowledge that all people are accorded the same right not to be discriminated against on the grounds of sex, but argue that this right is experienced differently by different people, and that the difference could be measured and scaled according to how close one's life is located to the centre of white privilege. They argue that the experience of discrimination by Aboriginal people means that the primary focus must be directed to the issue of race. Watson and Venne present a critique of the recent UN Declaration on the Rights of Indigenous Peoples as the key international human rights instrument. Their prognosis as to how valuable it might be is, however, not propitious in light of a return to assimilationist policies in Australia.

Bibliography

Books and articles

Brown, Wendy, *Edgework: Critical Essays on Knowledge and Politics*, Princeton University Press, NJ, 2005.

Merrit, Chris, 'A-G pulls plug on charter of rights', *The Australian*, 21 April 2010, p. 7.

Summers, Anne, *The End of Equality: Work, Babies and Women's Choices in 21st Century Australia*, Random House, Sydney, 2003.

Thornton, Margaret, 'Sex Discrimination, Courts and Corporate Power' (2008) 36(1) *Federal Law Review*, 31.

Thornton, Margaret, 'Auditing the *Sex Discrimination Act*' in Marius Smith (ed.), *Human Rights 2004: The Year in Review*, Castan Centre for Human Rights Law, Monash University, Melbourne, 2005.

Legislation

Age Discrimination Act 2004 (Cth)

Disability Discrimination Act 1992 (Cth)

Equality Act 2010 (UK)

Equal Opportunity Act 2010 (Vic.)

Racial Discrimination Act 1975 (Cth)

Cases

Ansett Transport Industries (Operations) Pty Ltd v Wardley (1980) 142 CLR 237

Australian Iron & Steel Pty Ltd v Banovic (1989) 168 CLR 165

IW v City of Perth (1997) 191 CLR 1

New South Wales v Amery (2006) 226 ALR 196

Purvis v New South Wales (Department of Education and Training) (2003) 21 CLR 92

Qantas Airways Limited v Christie (1998) 193 CLR 280

Wik Peoples & Thayorre People v Queensland (1996) 141 ALR 129

X v Commonwealth (1999) 200 CLR 177

Reports and miscellaneous primary sources

Attorney-General Hon. Robert McClelland MP and Minister for Finance and Deregulation Hon. Lindsay Tanner MP, Reform of Anti-discrimination Legislation, Media release, 21 April 2010, Parliament House, Canberra.

Australian Human Rights Commission, *Annual Report 2008–09*, Australian Human Rights Commission, Sydney, 2009, <http://www.humanrights.gov.au/about/publications/annual_reports/2008_2009/chap4.html#>

Australian Senate Committee on Legal and Constitutional Affairs, *Effectiveness of the* Sex Discrimination Act 1984 *in Eliminating Discrimination and Promoting Gender Equality,* Commonwealth of Australia, Canberra, 2008.

Commonwealth of Australia, *National Human Rights Consultation Report*, Attorney-General's Department, Canberra, 2009 [*Brennan Report*].

United Nations Convention on the Elimination of All Forms of Discrimination Against Women, United Nations, New York.

Part I

A Silver Anniversary

Opening Address I

Dr Helen Watchirs OAM

Introduction

We are here to honour the twenty-fifth anniversary of the *Sex Discrimination Act 1984* (Cth) (*SDA*) in the place where the legislation laboured in debate and was born (although conception took place in many minds and hearts around the country). It is fitting that we have the mother/s and midwives here to celebrate and speak. Just as interesting as the legislation are the individual feminists who have applied it to real life—people who have been brave enough to complain to equal opportunity agencies when their rights have been breached, women's groups who have consistently lobbied on important gender issues, lawyers and supportive advocates who have fought for its enforcement, the women and men who routinely implement it in their everyday lives, and the pioneer commissioners (and of course staff); some moderates on appointment became activists by the glaring evidence of inequality they saw close up.

All sex discrimination commissioners are very memorable, committed and successful, and I pay equal tribute to their work. Governor-General, Quentin Bryce, has a special place and Pam O'Neil was the inaugural commissioner. I have personally worked with Pru Goward during her consultations for the 2007 report, *It's About Time: Women, men, work and family*, which was preceded by the landmark 2002 report, *A Time to Value*. Elizabeth Broderick is here for the implementation of a national paid parental leave scheme to be introduced in 2011 paying the minimum wage ($543.78) for a maximum 18 weeks, leaving only the United States as the last developed country not to have a national scheme.

Employment

The public area of employment has been the greatest area of change as most workplaces were designed for men by men of another generation. Only in 1969 was the marriage ban removed for federal public servants (I remember this happened while I was in primary school, as my godmother was a secretary in the Tax Department in Parramatta). At the personal level, in my first job interview with a large Sydney law firm in 1982 (at the age of twenty-two), the second question I was asked was what form of contraception I was using. I was shocked and told them it was private information. Needless to say, I did not get the job (it was pre-1984), but fortunately I was soon employed by the Australian Law Reform Commission and met Michael Kirby, who has been a lifetime mentor. In 1984, some changes did happen overnight: newspaper and other job advertisements could not specify 'men only to apply'. You will read much more from contributors Marian Sawer, Sara Charlesworth and Beth Gaze.

Equality and Human Rights Legislation

Like most ground-breaking laws—as can be seen from the debate—for the *SDA*, there were dire prophecies; these had earlier been made in the case of the 'new' administrative law and now human rights acts. No law can be a magic bullet for implementing human rights and solving complex social justice issues, but it can be a workable step forward in strengthening compliance. The *SDA* has had substantive and symbolic impact—as a source of focus for social change, a specific framework to debate equality and a measure against which decisions and actions can be compared with international standards in order to prevent backsliding in human rights. Implementation of the UN Convention on the Elimination of All Forms of Discrimination Against Women (CEDAW) requires other legal mechanisms, such as those relating to industrial relations, super, tax, social security, family and criminal law (domestic violence and sexual assault). There has been real progress on attempting to remove two CEDAW reservations: paid maternity leave following the Productivity Commission report, and exclusion of women from combat duties, with the review of physical capabilities in new employment standards by the Minister for Defence Personnel, Greg Combet.

We have probably expected too much from one law. The *SDA* does not cover law-making, but a national Human Rights Act would, if it were based on the ACT, Victorian and UK legislative models, as laws are scrutinised not only by a parliamentary committee, the Attorney-General must also issue a compatibility statement for all new bills (as well as the administrative practice of requiring details of human rights impacts in draft cabinet submissions). In building a human rights culture, the biggest impact of the *ACT Human Rights Act* has been in the formulation of government policy and new legislation (for example, covering children and corrections). Chairman Professor Frank Brennan and members Mary Kostakidis, Mick Palmer and Tammy Williams held more than 65 community meetings and received more than 35 000 submissions, with organised campaigns by Get-Up, Amnesty International and others.

I think that it could be time to move to a generic equality law that includes sex as well as other forms of discrimination, such as sexuality, religion, disability, race, and so on. This is the structure of State and Territory legislation, as well as the UK *Equality Act 2006* model. The Standing Committees of Attorneys-General are working on harmonising State and Territory anti-discrimination laws. My five and a half years' work at the ACT Human Rights Commission influences my view, primarily because we often receive complaints under the *Discrimination Act 1991* (ACT) on multiple grounds; women are a diverse group and sex is not the only ground, as race, disability, sexuality and caring responsibilities can be entwined in the complainant's case. We also provide community education on discrimination and human rights issues, reviewing laws and providing reports to the ACT Attorney-General under the *Human Rights Commission Act 2005* (ACT) and the *Human Rights Act 2004* (ACT). This is effectively the full jurisdiction of the Australian Human Rights Commission, but of course on a small scale. I have power to seek leave to intervene in human rights court cases and conduct human rights audits—for example, of the Quamby Youth Detention Centre, which I will talk about later.

Senate Committee Report

In December 2008, the Senate Standing Committee on Legal and Constitutional Affairs released its report on the effectiveness of the *SDA* in eliminating discrimination and promoting gender equality. Its recommendations are very sensible and practical, using models of other federal, as well as State/Territory, provisions to call for

- the inclusion of marital and relationship status (same sex) as grounds of complaint

- the removal of the comparator test for discrimination (for example, ACT *Discrimination Act 1991* 'unfavourable treatment' test)

- changing 'reasonableness' to 'proportionality' test for indirect discrimination

- the inclusion of a general equality provision (for example, *Racial Discrimination Act* [s. 10] and *Human Rights Act* (ACT) [s. 8])

- the inclusion of breastfeeding specifically

- the inclusion of a positive obligation to reasonably accommodate flexible work (for example, as in Victoria)

- strengthening the sexual harassment provisions and listing of relevant factors (for example, as in Queensland)

- better funding for advocate/support services and the Australian Human Rights Commission

- the removal of some exceptions—for example, voluntary bodies—and narrowing of others, such as religious

- the empowerment of the Australian Human Rights Commission to join cases with intersecting grounds

- the inclusion of a requirement to consider objects of the *SDA* when deciding whether to grant exemptions

- the inclusion of the power to make legally binding standards (as with the *Disability Discrimination Act 1992* [Cth])

- the Sex Discrimination Commissioner to have an 'own motion' power, as well as intervener/amicus roles

- amendments to the *Equal Opportunity for Women in the Workplace Act 1999* (Cth)—for example, positive duty to promote equality

- regular reports to Parliament (for example, Social Justice Commissioner)

- the Attorney-General's Department to consult and the Australian Human Rights Commission to hold an inquiry into the need for an equality law and report by 2011.

The committee acknowledged that the *SDA* had been more successful in addressing overt cases of sex discrimination than systemic or structural disadvantage issues. It does not have comprehensive enforcement powers like those used by other regulators in the field of employment, such as the Workplace Ombudsman and occupational health and safety bodies—for example, to issue improvement notices. It uses an individual complaints-based model of regulation, which relies on investigation and private conciliation, then moving to public hearings in the federal courts using an adversarial model, following the *Brandy* case.[1] The awarding of damages is traditionally not high— for example, for sex discrimination: *Hickie v Hunt and Hunt* ($160 000).[2] With expensive legal representation, many complainants are deterred and most of the strong cases are settled—for example, a sexual harassment case in the Australian Capital Territory was conciliated for the amount of $65 000. Although not really comparable, I felt the shock when the ACT Human Rights Commission appealed a defence industry race discrimination exemption case in the Supreme Court and was hit with $18 000 legal costs when we were unsuccessful. In the Australian Capital Territory, we had an appalling decision of the Discrimination Tribunal

---

1   *Brandy v Human Rights & Equal Opportunity Commission* (1995) 183 CLR 245; [1995] HCA 10.
2   *Hickie v Hunt & Hunt* (1998) EOC 92-910.

(thankfully its last) on 3 August 2009 in *Paterson v Clarke*[3]—a very old case (13 years)—in which an award of only $1000 was made for a shockingly named 'hands down the pants incident'. I have not highlighted the case in the media, as it could deter other complainants as well as embolden potential respondents; also, the new ACT Civil and Administrative Tribunal has been established.

ACT Jurisdiction

Australia's combined 6/7th report on the implementation of CEDAW of July 2008 sets out the need to improve our treatment of women in correctional facilities and refers to our human rights audits of ACT juvenile (2005) and adult (2007) detention facilities. This need is highlighted by our recent accession to the Convention Against Torture Optional Protocol (as well as CEDAW). One major gender issue we discovered through regular visits (now a power to inspect under the ACT *Corrections Management Act 2008*, but without any funding attached), including of periodic detention on weekends, was the practice of bussing women between facilities on weekends. This amounted to systemic sex discrimination as women were subjected to more strip searches, had difficulty making professional appointments (for example, medical), had fewer visits (for example, from children and family) and work opportunities and were required to clean out their cells—for example, removing vomit and urine—when they relocated due to some weekend male detainees detoxing there. The government agreed and the practice was stopped, even when our ACT facilities were overcrowded (the new prison, the Alexander Maconochie Centre, was delayed and NSW prisons were full).

The most controversial recommendation in the audit was to pilot a needle and syringe program (NSP) based on a harm-reduction approach that protects the rights to life and health, and recognises the principle of 'equivalence'. There are already community-based NSPs, and many global studies have demonstrated their efficacy in communities as well as in prisons in some countries. To deny protection against disease transmission in a closed population in prison could be viewed as inhumane. NSW research indicates that 63.3 per cent of males and 74.5 per cent of females abuse or are dependent on drugs or alcohol. The rate of hepatitis C in the general community is 2 per cent, but the rate for male inmates is 35–40 per cent and is even higher for female inmates—55–56 per cent. The rate of spread of these preventable infections could be exponential, considering that detainees return to the community quickly; the average length of stay is seven months.

---

3 *Paterson v Clarke* [2009] ACTDT 3.

Wide Range of Issues

Gender equality has had something of a roller-coaster ride—cases such as: *Proudfoot* in 1992 (Chris Ronalds appeared as counsel), in which President Ron Wilson found that ACT women's health centres were a special measure,[4] exemption applications for Catholic teachers' scholarships in 2004, the Club Pink breastfeeding case in 2005 and Virginia Haussegger's call to 'ban the burqa' in 2009. Maybe the colour of children's ballet uniforms will be next! The future is unclear about the interaction with discrimination law through the impact of the new Fair Work Ombudsman, which started on 1 July 2009 (under the *Fair Work Act 2009*). It receives about 30 complaints a week, many in the area of pregnancy and family responsibilities. Its resources are phenomenal compared with human rights agencies, with 26 offices nationally and about 800 staff.

The Australia Institute's report *The Impact of the Recession on Women* shows the impact is disproportionate, as women are the hidden underemployed (80 per cent of those in the twenty-five to thirty-four-year-old group), with many working part-time.[5] There are many more women's human rights issues, including the glass ceiling in employment (although we continue to batter away), the gender pay gap with over-representation in casual, part-time and low-skilled or low-valued caring work (for example, teaching, child care, health care and hospitality), the feminisation of poverty and women's insufficient superannuation. The new workplace relations system has collective bargaining as a central feature, but the Workplace Research Centre at the University of Sydney recently found that women are often in service industries under awards with fewer pay increases. I look forward to the finding of the House of Representatives Standing Committee on Employment and Workplace Relations inquiry into 'Pay Equity and Associated Issues Related to Increasing Participation of Women in the Workforce'. No wonder it's being called 'Are we there yet?'.

It is very important that equal employment opportunity (EEO) agencies work with academic and other researchers to analyse discrimination trends. For example, Professor Margaret Thornton from The Australian National University has researched our de-identified old case files, as has Professor Patricia Easteal from the University of Canberra, whose work '"She said, He said": Credibility and Sexual Harassment Cases in Australia' has been published.[6] Academics have also been good promoters of the need to collect disaggregated data. While we are world leaders in levels of educational attainments for women, this does not

---

4   *Proudfoot v ACT Board of Health* (1992) EOC 92-417.
5   David Richardson, *The Impact of the Recession on Women*, The Australian Institute, 2009, p. 8 (<http://www.security4women.org.au/wp-content/uploads/IP-3-Women-in-the-recession-S4Wl.pdf>).
6   In (2008) 31(5) *Women's Studies International Forum* 336–44.

translate into pay equality. The ACT Human Rights Commission has also been doing its own work on community attitudes using Survey Monkey; local non-governmental organisations (NGOs), such as the ACT Women's Centre for Health Matters, are also using this cheap methodology.

Conclusion

I agree with Pru Goward's statement at the twentieth anniversary conference that the *SDA* 'deals with gender relations, an issue at the heart of all cultures. The *SDA* will only ever be as strong as our commitment to it.' The Act is aspirational, but the ideal situation is when there is no need for the *SDA*, which has not yet occurred. I will finish with the words of Martin Luther King Jr: 'if you start treating equally people who have been treated unequally, you capture them forever in their inequality.'

Bibliography

Article

Easteal, Patricia and Judd, Keziah 2008, '"She Said, He Said": Credibility and Sexual Harassment Cases in Australia' (2008) 31(5) *Women's Studies International Forum* 336–44.

Legislation

Corrections Management Act 2008 (ACT)

Disability Discrimination Act 1992 (Cth)

Discrimination Act 1991 (ACT)

Equal Opportunity for Women in the Workplace Act 1999 (Cth)

Equality Act 2006 (UK)

Fair Work Act 2009 (Cth)

Human Rights Act 2004 (ACT)

Human Rights Commission Act 2005 (ACT)

Racial Discrimination Act 1975 (Cth)

Sex Discrimination Act 1984 (Cth)

Cases

Brandy v Human Rights and Equal Opportunity Commission (1995) 183 CLR 245

Hickie v Hunt & Hunt (1998) EOC 92-910

Paterson v Clarke [2009] ACTDT 3

Proudfoot v ACT Board of Health (1992) EOC 92-417

Reports and miscellaneous primary sources

Australia Institute n.d., *The Impact of the Recession on Women*, Australia Institute, Canberra, <http://www.security4women.org.au/wp-content/uploads/IP-3-Women-in-the-recession-S4Wl.pdf>

Commonwealth of Australia, *National Human Rights Consultation Report*, Commonwealth of Australia, Canberra, 2009 [*Brennan Report*].

Human Rights and Equal Opportunity Commission, *A Time to Value: Proposal for a national scheme of paid maternity leave*, Human Rights and Equal Opportunity Commission, Sydney, 2002.

Human Rights and Equal Opportunity Commission, *It's About Time: Women, men, work and family*, Human Rights and Equal Opportunity Commission, Sydney, 2007.

Richardson, David, *The Impact of the Recession on Women*, The Australian Institute, 2009, p. 8 (<http://www.security4women.org.au/wp-content/uploads/IP-3-Women-in-the-recession-S4Wl.pdf>).

United Nations Convention Against Torture (Optional Protocol), United Nations, New York.

United Nations Convention on the Elimination of All Forms of Discrimination Against Women, United Nations, New York.

Opening Address II

Hon. Susan Ryan AO

It is reassuring to me as a former legislator—and one who copped more than a fair share of controversy—that the conference on which this collection is based is being held to mark the twenty-fifth anniversary of the *Sex Discrimination Act 1984* (Cth) (*SDA*). To those who believe that it is the basic responsibility of Parliament to use its legislative powers to advance fairness and justice, the *fact* of this conference is reassuring in itself. Of the many hundreds, perhaps thousands of bills passed in the 13 years that I sat in the Senate, very few have attracted positive attention and significant reconsideration 25 years after gazettal.

Why does the *SDA* continue after 25 years to attract this attention?

Because it addressed fundamental inequalities and unfairness, it did so with considerable effectiveness and it has produced outcomes that can easily be measured to establish success. The numbers always help.

It did change Australia—for the better. Such laws deserve the continuing attention of senior academics and activists alike. So I congratulate Margaret Thornton and all who have made the conference happen.

It is more than a coincidence that the last time I stood at a podium in Old Parliament House was in December last year, to mark the anniversary of another, even more significant legal initiative: an instrument aimed at improving justice and fairness *globally*.

Last December, we held a forum in Old Parliament House to mark the sixtieth anniversary of the Universal Declaration of Human Rights. We did that on the eve of the announcement by Attorney-General, Robert McClelland, of a national consultation to report to government our community's views and wishes in relation to a Human Rights Act for Australia. I hope, as do many Australians, that the release of the national consultation report will lead to a new Act of the Parliament that puts into national law all those responsibilities Australia agreed to when we signed up for the Universal Declaration 60 years ago and the major UN human rights instruments—civil and political, economic and social— and the other conventions that were built on the Universal Declaration's strong foundations.

As well as all these broad protections, a Human Rights Act would strengthen and reinforce the effectiveness of the *SDA* and reach even further in combating sex discrimination.

But let us go back 25 years, when we lacked both an umbrella Human Rights Act and any specific national protection of women against the sex discrimination that was widespread and extremely destructive. Entrenched sex discrimination, especially in education, employment and the economy, had produced extensive poverty and other serious disadvantage among female Australia. Australia had the most sex-segregated labour market of any Organisation for Economic Cooperation and Development (OECD) country, so that women were in general restricted to work ghettos of low pay and poor conditions. No woman had sat on the High Court or headed a university, a Commonwealth department or a major corporation. By 1984, only two women had held cabinet posts in a federal government.

A number of factors explain the dramatic move from where we were in 1984, with no national protection, to where we are now, marking 25 years of the *SDA*, living in an economy in 2009 in which women are everywhere, including in many (though not enough) leadership positions. The *SDA* was crucial to this change. Many individuals played a role in achieving this progressive measure: my own parliamentary colleagues in 1983–84, as well those expert lawyers who helped put our political objective into a constitutionally robust and workable law.

The most important of those lawyers is Chris Ronalds AM, SC. Chris had the dedication, skills and imagination to draft the original Private Member's Bill (1981), which I introduced while in opposition to prepare the way, and her work was crucial in securing the form of the much amended Bill that eventually became the *SDA*.

We worked together but our roles were different; mine concerned politics—the politics of reform. Fundamental to my purposes in entering Parliament was the belief that I should, with my colleagues, use all available powers of the Parliament to reduce discrimination and promote fairness and equality. As I saw it, that was at the core of what I was elected to do. Of course, we had other tasks: deregulating the economy, restructuring the labour market, remaking foreign, defence and social policy—all massively important but none more so than fighting discrimination against women. Coming as I did from the women's movement, I was aware on every level of widespread sex discrimination that kept women out of good jobs, severely limited their income and standard of living and reduced their lives to unhappy and unhealthy servitude.

Redistributing power and opportunity is an objective that always provokes resistance and hostility. Those who are well served by the status quo will do everything they can to hang on to their advantage. And so it was with the *SDA*. The 're-enactment' was a reminder of what lengths—of absurdity and vitriol—our opponents, inside and outside the Parliament, were prepared to go to to maintain the inferior position of women in all aspects of our public and private lives.

For younger people, looking back on it all now, it seems unbelievable that there was such vicious opposition to a law that in essence required simply that women should not be sacked or refused education, loans or leases simply because they were female, pregnant, married or unmarried as the case may be. But the opposition was intensely serious. The 'Ryan Act', as it came to be called—as a term of abuse—represented change at a basic level of society and resonated with all the fears of the dominant groups that their values would have to be modified a little to make way for fairness and give women a chance to contribute on the basis of merit.

Who were our opponents?

Business large and small feared having to pay female workers more; the commercial media saw the chance to sell more papers and increase advertising revenue by stirring up fear of change; conservative politicians of all kinds saw a direct link between my modest proposal and the communist USSR and its tyrannies. Churches, including the ever-powerful Catholic Church, were concerned about maintaining their discriminatory employment rights—and they did. The trade unions were not entirely shoulder-to-shoulder with us, though most were.

Many women were opposed. The wonderfully named 'Women Who Want to be Women'—the '4Ws'—were numerous, vociferous and very well organised, arranging for thousands of petitions against the Ryan Act to be shovelled into the chambers each day, typically on pink paper. Other women's groups of the right saw the idea of removing sex barriers to jobs as scary and undermining of their comfortable stay-at-home arrangements with their husbands.

On the left, the Women's Electoral Lobby (WEL) was strongly in support, but other feminists decided we were compromising too much and that an imperfect law was worse than no law. Although I had and still have friends—scholars I admire—who took this view, I have to reject it.

In our sort of democracy, with our parliamentary structure of two chambers in which the government rarely controls the Senate, perfect laws are not possible. Radical or progressive reforms will always need to be modified. Ask Penny Wong! Our Bill was a quintessential example of this reality: in its first consideration in the Senate, it attracted huge numbers of amendments—some good, some loopy. We had to deal with them all. We withdrew the Bill and redrafted it, and re-presented what we judged was a fair compromise. No go. Dozens more amendments had to be negotiated.

We recognised the realities of our circumstances. In an atmosphere in which the milder predictions of the effects of the Act included

- the death of the family
- the destruction of the labour market
- the wrecking of the economy
- the end of marriage
- the imposition of compulsory 24-hour child care
- the collapse of Christianity
  the Bill was passed.

It became an act and was gazetted and in operation by August 1984 (with, I must confess, none of those predictions coming to pass).

Since all that drama, the *SDA* has provided effective protection to women for 25 years. At this point, I must acknowledge the terrific work of all the sex discrimination commissioners, including our much admired Governor-General, Quentin Bryce AC. They implemented the protections with total commitment, imagination and skill, as does the current Commissioner, Elizabeth Broderick.

The huge numbers of complaints conciliated each year, the rarity of court hearings and the valuable amendments generated by two major parliamentary reviews illustrate how well evolutionary reform of this kind can work. Despite two attempts to reduce the coverage of the *SDA*—one by the Catholic Church in relation to its proposal for male-only teacher scholarships and one by the Howard Government seeking to exclude single women and lesbians from access to IVF— the Act has never been weakened. Does it need to be further strengthened? I expect we all would say yes. I hope that the recommendations from current Commissioner Broderick to the recent senate review will be adopted.

My point is this: *we are better off since 1984 having the* SDA, *with all its imperfections, than we would have been without it*. I cannot state too strongly my belief that Parliament must seize the day, use its powers and deliver what it can of value to the people. Where reform is urgently needed, it is not an acceptable strategy, in my view, to wait for complete consensus or to defer a bill until its drafting is beyond any criticism. Such pursuit of the perfect constitutes a failure of representative democracy.

Compromise, accepting less than useful amendments as a trade-off to secure the main objectives—well, if that is what you have to do, do it. Of course, academics and other experts should continue to point to weaknesses and flaws and call for better, but not to the point of actually obstructing a generally needed and wanted reform.

As I make these assertions, I am struck by the parallel situation we seem to be in between the story of securing the *SDA* and the story to date of the yet to be achieved Human Rights Act. With the human rights consultation, again we have a high-temperature public debate, lots of controversy, passionate supporters and opponents, a measure of genuine disagreement among serious lawyers and lots of fear tactics and exaggerations, amplified by a relentlessly negative campaign by *The Australian* newspaper.

The Hawke Government in 1983 had the boldness to discount critics and take legislative action. Will the Rudd Government show similar leadership and purpose and introduce a Human Rights Act? We do not know yet, but we live in hope. Just as 25 years ago, all women needed protection against damaging discrimination, all of us now need a law to embody our basic human rights and to protect vulnerable individuals against violations of these rights by state power.

I am convinced that all of us—who, undeterred by controversy and wild criticisms, put our shoulders behind the achievement of the *SDA* one-quarter of a century ago—did the right thing by the people. Not too many would disagree these days. I do not even hear any whinges from the 4Ws.

I conclude by stating the hope that the *SDA* is not only recognised and maintained for the next 25 years as a vital reform in its own right, but that it can serve as an inspiration and practical example to today's legislators, so that the valuable impacts of the *SDA* will soon be reinforced by a Human Rights Act for Australia.

Opening Address III

Chris Ronalds AM, SC

When I look back now to matters that were so controversial in 1983–84, I note with a tinge of satisfaction/amusement/curiosity that most are matters that attract little or no controversy at all these days. Those colourful and controversial debates of the 1980s were instrumental in forming the ground on which so much important current legislation and freedoms for women have been built. It was a privilege to be engaged to work on issues that were truly 'new ground' and that would serve to support future generations of Australians. That is not to say also that there is no need for change going into the future.

To take you back briefly to those turbulent, historic and often exciting early 1980s…

The Hawke Government was elected on 5 March 1983 with a commitment to passing sex discrimination legislation. One of the first steps was the ratification of the UN Convention on the Elimination of All Forms of Discrimination Against Women (CEDAW), on 28 July 1983, and it became operative one month later.

There were two reservations that caused controversy from the women's movement and others: 1) on paid maternity leave, and 2) on women banned from combat and combat-related positions in the armed forces. Both continue to be controversial topics 25 years later.

That UN convention was the basis for many false accusations and wonderful inventions about women at the time.

Here is a copy of my all-time favourite advertisement from October 1983: 'Stop Ryan—Australia's feminist dictator—Stop Ryan's ruthless juggernaut and anti-female Sex Bill' (Figure 1).

The constitutional basis for the *SDA* was in hot dispute in 1983. The Solicitor-General—appointed by the previous government—held a strong view that international treaties could not be the basis for domestic legislation. The Attorney-General, Senator Gareth Evans, and I held diametrically opposite views to those of the Solicitor-General; our 'side' won after some feisty debate with much mutterings and warnings of defeat in the High Court. In such matters, there was no room for compromise or 'middle' positions to be taken. I always thought it was worth the risk—and it was. There is now a raft of legislation relying on the foreign affairs powers and treaties to provide a constitutional basis, but 25 years ago this was a far from settled debate.

Figure 1.1

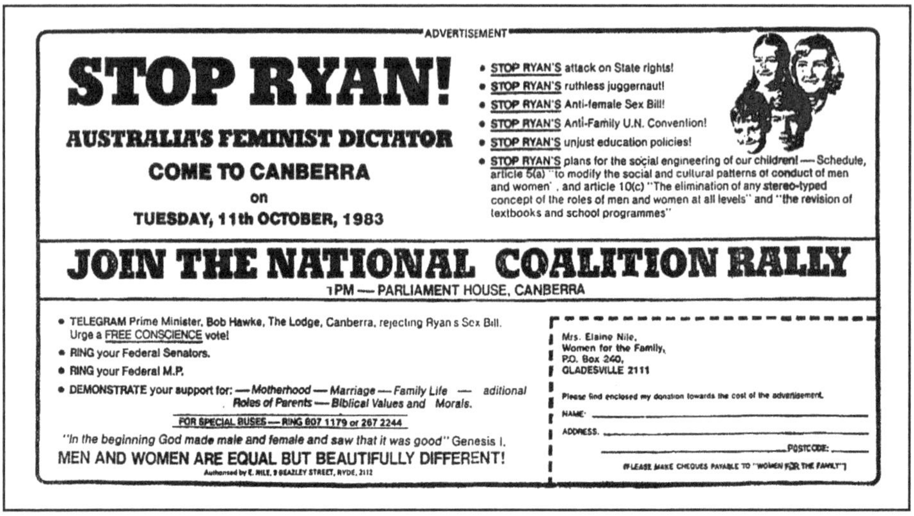

Sydney Morning Heald, 8th October 1983

Using the corporations power to cover the private sector was also then a novel approach to the use of the *Constitution* and much resisted by conservatives.

Curiously, great condemnation arose from the women's movement in response to these discrimination initiatives—condemnation almost as big as the opposition from the conservatives. Obviously, this was hugely disappointing. There was a primary focus on the exemptions, particularly the genuine occupational qualification (GOQ) in Section 30. Much heat was generated. Some women contended that the Act should not be passed, as the exemptions meant it was worse than nothing. I did not agree. I considered it was better to have it on the statute books and then improve it over time.

Once I arrived home in Sydney after a tumultuous week in Canberra to find a message from a woman—who identified herself, who I knew and who was a university lecturer and leftie—to say I should be ashamed of myself and resign immediately, that I was destroying women's rights in Australia and various other robust character assessments. So it was pretty up-close and personal. While feeling extremely confronted and disappointed at such a display of 'support', I—and others working on these issues—ploughed on. I hope (and believe) that we have been vindicated in our stance by history; since 1983, there has been no case under the *SDA* in which an employer has relied on the GOQ exemption to avoid their liability. The exemption turned out to be a damp squib.

The proposed exemptions on superannuation and insurance were also seen as the government giving in to big business and a serious erosion of women's rights. Time has shown that the problems with superannuation arose from a raft of issues tied to women's participation in the labour market and there has been a huge community shift since then. The idea of superannuation for all is now a commonly accepted part of the Australian wage packet. In terms of complaints and real issues for women, neither proved a major impediment to the effective implementation of the law.

It was the real ambit of the legislation that I always considered important. The drafting of the Sex Discrimination Bill presented some large problems. The bureaucracy was generally—but not universally—opposed to trying to put what many considered social policy into an inappropriate framework of legislation. The Office of Parliamentary Counsel (OPC) in 1983 was—to be polite—less than helpful. While there were legislative models operating in various States and overseas, the OPC decided to reinvent the wheel and, with a lack of appreciation of the fundamental principles and the objectives, they prepared a draft bill that was not suitable. Getting them back to first principles involved more heated debates and having to drag Gareth Evans into a conference at midnight as the only way to win.

The sexual harassment provisions were the tinderbox. I was determined that there would be specific provisions covering sexual harassment. This was the first legislation in the world to use the term 'sexual harassment'. Evans was initially unconvinced but Susan Ryan and I persuaded him.

Convincing the drafters was another issue until, at 3.30 one morning, they gave in while claiming that the judges would throw the provision out as being unworkable and unclear. This has never happened, and the Federal Court has never had any difficulty in applying the provisions in an effective way.

The model of conciliation before litigation was also controversial and was criticised many times over the years by some academics as taking the power away from female complainants. I did not and do not agree at all. Many complaints have been settled with great outcomes for the complainant without the trauma of a litigated outcome. Now the federal Attorney-General and all the chief justices around Australia are pushing for alternative dispute resolution instead of litigation. This model of conciliation before litigation has held up well over the years and provides an effective model on which current dispute-resolution practices can be built.

An important occasion such as this must necessarily represent a celebration of achievements as well as a milestone for future developments and progress. We should remember the real heroines: those courageous women who were represented in the first test cases and endured relentless, front-page news and commentary, which was often ill informed, vicious or just plain wrong.

- Deborah Wardley, who Ansett dragged all the way to the High Court in 1980 under the Victorian discrimination laws to win a job as a pilot.[1] This led to the first and only successful 'girl-cot': businesses were encouraged by women to transfer their travel accounts from Ansett to Qantas and, in the first six months, Ansett lost more than 50 per cent of its business travel and a lot never returned. We all virtuously flew Qantas, who ironically had no women pilots and did not for many years. Ansett, having fought and lost, then continued to employ women and participate in the affirmative action pilot program until the company went broke.

- Sue O'Callaghan brought the first case of sexual harassment in 1983 under the NSW law against the Commissioner of Main Roads, Bruce Loder.[2] She was the driver of his personal lift. She lost on a technicality but did much to make the issue an area of hot debate and confirmed my view that we needed a specific provision addressing sexual harassment and should not rely on using the sex discrimination provisions.

- Lynette Aldridge brought a complaint of sexual harassment against Grant Booth when working at the 'Tasty Morsel' cake shop in Brisbane, which went all the way to the Federal Court in 1988.[3]

- Three young women—Susan Hall, Dianne Oliver and Karyn Reid—all made remarkably similar allegations of sexual harassment against Dr Sheiban, a sixty-five-year-old medical practitioner.[4] After a heavily publicised hearing before the Human Rights and Equal Opportunity Commission, the then President, Marcus Einfeld, found the complaints of sexual harassment sustained and made no order for damages, as he considered that 'the public exposure of these complaints and the findings I have made are sufficient relief in these matters'. Having dismissed the women's evidence of pain and suffering, he awarded no compensation. There was a huge outcry. An appeal to the Federal Court was successful and Einfeld's views were comprehensively trashed by his brother judges. Such a trade-off was resoundingly rejected as an improper way of assessing damages.

- Helen Styles, who unsuccessfully took on the Department of Foreign Affairs and Trade about a promotion to an overseas posting as a journalist in 1988.[5]

- Marea Hickie was a partner in the law firm Hunt & Hunt.[6] She successfully challenged the decisions made about her position on her return from maternity leave when she wanted to work part-time. This was the first high-

---

1 *Ansett Transport Industries (Operation) Pty Ltd v Wardley* (1980) 142 CLR 237; [1980] HCA 8.
2 *O'Callaghan v Loder* (1984) EOC 92-023 (NSW EOT).
3 *Aldridge v Booth* (1988) 80 ALR 1.
4 *Hall v Sheiban* (1989) 85 ALR 503.
5 *Secretary, DFAT v Styles* (1989) 23 FCR 251; 88 ALR 621.
6 *Hickie v Hunt & Hunt* (1998) EOC 92-910.

profile case involving a professional woman and it generated controversy within the legal and other professions such as accountancy. Suddenly, they felt vulnerable to claims of sex discrimination when they had previously viewed this as unlikely.

There were many other women who pioneered their way through the courts—and we should remember them for their bravery in the face of an often hostile media and the joys of being torn apart by ill-informed shock jocks and misogynist callers.

Where Now?

There are a few pressing areas that I consider need review.

One is the sexual harassment law and I am surprised that none of the papers tomorrow, by their abstracts, appear to address this issue. In my view, there are very real issues that arise with the changes of technology, especially in two important areas: social networking sites such as Facebook and MySpace and the readily accessible camera in every mobile phone, which means no moment in life can now be assumed to be private. The distinction between work and after-hours is no longer as clear as it was and otherwise private conduct now bleeds into the workplace. There is some confusion around the new rules of engagement in the workplace and what is and is not appropriate behaviour. Gen Y women have different expectations and the way they interact with society and recognise sexual power and seek to use it to their advantage create new challenges. More women in more diverse workplaces presents new issues or a new focus on the old ones. There needs to be a recognition that the limitations as well as the protections apply to all women. An objective assessment of conduct within the workplace and other environments is needed.

The second area is the level of damages awarded by the courts. To date, with few recent exceptions, they have been low and are often not a proper recognition of the immense psychological damage a person might have suffered from, for example, a year of revolting sexual harassment. When compared with even the newly restricted areas of damages for, say, defamation at a maximum of $250 000, one nasty newspaper article is worth considerably more in compensation than a devastating life experience from which a woman might struggle to recover and return to work.

The third area is the capacity for businesses to provide part-time work to parents, usually mothers, returning from parental leave. While large organisations with a number of people performing similar roles can readily make adjustments, the same cannot be said for small or medium companies with only one person performing a particular role. As a society, we must make an assessment of the way resources are to be provided in that situation and it will be interesting to see the way the new provisions in the *Fair Work Act* requiring flexible work arrangements around reasonable business grounds will work out over time.

Remember

When critically examining the operation of the *SDA*, it is important to remember that it was always designed for individual rights and not collective rights. The *Affirmative Action Act* was intended to have a broader focus and develop a strategic approach. It provides important protections for women. Certainly, it deserves, and indeed needs, active review and amendment, to strengthen it from the ravages of time—changing cultures and societal values. So as we move forward boldly into a new world, let us not abandon the legislated principles that we have. Let us build on them.

In the words of Tom Keneally, referring to a conversation he had with Stephen Spielberg's mother about the film *Schindler's List*, 'never forget to remember'.

So, in closing, I leave you with this one thought: our girl has grown up and, while she might need a new frock by Sass and Bide, her bone structure is still solid and a sturdy cloak made of supportive social policy and industrial muscle and funded child care will improve her health and wellbeing. She has stood the test of time with continuing changes and there should be more, but let us be cautious about throwing her away in our enthusiasm and indignation. Let us give her a little sister in an Equality Act—so she can grow up too.

Bibliography

Cases

Aldridge v Booth (1988) 80 ALR 1

Ansett Transport Industries (Operation) Pty Ltd v Wardley (1980) 142 CLR 237; [1980] HCA 8

Hall v Sheiban (1989) 85 ALR 503

Hickie v Hunt & Hunt (1998) EOC 92-910

O'Callaghan v Loder (1984) EOC 92-023 (NSW EOT)

Secretary, DFAT v Styles (1989) 23 FCR 251; 88 ALR 621

Part II
Then and Now

1. The *Sex Discrimination Act* and its Rocky Rite of Passage

Margaret Thornton and Trish Luker

Through an analysis of the parliamentary debates on the Sex Discrimination Bill 1983–84, this chapter underscores the anxiety that preoccupied the opponents of the Bill. Their fear that the Bill would give rise to a totalitarian regime, reminiscent of an Eastern bloc country, is clearly apparent from their own words. Not only would the passage of the Bill signal a blow to democracy, it would result in the creation of a unisex society and, most significantly, the demise of the nuclear family.

Introduction

Will the Prime Minister give an assurance to Australian women that neither the Government's proposed sex discrimination Bill nor ratification of the United Nations Convention on the Elimination of All Forms of Discrimination Against Women will in any way discriminate against women who choose life within the family, will not force them to go out to work, separate them from their children or break up their families, as some people have recently been suggesting?[1]

The passage of the *Sex Discrimination Act 1984* (Cth) (*SDA*) represents a high political moment in the history of gender relations in Australia. The seemingly protracted debates of 1983–84[2] were marked by a deep anxiety about sex roles, the patriarchal family and the wellbeing of children. The hysterical propaganda campaign and the fear engendered by the Bill were out of all proportion to its modest liberal intent that women be 'let in' to certain domains of public and quasi-public life, including employment, on the same terms as men.

Reliance on the external affairs power (*Constitution*, s. 51 [xxix]) to implement legislation in the absence of an express head of power had only recently been

---

1   Mrs Elaine Darling, Member for Lilley (ALP), Question without notice, *House Hansard*, 10 May 1983, p. 349.

2   Sawer debunks the myth that the debate on the Sex Discrimination Bill was 'the longest in the Australian Parliament'. In fact, it was only the eleventh longest, involving 17 hours of debate, compared with almost 70 hours on the two Communist Party Dissolution Bills. See Marian Sawer with Gail Radford, *Making Women Count: A History of the Women's Electoral Lobby in Australia*, UNSW Press, Sydney, 2008, p. 184.

held to be constitutional by the High Court.[3] The relevant international treaty on which the *SDA* was based was the UN Convention on the Elimination of All Forms of Discrimination Against Women (CEDAW). For some parliamentarians, recourse to an international treaty as the constitutional basis of domestic law represented not only a derogation of Australian sovereignty, but also a backdoor mechanism for augmenting federal power at the expense of the States,[4] thereby fanning the residual resentment regarding the attempts by the Whitlam Government to modernise the Australian nation-state.[5] It is nevertheless apparent that more than constitutionality was at stake. Not only was the shadow of the Cold War discernible in the denunciation of CEDAW as a communist plot, but, by a convenient sleight of hand, the misogyny underpinning opposition to the Bill became imbricated with the bogeys of totalitarianism, including the suggestion that children would be confined to drab childcare centres while their mothers entered forced labour camps. The suspicion of UN member states that did not espouse Western liberal-democratic capitalism also evinced a deep ethnocentrism and fear of the Other.

The question of whether law can change hearts and minds in the face of intransigent opposition remains an enigma. It encouraged us to revisit the debates on the *SDA* in 2009—the year of its silver anniversary—because similar issues are on the agenda once more as we contemplate the *National Human Rights Consultation Report (Brennan Report)*,[6] the key recommendation of which is that a federal Human Rights Act be enacted. It is already clear that such an Act would be highly contentious, not only because it would depend for its validity on seven international treaties, including CEDAW, but because it would also include a wide-ranging equality prescript—an idea that continues to be viewed as destabilising by conservatives, particularly in the case of sex and sexuality. Indeed, any suggestion of legislating for human rights is being trenchantly opposed by right-wing Christian lobby groups even before a bill has been tabled.[7] Objections are couched in terms of freedom of conscience and opposition to vesting judges with 'unfettered discretion'. It is notable that an

---

3   *Koowarta v Bjelke-Petersen* (1982) 153 CLR 168 (*Koowarta*); *Commonwealth v Tasmania* (1983) 158 CLR 1 (*Tasmanian Dams*). *Koowarta* upheld the validity of *Racial Discrimination Act 1975* (Cth), which was based on the Convention on the Elimination of All Forms of Racial Discrimination.

4   Queensland Senator Boswell (NP) alleged that the government was using 'a United Nations treaty to come in right over the top of the States…taking sovereignty away from the States of Australia' (*Senate Hansard*, 29 November 1983, p. 2963). Senator Walters (LP) claimed that the Hawke Government had 'altered the Constitution by the backdoor method' by trying to 'take over the rights of one of the small States'—namely, her state of Tasmania (*Senate Hansard*, 16 December 1983, p. 3959). See also Senator Crichton-Browne (LP), *Senate Hansard*, 16 December 1983, p. 3960.

5   See, for example, *Commonwealth v Queensland* (1975) 134 CLR 298 (Queen of Queensland Case).

6   Commonwealth of Australia, *National Human Rights Consultation Report*, Commonwealth of Australia, Canberra, 2009 [*Brennan Report*].

7   For example, Patrick Parkinson, Christian concerns with the charter of rights, Paper presented at Cultural and Religious Freedom under a Bill of Rights Conference, Canberra, 2009.

attempt to effect an amendment to the *SDA* in 1983 to include an exception on the ground of freedom of conscience (to discriminate) was rejected in the course of the debates.

Even though there is no established church in Australia and the most recent census figures reveal that 15.5 per cent of the population professes no religion,[8] Christianity and religious values continue to play a central role in shaping gendered norms. These values, which are based on ancient texts, including the Bible, are often patriarchal and misogynistic, necessarily conflicting with the egalitarian secularism underpinning the legislation. This tension between secularism and religion is now being routinely played out in law.[9] Accordingly, it is salutary to reflect on the role of law when it crosses the imaginary line between law and morality. If law is confined to a purely functional role, that is unproblematic, but, as soon as its focus shifts to the normative realm, it becomes contentious because unanimity is unattainable in a pluralistic society.

Of course, the *SDA* was not the first occasion on which the federal government had sought to alter social norms in ways that challenged conservative religious beliefs by legislative fiat. The *Family Law Act 1975* (Cth) is a notable example, and there are many others. The *SDA* was, however, widely believed to be revolutionary because of its potential to disrupt the prevailing social order. While many saw this as a social good, a vociferous minority was adamantly opposed.

The Politics of Reform

The 1970s was a distinctive period in Australian political history. The social liberalism associated with Gough Whitlam marked the beginning of a new era. There was a rejection of classical liberalism, moral conservatism and the 'British to the bootstraps' ideology of the Menzies years. The Whitlam era involved a dynamic period of law reform that included no-fault divorce, Aboriginal rights, environmental protection, free tertiary education and a range of other distributive justice policies associated with the modernisation of the Australian state. Law was seen as a positive force for change despite its past sins, and feminist activists wanted to play a central role in the transformation.

Social liberalism's concern with equity and the collective good underscored the starkness of the marked under-representation of women in many facets of public and economic life. A robust civil society enabled feminism in its many guises to emerge and establish itself as a political force for change. The Whitlam

---

8   Australian Bureau of Statistics, *Year Book Australia 2006*, Australian Bureau of Statistics, Canberra, 2007. This figure is taken from the 2001 Census.

9   For example, *Members of the Board of the Wesley Mission Council v OV & OW (No. 2)* [2009] NSWADTAP 57.

Government responded positively to the reform agenda. Its initiatives had been supported by the establishment of a formal role for feminist advisors within government bureaucracies, which gave rise to the Australian neologism the 'femocrat'. The functional and the normative came to be intimately intertwined under social liberalism.

The element of bipartisanship associated with the *SDA* puts paid to the suggestion that it was only the Australian Labor Party that favoured reform. It was Liberal Party policy to support the Bill after CEDAW was signed in Copenhagen in 1980 on behalf of Australia by Liberal MP R. J. Ellicott QC, although the convention was not ratified until the Labor Party came into office in 1983. Liberal MPs Ian Macphee and Peter Baume were among the staunchest supporters of the Bill. Sustained opposition emanated from the right wing of the Liberal Party, as well as the National Party. So passionate were the sentiments aroused by the Bill that it is credited with having caused a philosophical split within the Coalition.[10] Maverick independent Senator Brian Harradine relentlessly campaigned against the Bill, zealously pursuing the issue of abortion, to which we will return.

Despite the efforts of feminist reform groups, such as the Women's Electoral Lobby (WEL), to pressure political parties to include issues of concern to women in their election platforms, there was a dearth of women in Parliament before International Women's Year, 1975. A record number of female candidates stood in the Australian federal election of 1983,[11] but the number of women elected remained minuscule, which meant that the *SDA* was debated in an overwhelmingly masculinist environment. Of the 125 members in the House of Representatives, there were only six women, all of whom were on the Labor side; in the Senate, there were 13 women and 51 men across all parties. Somewhat ironically in light of the substance of the *SDA*, women were still reliant on the good graces of men to alter entrenched gender norms.

In fact, only a minority of parliamentarians opposed the Bill, but those who did were loud in their denunciation of it. Opposition was galvanised by a deluge of petitions—almost 80 000 opposing the legislation and a mere 1400 in favour. The ultra-conservative lobby groups that orchestrated the campaign against the Bill bombarded parliamentarians with literature, much of it misinformed, as well as lobbying them in person. The most assiduous of these groups was the curiously named Women Who Want to be Women (WWWW), founded and led by Babette Francis of Victoria.[12]

---

10 Philippa Hawker, 'A plain person's guide to that sex bill', *Sydney Morning Herald*, 6 October 1983, p. 38.
11 Marian Simms, '"A Woman's Place is in the House and in the Senate": Women and the 1983 Elections' in Marian Simms (ed.), *Australian Women and the Political System*, Longman Cheshire, Melbourne, 1984.
12 WWWW had close links with the National Party. Sawer reports that Francis ran as a National Party candidate in the 1984 federal election against a sitting Liberal who had supported the *SDA*. See Marian Sawer and Marian Simms, *A Woman's Place: Women and Politics in Australia*, Allen & Unwin, Sydney, 1993, p. 226.

Irene Webley published an insightful piece in 1983 analysing the role of WWWW in the context of the emergence of the New Right in Australia.[13] Webley suggests that anti-feminist groups, such as WWWW, grew out of resentment over the fact that while government recognised women as a new political constituency, the territory had been commandeered by reformist feminist groups, such as WEL.[14] New Right anti-feminist lobby groups, including WWWW and the Festival of Light, campaigned against the reformist initiatives, claiming to speak for the 'silent majority'—the women who 'chose' to remain at home and were in danger of being seduced by feminist rhetoric. The New Right lobby sought to abolish government consultative groups such as the National Women's Advisory Council,[15] it attacked the validity of women's studies courses in universities and arranged for prominent US Moral Majority campaigners to come to Australia to lend their voices to the anti-progressive campaigns. Webley describes the New Right lobby as a loosely organised coalition with a platform that was essentially 'pro-life, pro-family and pro-Christian'.[16]

Legislating for Social Change

Susan Ryan introduced the first Sex Discrimination Bill as a Private Member's Bill in the Senate in 1981 but it was adjourned without a vote. The affirmative action provisions were particularly contentious and did not form part of the revised Bill, which the Labor Party introduced soon after coming into office in 1983. These provisions were set aside and, with the support of Prime Minister, Bob Hawke, became the subject of separate legislation—viz., *Affirmative Action (Equal Employment for Women) Act 1986* (Cth).

Despite the hysteria surrounding the Sex Discrimination Bill, its aims were in fact extremely modest and unlikely to bring about the end of civilisation, as detractors predicted. Indeed, a similar model had been operating in New South Wales, Victoria and South Australia for some years. First of all, the ambit of the legislation was confined to certain areas of public and quasi-public life—viz., employment, education, goods and services, accommodation, land, clubs and the administration of Commonwealth laws and programs. Sexual harassment was expressly proscribed, albeit only in employment. Various exemptions were included, such as those pertaining to educational institutions established by religious bodies—a continuing source of contention on which we will elaborate.

---

13   Irene Webley, 'The New Right and Women Who Want to be Women in Australian Politics in the 1980s' (1983) 9(1/2) *Hecate* 7.
14   For a history of WEL, see Sawer, *Making Women Count*.
15   Lyndsay Connors, 'The Politics of the National Women's Advisory Council', in Simms, *Australian Women and the Political System*.
16   Webley, 'The New Right and Women Who Want to be Women in Australian Politics in the 1980s' 15.

What is significant about the ambit of operation in light of the predicted demise of the family is that the private sphere qua family was immunised from scrutiny. No legislature has been brave enough to cross this line.

Second, the legislation was complaint based, not proactive, which meant that the onus was on an aggrieved individual, male or female, to lodge a complaint with the Human Rights Commission (HRC) alleging discrimination.[17] The HRC would endeavour to conciliate the complaint in private. If this was unsuccessful, the HRC had the power to conduct a formal public hearing. At the hearing, the complainant would bear the onus of proving the discrimination according to the civil standard. The HRC did not have the power to make binding orders. Thus, even if the heroic complainant were successful at the HRC hearing, she could find herself confronted with a hearing de novo before the Federal Court in pursuit of binding orders. The debates contained no inkling of just how difficult this would prove to be.

The aim of the legislation was to effect equal opportunity for women to enable them to compete for jobs and other social goods on the same terms as men. There is no suggestion of preferential treatment; it was anticipated that the best person for the job would be appointed without regard to sex. The approach comported with the liberal principles of formal equality.[18] While there was no express proposal to alter the workplace profile in order to secure substantive equality, it was nevertheless hoped that the resolution of each complaint would have a ripple effect within the community and contribute to the 'elimination' of discrimination in accordance with CEDAW. As argued elsewhere, however, this hope was naive as it is predicated on a belief that discrimination is finite and ignores the way that it is perennially being reconstituted and revived in an ever-changing socio-political context.[19]

Sex discrimination was only inferentially rendered unlawful by the Act (although the proscription of sexual harassment was explicit), as what constitutes discrimination is always contested and must be determined with regard to a particular social and temporal context. Despite limitations in the form of the *SDA*, it possessed great symbolic value. It might not have been able to change attitudes directly, but its proponents hoped that the ripples from each complaint would cause the deeply ingrained prejudice towards women in the public and quasi-public spheres to recede in time. The prospect of a utopian

---

17   The HRC became the Human Rights and Equal Opportunity Commission in 1986 and the Australian Human Rights Commission in 2009.

18   Margaret Thornton, *The Liberal Promise: Anti-Discrimination Legislation in Australia*, Oxford University Press, Melbourne, 1990, Ch. 1.

19   Margaret Thornton, 'Auditing the *Sex Discrimination Act*' in Marius Smith (ed.), *Human Rights 2004: The Year in Review*, Castan Centre for Human Rights Law, Monash University, Melbourne, 2005, pp. 21–56.

society in which gender would have as much significance as eye colour,[20] according to the assimilationist vision, filled the breasts of conservatives with a deep atavistic fear.

The United Nations as Marxist Tyranny: Responses to CEDAW

CEDAW was adopted by the UN General Assembly in 1979[21] and came into force in 1981. The convention is powerfully worded: state parties 'condemn discrimination against women in all its forms' and agree to take 'all appropriate measures' for its elimination 'by all appropriate means and without delay'.[22] A very broad definition of discrimination is included to mean 'any distinction, exclusion or restriction made on the basis of sex',[23] and the convention goes on to enumerate specific areas of private as well as public life on which state parties should focus. The overarching principle is one of effecting equality between men and women in all facets of political, social, economic and cultural life.[24] To accelerate the achievement of this end, express reference is made to the acceptability of temporary special measures,[25] which include affirmative or positive action. In addition, state parties are required to report regularly to a 23-member committee.

While CEDAW is potentially radical, Australia has interpreted its injunctions narrowly.[26] First of all, the focus of the *SDA* is on formal rather than substantive equality. Second, as already mentioned, a strict line of demarcation is maintained between public and private life. Third, the affirmative action provisions disappeared from the Bill at an early stage, which meant that the responsibility for initiating action and proving discrimination rested with individual complainants. Fourth, the Act is sex neutral not sex specific, as is the case with CEDAW—that is, the underlying presupposition of the *SDA* is that men and

---

20   Richard A. Wasserstrom, 'On Racism and Sexism' in Richard A. Wasserstrom (ed.), *Today's Moral Problems*, Third edition, Macmillan, New York, 1985, pp. 20–1.

21   Resolution 34/180, 18 December 1979.

22   CEDAW, Article 2.

23   CEDAW, Article 1.

24   The shift from a focus on protection and correction in earlier UN instruments to non-discrimination in CEDAW represented a significant change of direction. See Natalie Kaufman Hevener, 'An Analysis of Gender Based Treaty Law: Contemporary Developments in Historical Perspective' (1986) 8 *Human Rights Quarterly* 70.

25   CEDAW, Article 4.

26   Cf. Louise Chappell, 'Winding back Australian Women's Rights: Conventions, Contradictions and Conflicts' (2002) 37(3) *Australian Journal of Political Science* 475–88. For evaluation by former CEDAW Committee Chair Elizabeth Evatt, see Elizabeth Evatt, 'Eliminating Discrimination against Women: The Impact of the UN Convention' (1991–92) 18 *Melbourne University Law Review* 435.

women are already similarly situated, a factor that heightens the burden of proof for complainants. Finally, the Australian Government reserved in two respects: the participation of women in armed combat and paid maternity leave.[27]

It might also be noted that the constitutionality of the *SDA* did not depend on the external affairs power alone, but on a range of designated powers within the *Constitution*, including trade and commerce (s. 51[i]), banking (s. 51[xiii]), insurance (s. 51[xiv]), corporations (s. 51[xx]) and Territories (s. 122). Susan Ryan recounts how, with the help of Chris Ronalds, every constitutional power that could be used was included in the drafting of the Bill.[28] Nevertheless, the entire focus of the attack in the course of the debates in regard to constitutionality is directed towards CEDAW and the use of the external affairs power.[29]

It is the preponderance of non-Western nation-states among the ratifying states that most disturbed the conservative parliamentarians. At the time of the debates, 55 countries had ratified CEDAW: eight from Africa, six from Asia, 11 from Eastern Europe, 20 from Latin America and 'only' 10 Western countries (including Australia).[30] Underscoring the non-Anglo-centric orientation of CEDAW was the composition of the 23-member UN overseeing committee. Elected by secret ballot were four members from the Western Bloc, seven from the Eastern Bloc, six from Latin America, two from Africa and four from Asia.[31] The chair was from Mongolia.[32] The identity of the state parties and the composition of the committee underscored the suggestion that the anxiety of the conservative parliamentarians was not just because Australian sovereignty was being compromised by adherence to a UN treaty, but because of the xenophobia arising from the prominence of non-Western influences.

Such anxiety was expressed with recourse to Cold War rhetoric, which retained continuing resonance for conservatives and served as a trigger to reject the social progressivism represented by the Bill. The suggestion that the United Nations was a pretext for the spread of communism was articulated by Senator Ron

---

27　The reservation in respect to women in combat duties was partially withdrawn on 30 August 2000 (<http://treaties.un.org/doc/Publication/MTDSG/Volume%20I/Chapter%20IV/IV-8.en.pdf>). The Rudd Government enacted the *Paid Parental Leave Act 2010* (Cth), which established a scheme to begin in January 2011.

28　Susan Ryan, *Catching the Waves: Life in and out of Politics*, HarperCollins, Sydney, 1999, p. 201.

29　Ian Macphee, Member for Balaclava (LP), said: 'No one would deny, for example, that the Bill should rest on the powers that are properly conferred on the Government in respect of interstate trade and commerce, corporations, financial corporations, or banking and insurance, but there is a great deal of disquiet about the use of the external affairs power as a safety net to provide residual validity in case the High Court should find that the more conventional heads of power were inadequate' (*House Hansard*, 5 March 1984, p. 502).

30　Margaret E. Galey, 'International Enforcement of Women's Rights' (1984) 6 *Human Rights Quarterly* 463, 483.

31　Ibid., 476.

32　Ibid.

Boswell (LP), who, in a veiled reference to the chair of the CEDAW Committee, announced that '[t]he women of Australia do not want legislation that is drafted by the public servants of Mongolia'.[33]

Parochial anxiety about Australia's increased participation on the international stage elicited resentment that 'we should be dragged by the nose to some international convention to be reminded of our derelictions in this country'.[34] Peter Drummond (LP) declared that many of the UN member states were 'ruled by Marxist tyrannies. Hypocrisy and humbug are their stock in trade.' He maintained that UN conventions were acceptable only to the extent that they expressed 'innocuous sentiments' and did not 'interfere with the lives of Australians':

> The United Nations has some value in providing an international talking-shop, a safety valve, and some useful mechanisms and agencies. However, I think the people of Australia would be horrified to think of it as some kind of incipient world government, whose decrees and conventions are morally superior to the laws of this country.[35]

Resistance was also expressed as xenophobia, for, according to some senators, CEDAW was not relevant in Anglo-Celtic society, but 'makes perfectly good sense if it relates to the removal of social and legal repression of women as it exists in many Third World countries'.[36] Senator Flo Bjelke-Petersen (NP) announced that the Bill would be more appropriate for 'the Middle East'[37]—an ethnocentric sentiment echoed by future prime minister John Howard, who supported the Bill because 'amongst ethnic groups, there are incidences of discrimination and disadvantage against women which are not present within some of the more conservative or Anglo-Saxon elements of our society'.[38] Such attitudes were not limited to the conservative side of politics—for example: Senator Michael Tate (ALP) stated that CEDAW was 'designed to liberate women in quite different cultures from our own who quite often are the slaves and victims of very chauvinistic societies'.[39]

---

33   Senator Boswell (LP), *Senate Hansard*, 29 November 1983, p. 2963.
34   Mr Clarrie Millar, Member for Wide Bay (NP), *House Hansard*, 5 March 1984, p. 472.
35   Mr Peter Drummond, Member for Forrest (LP), *House Hansard*, 1 March 1984, p. 344.
36   Ibid.
37   Senator Flo Bjelke-Petersen (NP), *Senate Hansard*, 6 December 1983, p. 3335.
38   Hon. Mr John Howard, Member for Bennelong (LP), *House Hansard*, 7 March 1983, p. 671.
39   Senator Michael Tate (ALP), *Senate Hansard*, 21 October 1983, p. 1923.

Feminists in the House

Often characterised by rhetorical flourishes that would be the envy of contemporary political speechwriters, the proposed legislation was condemned by conservatives, who alleged that it was evidence of the newly elected Hawke Labor Government's affiliation with communism. In a surprising display of familiarity with Marxism, Senator Boswell quoted Friedrich Engels as the source of the 'movement towards a unisex society'.[40] It was claimed the Bill was fundamentally flawed because it undermined traditional values and individual rights, which conservatives claimed were the hallmarks of a liberal democracy. The challenge to these principles was said to emanate chiefly from feminists on the left of the ALP whose recent arrival in the parliamentary chambers had unsettled the chauvinistic culture among conservatives in the Liberal/ National Coalition parties. According to Michael Hodgman (LP), the Bill was 'an appalling piece of legislation', which was promoted by 'arrogant minority pressure groups' to be 'inflicted upon the people of Australia by the Hawke socialist Government'. When announcing his intention to vote against the Bill, he said:

> Whilst conceding that there are parts of the Bill with which I have no quarrel whatsoever, I have to say that the legislation as a whole is tainted with the pseudo-intellectualism of selfish and unrepresentative feminism and doctrinaire marxist-socialist precepts of contrived equality—defying even the laws of nature. This Bill, in so many ways, brings down upon itself the maxim reductio ad absurdum. It therefore does a grave disservice to the principle it espouses. [41]

The increased visibility of feminists in parliamentary politics and in senior positions in the public service in Australia from the mid-1970s generated bewilderment and antipathy among conservatives who feared their power would be diminished. Rather than extending equality of opportunity to women, the *SDA* was characterised as representing an attack on fundamental Christian values. The hostile response to progressive social change took the form of reactionary backlash, with denigrating—and often farcical—attacks on progressive women. Feminist politics was dismissed as an incomprehensible fad.

The Member for Franklin, Bruce Goodluck (LP), announced that he had conducted an investigation of WEL and concluded that most of the members

---

40 Senator Ron Boswell (LP), *Senate Hansard*, 29 November 1983, p. 2963, quoting *The Origin of the Family* (1884).

41 Hon. Mr Michael Hodgman, Member for Denison (LP), *House Hansard*, 5 March 1984, p. 489.

were 'given-up Catholics'. While acknowledging that there were some women in the Liberal Party who supported the Bill, he flippantly dismissed women in the Labor Party because they advocated progressive political positions:

> I have looked at the four women on the Government side. They are nice ladies…But they are all the same. They are always campaigning to save the cats, save the dogs and save the whales. They are anti-nuclear and pro-abortion…They are anti the flag and anti the dam…That is predominantly what Labor Party women are like. But they can talk; they are dashed good talkers. We have a few Liberal women who cross those lines and who are called trendy. But the majority of Liberal women are quiet and do not say much…I have nothing against Labor women personally but they all seem to take up this role and I am afraid that everybody is starting to think that that role is the norm. [42]

Creating a Unisex Society

The suggestion that the *SDA* was an inappropriate mechanism for liberal-democratic capitalist states such as Australia functioned to augment a parallel argument that asserted that it threatened to destabilise traditional sex roles, reflecting a more general anxiety about the impact of second-wave feminism on social norms. Indeed, the *SDA* was credited with significant transformative power; it was said to threaten to effect the eradication of sexual difference altogether. During the course of the parliamentary debates, the conservative think tank the Institute of Public Affairs published the opinion of a prominent paediatrician in which it was claimed that 'the basic philosophy of this Bill is to remove as far as possible all differences between men and women'.[43]

Senator Pat Giles pointed out that it was beyond the government's power to 'legislate to eradicate gender differences',[44] but the commitment in CEDAW to the elimination of sexism based on sex-role stereotypes[45] was characterised by conservative lobby groups and parliamentarians as evidence of a desire to create a 'unisex society'. The use of the term 'unisex'—which had entered the lexicon to mean the provision of services to both men and women—demonstrates a

---

42 Mr Bruce Goodluck, Member for Franklin (LP), *House Hansard*, 2 March 1984, p. 391. Although Goodluck strongly opposed the *SDA*, he was subsequently reported as saying that he did not want his five daughters to be discriminated against. See Mary-Louise O'Callahan, 'Equality bill sparks a war cry', *Sydney Morning Herald*, 19 February 1986, p. 15.

43 Opinion of Dr Clair Isbister, published by the Institute of Public Affairs and cited by Senator Haines (Democrat), *Senate Hansard*, 21 October 1983, p. 1928.

44 Senator Pat Giles (ALP), *Senate Hansard*, 26 November 1983, p. 405.

45 Article 5(a) commits state parties '[t]o modify the social and cultural patterns of conduct of men and women, with a view to the elimination of prejudices and customary and all other practices which are based on the idea of the inferiority or the superiority of either of the sexes or on stereotyped roles for men and women'.

fundamental misunderstanding of the concept of gender neutrality underlying liberal feminist claims to equal opportunity, suggesting a far more powerful role for law in subverting prevailing social norms.

Far from embracing gender neutrality, conservative politicians echoed the thesis of gender complementarity according to which women and men perform different social roles on the basis of their biological uniqueness. This thesis is entrenched within the Western intellectual tradition and can be traced back to Aristotle.[46] Its crude socio-biology enabled a clear gender division between public and private spheres to be maintained. This was now being threatened, according to conservative politicians.

Ray Groom (LP) argued that '[t]he philosophy from which this Bill springs does not recognise any innate differences between male and female'; 'the sexes are not in competition but, according to the rules of nature, complement each other'.[47] Such claims were illustrated with reference to overstated examples of women performing non-traditional roles, such as 'digging drains, shearing sheep, slaughtering beasts or occupied as undertakers, [and] sawmill operators'.[48] Contrary to such images, Senator Archer announced that '[m]en, by nature, are more likely to be leaders, providers and protectors. We can legislate all we like, but we will not change that…Why do women want to be like men, or men want to be like women…What has become wrong with being what nature provides?'[49]

The resistance provoked by the prospect of women working in male-dominated fields highlights the threatening presence of the feminine in the public sphere and its emasculating effect on men. The suggestion that the *SDA* would facilitate the mass entry of women into archetypal 'masculine' areas of work—where resistance to the feminine remains pronounced—was, however, also a rhetorical device intended to undermine the legislation's appeal to the Western liberal principle of equality. It conjures up Cold War images of women in Eastern Bloc countries working in industries absent the trappings of Western notions of femininity. Senator Bjelke-Petersen described the removal of gender stereotypes as 'social engineering'[50]—not only exemplifying the attempt to associate the *SDA* with totalitarianism, but also suggesting the insidious power of law to disrupt conventional norms of gender relations.

---

46   Londa Schiebinger, *The Mind Has No Sex? Women in the Origins of Modern Science*, Harvard University Press, Cambridge, Mass., 1989, pp. 216–22.

47   Hon. Mr Ray Groom, Member for Braddon (LP), *House Hansard*, 1 March 1984, p. 367.

48   Senator Brian Archer (LP), *Senate Hansard*, 8 November 1983, p. 2299.

49   Ibid.

50   Senator Flo Bjelke-Petersen (NP), *Senate Hansard*, 6 December 1983, p. 3335.

Despite the significant feminist theoretical challenges to the nature/culture dualism of sexual difference,[51] biological determinism animated the parliamentary debates. According to Senator Archer, the proposed legislation would make it an offence to take into account the sexual characteristic of 'most ordinary, natural women', who are 'homely and caring...not wildly ambitious... not naturally dominating...and mostly inclined to avoid authority...by nature, more cautious and more considerate'.[52]

By the early 1980s, women had entered the paid workforce in Australia in significant numbers, but participation was concentrated in the occupational categories of clerical, sales and services, as had been the case for most of the twentieth century.[53] In these occupations, it is assumed that 'natural' feminine characteristics such as subservience and compassion are demanded. The feminisation of these traditional roles, particularly when part-time and/or at junior levels, does not unduly disrupt the patriarchal construction of subordination in which full citizenship is withheld from women. As Pateman pointed out: 'The civil right to "work" is still only half-heartedly acknowledged for women. Women in the workplace are still perceived primarily as wives and mothers, not workers.' [54]

Resistance to the *SDA* reflected this perception, as we will go on to discuss.

The Disintegration of the Patriarchal Family

Undoubtedly, the most menacing ramification of the *SDA* was that it was bound to contribute to the disintegration of the patriarchal nuclear family. The Bill was described as an attack on 'the importance of the family as the fundamental unit of society, and our traditional Australian way of life'.[55] Innumerable petitions were tabled in both houses of parliament alleging that the commitment within CEDAW to the elimination of stereotyped roles for men and women[56] was likely to contribute to 'further marriage insecurity and breakdown', as well as disrupting

---

51   For example, Simone de Beauvoir, *The Second Sex*, Translated and edited by H. M. Parshley, Four Square Books, New English Library, London, 1960; Sherry B. Ortner, 'Is Female to Male as Nature is to Culture?' in Michelle Zimbalist Rosaldo and Louise Lamphere (eds), *Woman, Culture and Society*, Stanford University Press, Calif., 1983.

52   Senator Brian Archer (LP), *Senate Hansard*, 8 November 1983, p. 2299.

53   Margaret Power, 'Women's Work is Never Done—by Men: A Socio-economic Model of Sex-typing in Occupations' (1975) 17 *Journal of Industrial Relations* 225.

54   Carole Pateman, *The Disorder of Woman: Democracy, Feminism and Political Theory*, Polity Press, Cambridge, 1989, p. 190.

55   Hon. Mr Michael Hodgman, Member for Denison (LP), *House Hansard*, 5 March 1984, p. 489.

56   Part III, Article 10(c) commits state parties to '[t]he elimination of any stereotyped concept of the roles of men and women at all levels and in all forms of education by encouraging coeducation and other types of education which will help to achieve this aim and, in particular, by the revision of textbooks and school programmes and the adaption of teaching methods'.

traditional parental roles leading to 'emotional disturbances of childhood'.[57] In the wake of second-wave feminism and no-fault divorce, reactionary responses crystallised in regard to the increasing instability of the patriarchal nuclear family. By the early 1980s, the introduction of no-fault divorce under the *Family Law Act 1975*, together with increasing numbers of single-parent families headed by women, had a significant impact on the constitution of the family. To counteract the disorder arising from 'unmanned' women usurping the proper role of the pater familias, conservative organisations—notably, WWWW—trenchantly advocated for the primacy of the heterosexual nuclear family.[58] WWWW was also supported by the wives of prominent conservative politicians, such as Margot Anthony, wife of the National Party leader, who argued that the *SDA* would 'encourage the breakdown of the family unit'.[59]

It was repeatedly alleged that the principle of non-discrimination enshrined in CEDAW imposed a requirement on women to reject their traditional role within the family. Senator Crichton-Browne (LP) claimed that the convention 'seeks to assert that many women who consider themselves to be both happy and equal in their roles as mothers and wives are not happy, and that the steps set out in the Convention requiring a change in their roles are necessary to make them equal'. He declared that '[t]he real intention and purpose of this legislation…is a not too subtle attempt to destroy the structure, the fabric, the values and the intrinsic role of the family unit which for centuries has been the foundation of our orderly and disciplined society and culture'. [60]

Ray Groom (LP) claimed that almost every provision in the convention 'attempts to encourage women to leave home and go into the workforce', but it 'is high time we did more to give proper support to the woman who chooses to remain at home to look after her family'.[61] Despite attempts by supporters of the Bill to make clear that neither CEDAW nor the *SDA* 'obliged anyone to enter the paid work force or to alter people's views of their responsibilities towards their spouses or children',[62] the legislation was repeatedly said to force mothers out to work, with 'no choice…except for short maternity leave'.[63]

Women would lose their 'right to choose' to prioritise their role as wives and mothers over paid work. According to Senator Shirley Walters, it was 'quite

---

57   For example, petition tabled by Senator Sir John Carrick, *Senate Hansard*, 1 November 1983, p. 1976; petition tabled by Senators Button, Sir John Carrick and Collard, *Senate Hansard*, 2 November 1983, p. 2041.
58   WWWW, which has since changed its name to Endeavour Forum, continues to be active in lobbying governments on a range of issues. It claims to have been set up to 'counter feminism, defend the unborn and the traditional family' (<http://www.endeavourforum.org.au/>)
59   Jenny Cooke, 'Strong advice for Flo, Mrs Anthony', *Sydney Morning Herald*, 21 September 1983, p. 3.
60   Senator Noel Crichton-Browne (LP), *Senate Hansard*, 9 December 1983, p. 3628.
61   Hon. Mr Ray Groom (LP), Member for Braddon, *House Hansard*, 1 March 1984, p. 367.
62   Senator Peter Durack (LP), *Senate Hansard*, 21 October 1983, p. 1919.
63   Pamphlet distributed by WWWW, cited by Mr Leonard Keogh (ALP), Member for Bowman, *House Hansard*, 2 March 1984, p. 406.

incorrect' that Australian women were 'paid less for equal work and equal time' because 'women choose different careers from men'. She claimed that the reason women earn less than men is because '[w]omen make choices. The facts prove that they choose to have a family…96.1 per cent of married women choose to have babies. Obviously they make it a greater priority than a career.' [64]

The use of the rhetoric of 'choice' resonates with contemporary debates over abortion—another issue that was tenaciously pursued, as we will discuss.

The emotive power of the mother–child relationship was not lost on opponents of the *SDA*, who made dire predictions that motherhood would become a 'second class calling or profession', leaving the state with the responsibility for the 'care and control of the child from infancy to maturity with the opportunity to mould its emotional life and its thinking'.[65] Rather than a progressive move that would facilitate the entry of women into the paid workforce, child care was described as 'a disgrace', where young children suffered maternal deprivation, 'their thumbs stuck in their mouths, all trying to rock themselves to sleep'.[66]

In the face of such rhetoric, supporters of the legislation recognised the necessity of affirming the legislation's inability to effect significant changes in the structure and organisation of the traditional family. Senator Giles acknowledged that '[s]ome of the less palatable aspects of the family—its nuclear structure and its patriarchal dominance—are already in the process of modification'. Moreover, anti-discrimination legislation would 'lead to a greatly enhanced quality of relationships within that very resilient institution, the family'.[67] Among members of the Coalition, significant divisions emerged. Senator Teague saw cause to table a statement outlining the Liberal Party's policy on the family as 'the fundamental and most important social and cohesive force in society'.[68] Nevertheless, the level of antipathy from some members, particularly the Nationals, resulted in the Coalition allowing a conscience vote on the *SDA*.

Conscientious Objection: The Right to Discriminate

The tension between law and morality was revealed most starkly in the proposal that emerged during debates that a conscientious objection clause be included in the *SDA* itself in respect of its areas of operation. Such a clause would provide exemption where there are 'any conscientious beliefs, whether the grounds for

---

64   Senator Shirley Walters (LP), *Senate Hansard*, 29 November 1983, p. 2950.
65   Document signed by Dr Rendle-Short, Mrs Butler and Mrs Sully, tabled by Senator Baden Teague (LP), *Senate Hansard*, 29 November 1983, p. 2954.
66   Senator Austin Lewis (LP), *Senate Hansard*, 6 December 1983, p. 3329.
67   Senator Pat Giles (ALP), *Senate Hansard*, 8 November 1983, p. 2311.
68   Senator Baden Teague (LP), *Senate Hansard*, 29 November 1983, p. 2954.

the beliefs are or are not of a religious character and whether the beliefs are or are not part of the doctrine of any religion'.[69] According to Evan Adermann (NP), such an exemption was necessary in a situation in which, for example, he decided to sell property and would otherwise be unable to prevent a prospective buyer who 'intended to institute a brothel, a witches' coven, a temple for Satan worship' if it could be 'alleged anywhere that sex, marital status or the like had any part in my decision'.[70] Mr Groom announced: 'As I understand the Bill, it requires a person to decide between what his conscience tells him and what the law tells him. I think this is placing a very unfair pressure upon individuals in the community.'[71]

The government resisted pressure, however, to include a conscientious objection clause, because, as Senator Ryan pointed out, it would provide that 'one does have the right to discriminate if one's conscience tells one that women are inferior, unable to be trusted, or anything else'.[72]

Nevertheless, the thin edge of the wedge was apparent, for the government was prepared to concede an exemption for church-run educational institutions to discriminate in employment on the grounds of sex, marital status or pregnancy, 'where the discrimination is in accordance with the doctrines of the religion or creed and the discrimination occurs in good faith…The discrimination itself has to flow from the ethos, the creed, the values, of that particular educational institution'.[73] The Opposition did not believe this went far enough—proposing an amendment to exempt non-denominational schools that were 'conducted in accordance with stated moral principles which are not, in fact, dictated by the teachings or beliefs of a particular religion'.[74] This amendment was defeated in committee.[75] The exemption in favour of religious schools accords with the general practice of the secular state in deferring to religious freedom. The anomaly in the Australian context is that religious schools are not strictly 'private' as they are the recipients of substantial state funding. No regard was paid to this factor in the debates, although the *Defence of Government Schools* (*DOGS*) case, in which state aid for private schools had been unsuccessfully challenged in the High Court,[76] had been a matter of public controversy only a couple of years earlier.

---

69   Senator Brian Harradine (Ind.), *Senate Hansard*, 16 December 1983, p. 3994.

70   Mr Evan Adermann, Member for Fisher (NP), *House Hansard*, 5 March 1984, p. 485.

71   Hon. Mr Ray Groom, Member for Braddon (LP), *House Hansard*, 1 March 1984, p. 367.

72   Senator Susan Ryan (ALP), *Senate Hansard*, 16 December 1983, p. 3997.

73   Senator Michael Tate (ALP), *Senate Hansard*, 21 October 1983, p. 1923. Under the *Sex Discrimination Act 1984* (s. 38), there is exemption in the area of employment, including contract workers, in situations where this is conducted 'in good faith in order to avoid injury to the religious susceptibilities of adherents of that religion or creed'.

74   Senator Peter Durack (LP), *Senate Hansard*, 29 November 1983, p. 2948. The Australian Parents' Council (representing private schools) also attacked the government for not going far enough. See Amanda Buckley, 'Parents criticise sex bill changes', *Sydney Morning Herald*, 13 October 1983, p. 5.

75   Amendment proposed by Hon. Mr Ian Macphee, Member for Balaclava (LP), *House Hansard*, 7 March 1984, p. 627.

76   *A-G (Vic) Ex rel Black v Commonwealth* (1981) 146 CLR 559.

Undoubtedly, the biggest 'red herring' of the *SDA* debate was the issue of abortion.[77] Despite the fact that neither CEDAW nor the Bill made any reference to abortion—which hardly falls within the sex-neutral provision of goods and services—the prospect that the legislation could 'convert a woman's decision to have an abortion into a right to demand that abortion' was addressed in thousands of petitions and repeatedly raised in the parliamentary debates. Senator Ryan clearly explained that anti-discrimination legislation could not be used in this context because '[o]ne cannot say that it is discriminatory to refuse a man an abortion since in the nature of that service it is not available to be offered to a man'.[78] This was supported by legal advice to the Right to Life Association of Victoria.[79] Nevertheless, as a result of Senator Harradine's relentless pursuit of the issue,[80] an amendment was included to clarify concern that the Bill did not apply to the 'provision of services the nature of which is such that they can only be provided to members of one sex'.[81]

The passage of the *SDA* represented the triumph of social liberalism in Australia. Far from persuading others through their rhetoric, Senator Harradine and those conservative Liberal and National Party members who opposed the Bill succeeded only in alienating their colleagues with their filibustering and hyperbolic claims. Similarly, groups such as WWWW vigorously garnered opposition to the *SDA* in the broader community, but the final votes suggest that they exercised little impact on the mainstream. In the Senate on 16 December 1983, there were 40 ayes and 12 noes; in the House of Representatives on 7 March 1984, there were 86 ayes and 26 noes.[82] Susan Ryan noted in her autobiography that the *SDA* was probably the most useful thing she had done in her life.[83]

Conclusion

The tension between equality and liberty—the constituent elements of liberalism—is very clearly illustrated by the passage of the *SDA* and the subsequent backlash.[84] Any attempt to implement policies of equality and distributive justice under social liberalism is likely to induce a sense of

---

77 Senator Susan Ryan (ALP), *Senate Hansard*, 16 December 1983, p. 3964.

78 Ibid., p. 3964; *SDA*, s. 32.

79 Advice provided by P. J. O'Callaghan (30 November 1983), tabled by Senator Michael Tate (ALP), *Senate Hansard*, 16 December 1983, p. 3987.

80 Concern was also expressed by Senator Austin Lewis (LP) (*Senate Hansard*, 6 December 1983, p. 3329) and Senator Flo Bjelke-Petersen (NP) (*Senate Hansard*, 6 December 1983, p. 3335).

81 Senator Kathy Martin (LP), *Senate Hansard*, 16 December 1983, p. 3966.

82 *Senate Hansard*, 16 December 1983, p. 4011; *House Hansard*, 7 March 1984, p. 677.

83 Ryan, *Catching the Waves*, p. 243.

84 As Sawer shows, the retreat from EEO was not confined to the conservative political parties. See Marian Sawer, *Sisters in Suits: Women and Public Policy in Australia*, Allen & Unwin, Sydney, 1990, pp. 212–26.

ressentiment[85] among conservatives. As Wendy Brown argues, they feel that their freedom has been attenuated, which causes them to campaign against equality for increased liberty.[86] When conservatism is in the ascendancy, egalitarianism contracts and the *ressentiment* of the left causes the pendulum to swing in the other direction.

The *ressentiment* of the right over social-liberal initiatives of all kinds, including the *SDA*, led to the fervent embrace of neo-liberalism within little more than a decade of the passage of the *SDA*. The feminist agenda quickly became passé within the wider community as the discourse of the market became the meta-narrative of the millennial moment. An intimate liaison was effected between the state and the market. Although secularism was ostensibly in the ascendancy, the state's embrace of neo-conservatism allowed greater cognisance of and deference to religion.[87]

The category 'woman', which was central to the political power of the women's movement in the period leading up to the passage of the *SDA*, also began to disintegrate. Instead of the one-dimensional woman of feminist discourse, a more nuanced heteroglossic symbol emerged in which greater attention was paid to difference, particularly with regards to race, sexuality and disability. A notable manifestation of the phenomenon was the way women's studies courses began to disappear from the academy in favour of gender studies or diversity studies. With feminism no longer in the ascendancy, the neo-conservative disciplining gaze could be directed to the family in its traditional nuclear incarnation, together with sexuality and extramarital pregnancy.

The *SDA* signified a major rift between secularism and religion in terms of gender norms. The rift highlights the aporia between equality and liberty that is central to liberal theory. On the one hand, as Julian Rivers suggests, gender equality requires the 'complete androgynisation of law',[88] which has profound moral consequences for understandings of sex and gender. On the other hand, freedom of religion is one of the manifestations of liberty, along with freedom of speech, property and the person, to say nothing of freedom of the market, which is accentuated by conservatism. The struggle over the androgynisation of law, which began with the *SDA*, has become the new site of struggle within liberalism. Rather than a focus on sex per se, attention has, however, subtly shifted to race, religion or age, so that the issues of sex, sexuality and

---

85 Nietzsche uses this term to capture the desire of a victim to retaliate by inflicting harm on the perpetrator in order that the victim might lessen his or her own pain. See Friedrich Nietzsche, *On the Genealogy of Morals*, Translated by W. Kaufman and R. J. Hollingdale, Vintage Books, New York, 1969, p. 127.

86 Wendy Brown, *States of Injury: Power and Freedom in Late Modernity*, Princeton University Press, NJ, 1995, p. 67.

87 Marion Maddox, *God Under Howard: The Rise of the Religious Right in Australian Politics*, Allen & Unwin, Sydney, 2005.

88 Julian Rivers, 'Law, religion and gender equality' (2007) 9 *Ecclesiastical Law Journal* 33, 50.

marital status are occluded, other than in instances where corporeality is to the fore: sexual harassment, pregnancy and caring for children. This shift in the prioritisation of grounds instantiates the conservative orthodoxy that sex discrimination is now passé.

Bibliography

Books and articles

Brown, Wendy, *States of Injury: Power and Freedom in Late Modernity*, Princeton University Press, NJ, 1995.

Buckley, Amanda, 'Parents criticise sex bill changes', *Sydney Morning Herald*, 13 October 1983, p. 5.

Chappell, Louise, 'Winding Back Australian Women's Rights: Conventions, Contradictions and Conflicts' (2002) 37(3) *Australian Journal of Political Science* 475–88.

Connors, Lyndsay, 'The Politics of the National Women's Advisory Council' in Marian Simms (ed.), *Australian Women and the Political System*, Longman Cheshire, Melbourne, 1984.

Cooke, Jenny, 'Strong advice for Flo, Mrs Anthony', *Sydney Morning Herald*, 21 September 1983, p. 3.

de Beauvoir, Simone, *The Second Sex*, Translated and edited by H. M. Parshley, Four Square Books, New English Library, London, 1960.

Evatt, Elizabeth, 'Eliminating Discrimination Against Women: The Impact of the UN Convention' (1991–92) 18 *Melbourne University Law Review* 435.

Galey, Margaret E., 'International Enforcement of Women's Rights' (1984) 6 *Human Rights Quarterly* 463.

Hawker, Philippa, 'A plain person's guide to that sex bill', *Sydney Morning Herald*, 6 October 1983, p. 38.

Hevener, Natalie Kaufman, 'An Analysis of Gender Based Treaty Law: Contemporary Developments in Historical Perspective' (1986) 8 *Human Rights Quarterly* 70.

Maddox, Marion, *God Under Howard: The Rise of the Religious Right in Australian Politics*, Allen & Unwin, Sydney, 2005.

Nietzsche, Friedrich, *On the Genealogy of Morals*, Translated by W. Kaufman and R. J. Hollingdale, Vintage Books, New York, 1969.

O'Callahan, Mary-Louise, 'Equality bill sparks a war cry', *Sydney Morning Herald*, 19 February 1986, p. 15.

Ortner, Sherry B., 'Is Female to Male as Nature is to Culture?' in Michelle Zimbalist Rosaldo and Louise Lamphere (eds), *Woman, Culture and Society*, Stanford University Press, Calif., 1983.

Parkinson, Patrick, Christian Concerns with the Charter of Rights, Paper presented at Cultural and Religious Freedom under a Bill of Rights Conference, Canberra, 2009.

Pateman, Carole, *The Disorder of Woman: Democracy, Feminism and Political Theory*, Polity Press, Cambridge, UK, 1989.

Power, Margaret, 'Women's Work is Never Done—by Men: A Socio-economic Model of Sex-typing in Occupations' (1975) 17 *Journal of Industrial Relations* 225.

Rivers, Julian, 'Law, Religion and Gender Equality' (2007) 9 *Ecclesiastical Law Journal* 33.

Ryan, Susan, *Catching the Waves: Life in and out of Politics*, HarperCollins, Sydney, 1999.

Sawer, Marian, *Sisters in Suits: Women and Public Policy in Australia*, Allen & Unwin, Sydney, 1990.

Sawer, Marian and Simms, Marian, *A Woman's Place: Women and Politics in Australia*, Allen & Unwin, Sydney, 1993.

Sawer, Marian with Radford, Gail, *Making Women Count: A History of the Women's Electoral Lobby in Australia*, UNSW Press, Sydney, 2008.

Schiebinger, Londa, *The Mind Has No Sex? Women in the Origins of Modern Science*, Harvard University Press, Cambridge, Mass., 1989.

Simms, Marian, '"A Woman's Place is in the House and in the Senate": Women and the 1983 Elections' in Marian Simms (ed.), *Australian Women and the Political System*, Longman Cheshire, Melbourne, 1984.

Thornton, Margaret, *The Liberal Promise: Anti-Discrimination Legislation in Australia*, Oxford University Press, Melbourne, 1990.

Thornton, Margaret, 'Auditing the *Sex Discrimination Act*' in Marius Smith (ed.), *Human Rights 2004: The Year in Review*, Castan Centre for Human Rights Law, Monash University, Melbourne, 2005.

Wasserstrom, Richard A., 'On Racism and Sexism' in Richard A. Wasserstrom (ed.), *Today's Moral Problems*, Third edition, Macmillan, New York, 1985.

Webley, Irene, 'The New Right and Women Who Want to be Women in Australian Politics in the 1980s' (1983) 9(1/2) *Hecate* 7.

Legislation

Racial Discrimination Act 1975 (Cth)

Sex Discrimination Act 1984 (Cth)

Cases

A-G (Vic) Ex rel Black v Commonwealth (1981) 146 CLR 559 (*DOGS case*)

Commonwealth v Queensland (Queen of Queensland) (1975) 134 CLR 298

Commonwealth v Tasmania (1983) 158 CLR 1 (*Tasmanian Dams*)

Koowarta v Bjelke-Petersen (1982) 153 CLR 168

Members of the Board of the Wesley Mission Council v OV & OW (No. 2) [2009] NSWADTAP 57

Reports and miscellaneous primary sources

Commonwealth of Australia, *National Human Rights Consultation Report*, Commonwealth of Australia, Canberra, 2009 [*Brennan Report*].

Parliament of Australia, *Hansard: House of Representatives*, Parliament of Australia, Canberra, 1983–84.

Parliament of Australia, *Hansard: Senate*, Parliament of Australia, Canberra, 1983–84.

United Nations Convention on the Elimination of All Forms of Discrimination Against Women, United Nations, New York.

United Nations Convention on the Elimination of All Forms of Racial Discrimination, United Nations, New York.

2. A Radical Prequel: Historicising the Concept of Gendered Law in Australia

Ann Genovese[1]

Anniversaries are about remembering—about reiterations and critiques, as well as about reflections and celebrations. In this way, an anniversary essay about the Commonwealth Sex Discrimination Act 1984 *(SDA) is an invitation to think historically from different purviews of the past. What I would like to consider therefore in response to such an invitation, as a historian of legal ideas, is not a story about the legislative process in making the Act a reality or a story of the contests and challenges to its subsequent legal meanings. Instead, what I would like to offer to this collection is a prequel: a story of how it became possible to use gender as a conceptual frame for thinking about law in Australia—as the SDA exemplifies— and how that history exposes an experience of radical, countercultural feminist praxis that is often hidden by, but constitutive of, the more familiar teleological stories of feminisms, and of law itself.*

'Gender: A Useful Category for Historical Analysis'

In considering how to approach historicising the concept of gendered law in Australia in this way, it is worth reflecting on the fact that it was not until the mid-1980s that gender was theorised, let alone operationalised, as a conceptual category in law, history or other disciplinary traditions. For historians, one of the most influential essays that argued for a theoretical approach to using gender in ways that went beyond descriptive or causal techniques was US historian and theorist Joan Wallach Scott's 'Gender: a useful category for historical analysis' in the *American Historical Review*. Scott suggested 'we must constantly ask not only what is at stake in proclamations or debates that invoke gender to explain or justify their positions but also how implicit understandings of

1   I thank Ann Curthoys and Margaret Thornton for engagement and dialogue with the historiographical and jurisprudential arguments offered here, as well as with the historical content. I also thank the two reviewers for their helpful clarifications.

gender are being invoked and reinscribed'.[2] This is particularly important and useful, Scott argues, for thinking through how representations about, and also made by, women are often re-inscribed as normative *concepts* within discourses, and how that process then 'limits and contains their metaphoric possibilities'. These limits, as has been well understood in much scholarship since then, are often predetermined by the inherent binary oppositions within Enlightenment thought, re-inscribed through particular doctrinal givens.[3] The task for *historians*, Scott contended, was nevertheless specific: to refuse to accept those normative concepts and languages, exposed through the archive, as anything but the product of social contest. Through such a refusal, what could be opened up are the spaces that lie between the processes, languages or structures that overwrite and describe concepts in the first place. This enables some room for human agency in normative discourse and therefore suggests rather than forecloses the possibility of change. From this perspective, asking questions about how concepts (such as gender) developed within the legal praxis of a country such as Australia in the immediate past has the potential to be useful in the present, as they can be directed towards 'the possibility for negation, reinterpretation, the play of metaphoric invention and imagination'.[4]

Thinking about Scott's 1986 essay is important for this prequel for two reasons. The first reason is this key question about centralising gender as a category of analysis. Scott's 'Gender' essay is contemporaneous with the *SDA*'s genesis; it reminds us, as noted already, that the mid to late 1980s marks a key moment in the development of thinking about how gender operates normatively in society. To the earlier focus of 'writing women in' (be it to historical narrative or legislative instruments) was now added an interest in the ways in which conceptual categories (such as discrimination) were constructed and perpetuated.[5] As others in this volume and elsewhere attest in their analyses of the emergence of the *SDA* in Australia—but for one example—these conceptual concerns were, and remain, clearly evident.[6] Scott's theorising of gender therefore refracts the content of both a legislative instrument such as the *SDA* and its political context, and makes an important reiteration that the mid-1980s was an epoch

---

2   Joan W. Scott, 'Gender: A useful Category of Historical Analysis' (1986) 91(5) *American Historical Review* 1053, 1074.

3   In that same year, Margaret Thornton made a similar case contributing to the development of feminist jurisprudence in this country: Margaret Thornton, 'Feminist jurisprudence: Illusion or Reality?' (1986) 3 *Australian Journal of Law & Society* 5.

4   Scott, 'Gender' 1067.

5   For general examples, see: Genevieve Lloyd, *The Man of Reason: 'Male' and 'Female' in Western Philosophy*, Methuen, London, 1984; Catherine Mackinnon, *Feminism Unmodified: Discourse on Life and Law*, Harvard University Press, Cambridge, Mass., 1987; Carol Smart, *Feminism and the Power of Law*, Routledge, London, 1989; Elizabeth Grosz, 'The In(ter)vention of Feminist Knowledges' in Barbara Caine, E. A. Grosz and Marie de Lepervanche (eds), *Crossing Boundaries: Feminism and the Critique of Knowledges*, Allen & Unwin, Sydney, 1988.

6   See Sawer, Magarey, Thornton and Luker, Ronalds and Ryan, this volume.

in which earlier manifestations of thinking about the state's construction of women, and its response to discrimination based on sex (be it in Australia, the United Kingdom, Europe or the United States), shifted.

The second reason—and the one that primarily concerns me in this chapter— is a question of interrogating politico-legal questions from the traditions offered by critical history. This tradition—as argued by Scott and of course Foucault and others—is to think about *how* concepts change and to look for ways of engaging with the process of change beyond single origins. As Scott identified, this involves interrogating a range of different, yet intermingled, political, cultural and intellectual trajectories. This suggests a slightly different history from the other stories of the Act's passage included in this book, which cover the predominant and more chartered territory of understanding how feminists, through WEL and within the state in the 1970s and 1980s, argued for the legislative right to be equal (as Jocelynne Scutt described it, in 1988).[7] The specific *causative* history of the *SDA* is importantly very much about the relationship between WEL's focus on making sex discrimination politically visible from 1972 onwards and a state at the high point of its commitment to legislating against disadvantage, as Marian Sawer has made very clear.[8] My point, however, is that there are other histories to remember here too. One of these—complementary to those offered in this book—I want to bring to light in this spirit of disrupting a fixed historical gaze, or a belief in single origins, inhered in problematic ways in normative concepts.

This other history involves traditions that ran alongside yet in partnership with those in WEL: Marxism and, less frequently identified in stories about law, radical libertarianism with a commitment to situational exposure of harms to women in the criminal justice system. How these other traditions within feminism met and influenced a nascent Australian feminist legal praxis is my focus. It is a story that centres on the emergence of the Feminist Legal Action Group (FLAG), a group that took gender as a concept seriously and that emerged during the maelstrom of political-cultural radicalism that preceded the passing of the *SDA* in 1984.

This might seem an esoteric or unorthodox contribution, or indirectly related, to a collection dedicated to reflection about this important piece of Australian legislation. This could even be exacerbated for some by my commitment to write about law using the theory and method of critical history. If, however, we want to continue to take seriously the question of gender for law, we cannot resort to

---

7   Jocelynne Scutt, 'Legislating for the Right to be Equal: Women, the Law and Social Policy' in Cora Baldock and Bettina Cass (eds), *Women, Social Welfare and the State in Australia*, Allen & Unwin, Sydney, 1988. See also Jenny Morgan, 'Women and the Law' in Refractory Girl Collective (eds), *Refracting Voices: Feminist Voices from Refractory Girl*, Southwood Press, Sydney, 1993.
8   Sawer, this volume.

descriptive analysis of our past, for gender does not reside in our past—legal or otherwise—in an assumed position of liberal privilege. We should also not become caught in the trap of a historical presbyopia, which Margaret Thornton, in a 2004 essay about crises in feminist legal thinking, describes as the inevitable loss of ability by individuals or communities to focus on what is nearest to them, in all its messy dimensions.[9] In offering this other history—this prequel about gender as a concept for feminist legal praxis—I want to suggest, instead, that there are always subsumed or forgotten spaces in feminist cultural politics that can be of value when considering how to engage with the *SDA* today, as these spaces carry the possibilities of re-inscription or resistance beyond the normative boundaries of the law itself.

Discrimination and Australian Laws

It is important to acknowledge at the outset that the *SDA* was not without immediate legislative predecessors. Federally, the Commonwealth had enacted the *Racial Discrimination Act* in 1977, as well as testing its constitutional reliance on UN treaties and conventions, and hence its validity, in *Koowarta v Bjelke-Petersen*.[10] At the State level, there had been of course legislative instruments enacted (the ill-fated *Prohibition of Discrimination Act 1966* [SA], as well as the more successful *Sex Discrimination Act 1975* [SA], the *Anti-Discrimination Act 1977* [NSW] and the *Equal Opportunity Act 1977* [Vic.]), which also attempted to grapple in law with the paradox of equality as exclusion.[11] The language in these predecessors to the *SDA* reflected a concern present in political culture in Australia at the time: a principle of equality understood as opportunity that emerged from the political rubric of trade unionism and spilled into other areas of political contestation.[12] These earlier instruments—unsurprisingly perhaps because of that foundation in industrial politics—were very much about addressing the effects of discriminatory conduct as the result of workplace exclusion. (That language is clearly replicated in the *SDA* and continues to define

9   Margaret Thornton, 'Neoliberal Melancholia: The Case of Feminist Legal Scholarship' (2004) 20 *Australian Feminist Law Journal* 7.

10   (1982) 34 ALR 417.

11   Margaret Thornton, *The Liberal Promise: Anti-Discrimination Legislation in Australia*, Oxford University Press, Melbourne, 1990, p. 36.

12   See Marian Sawer, *Making Women Count: A History of the Women's Electoral Lobby in Australia*, UNSW Press, Sydney, 2008, p. 51; Elizabeth Reid and Denis Altman, *Equality: The New Issues*, Fabian's Winter Lecture Series: Equality under Labor, Victorian Fabian Society, Melbourne, 1973. This point is fully developed in Marian Sawer, *The Ethical State?*, Melbourne University Press, Carlton, 2003. This idea of equality was in circulation therefore beyond women's campaigns for justice. It can be seen as deployed strategically, for example, in the 1967 referendum by the Federal Council for the Advancement of Aborigines and Torres Strait Islanders (FCAATSI). See Bain Attwood and Andrew Markus, *The 1967 Referendum: Race, Power and the Australian Constitution*, Second edition, Aboriginal Studies Press, AIATSIS, Canberra, 2007.

its use and limits, as Sara Charlesworth has argued).[13] There was also as part of that material focus an intended educative function—that law could lead social change in relation to work practices by example, and by coercion if necessary. What was distinct about the *SDA*, unlike these legislative predecessors, was that its framers and champions—women such as Susan Ryan—also sought for the first time to cast it as resolutely embodied. This focus ensured that the incipient legislative language of discrimination was confronted by a specifically feminist legal critique that could be articulated by the mid-1980s, through the indirect discrimination and sexual harassment provisions of the Act.

How had this happened? Partly, through the experience of lawyers working with feminist lobby groups in bringing cases to the anti-discrimination agencies in their respective States, as under the existing legislative schemes there was a growing understanding of what the possibilities and limits of discrimination could mean when incorporated within the conceptual framework of law. The campaigns by the Women's Trade Union Commission and the Working Women's Charter to bring to public notice the indirect discrimination against migrant women workers by Australian Iron and Steel are a case in point. The campaigns (which culminated in the testing of the NSW legislative scheme by the NSW Anti-Discrimination Board in *Nadjovska v AI & S* in 1985,[14] leading to a decision by the High Court in *AI & S v Banovic* in 1989)[15] had made clear the need for more specific indirect discrimination provisions, based on recognising barriers to women's advancement at work, because of their circumscribed choices elsewhere. Perhaps more importantly for the historical narrative told here—intended to be distinct but complementary to that of the history of equal rights in work—are the hard-fought-for provisions that identified sexual harassment as a form of discriminatory practice. The NSW case of *O'Callaghan v Loder*—although the plaintiff was ultimately unsuccessful—did result in an Australian tribunal identifying for the first time, albeit problematically, that sexual harassment could be understood as a form of discrimination.[16] The critique of the reasoning in the decision, however, was important, as it raised

---

13 Charlesworth, this volume.

14 (1985) EOC 92-140.

15 (1989) 168 CLR 165. See also Rosemary Hunter, *Indirect Discrimination in the Workplace*, Federation Press, Leichhardt, NSW, 1992, p. 184; Women's Trade Union Commission, *Women's Unions*, Booklet, Women's Trade Union Commission, Sydney, 1976; The First Ten Years of Sydney Women's Liberation Collection, Mitchell Library, Sydney (hereafter, ML), 388/81.

16 *O'Callaghan v Loder* (1984) EOC 92-024 (NSW EOT). Justice Jane Mathews defined sexual harassment as 'occurring where a person is "subjected to unsolicited and unwelcome sexual conduct by a person who stands in a position of power in relation to him or her" or must have been accompanied by (tangible) adverse employment consequences to the complainant, such as dismissal or reduction in hours worked' (at 505, 506). This amounted to less favourable treatment of a person on the ground of their sex, when compared with a person of the opposite sex, in similar circumstances. In the preceding decision regarding interpretation of the NSW Act (1984, EOC 92-023), Mathews J made it clear that jurisprudentially she was reliant on North American cases, which made it explicit that harassment based on women's embodiment was an 'unwelcome feature of employment' (as per s. 25 [2]). At 75, 505, she noted that intangible effects were enough to invoke

questions about the need for how power is used by men against women in workplaces to be seen not only as a question of employment hierarchy, but as a question of gender—a question that was open for vigorous debate in the subsequent legislation.[17] The sexual harassment provision in the *SDA* (section 28A) was premised therefore on the idea that there should be a category of harm arising from women's *embodied* experience, although it was phrased in gender-neutral language and did reiterate a key fiction of liberal legalism that standards of reasonableness are objectively neutral.[18] Nevertheless, the political intent and context of this provision reflected a genuine shift in thinking about 'discrimination', which was different from the applied language of opening up opportunities that circulated in political rubric of the broad left in Australia at the time, and that feminists were now applying to the case of women's equality. This shift was about thinking how to use law to combat its own constructions and limitations of sexed bodies, rather than seeing law only as a straightforward means of engaging in state reform in order to achieve equal measures, and was about the relationship between feminist politics and legal practitioners, and the development of a subset between the two.

Feminism, Marxism and Law

Kathleen Lahey has noted of North American feminist theorising about law in the 1970s that it was an 'uncatalogued item, a yet to be recognised experience'.[19] This was mirrored, to greater and lesser degrees, in the Australian context during the same period. Although Joan Scott's point that gender remains a constantly renegotiated value in normative constructions and repressions can be aptly applied to Australian politics in the 1970s, this conscious questioning of gender was slower to be identified within law than in other fields of life and work. One reason for this was that there were fewer women participating in the law in the early 1970s. As Jane Mathews has argued: 'When I went to law school

---

the section and made clear that there was to be a factual/contextual examination of actions that lead to detriment that encompassed bodily harm or perceived harm. The critique of the judgment, however, rested on the objective test of whether the employer should have realised that their approaches were unwelcome.

17   See Thornton, *The Liberal Promise*, pp. 58–61. For discussion of this ruling in conjunction with existing NSW provisions and debates, see Gail Mason and Anna Chapman, 'Defining Sexual Harassment: A History of the Commonwealth Legislation and its Critiques' [2003] *Federal Law Review* 6—especially their reflection on the contemporaneous critique of the judgment. The interaction between Australian and US feminist legal scholars and activists is of course important here, noting, however, the distinctiveness of the Australian political context: see Catharine A. Mackinnon, *Sexual Harassment of Working Women*, Yale University Press, New Haven, Conn., 1979.

18   *SDA*, s. 28A. See Mason and Chapman ('Defining Sexual Harassment') for an overview of this point and the subsequent critique regarding amendment.

19   Kathleen Lahey, 'Until Women Themselves Have Told All That They Have To Tell' (1985) 23 Osgoode Hall law Journal 519.

at the end of the fifties and early sixties, there were very few female students indeed…But the 1970s saw a steady and ultimately dramatic increase in the number of women law students.'[20]

Adding women to law was a breakthrough for 'getting equal' politics—a breakthrough for Mary Wollstonecraft's and later feminists, incorporating John Stuart Mill's articulation that education for women enables and promotes social betterment for the individual and the society.[21] Adding *feminism* to law is, however, something quite different.

The early engagement of feminists with the law in the 1970s did not occur in a straightforward way. For some, engaging with law—even around significant questions of abortion law reform—was problematic, as it suggested a relationship to the state or police that was antithetical to radical politics at the time. For others, it was about using law strategically to effect specific, material change for women.[22] This recognition of law's role—as part of the state—came in two forms. One was the conscious lobbying of grassroots groups, often drawn from a more radical base than WEL, asking lawyers to assist in their campaigns to lobby the government for provisions of resources for women-specific services (especially domestic violence refuges and medical services).[23] The second, as already mentioned, was the more strenuous use of law as a lobby or reform vehicle for state intervention, as mobilised by WEL. This kind of attention, however, to the instrumental function of law as it directly translated to the organisation of holistic legal services or practitioner advice, no matter how crucial, was in many ways a continuation of earlier periods of feminist-identified campaigning around equal pay, property rights or social security provisions.[24] It was a turn to law by feminist groups, not a specifically 'feminist legal' response to identified harms, and did not necessarily engage an analytical focus of the law's epistemological construction of women as legal subjects, or therefore of how gender operated in law.

By 1975 there was, however, the beginning of a theorised recognition of the barriers preventing the emergence of a legal identity for women, which would

---

20   Jane Mathews, 'Women in the Law' (1991) 41 *Refractory Girl* 27.

21   Mary Wollstonecraft, *A Vindication of the Rights of Woman*, Penguin Books, Harmondsworth, UK, 1982 [1792]. See also Wendy Brown, 'Tolerance as Supplement: The "Jewish Question" and the "Woman Question"', *Regulating Aversion: Tolerance in the Age of Identity and Empire*, Princeton University Press, NJ, 2008.

22   I thank two of my reviewers for pointing out these opposing nuances in the general claim.

23   This is not to suggest that 'lawyers' and 'women's groups' were always distinct, but, as noted by FLAG in 1981, there was a 'dearth of lawyers with feminist sympathies'. See Kim Ross, 'F.L.A.G.' (1979) 4(3) *Legal Services Bulletin* 123. For examples of the kind of engagement suggested here, see: Ann Genovese, The Battered Body: A Feminist Legal History, PhD thesis, University of Technology, Sydney, 1998, pp. 152–5, <utsescholarship.lib.uts.edu.au/dspace/handle/2100/276>

24   See generally: Marilyn Lake, *Getting Equal: The History of Australian Feminism*, Allen & Unwin, St Leonards, NSW, 1999; Patricia Grimshaw, Marilyn Lake, Ann McGrath and Marian Quartly, *Creating a Nation 1788–2007*, Second edition, API Network, Perth, 2007.

suggest gender as a conceptual basis for extending the existing legislative understanding of discrimination. An incipient Marxist feminism provided the foundation for a critique of law as a product of capitalism qua patriarchy that was allegedly committed to equality for all, yet which operated overtly to prevent women from enjoying equitable protection for their legal injuries and legal entitlements. In an indirect fashion, by recognising the operation of laws in Australia that used sex as the basis for their determination, on matters such as the right to a minimum wage, custody of children or legal abortion, some lawyers, who also were part of the women's liberation movement, such as Deirdre O'Connor, started to make more critical claims for women's legal equality and consequently their autonomy. O'Connor, in a submission to the Sydney Women's Commission in 1975, envisaged this process in the same language as that used by WEL, through direct agitation by women, in terms of campaigning directly against discriminatory legislation, as well as campaigning for sex discrimination laws 'either as a basic constitutional guarantee or as a normal legislative enactment'.[25] O'Connor also tried, however, to problematise the question of reliance by the women's liberation movement, or WEL, on law reform 'as a major weapon in their struggle'.[26] As she explained in her paper:

> The legal system reflects and reinforces the social system in which it operates. Marx went so far as to assert that as law was a reflection of the economic base of society, it was incapable of being innovative except to the extent that laws could react back on the base, and impede change and/or progress. Even without a total adoption of the Marxian view, it must be conceded that in every area legal change has followed rather than promoted social and economic change.[27]

This Marxist foundation, bolstered by supportive Labor politics of the period committed to understanding disadvantage as socially embedded, enabled important material developments in relation to Australian women's experience within existing law, as well as gaining better access to its protections (such as the aforementioned state-based discrimination legislation).[28] It did not yet embody the idea of gendered discrimination that galvanised politics in the 1980s.

---

25 Deirdre O'Connor, Should the Women's Movement rely on law reform as a major weapon in their struggle?, Unpublished paper, Women's Commission, Sydney, 1975, p. 41; The First Ten Years of Sydney Women's Liberation Collection, ML 388/81.

26 This intellectual debate between feminists who advocated reform and those who did not has been legion, and is still constantly negotiated. See: Margaret Thornton, 'Feminism and the Contradictions of Law Reform' (1991) 19 *International Journal of the Sociology of Law* 453 and more recently, Susan Armstrong, 'Is Feminist Law Reform Flawed? Abstentionists & Sceptics' (2004) 20 *Australian Feminist Law Journal* 43.

27 O'Connor, Should the Women's Movement rely on law reform as a major weapon in their struggle?, p. 41.

28 For an assessment of these early changes, see Anne Maree Lanteri, 'Woman and The Law' in Jan Mercer (ed.), *The Other Half: Women in Australian Society*, Penguin, Ringwood, Vic.,1975

The politics of feminism and the interactions between the increase of women law students throughout the 1970s and their exposure to the politics and ideas of their time, however, helped give shape to this emergent feminist jurisprudence. This is not to suggest that all female law students or even lawyers who wanted to think about questions such as equality or disadvantage identified as feminist. Nevertheless, it is important to acknowledge that for those who did, their legal education remained normatively bound.[29] As such, ideas about law were informed as much by conversation about the role of the state and other prevailing questions of governance, in other disciplines and in other grassroots campaigns—some of which did not originate in the politics of WEL or women's liberation.

Left Lawyers and Libertarians

Political historian John Chesterman has argued that the amorphous nature of left-wing political cultures in Australia in the 1970s was linked by one common theme: the 'rejection or at least the appearance of rejection, of mainstream culture'.[30] This is significant. Mainstream culture itself became a site of protest and, for young legal academics and law students, men and women, such protest—or confrontation—was manifested through a critique of the manipulation of people by authority and the lack of access to the law for those on low incomes. O'Connor's Marxist analysis of law in 1975 clearly showed this and was a contributing intellectual tradition to the emergence of a specifically legal enclave within New Left politics in Australia in the 1970s. The New Left lawyers—a loose, unstructured grouping of practitioners with similar political beliefs about law's negative impacts on the socially marginalised—were broadly interested in the provision of legal services to all citizens denied fair and equal access to its protection. The focus of many of these practitioners was the establishment of community legal centres in inner-city Melbourne and Sydney, in the early 1970s, underpinned by a broader imperative to engage law with the general question of disadvantage, particularly as it related to Indigenous peoples.[31] In doing so, there

---

29   See Margaret Thornton, *Dissonance and Distrust: Women in the Legal Profession*, Oxford University Press, Melbourne, 1996, pp. 73–9; Lorraine Elliot, 'Inequalities in the Australian Education System. Part 2: Women in the Professions' in Mercer, *The Other Half*.

30   John Chesterman, 'The Making of the Australian New Left Lawyer' (1995) 1 *Australian Journal of Legal History* 37, 43. For a discussion of the New Left in general, reflecting on their intellectual antecedents and politics, and a contemporaneous assessment of John Anderson's influence on Push politics and agendas, see John Docker, *Australian Cultural Elites: Intellectual Traditions in Sydney and Melbourne*, Angus and Robertson, Sydney, 1974; Richard Gordon and Warren Osmond, 'An Overview of the Australian New Left' in *The Australian New Left: Critical Essays and Strategy*, William Heinemann Australia, Melbourne, 1970.

31   In particular, the establishment of the Aboriginal Legal Service in Sydney, in 1972. See, for example: John Basten, 'Legal Services: Looking into the 1980s' (1980) 5(6) *Legal Service Bulletin* 282–5. Basten's article is an overview of a public meeting held at the Redfern Town Hall on 1 October 1980, organised by the Australian Legal Workers' Group, on the topic 'Legal Services in the Eighties'. The panel consisted of Justice Lionel

was an implicit recognition of liberal law's contradictions, its claims to provide equal treatment and protection for all and its different standard of delivery of services to different citizens. Despite constructing themselves in opposition to mainstream legal practice and culture, many lawyers who identified as part of the New Left were by default implicated in the process of liberal reformism. Like feminists beginning to find a critical engagement with state doctrine and practice, the left legal community from the early to mid-1970s had to engage with the law to attempt to transform its operation. These efforts showed, at first, a concern with theorising how the law constructed some subjects as disadvantaged to begin with. At the same time, however, they sowed the seeds for understanding some of the epistemological limits of transformative legal critique that were to come in the 1980s. The centres, and the broad philosophy of working collectively and actively through community education as well as the provision of legal services to alter their society, was important at this time as it brought a genuinely pluralist political community within the auspices of legal service provision. Slowly, and correlatively, this broadened thinking about law that started to escape the traditional binds of professional solidarity or formalist jurisprudence about legal subjects that had previously prevailed in Australian legal culture.[32]

The Redfern Legal Centre (RLC) in Sydney provides perhaps the best example of the practicalities of these connections and influences and how they, in turn, impacted on specifically feminist praxis also.[33] The story of the RLC is of course a distinctly Sydney history. This is, however, important: the micro-histories of people and political organisations, and the philosophies that drive them, in each state are too often glossed over in an attempt to reflect what is perceived to be a national or transnational experience. Often the specificities of time and place contribute greatly to the social contests that influence conceptual developments within discourses such as law; and paradoxically, looking closely at such contests can only help reveal the interplay of ideas and political currents that emerges from international intellectual exchange, and that assists in creating a uniquely national political experience. This is particularly the case, I would

Murphy, who initiated the Australian system of legal aid in 1972, when he was Attorney-General of Australia, Mary Gaudron, Chairwoman of the NSW Legal Services Commission, and Paul Coe, Chairman of the NSW Aboriginal Legal Service.

32   Chesterman, 'The Making of the Australian New Left Lawyer', p. 47. The implication that the left legal community of the 1980s was 'non-theoretical' is made contextually. In comparison with the nature of theoretical and critical jurisprudence in the 1990s, the emphasis in the 1980s was placed heavily on securing actionable methods by which citizens could receive access to justice. As the papers to a 1982 conference organised by the Australian Legal Workers' Group indicate, however, a theoretical perspective on these issues was evident. See: John Basten, Mark Richardson, Chris Ronalds and George Zdenkowski, 'The Criminal Injustice System', *ALWG and Legal Service Bulletin*, with the Law Foundation of New South Wales, Sydney, 1982.

33   For the Victorian history, see: John Chesterman, *Poverty Law and Social Change: The Story of the Fitzroy Legal Service*, Melbourne University Press, Carlton. Note, however, that the politics of libertarianism was predominantly a Sydney phenomenon.

argue, in relation to recognising gendered embodiment within Australian law. In this prequel to the history of the *SDA*, a close examination of Sydney radical politics that engaged with law in the period before 1984 is important, for the simple fact that many of the people involved in codifying or later analysing that law were part of that political community. They can be viewed, then, as Gilles Deleuze and Felix Guattari suggest, as 'conceptual personae' or 'thought figures' that enable and contribute to social and intellectual genealogy.[34]

Many volunteers at the RLC, about the time of its opening in 1976, were still in law school or had just completed their law degrees. Robyn Lansdowne, later a member of FLAG, reflecting on the initial organisation of that centre, characterised the informing perspectives of its original membership as products of the more radical new law curriculum at the University of New South Wales and of the political climate of 'expansion and optimism'.[35] There was a sense of energy to harness the changes to legal aid and law reform that had occurred under the Whitlam administration—an administration that had also opened up entry to the legal profession for many through its egalitarian policy on free tertiary education. Other members of the original Redfern Legal Centre Collective brought quite different expectations and experience to this new quest to grant accessible legal services for those who generally fell outside the law's protection. The RLC also drew the involvement of those with libertarian anarchist backgrounds—in particular, the criminal justice collective known as the Prisoners' Action Group (PAG).

Libertarianism in Sydney was idiosyncratic and deeply nihilistic. Influenced by Sydney University philosopher John Anderson, the Sydney Push (as the older-style libertarians identified it) was committed to disrupting traditional notions of morality through lived experience, critiquing the suppression of internal dissent virulent in political organisation and confronting difficult and contradictory aspects of more mainstream, as well as Marxist platforms. That said, the lived experience of flouting mores—the practice of permanent protest—did not translate to direct confrontation of changing the systemic ways in which those cultural mores flourished and were constantly politically perpetuated. For younger members of the Push, the Vietnam War provided a significant break with the ethic of permanent protest as lifestyle. The new group, originally self-titled the Kensington Futilitarians (after the suburb in which the University of New South Wales had been built, which many attended), was less devoted to the philosophical ramparts of the old Push (Reich, Pareto) than to

---

34 Gilles Deleuze and Felix Guattari, *What is Philosophy?*, Translated by Graham Burchell and Hugh Tomlinson, Verso, London, 1999, p. 73. A similar idea is expressed by Hannah Arendt, *Men in Dark Times*, Jonathon Cape, London, 1970. I thank Ann Curthoys and John Docker for this point (see Ann Curthoys and John Docker, *Is History Fiction?*, UNSW Press, Sydney, 2006, p. 10).

35 Genovese, The Battered Body, p. 191. See also John Basten and Robyn Lansdowne, 'Community Legal Centres: Who's in Charge' (1980) 5(2) *Legal Service Bulletin* 52.

the intellectual movement situationism then emerging in France, and key to the events of May 1968 in Paris. Influenced by the writings of Marx and of Guy Debord, situationists believed in 'subverting accepted norms, in spontaneous and haphazard anarchism, in using art to turn society on its head to reveal the emptiness of public rhetoric'.[36] The Kensington Futilitarians (later Libertarians) were to extend this project, marrying the ethic of haphazard performative anarchism to more concrete struggles (such as the battle to save Victoria Street in Kings Cross from redevelopment, and anti-censorship.) Their political actions inevitably resulted in their own arrests and a personal lived experience of the criminal justice system from the inside, which culminated in the formation of PAG in 1973.

PAG was therefore a unique alliance that would be hard to imagine in our own regulated and politically demarcated times. It included ex-prisoners, UNSW legal academics such as George Zdenkowski and David Brown, libertarians and civil liberties members—all committed to exposing the horrendous conditions in NSW jails.[37] They wanted to transform the criminal justice system itself, with a long-term goal of abolishing jails altogether, and employed the intellectual framework and street performativeness of situationism to great effect in the politics surrounding the Bathurst Jail riots and Nagle Royal Commission into the NSW prison system in the 1970s.[38] As a theoretical proposition, PAG advocated 'breaking through categorisations of "practitioners", "theoreticians", "political activists" and also acknowledging the different contributions that organizations and individuals can make and the alliances that can be formed around specific issues' (this was of course an important lesson of feminism also). From a criminology/penology perspective, Zdenkowski and Brown also began to refer to the work of Michel Foucault, especially *Discipline and Punish* (1977), in order to explain the regime of regulation that gave the criminal justice system its sense of authority—adding new intellectual directions for an emerging Marxist/ anarchist critique of criminal law, if not law more generally.[39]

---

36   Anne Coombs, *Sex and Anarchy*, Viking/Penguin, Ringwood, Vic., 1996, p. 232. See also John Docker, 'Sydney Intellectual History and Libertarianism' (1972) 7(1) *Australian Political Studies Association Journal* 42; A. J. Baker, 'Sydney Libertarianism and the Push', *Broadsheet*, no. 81,(March, 1970), p. 5.

37   Coombs, *Sex and Anarchy*, pp. 186–7; Ken Buckley, 'Our Meeting With The Premier: The Nagle Report on Prisons', *Civil Liberty*, no. 79 (July/August, 1978), p. 6; George Zdenkowski, 'Civil Liberty', *Civil Liberty*, no. 68 (August/September, 1976), p. 4.

38   See generally: Prisoners' Action Group 1976, 'Bathurst Gaol and the Royal Commission into Prisons—A summary by the PAG' (1976) 2(3) *Alternative Criminology Journal* 142. Their activities included: broadcasting over prison walls; setting up and managing a halfway house for ex-prisoners in Glebe; publishing prison diaries and newsletters through their publishing arm, *Breakout*; working with trade unions to stop the construction of the maximum-security complex Katingal; and protesting the draconian and vicious imperatives behind the complex itself in the ultimately successful 'Close Katingal Campaign'. See generally: 'Editorial' (1978) 1(9) *Jail News*.

39   George Zdenkowksi and David Brown, *The Prison Struggle: Changing Australia's Penal System*, Penguin, Ringwood, Vic., 1982.

The Embodiment of Crime

Concomitant with this situationist attack against morality and authority in the criminal justice system there was burgeoning internal conflict within libertarianism itself, which resulted in the formation of a specifically feminist-focused prison reform group, in 1973: Women Behind Bars. Key to this development was a student called Wendy Bacon, who had arrived in Sydney in 1966 from Melbourne to study sociology with Sol Encel at the University of New South Wales. Bacon is of course a significant Australian journalist and academic, but at this time she was part of a vanguard of younger women who had been introduced to libertarian philosophy through their social and sexual relationships. They began, however, to challenge the old Push in a different way to their male contemporaries. Although libertarianism in any form appeared to accord women a sense of sexual freedom, and through this an identity that existed outside the cultural constraints imposed on the 1950s and 1960s woman, this freedom was extracted at a price. Like other women in more mainstream New Left politics at the time, whose ideas about feminism emerged from their firsthand experience of misogyny within the constraints of politics allegedly committed to equality, women such as Bacon began to question the terms on which their freedom was granted; their engagement with theories of women's liberation challenged the inherent misogyny of the Push.[40] It was this kind of cross-fertilisation of experience with ideas that created a new critical perspective for women-centred political action—a perspective that demanded constant and continuous opposition to authority as well as a need for broad social change; and the focus, increasingly, became the operation of the law.

In February 1972, Bacon was put on trial for obscenity charges relating to editing the UNSW paper, *Tharunka*. (These charges were exacerbated by demonstrating against the summons by parading outside the court wearing a nun's habit emblazoned with the infamous slogan 'I've been fucked by God's steel prick', which if nothing else showcased how disruptively potent a libertarian feminism might be.)[41] She chose to defend herself in 'an attempt to cut across accepted legal notions of what might be acceptable to an "average man"'.[42] Despite her efforts, she lost the case and was sentenced to Mulawa Women's Detention Centre for eight days. The experience of being in jail—as it had for those who formed PAG—undeniably sharpened Bacon's political focus and formed the experiential basis for her unfolding commitment to challenging and confronting the operation of the law, which had arguably ever broadening

---

40   Coombs, *Sex and Anarchy*, pp. 223–7; Wendy Bacon and Ken Maddock, 'Symposium on Does Women's Liberation Conflict with Human Liberation?', *Broadsheet* 67, 1971, p. 1.
41   Coombs, *Sex and Anarchy*, pp. 240–5.
42   Ibid., p. 245.

implications. On Bacon's release, and alongside women increasingly drawn from the women's liberation movement and, more broadly, the New Left legal community, Women Behind Bars (WBB) was formed.[43]

With a commitment to pluralism across theoretical and activist lines, WBB mirrored PAG. Its original and primary objective was, however, to critique the bases of imprisonment of women. Many women were in jail because they were poor; crimes such as prostitution or fine default were the result of class circumstances. For other women incarcerated for more serious offences, such as murder, manslaughter or infanticide, WBB began to argue that those crimes were precipitated by a history of violence and abuse, which in the face of a lack of other community resources, were played out to tragic ends in women's efforts to free themselves.[44] These arguments were informed and influenced by the cross-section of WBB members who had also been involved with grassroots feminist campaigns to establish women's refuges—campaigns for service provision that had caused domestic violence to be named and discursively identified as embodied crime for the first time. WBB was committed to arguing against the unequal and discriminatory effects of law as pertaining to women as a class, but was increasingly conscious of the need to make specific the ways in which law—in this case, criminal law and practices—enabled such unequal treatment for women, inscribed through their bodily difference to men and, more intangibly, the male legal subject.[45]

For example, the Bathurst riots in 1975 had illuminated the culture of violence and coercion horrifically enacted on the male prisoner through his body. For women, this level of violence was more insidiously inflicted on their bodies by a withholding of services, as opposed to daily beatings or floggings (although these also occurred). As Bacon mentioned later: 'Women in prison as elsewhere are controlled through their bodies in a very real way.'[46] Realising the extent to which embodiment, and gendered embodiment, rendered the operation of their treatment within prison was significant. In May 1976, WBB applied for and was granted legal aid for representation at the Nagle Royal Commission into NSW prisons. Lawyer Pat O'Shane (later one of Australia's first Indigenous

---

43 Wendy Bacon, *The Anne Conlon Memorial Lecture*, NSW Women's Advisory Council, Sydney, 1983, pp. 17–18.
44 Wendy Bacon, 'Women in Prisons', *Refractory Girl*, May, 1985, p. 2; Sandra Willson, 'Behind Bars' in Judy Mackinolty and Heather Radi (eds), *In Pursuit of Justice: Australian Women and the Law 1788–1979*, Hale & Iremonger, Sydney, 1979, pp. 173–6; Women Behind Bars, 'Who is in Gaol and Why are they There?', *Women Behind Bars (A Summary of Activities)*, 1983, Women Behind Bars, Sydney; The First Ten Years of Sydney Women's Liberation Collection, ML 388/81.
45 See also Anonymous, 'Prison Justice', *Sydney Women's Liberation Newsletter*, May, 1977, p. 7. Women Behind Bars, 'Women Behind Bars' (1976) 1(3) *Alternative Criminology Journal*, 21–2 (reprinted from *Mabel*, December, 1975); Willson, 'Behind Bars', p. 172.
46 Bacon, *The Anne Conlon Memorial Lecture*, p. 18.

magistrates) was employed to present the group's case.[47] The main focus of the submission was the inadequate medical treatment available to women in Mulawa. In July 1976, WBB held a demonstration outside the jail to highlight the nature of the complaints being prepared for the commission. A long banner with the words 'Mulawa Jail makes women sick' was stretched along the fence and a tape of medical information was broadcast for the benefit of the women inside. In 1976, WBB was successful in having its submission to the Nagle Royal Commission accepted as the basis for recommendations for reform.[48] That said, the campaign to improve medical treatment for women prisoners in New South Wales illuminated the distinct and somewhat contradictory character of WBB. The incursion of women from outside the original libertarian membership, from women's liberation and from the New Left legal community, and the nature of campaigns that showed clearly the need to confront law itself, ensured that the group began to have a reformist agenda inscribed on an anarchist foundation. This cross-fertilisation gave impetus to an increasingly critical focus on the negative, and adversely experienced, particulates of gendered difference inherent within the prison system and how those differences effected the unequal operation of criminal justice for men and women.

Wendy Bacon might have initially gone to jail, and been awakened to the injustice of the criminal justice system, because of an anti-authoritarian act that implicitly critiqued the practices of the law. Her journey, however—in some senses the journey of many women with radical political perspectives writ small—led her to a dissonant engagement with liberal reformism as an intellectual project. By 1978, Bacon had enrolled as a law student, and, along with Robyn Lansdowne, part of the New Left legal community, had been employed as a researcher by FLAG—Australia's first feminist collective committed to confronting gendered difference as experienced and also proscribed, and therefore as a paradoxical concept in the broader legislative project of getting equal.

An Australian Feminist Legal Praxis

In August 1978, at Sydney University, an academic conference dedicated to thinking about the possibilities suggested for feminism and law was held for the first time. The Australian Women and Law Conference drew participants

---

47 Women Behind Bars, 'Legal Visits to Mulawa' and 'Mulawa Jail Makes Women Sick', *Sydney Women's Liberation Newsletter*, May, 1977; Bacon, 'Women in Prisons', p. 7.

48 J. F. Nagle, *Report of the Royal Commission into New South Wales Prisons. Volumes I, II and III*, NSW Government Printer, Sydney, 1978, Recommendations 187–99. These included: the provision of antenatal and gynaecological treatment for all women prisoners; the relaxation of the practice of forcing mothers to surrender infants on their first birthday; the improvement of medical facilities; and the movement of psychiatric patients to more appropriate care. See also: Women Behind Bars, 'Demonstration at Mulawa' (1976) 1(4) *Alternative Criminology Journal* 71–2.

from history, sociology and, more tentatively, law. The conference covered a wide range of topics—from domestic violence, lesbian custody cases and a discussion of the recently introduced *Family Law Act1975* (Cth) to more historically grounded analyses of citizenship, professional legal participation and colonial law.[49] The number of women involved who had also been involved in early women's liberation campaigns was considerable. These women—a disproportionate number of whom were historians or postgraduate students in history (such as Anne Summers and Lyndall Ryan)—had instigated journals and newspapers such as *Refractory Girl* and *Mejane* and were themselves influential in developing a burgeoning theoretical focus on the nature of liberation, then feminism, itself.[50] The conference was the first conscious attempt within the nascent academic arm of Australian feminism to conduct an interdisciplinary forum on the development and operation of law as it affected women in contemporary Australian society. Lesley Lynch, in reviewing the conference for *Refractory Girl*, noted with interest and a clear sense of theoretical separation the focus and visibility of the 'new breed of feminist legal women'. Her reaction to them as a group was ambivalent:

> On the one hand I was admiring, even envious, of the talent, energy and more particularly of the confident optimism; on the other I was uneasy about what appeared to be the prevailing world view. It might just be the hoary old tension between the pragmatism of reform and revolution making, but I detected an unhealthy respect for the overall legal system…[T]hey seemed to regard this structure too reverentially.[51]

The talented young women starting to emerge within the legal profession at this time, and becoming inculcated into the procedural language and practice of the law, were not of course without theoretical or critical voice. As O'Connor's submission to the Women's Commission in 1975 indicates, there was an awareness among New Left lawyers of the *form* of disadvantage imposed on women as legal subjects by the law's instrumental bias and lack of recognition of their political equality, and of their claims to entrench that equality within other spheres, however cautiously that extended to theorising about the normative biases within law itself. As Lynch also observed, 'it must be difficult being both a lawyer and a feminist'.[52]

In July 1978, however, one month before the conference, Margaret Thornton, a recent graduate of the new and progressive law school at the University of New South Wales, and Joan Bielski of the WEL, sent a joint circular letter to call

---

49   Lesley Lynch, 'Women and Law Conference', *Refractory Girl*, March, 1979, p. 35.

50   Ann Curthoys, 'Visions, Nightmares, Dreams: Women's History, 1975' (1996) 27(6) *Australian Historical Studies* 1.

51   Lynch, 'Women and Law Conference', p. 35.

52   Ibid.

together a meeting of women interested in the law.[53] Despite the existence of a professional body for female practitioners (the Women Lawyers' Association) and despite the committed left praxis emerging from the community legal centre movement, Thornton and Bielski saw the need for a collective and organised group that 'did something for women in general'. The US group Women's Equity Action Lobby (WEAL) provided both a framework and an inspiration as a *feminist* group committed to researching and proposing legislation that affected women and developing test cases on women's rights.[54] Thornton and Bielski perceived the group—like the approach to pluralist membership of groups within the left in general at this time—to be inclusive of a wide range of women, not merely those within the legal profession, and directed their original circular to students and non-lawyers as well as practitioners. The group's members emerged from the New Left legal community—groups such as WBB, the refuge movement, WEL and broadly aligned women's liberationists. In keeping with this open spirit and the recognition of the need to draw together women with a wide range of perspectives and skills, 'lawyers' was carefully avoided in the process of naming the group (although in sharp contrast with today's political conservatism, 'feminist' was included). They called themselves the Feminist Legal Action Group (FLAG). In these terms, FLAG consciously constituted itself as a reactive body committed to investigating and researching from a multi-perspective basis what the law meant to women and how it controlled them.[55]

From the first meeting of FLAG (held in the boardroom of Coonan and Hughes) it was evident that the range of perspectives on the law brought from members trained in social work, counselling and grassroots politics, as well as law, meant that the group's aims and objectives stretched beyond ad-hoc, issue-by-issue campaigns directed towards instrumental law reform.[56] This was to be achieved practically through a range of actions. For example, FLAG perceived some of its short-term aims to be giving expert evidence at public hearings that related to women, commenting on legislation under consideration (specifically the *Anti-Discrimination Act 1977* [NSW]) and compiling a directory of lawyers sympathetic to women.[57] (As noted in a FLAG information sheet in 1979, 'an incipient directory exists but suffers from a dearth of lawyers with feminist

---

53   FLAG announced its formation at the conference: Lynch, 'Women and Law Conference' 36; Thornton, *Dissonance and Distrust*, pp. 213–15; Ross, 'F.L.A.G.' 123.

54   Ross, 'F.L.A.G.'.

55   Ibid., p. 123; Letter, Margaret Thornton to Sue Wills, 7 August 1991, The First Ten Years of Sydney Women's Liberation Collection, ML 388/81. Thornton also noted: 'I do remember an early meeting involving a ubiquitous discussion (maybe less so now) as to whether the word "feminist" should be included in the title or not. Some were opposed as it would be "too threatening" to the law reform bodies etc to which we proposed to make submissions.'

56   By 1979, it was noted that membership was drawn from a minority of practitioners, many legally qualified but non-practising women, a number of law students and many other women drawn from education, sociology, counselling and social work (Ross, 'F.L.A.G.').

57   Thornton to Wills, 7 August 1991; Ross, 'F.L.A.G.'. 123.

sympathies'.)[58] FLAG's longer-term objective was to conduct research into women's treatment by the law. This research-based focus was something new. It was to be the diversity of women who designed, executed and engaged with this idea of understanding through research how gender was conceptualised by law, with what reasons and with what effects, that opened up the space for a specifically Australian feminist legal praxis, which moved beyond the specificity of this group and of which the *SDA* became a beacon example.

Between July 1978 and June 1979, for example, FLAG worked on a number of small projects focusing on child welfare, family law and anti-discrimination. The major project initiated by the group, however, and the one that was to raise FLAG's profile within both the community of lawyers and legal reformers and the broader public, was their funded research on women convicted of homicide in New South Wales.[59] The wide objective behind the homicide project was to 'build up the presently deficient body of research relating to women and the law',[60] and the two researchers chosen to undertake this task, supervised by sociologist Roslyn Omodei, were Robyn Lansdowne and Wendy Bacon. Lansdowne, as a graduate lawyer involved with the Redfern Legal Centre, brought skill and political conviction to the task of law reform inherent in such a project. Bacon's involvement evidenced her continuing political commitment to find new methods for exposing the injustice of the prisons, which, in a libertarian sense, inappropriately incarcerated women for crimes derived from their own social dislocation.[61] The FLAG homicide report that resulted from their efforts was a watershed in Australian research into the law's treatment of women for several reasons, not least of which was the fact that it resulted from the synthesis of political and cultural currents operating within feminism and the wider political community at the time. Research undertaken before the FLAG report on homicide in New South Wales had followed a traditional statistical sociology/criminology methodology.[62] The FLAG report instead eschewed traditional criminological readings of offending women (analyses based objectively on their biology and psychology), preferring to investigate the subjective characteristics of each crime and the embodied experiences of each perpetrator. In accord with the political ethic of articulating the personal as political drawn from the women's liberation movement, female homicide offenders were interviewed to ascertain the personal histories that precipitated

---

58   FLAG, The First Ten Years of Sydney Women's Liberation Collection, ML 388/81; Ross, 'F.L.A.G.'.123.
59   Wendy Bacon and Robyn Lansdowne, *Feminist Legal Action Group Report: Women Homicide Offenders in NSW*, Feminist Legal Action Group, Sydney, 1982, pp. 44–5.
60   Ross, 'F.L.A.G.'.
61   Bacon, *The Anne Conlon Memorial Lecture*.
62   See, for example, the work undertaken in the field before the FLAG report: Therese Rod 1979, Murder in the Family in New South Wales 1958–1967, Master of Arts thesis, University of Sydney, NSW. For an explanation of the FLAG agenda and methodology, see Bacon and Lansdowne, *Feminist Legal Action Group Report*, pp. 8, 11–13, 26–8.

their crimes. The authors' view was that 'more insight is to be gained by seeing these women's acts as explicable in the light of their social and family situations than as expressions of individual deviance'. Overwhelmingly, the hidden experience of domestic violence, and women's inability to access avenues of assistance to free themselves, dominated the findings.

The wider effects and results of this research, which spearheaded and shaped the first successful challenge to the provocation defence in any Australian State, through the case of Violet and Bruce Roberts, I have written about elsewhere.[63] It is important to highlight in this context that the FLAG report, and the group itself, was of crucial importance in a developing feminist legal *theory*, as it pushed the boundary of a Marxist analysis of the law (in which women were constituted as a single, albeit disadvantaged class). Feminist thinking— especially about criminal law—could now also incorporate consideration of how law exerts power over women through a mythical objective ontology, yet correlatively subsumes the conceptual force of gender as diversely constituted and subjectively experienced.[64] Through the use of theoretically grounded and conceptualised research in specifically targeted legislative and community campaigning to force public recognition of the specificities of women's differences to men through this particular aspect of criminal law, FLAG also managed to challenge the bases on which law reform for and by women could be conceived. The pluralism of FLAG, evidenced through the Bruce and Violet Roberts campaign, knowingly combined reformist and activist skills and practical legal and theoretical positions on law reform. The group's formation and that particular project and its outcomes both demonstrated and exemplified, then, that a specifically critical feminist approach to law reform was possible. It also clearly identified that the pluralist politics of the feminist community, rather than a strictly lego-centric (law-centred) approach, was inherent in the exposure of the limits and contradictions of how gender was conceived of as a normative concept within law. This combination was to have significant consequences— not only for bringing the plight of the battered woman who kills to the attention of the wider public and in forcing legislative change in the light of common law intransigence (a question that dominated the feminist legal agenda in the 1980s and 1990s in Australia), but for broadening the parameters of feminist critical thinking about the law itself.

---

63   Genovese, The Battered Body.
64   Other work contributing to this shift in thinking about criminal law by feminists includes: Satyanshu K. Mukherjee and Jocelynne A. Scutt (eds), *Women and Crime*, George Allen & Unwin for Australian Institute of Criminology, Sydney, 1981.

Feminist Legal Thinking and Gendered Discrimination

It was not until the mid-1980s, then, concomitant with and broadly declared through the *SDA*, that an independent legal theory was fully articulated in the Australian feminist movement, as well as in the academic and legal circles, and beyond.[65] This specifically feminist legal thinking, influenced by similar intellectual shifts in the United States and the United Kingdom, asked questions, as Jenny Morgan has put it (echoing Scott), of 'how the law comes to know about women, and what women know'.[66] This kind of questioning, as Margaret Thornton noted in her own influential 1986 essay, was about recognising that paradox was always present in languages of discrimination, rights or equality for women. By the mid-1980s, this problem could be seen retrospectively as constantly present and under negotiation in all the feminist campaigns that had challenged domestic law to that date—not the least of which had been the work of and through FLAG around provocation. By the 1980s, as Thornton then elaborated in *The Liberal Promise* (1990) and Morgan and Graycar argued in their *The Hidden Gender of Law* (1990), it was possible to theorise from experience, research and philosophy that law was epistemologically constrained by its own systems of rationality and coherence. Law had great difficulty accepting a differentiated, sexed subject, bounded by legal and deeply held historical assumptions of corporeality, and hence social location and visibility. The choices for feminists wishing to open access for women within law's boundaries, and at the same time to recognise and contest those boundaries, by 1984 were perceived as constrained, and as always offering a compromised negotiation. To paraphrase political theorist Wendy Brown, any scrutiny by feminists of how gender is discursively constructed makes possible certain arguments about women's equality, yet forecloses others.[67]

---

65   Texts such as Ngaire Naffine, *Law and the Sexes: Explorations in Feminist Jurisprudence*, Allen & Unwin, Sydney, 1990; Regina Graycar and Jenny Morgan, *The Hidden Gender of Law*, Federation Press, Leichhardt, NSW, 1990, and Thornton's *The Liberal Promise* (also published in 1990) began to question the theoretical, as opposed to merely substantive, ways in which liberal law was built on claims to objectivity, neutrality as truth that denied recognition of women as a subject differentiated from the rational, benchmark 'reasonable man'. The questions raised in these texts—refracting and reflecting similar developments overseas—therefore acted as the 'next phase' of feminist legal thinking, building on the foundations of the focus in the fight for equal recognition, which dominated the feminist legal agendas of the early 1970s. They began to ask questions that attempted to understand women's difference as a tool for critique, even when this critique was inscribed on the binary conceptions of women that underpinned legal doctrine, and although in conversation with US, Canadian and British feminist legal scholars were importantly directed towards analysing a national experience and practice of law. For an analysis of this theoretical progression, see: Ngaire Naffine 1993, 'Assimilating Feminist Jurisprudence' (1993) 11 *Law in Context* 78.

66   Morgan, 'Women and the Law', p. 116; and generally Morgan and Graycar, *The Hidden Gender of Law*.

67   Brown, 'Tolerance as Supplement', p. 50.

This defining conundrum of feminist legal theory is embedded in the *SDA*. On the one hand, the purpose of the Act was about providing individual as opposed to collective avenues to legal address for harms caused in the workplace.[68] As Thornton has argued, this both reinforces legal liberalism's a priori assumptions about individual subjects—a benchmark man—and cordons off the domestic sphere from scrutiny by the Act. The legislation therefore 'effectively legitimises the public/private dichotomy of liberalism'.[69] Importantly, however, the *SDA* also recognised legislatively that harms occurred to women in a specifically embodied way because of their difference, inherently critiquing the dichotomised thinking of law through the indirect discrimination and sexual harassment provisions, and offering a gendered critique to law's construction and operation. One of the most significant achievements that can be identified in the *SDA* is that this paradox was implicitly recognised, but still formulated through legislation, despite the kinds of resistance articulated by Lesley Lynch in 1978 lingering within the feminist community at large. And, perhaps most importantly, this paradox was articulated by *lawyers* who also happened to be part of that much broader, diverse women's movement, emboldened by both intellectual critique of equality as offering negative and positive capabilities for women and a radical turn to situated, frontline engagement, unafraid of tackling sex as a differential.

Discrimination as a gendered concept in our law has therefore a complex past that cannot be reduced to what Scott identifies as fixity of historical gaze. A history must be interpolated through and by a multivalent, dissonant, sometimes maverick synthesis of feminist traditions and practices of the 1970s period of activism and theorising. What is clear is that the complex politics that led to the *SDA* not only incorporated the visions and skills of women who had infiltrated and upset the balance of the administration of the state (such as Susan Ryan) but also the more curious and somewhat slower articulation by other women of a jurisprudence of equality and difference that emerged through feminist legal theory and activism. The origins of the *SDA* should therefore read these histories of feminism of the 1970s and 1980s as complementary. Together, they open up spaces for different aspects of the conceptual as well as social-historical understanding of what was included in the Act in 1984, and why— and what was excised into affirmative action legislation. Such a history also, perhaps, offers ways of thinking, culturally and politically, about what remains unsaid about sexed discrimination in this country—the as yet unacknowledged legislation of an Equality Act, or the unheeded assumptions of future human rights instruments.

---

68   Ronalds, this volume.
69   Margaret Thornton, 'Equal Rights at Work' in Barbara Caine (ed.), *Oxford Companion to Australian Feminism*, Oxford University Press, Melbourne, 1998, p. 87.

Importantly, too, this short prehistory aims to caution against forgetting any of those origins, or conflicts, through which an Australian feminist legal thinking could be articulated. Despite the threats in the contemporary moment to the politics of naming and speaking questions of 'how the law comes to know about women, and what women know', it is easy to forget that Australian legal feminism was never lego-centric. It was never a praxis isolated within the profession or uncontaminated by intellectual challenges extant to traditional jurisprudence. Hard-fought skirmishes by lawyers over instruments such as the *SDA*, since 1984, by necessity, although inadvertently, narrow the political focus to legal discourse and experience. By remembering what the feminist legal community might have lost sight of in that process—the multiple, interconnected and often radical histories of how Australian feminism contested the public sphere—can only enliven law as a politics for present challenges, including, but not limited to, those about gendered discrimination.

Bibliography

Books and articles

Anonymous, 'Prison Justice', *The Sydney Women's Liberation Newsletter*, May, 1977, p. 7.

Arendt, Hannah, *Men in Dark Times*, Jonathon Cape, London, 1970.

Armstrong, Susan, 'Is Feminist Law Reform flawed? Abstentionists & Sceptics' (2004) 20 *Australian Feminist Law Journal* 43.

Attwood, Bain and Markus, Andrew, *The 1967 Referendum: Race, Power and the Australian Constitution*, Second edition, Aboriginal Studies Press, AIATSIS, Canberra, 2007.

Bacon, Wendy, *Anne Conlon Memorial Lecture*, NSW Women's Advisory Council, Sydney, 1983.

Bacon, Wendy, 'Women in Prisons', *Refractory Girl*, May, 1985, p. 2.

Bacon, Wendy and Lansdowne, Robyn, *Feminist Legal Action GroupReport: Women Homicide Offenders in NSW*, Feminist Legal Action Group, Sydney, 1982.

Bacon, Wendy and Maddock, Ken, 'Symposium on Does Women's Liberation Conflict with Human Liberation?', *Broadsheet*, no. 67 (1971), pp. 1–5.

Baker, A. J., 'Sydney Libertarianism and the Push', *Broadsheet*, no. 81 (March, 1975), pp. 5–10.

Basten, John 1980, 'Legal Services: Looking into the 1980s' (1980) 5(6) *Legal Service Bulletin* 282–5.

Basten, John and Lansdowne, Robyn, 'Community Legal Centres: Who's in Charge' (1980) 5(2) *Legal Service Bulletin* 52.

Basten, John, Richardson, Mark, Ronalds, Chris and Zdenkowski, George, 'The Criminal Injustice System', *ALWG and Legal Service Bulletin*, with the Law Foundation of New South Wales, Sydney, 1982.

Brown, Wendy, 'Tolerance as Supplement: 'The "Jewish Question" and the 'Woman Question'" in *Regulating Aversion: Tolerance in the Age of Identity and Empire*, Princeton University Press, NJ, 2008.

Buckley, Ken, 'Our Meeting with the Premier. The Nagle Report on Prisons', *Civil Liberty*, no. 79 (July/August, 1978), pp. 6–7.

Chesterman, John, 'The Making of the Australian New Left Lawyer' (1995) 1 *Australian Journal of Legal History* 37.

Chesterman, John, *Poverty Law and Social Change: The Story of the Fitzroy Legal Service*, Melbourne University Press, Carlton, 1996.

Coombs, Anne, *Sex and Anarchy*, Viking/Penguin, Ringwood, Vic., 1996.

Curthoys, Ann, 'Visions, Nightmares, Dreams: Women's History, 1975' (1996) 27(6) *Australian Historical Studies* 1.

Curthoys, Ann and Docker, John, *Is History Fiction?*, UNSW Press, Sydney, 2006.

Deleuze, Gilles and Guattari, Felix, *What is Philosophy?*, Translated by Graham Burchell and Hugh Tomlinson, Verso, London, 1999.

Docker, John, 'Sydney Intellectual History and Libertarianism' (1972) 7(1) *Australian Political Studies Association Journal* 42.

Docker, John, *Australian Cultural Elites: Intellectual Traditions in Sydney and Melbourne*, Angus and Robertson, Sydney, 1974.

Elliot, Lorraine, 'Inequalities in the Australian Education System: Part 2: Women in the Professions' in Jan Mercer (ed.), *The Other Half: Women in Australian Society*, Penguin, Ringwood, Vic., 1975.

Genovese, Ann, The Battered Body: A Feminist Legal History, PhD thesis, University of Technology, Sydney, 1998 <utsescholarship.lib.uts.edu.au/dspace/handle/2100/276>

Gordon, Richard and Osmond, Warren, 'An Overview of the Australian New Left' in The Australian New Left: Critical Essays and Strategy, William Heinemann Australia, Melbourne, 1970.

Graycar, Regina and Morgan, Jenny, The Hidden Gender of Law, Federation Press, Leichhardt, NSW, 1990.

Grimshaw, Patricia, Lake, Marilyn, McGrath, Ann and Quartly, Marian, Creating a Nation 1788–2007, Second edition, API Network, Perth, 2007.

Grosz, Elizabeth, 'The In(ter)vention of Feminist Knowledges' in Barbara Caine, E. A. Grosz and Marie de Lepervanche (eds), Crossing Boundaries: Feminism and the Critique of Knowledges, Allen & Unwin, Sydney, 1988.

Hunter, Rosemary, Indirect Discrimination in the Workplace, Federation Press, Leichhardt, NSW, 1992.

Jail News, 'Editorial' (1978) 1(9) Jail News..

Lahey, Kathleen, 'Until Women Themselves Have Told All That They Have To Tell' (1985) 23 Osgoode Hall Law Journal 519.

Lake, Marilyn, Getting Equal:The History of Australian Feminism, Allen & Unwin, St Leonards, NSW, 1999.

Lanteri, Anne Maree, 'Woman and the Law' in Jan Mercer (ed.), The Other Half: Women in Australian Society, Penguin, Ringwood, Vic., 1975.

Lloyd, Genevieve, The Man of Reason: 'Male' and 'Female' in Western Philosophy, Methuen, London, 1984.

Lynch, Lesley, 'Women and Law Conference', Refractory Girl, March, 1979 35.

Mackinnon, Catherine A., Sexual Harassment of Working Women, Yale University Press, New Haven, Conn., 1979.

Mackinnon, Catherine A., Feminism Unmodified: Discourse on Life and Law, Harvard University Press, Cambridge, Mass., 1987.

Mason, Gail and Chapman, Anna, 'Defining Sexual Harassment: A History of the Commonwealth Legislation and its Critiques' [2003] Federal Law Review 6 .

Mathews, Jane, 'Women in the Law' (1991) 41 Refractory Girl 27.

Morgan, Jenny, 'Women and the Law' in Refractory Girl Collective (eds), *Refracting Voices: Feminist Voices from Refractory Girl*, Southwood Press, Sydney, 1993.

Mukherjee, Satyanshu K. and Scutt, Jocelynne A. (eds), *Women and Crime*, George Allen & Unwin for Australian Institute of Criminology, Sydney, 1981.

Naffine, Ngaire, *Law and the Sexes: Explorations in Feminist Jurisprudence*, Allen & Unwin, Sydney, 1990.

Naffine, Ngaire, 'Assimilating Feminist Jurisprudence' (1993) 11 *Law in Context* 78.

Prisoners' Action Group (PAG), 'Bathurst Gaol and the Royal Commission into Prisons: A summary by the PAG' (1976) 2 (3) *Alternative Criminology Journal* 142.

Reid, Elizabeth and Altman, Denis, *Equality: The New Issues*, Fabians' Winter Lecture Series: Equality under Labor, Victorian Fabian Society, Melbourne, 1973.

Rod, Therese, Murder in the Family in New South Wales 1958–1967, Master of Arts thesis, University of Sydney, NSW, 1979.

Ross, Kim, 'F.L.A.G.' (1979) 4(3) *Legal Services Bulletin* 123 .

Sawer, Marian, *The Ethical State?*, Melbourne University Press, Carlton, 2003.

Sawer, Marian, *Making Women Count: A History of the Women's Electoral Lobby in Australia*, UNSW Press, Sydney, 2008.

Scott, Joan W., 'Gender: A Useful Category of Historical Analysis' (1986) 91(5) *American Historical Review* 1053.

Scutt, Jocelynne, 'Legislating for the Right to be Equal: Women, the Law and Social Policy' in Cora Baldock and Bettina Cass (eds), *Women, Social Welfare and the State in Australia*, Allen & Unwin, Sydney, 1988.

Smart, Carol, *Feminism and the Power of Law*, Routledge, London, 1989.

Thornton, Margaret, 'Feminist Jurisprudence: Illusion or Reality?' (1986) 3 *Australian Journal of Law & Society* 5.

Thornton, Margaret, *The Liberal Promise: Anti-Discrimination Legislation in Australia*, Oxford University Press, Melbourne, 1990.

Thornton, Margaret 1991, 'Feminism and the Contradictions of Law Reform' (1991) 19 *International Journal of the Sociology of Law* 453.

Thornton, Margaret, *Dissonance and Distrust: Women in the Legal Profession*, Oxford University Press, Melbourne, 1996.

Thornton, Margaret, 'Equal Rights at Work' in Barbara Caine (ed.), *The Oxford Companion to Australian Feminism*, Oxford University Press, Melbourne, 1998.

Thornton, Margaret, 'Neoliberal Melancholia: The Case of Feminist Legal Scholarship' (2004) 20 *Australian Feminist Law Journal* 7.

Willson, Sandra, 'Behind Bars' in Judy Mackinolty and Heather Radi (eds), *In Pursuit of Justice: Australian Women and the Law 1788–1979*, Hale & Iremonger, Sydney, 1979.

Wollstonecraft, Mary, *A Vindication of the Rights of Woman*, Penguin Books, Harmondsworth, UK, 1982 [1792].

Women Behind Bars (WBB), 'Women Behind Bars' (1976) 1(3) *Alternative Criminology Journal* 21–2 [reprinted from *Mabel*, December 1975].

Women Behind Bars (WBB), 'Demonstration at Mulawa' (1975) 1(4) *Alternative Criminology Journal* 71.

Women Behind Bars (WBB), 'Legal Visits to Mulawa' and 'Mulawa Jail Makes Women Sick', *Sydney Women's Liberation Newsletter*, May, 1977.

Zdenkowski, George, 'Civil Liberty', *Civil Liberty*, no. 68 (August/September, 1976), pp. 4–6.

Zdenkowksi, George and Brown, David, *The Prison Struggle: Changing Australia's Penal System*, Penguin, Ringwood, Vic., 1982.

Legislation

Anti-Discrimination Act 1977 (NSW)

Prohibition of Discrimination Act 1966 (SA)

Sex Discrimination Act 1975 (SA)

Sex Discrimination Act 1984 (Cth)

Cases

Australian Iron & Steel v Banovic (1989) 168 CLR 165

Koowarta v Bjelke-Petersen (1982) 34 ALR 417

Nadjovska v Australian Iron & Steel (1985) EOC 92-140

O'Callaghan v Loder (1984) EOC 92-023

O'Callaghan v Loder (1984) EOC 92-024

Reports and miscellaneous primary sources

FLAG 'Information sheet', 1979, The First Ten Years of Sydney Women's Liberation Collection, Mitchell Library, Sydney, MS388/81.

Letter, Margaret Thornton to Sue Wills, 7 August 1991, The First Ten Years of Sydney Women's Liberation Collection, Mitchell Library, Sydney, MS388/81.

Nagle, J. F., *Report of the Royal Commission into New South Wales Prisons. Volumes I, II and III*, NSW Government Printer, Sydney, 1978 [*Nagle Report*].

O'Connor, Deirdre, Should the Women's Movement rely on Law Reform as a Major Weapon in their Struggle?, Unpublished paper, Women's Commission, Sydney, The First Ten Years of Sydney, 1975, Women's Liberation Collection, Mitchell Library, Sydney, MS388/81.

Women Behind Bars, 'Who is in Gaol and Why are they There?', *Women Behind Bars (A Summary of Activities)*, Sydney, 1983, The First Ten Years of Sydney Women's Liberation Collection, Mitchell Library, Sydney, MS388/81.

Women's Trade Union Commission, *Women's Unions*, Booklet, Sydney, 1976, The First Ten Years of Sydney Women's Liberation Collection, Mitchell Library, Sydney, MS388/81.

3. Women's Work is Never Done: The Pursuit of Equality and the Commonwealth *Sex Discrimination Act*

Marian Sawer

The campaign for the Sex Discrimination Act 1984 *(Cth) (SDA) lasted more than a decade—or did it? In fact, the campaign for effective sex discrimination legislation has never ended. The champagne and cake of 1984 marked one victory in a continuing struggle. Continual effort has been required even to keep a specialist sex discrimination commissioner, while repeated budget cuts have depleted the resources needed to be effective. The two-decades-long campaign to enhance the statutory powers of the commissioner has also not yet borne fruit. Meanwhile, industrial relations changes contribute to new inequalities, while decision makers assume that discrimination has already been dealt with. This chapter will reflect on the history of the pursuit of equality by the organised women's movement in Australia and the changing nature of the obstacles in the path.*

The Prehistory of the *SDA*

It is now 25 years since the *SDA* came into force. The Act had a long prehistory and this chapter touches on the decades spent by women advocating for gender equality guarantees and then protecting the Act from sometimes unfriendly governments.

The modern history of demands for effective Commonwealth guarantees of gender equality starts in many ways with feminist campaigner Jessie Street. In 1942, when the Commonwealth Government began considering amendments to the *Constitution* to facilitate postwar reconstruction, Street wrote to Prime Minister John Curtin informing him that women in the Allied democracies were requesting constitutional change to 'extend to women all rights, status and opportunities enjoyed by men with provision that any sex discrimination prescribed in laws or regulations be invalid'.[1] She asked Curtin for a constitutional

---

1 Heather Radi, *Jessie Street: Documents and Essays*, Women's Redress Press, Sydney, 1990, p. 130. See also, Marian Sawer and Jill Vickers, 'Women's Constitutional Activism in Australia and Canada' (2001) 13(1) *Canadian Journal of Women and the Law* 9.

equality guarantee and this demand was included in the *Australian Women's Charter* drawn up in Sydney by a wartime conference of some 90 women's organisations. Despite Street's vigorous advocacy and the wartime mobilisation around the Australian Women's Charter, gender equality did not become part of the 1944 Constitutional Referendum on postwar reconstruction and democratic rights.[2] As has so often been the case in recent years, Street's advocacy for gender equality was to be more effective at the transnational than the national level. As an Australian delegate to the founding conference of the United Nations, she was one of a handful of feminist delegates that included Berta Lutz from Brazil and Minerva Bernardino from the Dominican Republic. They achieved the inclusion of a commitment to the equal rights of men and women in the Preamble to the Charter and of the word 'sex' in the phrase 'without distinction as to race, sex, language or religion', which appears in four different articles. Street was also effective in lobbying for Article 8 of the Charter on equal employment opportunity for men and women in the new organisation.[3] Bodil Bengtrup from Denmark successfully moved for the establishment of a UN Commission on the Status of Women (rather than the sub-commission originally decided on) and Street was elected its Vice-President in 1947.

Back in Australia, however, the Cold War brought Street into disrepute and demands for a general prohibition of sex discrimination receded from view, being widely regarded as having something to do with communism. This idea lingered on into the 1970s, resulting in members of the Australian Security and Intelligence Organisation (ASIO) lurking in the shrubbery outside women's liberation meetings.[4]

Meanwhile, women who felt dissatisfied with their lot as Brian's wife and Jenny's mum were famously being recommended to have a cup of tea, a Bex and a good lie down. In many areas of employment, including the Commonwealth Public Service, women continued to be subject to the infamous marriage bar and were fired if they committed the sin of matrimony, losing their superannuation in the process.[5] The Commonwealth marriage bar lasted until 1966, long after such bars had been removed elsewhere—that is, in all comparable countries except Ireland. Things began to move again in the 1960s, with the increased entry

---

2   It also did not become part of subsequent referendum proposals. Australia remains the only country that has amended its constitution (or introduced a new one) since World War II without incorporating the principle of gender equality.

3   Hilkka Pietilä, *The Unfinished Story of Women and the United Nations*, United Nations, New York, 2007, p. 11.

4   For ASIO photos of women arriving at a Canberra women's liberation meeting, see National Archives of Australia, Series No. A6122, Accession No. 2004/00686598.

5   Marian Sawer (ed.), *The Removal of the Commonwealth Marriage Bar: A Documentary History*, Centre for Research in Public Sector Management, University of Canberra, ACT, 1991, <http://pandora.nla.gov.au/pan/21883/20041011-0000/www.wel.org.au/issues/work/Marriage_Bar.pdf>

of women into higher education and the increased demand for women in the labour market. Attitudes were slow to shift, however, and were patronising in a way that would be totally unacceptable today.

Figure 3.1 Cover story, *The Bulletin,* **23 September 1967**

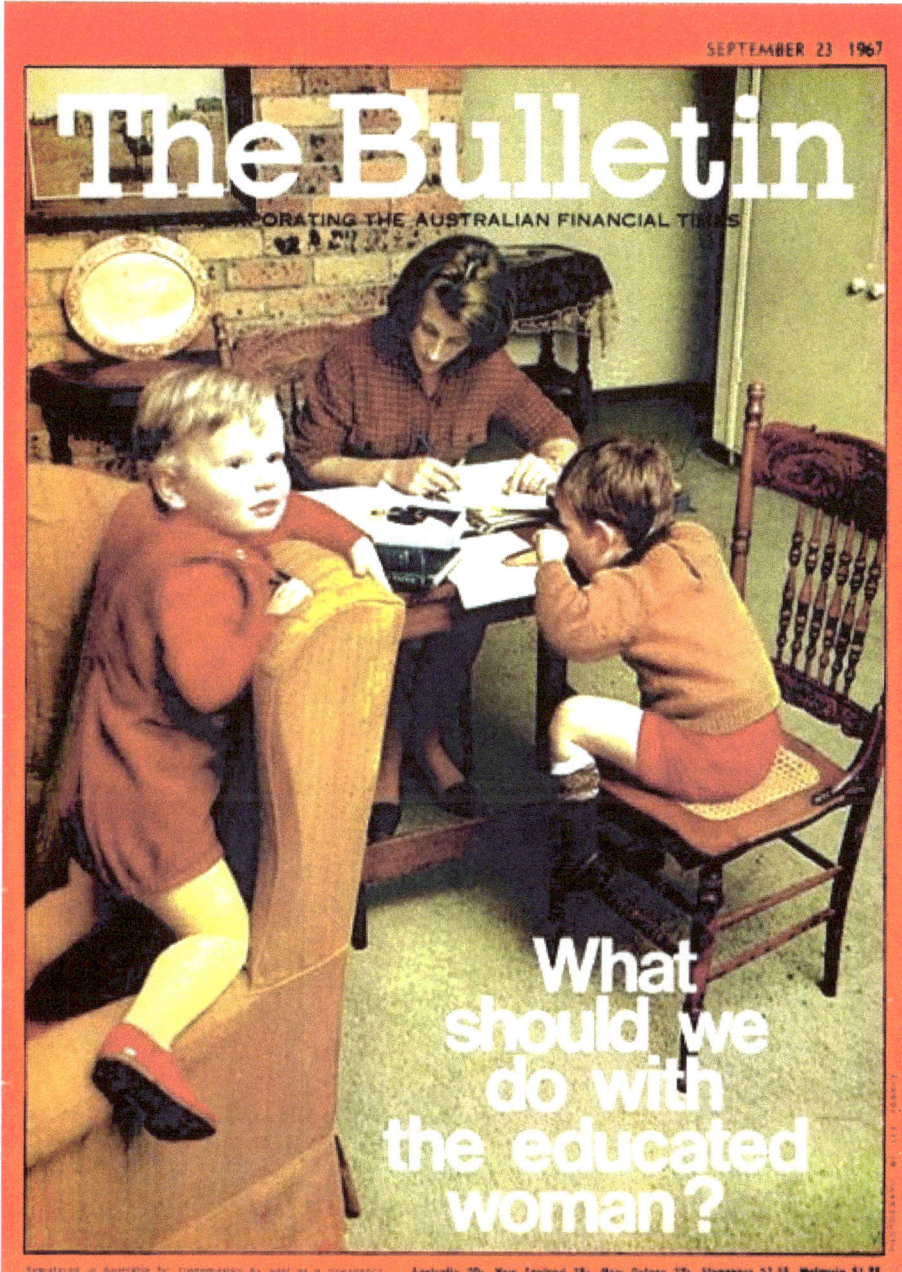

Courtesy APC Magazines

In 1967, a cover story, 'What shall we do with the educated woman?', appeared in the *The Bulletin*, the leading Australian current affairs journal of the period. It was about an influx of married women into Macquarie University in 1967, its first year. The women had formed a group to organise a creche and the article quoted the Vice-Chancellor's reaction: 'They don't have full permission yet, of course. They have yet to prove to us they can establish it, staff it, and keep it going. It just isn't possible for university funds to be used for a minority.'[6]

This view of married women as a minority and a request for a university childcare centre as novel and strange is a good illustration of the times. So too is the accompanying commentary by the journalist: 'Publicity has been showered on the Mums of Macquarie since the first mention of their childminding centre became known, and much of it has been a little absurd. They cannot, of course, take babies to lectures…They don't shell peas in the common-room or discuss the problems of napkin service.'[7]

Figure 3.2 WEL–Diamond Valley and women's liberation marching in 1973

Photo: Sandy Turnbull

This kind of trivialising of married women was indicative of the attitudes for which the new wave of the women's movement was shortly to invent a word: 'sexist'. Society had overlooked and wasted women's skills and talents, marooned them in the suburbs, expected them to spend the most productive

---

6   April Hersey, 'What shall we do with the educated woman?', *The Bulletin*, 23 September 1967, p. 23.
7   Ibid.

part of their lives in housework and then discounted their views as simply those of 'housewives'.[8] By the beginning of the 1970s, women's pent-up frustration at their treatment was about to explode.

A new wave of the women's movement swelled and in 1972 a new organisation, the Women's Electoral Lobby (WEL), succeeded in making sex discrimination a major campaign issue in the federal election. In response to WEL's agenda-setting work, Senator Lionel Murphy, soon to be Attorney-General, announced in November 1972 that '[t]he need to remove discrimination against women is obvious and will have early priority from a Labor government'.[9]

While the Whitlam Government moved quickly to ratify International Labour Organisation (ILO) Convention 111 on Discrimination in Employment and Occupation and to establish national and State employment discrimination committees, legislation took longer to appear. One must remember that this was before the adoption of the UN Convention on Elimination of All Forms of Discrimination Against Women (CEDAW) in 1979, so the constitutional grounds for federal legislation were less clear, quite apart from the enormous agenda of the Whitlam Government in the area of law reform. Nonetheless, in August 1975, the government did circulate a memorandum on a 'Proposed Bill to Prohibit Discrimination Against Persons by Reason of their Sex or Marital Status'.[10] By then, of course, it was too late and the dismissal of the government in November meant that the proposed Sex Discrimination Act did not eventuate.

Lobbying continued at the federal level, while women started gaining sex discrimination legislation at the State level—first in South Australia in 1975 and then in New South Wales and Victoria. The federal minister with responsibility for women's affairs, R. J. Ellicott, was persuaded of the need for sex discrimination legislation, as was the convenor of his National Women's Advisory Council, Beryl Beaurepaire. The National Party ministers in cabinet, however, were fiercely opposed and had support from the newly formed Women Who Want to be Women (WWWW). While Beaurepaire engaged in agenda setting on the need for anti-discrimination legislation, Babette Francis and Jackie Butler of WWWW were vociferous in opposition. Nonetheless, federal sex discrimination legislation was the centrepiece of the draft plan of action for the UN Decade of Women, drawn up after an unprecedented series of town hall meetings with

8   See Di Graham, 'Through Life in Pursuit of Equality' in Jocelynne Scutt (ed.), *Different Lives*, Penguin, Ringwood, Vic., 1987, pp. 179–87.

9   Jocelynne Scutt, 'Legislating for the Right to be Equal' in Cora V. Baldock and Bettina Cass (eds), *Women, Social Welfare and the State*, Allen & Unwin, Sydney, 1988 [1983], pp. 230–1.

10   In retrospect, the fact that the only bill to be enacted was the *Racial Discrimination Act* was perhaps a blessing in disguise; it made an ideal test case before the High Court for the use of the external affairs power as a constitutional base for federal human rights legislation (in *Koowarta*, 1982). This meant that the constitutionality of the use of the external affairs power to enact human rights legislation was established before the more controversial *SDA* came along.

women around Australia, culminating in a national meeting in the Academy of Science in Canberra in 1980. Despite being adopted by delegates whose election was overseen by the Australian Electoral Office, the Plan of Action was again blocked by the National Party.

At the mid-decade conference in Copenhagen, Minister Ellicott did manage to sign CEDAW, the new United Nation's Women's Convention. He achieved this despite WWWW trying physically to prevent him. They had acquired press accreditation for the conference from the *Ballarat Courier* and the *Toorak Times*. Ellicott and Andrew Peacock, as Minister for Foreign Affairs, issued a joint statement saying that signature of the Convention was an important indication of 'Australia's policy of equality for women and the elimination of discrimination'.[11] There was, however, no progress towards ratification of the Convention before the election of the Hawke Government.

Meanwhile, classified job advertisements in papers such as the *Sydney Morning Herald* continued to be divided between those for men and boys and those for women and girls. There was still an assumption that jobs that involved responsibility and had a career structure attached to them were for men, even though an increasing number of women had been able to take advantage of the Whitlam Government's abolition of tertiary fees to go to university. Often they had originally been trained as nurses or secretaries, as these were regarded as suitable jobs for women to have before they were married. Now these former nurses and secretaries were finding they had the brains to be brain surgeons or chief executive officers, and not only handmaidens as originally planned.

The *SDA* and its aftermath

Meanwhile, in Federal Parliament, the Labor Opposition was increasing the pressure on the issue and in 1981 Shadow Minister Senator Susan Ryan introduced her Sex Discrimination Bill as a Private Senator's Bill. This was a broad-ranging bill, drafted by early WEL member and barrister Chris Ronalds. Sex discrimination legislation became a major plank of the Labor Party's election policy, endorsed by representatives of some 26 national women's organisations, most of which had participated in Beaurepaire's UN Decade of Women consultation process. The momentum now seemed unstoppable and, with the election of the new Labor government in 1983, the way seemed clear for action at last. A Sex Discrimination Bill was introduced into Parliament in June 1983

11   *Australian Foreign Affairs Record*, July 1980, p. 240.

and CEDAW was ratified in July. By now the High Court had confirmed in the *Koowarta* case that the federal government was able to use its external affairs power to meet obligations under international human rights conventions.

It was at this point that a public furore erupted, as described by other contributors to the anniversary conference. While Elaine Nile, of the Festival of Light, made arrangements for busloads of opponents to come to Canberra to demonstrate against 'the Sex Bill' outside Parliament, supporters of the Bill were also busy. Pamela Denoon, the national coordinator of WEL, stitched together a coalition of women's organisations from across the political spectrum to support the Bill, ranging from the National Council of Women through to the Union of Australian Women. When the Bill finally passed through both houses[12]—after 53 amendments to placate seemingly implacable opponents—Denoon organised a large celebration party on the lawn in front of Parliament House to thank Susan Ryan and all the parliamentary supporters of the Bill, including Liberals such as Ian Macphee and Kathy Martin and Democrat Janine Haines, as well as tireless Labor advocates such as Senator Pat Giles. To go with the champagne there was a large purple, green and white cake in the shape of the women's symbol.

Once the legislation was through, what did it mean for women? For some it was empowering just to know there was now a law to prevent women being treated less favourably by employers because they were women, or because they were married women. Increasingly, women believed that they had the right to the same range of employment opportunities as men, the right not to be sexually harassed at work and the right to be paid equally—although the substantive achievement of the last two rights proved more elusive. In this new era, women became increasingly visible in public life—for example, in February 1986, Lynne Simons, the first woman Sergeant-At-Arms in the House of Representatives, led in the first woman Speaker, Joan Child. Women had come a long way in a Parliament, which until 1969, would not even employ a woman for the job of *Hansard* reporter, despite a lack of men with the shorthand skills required.

Despite such progress, Australia has been slipping down the Inter-Parliamentary Union's league table for representation of women in national parliaments for at least the past decade; today it ranks in thirty-third place along with Afghanistan.[13] This is because other countries, particularly since the United Nations' Fourth World Conference on Women (the Beijing Conference), have been taking more

---

12   While the passage of the bill was gruelling, the debate was far from being the longest in the Senate's history, as is sometimes claimed. The records of the Senate Table Office show that it was only the eleventh-longest debate in the period 1950–86. For example, while there were 17 hours of debate on the Sex Discrimination Bill, there were almost 70 hours on the Communist Party Dissolution Bill (Marian Sawer, *Making Women Count: A History of the Women's Electoral Lobby*, UNSW Press, Sydney, 2008, p. 184).

13   Inter-Parliamentary Union, *Women in National Parliaments*, 31 July 2009, <http://www.ipu.org/wmn-e/classif.htm>

vigorous action to ensure the presence of women in their parliaments, and more than 100 countries have adopted some form of electoral quota for women. The presence of women in elected office at local government level was even lower (28 per cent) than at the parliamentary level across Australia (31.6 per cent).[14] Nonetheless, it is now widely accepted in Australia, as elsewhere, that male-dominated political representation implies a democratic deficit, making it clear that there is 'something wrong with the picture' in cases such as the all-male 1992 Tasmanian Cabinet.

Figure 3.3 Tasmanian Cabinet. *The Mercury,* 19 February 1992, p. 2

Courtesy *The Mercury*

The survival of the *SDA* itself could also never be taken for granted. Already in 1986 there had to be an eleventh-hour effort to ensure there was a body to continue implementing the Act. The Human Rights Commission had been created in 1981 with a 'sunset' clause that came into effect after five years and the Attorney-General had delayed any action to replace it, because he was (unsuccessfully) trying to put through a Bill of Rights in the same package. On top of this, the Expenditure Review Committee of cabinet had decided in 1986 to abolish the commission, having temporarily overlooked the fact that it was responsible inter alia for implementing the government's new Act. Then Sex Discrimination Commissioner, Pam O'Neil, had to undertake a major campaign to ensure legislation was passed in time for a new body (the Human Rights and

---

14   Local government figures from October 2009, parliamentary figures from 9 April 2010—both from the Parliamentary Library, Parliament of Australia, Canberra.

Equal Opportunity Commission) to take over the functions of the old commission on its expiration at the end of 1986.[15] The commission was never really secure, however, being threatened with abolition by the Coalition's *Future Directions* manifesto released under the auspices of John Howard in 1988.

The *SDA* intermeshed with a range of sometimes challenging policies to address broad forms of discrimination against women. One of these was the failure of workplaces to acknowledge that employees had family responsibilities and that work practices needed to be more flexible to accommodate these responsibilities. Both men and women workers had such responsibilities and in 1983 the Hawke Government was elected with a commitment to ratify ILO Convention 156, which recognised that this was so. The Office of the Status of Women designed a 'Joe Average' poster to promote the Convention and to normalise the practice of male workers taking their share of family responsibilities.

Convention 156 was controversial because it required family-friendly work practices and conditions that would enable men to take a more equal role in raising their children. Although the Convention had been part of the Hawke Government's election policy, there were many delays in ratifying it, on the ground of States' objections. It again became part of Labor election policy in 1990 after determined advocacy by Labor feminists. At last, the Convention was ratified and the Office of the Status of Women led its implementation with a 'Sharing the Load' community education campaign that was highly commended by the United Nations. A Work and Family Unit was established in the industrial relations portfolio to continue policy development on ways to enable both parents to combine family responsibilities with paid work. The unit was abolished under the Howard Government in 2003, but the Rudd Government re-established an Office for Work and Family in the Department of the Prime Minister, with responsibility for paid parental leave and other 'work/life' issues.

The need to amend the *SDA* to prohibit both direct and indirect discrimination on the ground of family responsibilities has long been recognised—inside and outside government—and was once again recommended by the Senate Standing Committee on Legal and Constitutional Affairs, in 2008. At the time of the silver anniversary of the Act, the family responsibilities provision was still limited to termination of employment but, as we shall see below, this was one of the few recommendations of the committee endorsed in the Rudd Government's belated response in May 2010.

In one interesting development, soon after Australia's ratification of CEDAW in 1983, Justice Elizabeth Evatt took her place on the UN committee responsible for its oversight. Almost immediately, she began to play an important role in the development of CEDAW processes and jurisprudence.

---

15   Marian Sawer, *Sisters in Suits: Women and Public Policy*, Allen & Unwin, Sydney, 1990, pp. 212–13.

Figure 3.4 Justice Elizabeth Evatt

Courtesy Elizabeth Evatt

One of her most significant contributions was the drafting of the General Recommendation No. 19 (1992) on violence against women. The Convention text does not directly address the issue, so the General Recommendation is particularly important in clarifying that gender-based violence constitutes discrimination as defined under the Convention and that attitudes by which women are regarded as subordinate contribute to such violence. The General Recommendation also made it clear that because the concept of discrimination is not restricted to acts by or on behalf of government, states may be held responsible for private acts of violence if they fail to act with due diligence to prevent, investigate and punish such acts. In the case of *AT v Hungary* (2/03), the CEDAW Committee found that the state party was in breach of the Convention because it had failed to ensure the protection of 'AT' from her former common-law husband and had failed to enact specific domestic violence legislation to provide for protection orders and support services such as shelters.[16]

---

16   For discussion of this case, see: Bal Sokhi-Bulley, 'The Optional Protocol to CEDAW: First Steps' (2006) 6(1) *Human Rights Law Review* 143.

Reforming the *SDA*

Back at home, the women's movement was still working from both inside and outside government to improve the effectiveness of the *SDA*. These efforts bore fruit with successive amendments passed in 1992 and 1995. The amendments flowed from a House of Representatives inquiry of 1989–92. At first, the inquiry, put together quickly to take advantage of the fifth anniversary of the passage of the Act, looked unpromising—with an all-male committee and ambiguous terms of reference. The somewhat disturbing terms of reference included the formulation of 'the extent to which the objects of the *SDA* have been achieved or are capable of being achieved by legislative or other means'.[17] With the help of inquiry secretary Jon Stanhope, later Chief Minister of the Australian Capital Territory, feminists were, however, able to ensure a highly participatory inquiry process, including public seminars jointly sponsored by women's units.

The first public seminar was held in November 1990 and was co-hosted by the ACT Division of the Royal Australian Institute of Public Administration (of which Marian Sawer was then Vice-President). It was led off by discrimination expert Professor Margaret Thornton and included a dazzling cast of feminist legal and policy activists, from Justice Elizabeth Evatt to Jocelynne Scutt, Moira Rayner and Philippa Hall (for award issues) as well as John Basten, whose work on improving the definition of indirect discrimination was to be invaluable. Helen Styles of the Department of Foreign Affairs and Trade, a complainant in a major test case on the Act's indirect discrimination provisions, was asked by an industry representative whether voluntary EEO programs would not be less stressful than legal battles. She replied that if voluntary compliance worked, Moses would have handed down 'The Ten Guidelines'.

The report of the inquiry, *Half Way to Equal*, reflected much of what was learnt through such seminars and was promoted very effectively in the media by energetic committee chair, Michael Lavarch, later to be Attorney-General.[18] Not long before the tabling of the report in April 1992, a new coalition of national women's organisations called CAPOW! had been established, which proceeded to make the strengthening of the Act the subject of its first conference. Another element in this favourable configuration was the appointment of Anne Summers to the Prime Minister's Office. Prime Minister Paul Keating had been having 'women trouble', with the Opposition press boxing his maiden speech on the eve of International Women's Day 1992. As a new Member of Parliament in 1970, he had attacked the Gorton Government over the increased number of

---

17 House of Representatives Standing Committee on Legal and Constitutional Affairs, Inquiry into Equal Opportunity and Equal Status for Australian Women, 1989, Terms of Reference.
18 Lavarch had taken over as chairman of the Legal and Constitutional Affairs Committee after the 1990 election, when the inquiry was reinstated.

women in the workforce and asked what it was doing to 'put the working wife back in her home'. A bad press on women's issues, combined with his abysmal rating with women voters, led to the appointment of Summers to recapture the 'women's vote'.

The combination of insider and outsider advocacy brought success when the Prime Minister announced the first set of amendments to the Act at the CAPOW! conference in September and foreshadowed the second set, which was to come in 2005. The immediate changes included strengthening the sexual harassment provisions, making dismissal on the ground of family responsibilities unlawful and removing the exemption for industrial awards. The changes that had to wait until 2005 included strengthening the special measures provision and, most importantly, reversing the onus of proof in cases of indirect discrimination, so that an employer had to demonstrate the business necessity for requirements that disadvantaged women.

At the same conference, the Prime Minister announced the government's acceptance of the longstanding women's movement's demand for contract compliance to be introduced as an additional incentive for employers to comply with the *Affirmative Action Act*. This meant that from 1992, companies named in Parliament for non-compliance with the Act would be ineligible for government contracts or industry subsidies. Contract compliance is still part of the federal government procurement policy overseen by the Department of Finance, but has little effect on those named for non-compliance, which tend to be companies that do not have business with the government. The Coalition objected to the introduction of contract compliance and also to the removal of the exemption in the *SDA* for industrial awards. The Shadow Minister, Senator Jocelyn Newman, decried the new commitments with a press release headed 'Keating's sex speech a bit limp'.[19]

In a classic but unusual example of policy transfer, some of the improvements to the Commonwealth Act had already been trialled in the new ACT *Discrimination Act* of 1991. The developments in the Australian Capital Territory owed much to feminist advocates already involved in the federal inquiry, so the policy transfer was not really from a small jurisdiction to a national one, as much of the policy learning had already taken place.

Under the Howard Government elected in 1996, the women's movement was involved more in defensive actions than moving the agenda forward. It seemed clear that the new government was disinclined to have a Sex Discrimination Commissioner at all. Sue Walpole, then Sex Discrimination Commissioner, was described by the Prime Minister as a 'Labor stooge' and resigned early. She

---

19   Senator Jocelyn Newman, Press release, 19 September 1992.

was not replaced for 14 months. A cartoon by Cathy Wilcox depicted feminist frustration at this long wait and the uncertainty over the position being filled. It shows the Prime Minister delivering an answering-machine message.

Figure 3.5 Wilcox cartoon, *The Age,* 19 September 1997

Beeep! The office of the Commissioner for Sex Discrimination is currently unattended. If you're a woman and you have a complaint, well, that's just typical. Complain, complain, complain, it's all you women do. Not content to have a nice job and a few sisters in parliament, you want equal pay, childcare and protection as well! Next, you'll be wanting bloody land rights! Face it. Sex discrimination happens. In fact, it's something of a tradition in this country, and well, I'm an unashamed traditionalist. So on with the powder, there's a good love, freshen up your lippy, give up and go home. And sorry. We don't take messages. We only give them. Beeep.

Courtesy Cathy Wilcox

The position was finally filled soon after this very effective cartoon appeared.

Another high-profile campaign was to prevent the watering down of the marital status provisions of the *SDA*. The Federal Court had ruled that a Victorian law restricting access of single women to IVF treatment was inconsistent with the Commonwealth *SDA* and hence invalid. The Commonwealth Attorney-General, however, granted a fiat to enable the Australian Conference of Catholic Bishops to appeal to the High Court.[20] The challenge threatened not only single women's access to IVF, but also the marital status provisions of the *SDA* more generally and WEL–Victoria intervened along with the Human Rights and Equal Opportunity Commission. It was the first time a women's group had been granted status in the High Court. The bishops, who had not been a party to the original case, were unsuccessful.

---

20   *Ex parte Australian Catholic Bishops Conference* (2002) 209 CLR 372.

In the meantime, the government introduced a bill to amend the *SDA* to allow States and Territories to discriminate on the basis of marital status in the provision of 'assisted reproductive technology services'. Fortunately, the Senate Legal and Constitutional Affairs Committee was chaired by Senator Marise Payne, who helped hold the line against the various attempts by the Howard Government to weaken the Act. The committee found that the Bill was unable to achieve its objective of providing a child with the care and affection of a mother and father.[21]

The Howard Government also made unsuccessful attempts before and after the 2004 federal election to amend the *SDA* to provide an exemption for male-only teachers' scholarships—an initiative opposed by women's groups and by the then Sex Discrimination Commissioner, Pru Goward.

In addition, there were continuing struggles over the resourcing and structure of the Human Rights and Equal Opportunity Commission, which had responsibility for administering the Act. Resourcing of the commission and of the Sex Discrimination Commissioner became one of the recurrent themes of women's conferences. These struggles had begun under the Hawke Government but were exacerbated under the Howard Government, which straightaway made a 40 per cent cut to the commission's budget, meaning a loss of one-third of its staff in 1997–98. It went further by introducing successive bills to remove the specialist commissioners, including the Sex Discrimination Commissioner, and to require the commission to obtain permission from the Attorney-General before intervening in court proceedings. Fortunately, these bills were blocked in the Senate. WEL, along with feminist lawyers, wrote submissions and appeared before the Senate Legal and Constitutional Affairs Committee to argue the deleterious effects of losing specialist expertise.

WEL has continued to advocate the importance of the specialist commissioners and the overloading caused by the doubling up of responsibilities under the Howard Government. Rather than filling the vacant commissioner positions, however, the Rudd Government in 2008 formalised the doubling up of responsibilities, so that each commissioner carries two portfolios: the Sex Discrimination Commissioner is also the commissioner responsible for Age Discrimination. The Human Rights Commission also suffered disproportionately in the 2008 Budget, with the efficiency dividend resulting in a 14.5 per cent funding cut across the commission, including the sex discrimination area.

It should be noted here that with the abolition or muting of women's policy units in government, the role of a relatively independent Human Rights Commission in policy advocacy becomes increasingly important. This was particularly

---

21   Louise Chappell, 'Winding back Australian Women's Rights: Conventions, Contradictions and Conflicts' (2002) 37(3) *Australian Journal of Political Science* 475.

notable with Commissioner Goward's campaign for paid maternity leave and more recently with the campaigns of Commissioner Liz Broderick—both on paid maternity leave and on a range of gender equality issues.

Conclusion

So where are we now? The Rudd Government was elected in 2007 without a women's policy—the first time that the Australian Labor Party (ALP) had gone to an election without a women's policy since 1977. Like the Blair Government in the United Kingdom, it had been convinced that any trace of feminism would be an electoral turn-off for the blue-collar workers being wooed back to the party. Despite the absence of an overall plan on how to address gender inequalities, the ALP did have policies that included the strengthening of the Commonwealth *SDA*, the ratification of the Optional Protocol of CEDAW and strengthening the Office for Women (but without moving it back to the Department of Prime Minister and Cabinet or ensuring that the portfolio minister was in cabinet).

The loss of capacity within government to monitor policy for its impact on women and the loss of political will to act on such gender auditing had contributed to a range of adverse outcomes, particularly with WorkChoices and its impact on the pay and conditions of low-paid women workers. The Rudd Government legislated to undo the more extreme aspects of WorkChoices but without directly addressing the gender pay gap. The House of Representatives inquiry into pay equity reported in late 2009—well after the setting up of the new industrial relations system under Fair Work Australia. Meanwhile, the gender pay gap in the ordinary-time earnings of full-time workers increased to 17.2 per cent in Australia as a whole, and to 25.9 per cent in Western Australia.[22]

The Rudd Government legislated in 2010 for 18 weeks' paid maternity leave to take effect from 2011,[23] before which Australia remained one of only two Organisation for Economic Cooperation and Development (OECD) countries without such a basic entitlement at the national level. Childcare policy had also been in retreat since the 1990s. In late 2008, the collapse of ABC Learning, which had become the largest childcare corporation in the world, illustrated the dangers of using public money to subsidise the growth of a for-profit corporate childcare market. No resolute action was on the agenda—despite the findings

---

22   Australian Bureau of Statistics, Average Weekly Earnings, May 2009, ABS Cat 6302.
23   *Paid Parental Leave Act 2010* (Cth).

of the Australian Survey of Social Attitudes that for-profit child care was the least-preferred and government provision the most-preferred form of child care in Australia.[24]

Twenty-five years after the *SDA* came into force, our expectations have risen considerably. The Senate Legal and Constitutional Affairs Committee produced an excellent report in December 2008 on what needed to be done in the short term to strengthen the *SDA* and make it effective again. As we have noted, the Rudd Government was elected with a platform commitment to 'strengthen and improve the *SDA* and the powers of the Commissioner'. Despite this commitment, and another to respond to parliamentary committee reports within three months, a response to the senate committee report on the *SDA* did not appear until May 2010. And when it came, there were still no new powers for the Sex Discrimination Commissioner to take a more proactive role, as was the case with comparable commissions in Canada, New Zealand and the United Kingdom and as recommended by the senate committee. Women's organisations had been campaigning since the 1980s for such powers, to lift the burden of achieving change from the victims of discrimination. There was also no role for the Sex Discrimination Commissioner to monitor and report on progress towards gender equality—also recommended by the senate committee—let alone the resources to do so. All such matters were put off for the foreseeable future as part of the 'consolidation project'. The argument that a present reform would block the way for more sweeping measures in the future comes straight out of Cornford's classic compendium of tactics for resisting reform.[25]

By the time of the silver anniversary of the *Sex Discrimination Act*, many of those who had helped bring it into existence were themselves silver-haired. Nonetheless, it was clear that their work was far from over. The Act had required constant vigilance from the time of its difficult birth. And while the 2007 ALP National Platform had contained a specific commitment to 'strengthen and improve the *Sex Discrimination Act* and the powers of the Commissioner to protect women against discrimination on the basis of gender and family responsibilities', the 2009 National Platform had only a non-specific commitment to 'eliminate all forms of discrimination, vilification or harassment and to harmonise anti-discrimination laws and procedures'. As in the previous 25 years, now there was an easy assumption by government that sex discrimination was something that had already been dealt with. The achievement of strong accountability

---

24   Australian Survey of Social Attitudes 2009 (<http://aussa.anu.edu.au>). Of the respondents to this regular national survey, 35 per cent preferred government provision compared with 18 per cent preferring business provision, with other forms of provision (community organisations or family) coming in between.
25   F. M. Cornford, *Microcosmographia Academica: Being a Guide for the Young Academic Politician*, Bowes & Bowes, Cambridge, UK, 1908, p. 17.

frameworks and legislative instruments to ensure further progress was low on the agenda, and only continued campaigning by equality seekers was likely to change this. Indeed, women's work is never done.

Bibliography

Books and articles

Chappell, Louise, 'Winding back Australian Women's Rights: Conventions, Contradictions and Conflicts' (2002) 37(3) *Australian Journal of Political Science* 475.

Cornford, F. M., *Microcosmographia Academica: Being a Guide for the Young Academic Politician*, Bowes & Bowes, Cambridge, UK, 1908.

Graham, Di, 'Through Life in Pursuit of Equality' in Jocelynne Scutt (ed.), *Different Lives*, Penguin, Ringwood, Vic., 1987.

Hersey, April, 'What shall we do with the educated woman?', *The Bulletin*, 23 September 1967, p. 23.

Pietilä, Hilkka, *The Unfinished Story of Women and the United Nations*, United Nations, New York, 2007.

Radi, Heather, *Jessie Street: Documents and Essays*, Women's Redress Press, Sydney, 1990.

Sawer, Marian, *Sisters in Suits: Women and Public Policy*, Allen & Unwin, Sydney, 1990.

Sawer, Marian, *Making Women Count: A History of the Women's Electoral Lobby*, UNSW Press, Sydney, 2008.

Sawer, Marian (ed.), *The Removal of the Commonwealth Marriage Bar: A Documentary History*, Centre for Research in Public Sector Management, University of Canberra, ACT, 1997, <http://pandora.nla.gov.au/pan/21883/20041011-0000/www.wel.org.au/issues/work/Marriage_Bar.pdf>

Sawer, Marian and Vickers, Jill, 'Women's Constitutional Activism in Australia and Canada' (2001) 13(1) *Canadian Journal of Women and the Law* 9.

Scutt, Jocelynne, 'Legislating for the Right to be Equal' in Cora V. Baldock and Bettina Cass (eds), *Women, Social Welfare and the State*, Allen & Unwin, Sydney, 1988 [1983].

Sokhi-Bulley, Bal, 'The Optional Protocol to CEDAW: First Steps' (2006) 6(1) *Human Rights Law Review* 143.

Legislation

Paid Parental Leave Act 2010 (Cth)

Racial Discrimination Act 1975 (Cth)

Sex Discrimination Act 1984 (Cth)

Cases

Ex parte Australian Catholic Bishops Conference (2002) 209 CLR 372

Koowarta v Bjelke-Petersen (1982) 153 CLR 168

Reports and miscellaneous primary sources

Australian Bureau of Statistics, Average Weekly Earnings, May 2009, ABS Cat. 6302, Australian Bureau of Statistics, Canberra.

Australian Foreign Affairs Record, July 1980, p. 240.

Australian Survey of Social Attitudes, The Australian National University, Canberra, 2009 <http://aussa.anu.edu.au>

House of Representatives Standing Committee on Legal and Constitutional Affairs, *Inquiry into Equal Opportunity and Equal Status for Australian Women*, Parliament of Australia, Canberra, 1989..

Inter-Parliamentary Union, *Women in National Parliaments*, 31 July 2009, <http://www.ipu.org/wmn-e/classif.htm>

Newman, Senator Jocelyn, Press release, 19 September 1992, Parliament House, Canberra.

4. 'To Demand Equality is to Lack Ambition': Sex discrimination Legislation — Contexts and Contradictions[1]

Susan Magarey

From an acknowledgment of all that was achieved in the passage of the Sex Discrimination Act 1984, *this chapter moves on to consider the inherent contradiction in expecting government, which has legitimised discrimination against women, to redress such wrongs, and to consider a range of critiques advanced from the wider socio-political contexts of the early 1980s. Its second half focuses on the twenty-fifth anniversary of this legislation in its context of global recession and socio-political anxiety.*

Of course, it was an outstanding achievement: the *Sex Discrimination Act* passed in 1984, 25 years ago. That moment was one of exceptional confluence between the reforming goals of the Australian Labor Party (ALP) and the liberal commitment to equality between the sexes of the Australian women's movement. Both were personified in Susan Ryan, a member of the cabinet in the first Labor government of Bob Hawke and a longstanding member of the Women's Electoral Lobby (WEL).[2] This landmark legislation enjoyed enthusiastic support from all over Australia, from WEL and from a host of feminist organisations considerably older than WEL or women's liberation—from the Australian Federation of University Women, from the National Council of Women, from the UN Status of Women Committee, from the Union of Australian Women, from Women and Development Australia, from the Young Women's Christian Association and from Zonta.[3]

Even so, the women's movement was—and is—an umbrella term that groups together a host of very different experiences, beliefs, commitments and practices. That same moment was not a cause of rejoicing, or even attention, among all

---

1   My thanks to Sandra Lilburn for newspaper research, to Anne Edwards for editorial help, to Dianne Otto for discussion and encouragement, and to Sue Sheridan, always, for quality control.
2   Susan Ryan, *Catching the Waves: Life in and out of Politics*, Harper Collins, Sydney, 1999, pp. 241–4.
3   'Women's groups support Sex Discrimination Bill', *The Canberra Times*, 12 September 1983, p. 7; 'Sex discrimination ban "a must"', *The Courier-Mail* (Brisbane), 29 September 1983, p. 15.

feminists. Some saw contradictions in the whole project. Others, coming from extra-parliamentary commitments, had dreams of what feminism might achieve, which dwarfed notions of equality.

Margaret Thornton spelled out the central contradiction inherent in anti-discrimination legislation some years ago. She pointed out that while citizens of a democracy commonly assume that a fundamental norm is their equality, such equality is demonstrably 'imperfectly realised'. Comparison of one individual with another, one group of people with another, shows differences—and differences in hierarchical relationships to each other. At the peak of that hierarchy is an all too recognisable figure: 'a white, Anglo-Celtic, heterosexual male who falls within acceptable parameters of physical and intellectual normalcy, who supports, at least nominally, mainstream Christian beliefs, and who fits within the middle-to-the-right of the political spectrum.'[4]

Such men have power in our society and, Thornton went on to observe, 'they will invariably exercise it in their own interest'.[5] Accordingly, she concluded that the most positive case to be made for anti-discrimination legislation was that it rendered these characteristics of our society visible, so such legislation served 'an important symbolic and educative function'.[6] Sadly, though, only four years later, Thornton was compelled to note that legal discourse had remained largely immune to that function:

> [T]he benchmark male continues to be a powerful normative force within law, whose eminent reasonableness is used to disqualify the disorderly voices of women. This is the case with EEO, no less than with rape, wife-battering, provocation, pornography or with any of the manifold social harms to which women are subjected.[7]

Further, the benevolent intent of legislation with such a 'symbolic and educative function' depended on a generally liberal—small-'l' liberal—political and legal context. Such a context cannot, however, be assumed.

Context is the crucial factor in this whole consideration. That context, in 1984, included the opposition raised against Susan Ryan's Bill, which was, at the time, called 'the Ryan juggernaut'. One-quarter of a century on, people might find it difficult to credit the opponents' arguments and fervour. Most vociferous were the Women Who Want to be Women (WWWW), founded in 1979 by Babette

---

4   Margaret Thornton, *The Liberal Promise: Anti-Discrimination Legislation in Australia*, Oxford University Press, Melbourne, 1990, p. 1.

5   Ibid., p. 261.

6   Ibid.

7   Margaret Thornton, 'The Seductive Allure of EEO' in Norma Grieve and Ailsa Burns (eds), *Australian Women: Contemporary Feminist Thought*, Oxford University Press, Melbourne, 1994, pp. 215–16.

Francis, a scientist, to oppose feminist influence on government.[8] She and her supporters deluged Members of Parliament with letters written on pink paper, creating an illusion of a large organisation by writing dozens each. A Canberra member of the 4Ws, Betty Hocking, was also a member of the Family Team in the ACT House of Assembly. She issued a statement asking, 'Is there no-one who can see that the women who hate men are castrating them with their sex discrimination Bills and making them eunuchs in their own kingdoms?' Then, even more memorably, she observed: 'Delilah cut off Samson's hair and made him her slave. The Sex Discrimination Bill cuts off far more than that.'[9]

As an aside, I would note that it was not only the opponents of this Bill who found that questions about equality between women and men impelled them to allusions to people's sexual anatomy. What Margaret Thornton refers to as '[w]omen's indelible association with corporeality'[10] operated subconsciously, even among those who supported the Bill. Democrat spokeswoman, feminist Janine Haines, startled other members of the Senate when she observed that there had been 'many hysterical comments' about how the Bill would eliminate differences between men and women: 'Despite the Freudian remarks about assertive women, that they suffer only from penis envy, I have yet to meet a woman who suffers from that or who has any particular desire to acquire that section of the male anatomy.'[11]

No less a personage than Dame Roma Mitchell, inaugural chair of the then recently established Human Rights Commission, would find herself having to argue—a little more euphemistically—that the laws against sexual harassment would not 'rob Cupid of his arrow'.[12]

The 4Ws organised for two veterans of the struggle against the *Equal Rights Amendment Act* in the United States to visit. One was Phyllis Schlafly, a lawyer now acclaimed as the best-known advocate in the United States of the dignity and honour owed to the full-time homemaker,[13] the other Michael Levin, a professor of philosophy at the City College of New York. Both toured Australia speaking against the Sex Discrimination Bill. Levin accused feminists of becoming 'increasingly coercive', of endeavouring to institute 'a unisex society—that is not workable, and boring anyway', declaring that 'feminists are not women'

---

8   Emma Grahame, 'Anti-Feminism' in Barbara Caine, Moira Gatens, Emma Grahame, Jan Larbalestier, Sophie Watson and Elizabeth Webby (eds), *Australian Feminism: A Companion*, Oxford University Press, Melbourne, 1998, p. 380; Marian Sawer with Gail Radford, *Making Women Count: A History of the Women's Electoral Lobby in Australia*, UNSW Press, Sydney, 2008, p. 79.

9   'Are there men in Parliament?', *The Courier-Mail* (Brisbane), 27 September 1983, p. 13.

10   Thornton, 'The Seductive Allure of EEO', p. 223.

11   Amanda Buckley, 'Senate's uncomfortable Friday…and more to come', *Sydney Morning Herald*, 22 October 1983, p. 6.

12   *The Advertiser* (Adelaide), 27 August 1984.

13   Available online at: <http://www.eagleforum.org/misc/bio.html>

and announcing that '[s]exual harassment is a problem that simply does not exist'.[14] Local heavyweights who joined them included Lachlan Chipman, Founding Professor of Philosophy at the University of Wollongong, and the Very Reverend David Roberts, Anglican Dean of Perth. Roberts declared:

> Susan Ryan's drab and humourless Utopia…has lost sight of the complementary delights of being male and female…It would be tragic for our humanity if we allowed ourselves to be remodelled by an Amazonian reformism which legislates against the weakness of men and apparently counts as ineffectual the real strength of women—the humanising and civilising power of their femininity.[15]

'Whatever can the Dean have been reading as the Sex Discrimination Bill?' expostulated Dame Roma. 'Certainly not my copy.' 'Sometimes I wonder,' she went on, 'whether those who oppose the Sex Discrimination Bill accept women as human beings.'[16]

Other opposition to the Sex Discrimination Bill came from closer to the centre of the political spectrum. Margot Anthony, described as 'housewife and partner to the Leader of the National Party', and as 'one of the backroom campaigners of the National Party's fight against the Government's sex discrimination Bill', went to Sydney to hear Schlafly speak against the Bill at Macquarie University. She was horrified by the students' hostility to Schlafly and subsequently appeared in the *Sydney Morning Herald*, 'to put the intelligent conservative position from women who seldom get a hearing'. She thought that the Bill carried a subtle message that women were wrong if they wanted to stay at home, rather than seek work in the labour market, and she wanted to combat that. She lamented the decline of the family and traditional values.[17] Other wives of members of the parliamentary National Party joined her, including one wife—Flo Bjelke-Petersen—who was herself a senator.[18] The parliamentary Liberal Party, in contrast, was generally supportive. Its Deputy Leader, however, Shadow Treasurer, John Howard, leant, he said, 'towards the National Party position which opposed key aspects of the bill'.[19]

14   'US professor: what sexual harassment?', *West Australian*, 17 September 1983, p. 3; Mark Hooper, 'Professor invites fury by scorning feminists', *The Australian*, 7 September 1983, p. 3.

15   Roma Mitchell, Address at Monash University, 10 December 1983, State Library of South Australia, Adelaide, PRG 778/17/27.

16   Ibid.

17   Amanda Buckley, 'Why Mrs Doug Anthony is against the sex bill: is it wrong to stay at home?', *Sydney Morning Herald*, 16 September 1983, p. 1.

18   Kate Legge, 'Coalition split widens on sex discrimination Bill', *The Age* (Melbourne), 19 September 1983, p. 5; Editorial, 'Sex bill splits the opposition', *The Age* (Melbourne), 20 September 1983.

19   Amanda Buckley, 'Sex bill row to split Liberal Party room', *Sydney Morning Herald*, 19 September 1983, p. 1.

Of course, the context of the passage of this bill also included the presence or absence of feminisms committed to other forms of change in the world besides change directed towards equality between the sexes to be won through mechanisms of the state. Those feminisms were still present in 1984. In women's liberation, we used to wear badges that read 'To demand equality is to lack ambition'. We were not silly. We were simply drawing on ideas from another of the multifarious political components of the women's movement. Let me offer two sets of examples.

At much the same time as Susan Ryan was using all her energy and ingenuity to get the Sex Discrimination Bill through its final moments in the Senate, a considerable number of other feminists were engaged in the Close the Gap Women's Peace Camp at Pine Gap in the Northern Territory. The changes that those women sought were the removal of US nuclear bases from Australia; land rights, autonomy and self-determination for Aboriginal people; removal of Pershing missiles from England and Europe; and unity of women of all cultures acting against global violence.[20] These, surely, were immense goals—way beyond the capacity of any government, however benevolent.

At about the same time, I was taking up a new post to set up a Research Centre for Women's Studies at the University of Adelaide. Women's studies was engaged with some quite electrifying ideas. Recall, for a moment, American Kate Millett linking power—the core concept of any kind of politics—to sex.[21] Remember expatriate Australian Germaine Greer elaborating a similar connection, declaring women to be sexual eunuchs.[22] Another American, Shulamith Firestone, urged the abolition of sex differentiation altogether, arguing that reproduction and child rearing should be disengaged from biology, rendering the biological family unnecessary and making possible sexual freedom, economic independence and self-determination for everyone—women as well as men, and children too.[23] English feminist theorist Juliet Mitchell exclaimed: 'The longevity of the oppression of women must be based on something more than conspiracy, something more complicated than biological handicap and more durable than economic exploitation.'[24]

Her endeavour to explain such oppression became a very fat book called *Psychoanalysis and Feminism*.[25] Joan Kelly demonstrated just how different writing history must become (in terms of periodisation, categories of social

---

20   Emma Grahame, 'Anti-Nuclear Activism', in Caine et al., *Australian Feminism*, pp. 381–2.
21   Kate Millett, *Sexual Politics*, Rupert Hart-Davis, London, 1971.
22   Germaine Greer, *The Female Eunuch*, Paladin, London, 1971.
23   Shulamith Firestone, *The Dialectic of Sex: The Case for Feminist Revolution*, Paladin, London, 1972.
24   Juliet Mitchell, *Psychoanalysis and Feminism*, Allen Lane, London, 1974, p. 362.
25   Ibid.

analysis and theories of social change) if histories were to include women.[26] Eleanor Maccoby and Carol Jacklin dismantled seemingly timeless assumptions about the psychology of sex differences.[27] Michelle Rosaldo and Louise Lamphere explored and exploded longstanding analogies that anthropologists drew between men and 'culture', women and 'nature'.[28]

These ideas were part of a radical intellectual transformation, challenging a host of taken-for-granted assumptions into which we had all been inculcated. Some of them had thoroughly practical consequences as well. Here in Australia, human geographer Fay Gale pointed out one of the consequences of social scientists assuming that the human is male. This was the story of Werlatyre-Therre, a place near Alice Springs where the city fathers wanted to build a recreational lake. Government officials—planners, engineers, construction managers (all men)—consulted the local Aboriginal men. The Aboriginal men had nothing particular to say about it, so construction was about to begin. Then, however, 'a number of Aboriginal women…moved in to protest loudly and visibly. They set up camp at the site and effectively called a halt to construction, demanding that they be recognised, just as Aboriginal men would have been considered if it had been a men's site.'[29]

For this was a very important women's site—a 'crucial site in the whole women's Dreaming pattern of central Australia'. White male Australia's sexist assumptions about Aboriginal landownership giving all authority over land to men had, here, cost the government—us, taxpayers, as Gale did not shrink from pointing out—a great waste of hard cash.[30] Engagement with intellectual transformation of this order promised all-encompassing change.

I was not dismissing the *Sex Discrimination Act*'s achievement by wearing a badge declaring that 'To demand equality is to lack ambition' as I went about setting up women's studies at the University of Adelaide. Rather, I was trying to make people think about what equality meant in the wake of the Sears case in the United States, a case that pitted equality against, not in-equality, but difference[31]—another of the debates addressed in women's studies.

---

26   Joan Kelly-Gadol, 'The Social Relation of the Sexes: Methodological Implications of Women's History' (1976) 1(4) *Signs: Journal of Women in Culture and Society* 809.

27   Eleanor Maccoby and Carol Jacklin, *The Psychology of Sex Differences*, Oxford University Press, UK, 1974.

28   Michelle Rosaldo and Louise Lamphere (eds), *Woman, Culture and Society*, Stanford University Press, Calif., 1974.

29   Fay Gale, 'Seeing Women in the Landscape: Alternative Views of the World Around Us' in Jacqueline Goodnow and Carole Patemen (eds), *Women, Social Science and Public Policy*, George Allen & Unwin, Sydney, 1985, p. 65.

30   Ibid., pp. 63–5.

31   See, for example, Joan Wallach Scott, 'The Sears Case', *Gender and the Politics of History*, Columbia University Press, New York, 1988.

Today, one-quarter of a century later, we inhabit markedly different contexts. There have been gains in the position of women. Such pride we can take in the appointment of Quentin Bryce as Governor-General; in the front bench of the first Rudd Government, with Julia Gillard as Deputy Prime Minister and three other women with major portfolios; in the election of Anna Bligh, the first woman to be elected as a State premier. Fay Gale was a vice-chancellor. Women's studies has been mainstreamed or has become gender studies. Events have overtaken one of the Pine Gap protesters' goals: the US Pershing missiles have been removed from England and Europe. And yet, and yet—there is still an immense gulf between the optimism of 25 years ago and the position of women today.

Economic and political change from the early 1990s on made us all familiar with neo-liberal social ideology emphasising the individual, profound economic conservatism emphasising the primacy of market freedom, joined with a moral vacuity in which advertisements tell each of us to 'Put yourself first', which fosters the concept of 'retail therapy', even 'retail fun'—currently blamed for a greed-is-good culture and its consequences. As La Trobe University academic Mark Furlong observed recently: 'The personal pronoun has taken dominion in our period: there is the iPod and the iPhone; one spends time on MySpace or YouTube; universities simulate small group interactions using i-peer; you can even buy MyDog food.'[32]

In such a context, the feminisms of the 1970s and 1980s could be dismissed as having failed to provide to young women all that they wanted to have, while the market, if allowed free rein, would do just that. Any voices reminding that what such feminism had been about was not about having but, rather, about what women could do, or were being prevented from doing, were few and drowned out by advertising jingles.

Women are still victims of rape, domestic violence and trafficking. The sexual division of labour within households stretches women to snapping point, as women continue to provide most of the unpaid, usually unrecognised 'caring work' for members of the household, even when they are themselves employed in the labour market.[33] It is worth recalling that estimates of the market value of women's 'vast non-market contributions to family and community welfare' have shown it to be worth approximately 60 per cent of gross domestic product

---

32   Mark Furlong, 'i-dolatry', *Arena: The Australian Magazine of Left Political, Social and Cultural Commentary*, 101(8 September 2009) 12–13.

33   Adele Horin, 'Women stretched to snapping point', *Sydney Morning Herald*, 4–5 July 2009.

(GDP).[34] So much for considerations of work/life balance.[35] Paid parental leave is still no more than a promise.[36] Current legislation relating to the children of divorced couples operates starkly to women's disadvantage.[37] And Equal Pay Day, 1 September 2009, brought acknowledgment that in 2008, female university graduates started work on $2000 less than their male peers and that an average woman at the end of her earning life will have brought in $1 million less that the average man, which means that 'Australia's gender pay gap averages 17.4%, which is only a 1.1% improvement from 25 years ago'. As a consequence, women retire with less than half the amount in their superannuation accounts compared with men and are two and a half times more likely than men to live in poverty in their old age.[38]

This is a list prompting despair. Yet there are those who will argue that today we face far more alarming prospects affecting not only the women of Australia but the whole world: the global economic crisis and the threat that climate change poses not only to human life but to all life. Against that argument, I would contend that the present crises offer us unprecedented opportunities. Anthropologist Peter Sutton observed recently: 'Deep changes in culture are normally and, in most of human history, unintentionally generated in contexts such as substantial economic changes, radical ideological shifts such as mass conversion to an evangelical religion or social reconstruction following epidemics, warfare or environmental catastrophes.'[39]

Former Prime Minister Kevin Rudd identified the present economic crisis as having 'called into question the prevailing neoliberal economic orthodoxy of the past 30 years—the orthodoxy that has underpinned the national and global regulatory frameworks that have so spectacularly failed to prevent the economic mayhem which has now been visited upon us'.[40]

So we are amid one of Sutton's 'radical ideological shifts', one that, in Prime Minister Rudd's words, repudiates 'the neoliberal extremism that has landed us in this mess' and instead demonstrates that the social-democratic state—the government—offers the best guarantee of preserving the productive capacity

---

34 For example: Anne Edwards and Susan Magarey, 'Introduction' in Anne Edwards and Susan Magarey (eds), *Women in a Restructuring Australia: Work & Welfare*, Allen & Unwin in association with the Academy of Social Sciences in Australia, Sydney, 1995, p. 7.
35 Barbara Pocock, *The Work–Life Collision: What Work is doing to Australians and what to do about it*, Federation Press, Annandale, NSW, 2003.
36 The *Paid Parental Leave Act 2010* (Cth) was passed by the Rudd Government in June 2010 [Ed.].
37 Caroline Overington, 'Fair share?', *The Weekend Australian Magazine*, 5–6 September 2009, pp. 15–17.
38 'Issue of the week: the gender pay gap', *The Week*, 4 September 2009, p. 37; Eva Cox, 'Financing our Futures—How Privatising Retirement Discriminates Against Women' (2007) 26(3) *Dialogue: Academy of the Social Sciences in Australia* 42; Australian Council of Trade Unions, Media release launching an alliance of 135 organisations to mark Equal Pay Day, 31 August 2009.
39 Peter Sutton, 'Culture Worriers' (2009) 4(5) *Australian Literary Review* 4.
40 Kevin Rudd, 'The Global Financial Crisis', *The Monthly*, February 2009, p. 20.

of competitive markets because the government (not the market) will be the regulator, the government (not the market) will provide necessary public goods and the government (not the market) will 'offset the inevitable inequalities of the market with a commitment to fairness for all'. Does this suggest a commitment to change from a liberal-market society like Britain, the United States and New Zealand to a social-democratic society as in Scandinavia? If it does then it signals a historic transformation. And perhaps it does. Rudd observed, trenchantly: 'Social democracy's continuing philosophical claim to political legitimacy is its capacity to balance the private and the public, profit and wages, the market and the state. That philosophy once again speaks with clarity and cogency to the challenges of our time.'[41]

The former Deputy Prime Minister, Julia Gillard, signalled one way in which these optimistic principles are to be implemented when, at a recent conference of industrial relations practitioners, she called for a 'new focus on *cultural* change' (my emphasis). Having achieved the passage of the *Fair Work Act* through the Parliament, she wanted to move the reform process further forward, she said, by developing 'a new focus on cultural change in the workplace. We need to build partnerships between management and workers and their unions that operate for the benefit of all'[42]—an aspiration directed away from the neo-liberal market society and towards a Scandinavian social-democratic balance between capitalism and welfare.

Such culture change can be achieved only if it includes genuine sharing of the caring work of our society, with greater flexibility in workplace structures and procedures to allow both parents to participate in child care and housework, protections against the harms to which women can be subjected and proper parity in payment for work done. This is not simply a matter of justice for women; it is, rather, a rational deployment of *all* of our social resources. No society can afford the wasteful misuse of the resources that the female half of the population can bring to the whole society's endeavours. The women's movement—continuing in whatever form it might assume now—will demand nothing less. It should never again be possible for anyone to wonder, as did Dame Roma Mitchell, if there are people who cannot 'accept women as human beings'.

To conclude: a study recently published in Britain points out the 'life-diminishing results of valuing growth above equality in rich societies'. So, much as we might hope for growth to be restored in the economies that determine our employment levels, it will need to be growth regulated by government—a government committed to equality for all. As the British study observes:

---

41   Ibid., p. 21.
42   Ewin Hannan, 'Only the beginning', *The Weekend Australian*, 29–30 August 2009, p. 17.

Inequality causes shorter, unhealthier and unhappier lives; it increases the rate of teenage pregnancy, violence, obesity, imprisonment and addiction; it destroys relationships between individuals born into the same society but into different classes; and its function as a driver of consumption depletes the planet's resources.[43]

So let us insist that, while members of the Rudd Government traverse the world to ensure that Australia's social-democratic principles contribute to the future shape and nature of the economies of the G20, so, too, must members of the Rudd Government ensure that those principles include equality—yes, equality (I have abandoned my old badge)—for *all* of its citizens, women as well as men. We might then be able to agree on what to do about climate change as well.

Bibliography

Books and articles

Buckley, Amanda 1983, 'Why Mrs Doug Anthony is against the sex bill: is it wrong to stay at home?', *Sydney Morning Herald*, 16 September 1983, p. 1.

Buckley, Amanda 1983, 'Sex bill row to split Liberal Party room', *Sydney Morning Herald*, 19 September 1983, p. 1.

Buckley, Amanda 1983, 'Senate's uncomfortable Friday…and more to come', *Sydney Morning Herald*, 22 October 1983, p. 6.

Cox, Eva 2007, 'Financing our Futures—How Privatising Retirement Discriminates Against Women' (2007) 26(3) *Dialogue, Academy of the Social Sciences in Australia* 42.

Edwards, Anne and Magarey, Susan, 'Introduction' in Anne Edwards and Susan Magarey (eds), *Women in a Restructuring Australia: Work & Welfare*, Allen & Unwin in association with the Academy of the Association of the Social Sciences, Sydney, 1995.

Firestone, Shulamith, *The Dialectic of Sex: The Case for Feminist Revolution*, Paladin, London, 1972.

Furlong, Mark, 'i-dolatry', *Arena: The Australian Magazine of Left Political, Social and Cultural Commentary*, no. 101, 8 September 2009.

---

43   Richard Wilkinson and Kate Pickett, *The Spirit Level: Why More Equal Societies Almost Always Do Better*, Allen Lane, London, 2009 (reviewed by Lynsey Hanley in the *Guardian Weekly*, 27 March–2 April 2009).

Gale, Fay, 'Seeing Women in the Landscape: Alternative Views of the World Around Us' in Jacqueline Goodnow and Carole Patemen (eds), *Women, Social Science and Public Policy*, George Allen & Unwin, Sydney, 1985.

Grahame, Emma, 'Anti-feminism' in Barbara Caine, Moira Gatens, Emma Grahame, Jan Larbalestier, Sophie Watson and Elizabeth Webby (eds), *Australian Feminism: A Companion*, Oxford University Press, Melbourne, 1998.

Grahame, Emma, 'Anti-nuclear Activism' in Barbara Caine, Moira Gatens, Emma Grahame, Jan Larbalestier, Sophie Watson and Elizabeth Webby (eds), *Australian Feminism: A Companion*, Oxford University Press, Melbourne, 1998.

Greer, Germaine, *The Female Eunuch*, Paladin, London, 1971.

Hannan, Ewin, 'Only the beginning', *The Weekend Australian*, 29–30 August 2009, p. 17.

Hooper, Mark, 'Professor invites fury by scorning feminists', *The Australian*, 7 September 1983, p. 3.

Horin, Adele, 'Women stretched to snapping point', *Sydney Morning Herald*, 4–5 July 2009.

Kelly-Gadol, Joan, 'The Social Relation of the Sexes: Methodological Implications of Women's History' (1976) 1(4) *Signs: Journal of Women in Culture and Society* 809.

Legge, Kate, 'Coalition split widens on sex discrimination bill', *The Age* (Melbourne), 19 September 1983, p. 5.

Maccoby, Eleanor and Jacklin, Carol, *The Psychology of Sex Differences*, Oxford University Press, UK, 1974.

Millett, Kate, *Sexual Politics*, Rupert Hart-Davis, London, 1971.

Mitchell, Juliet, *Psychoanalysis and Feminism*, Allen Lane, London, 1974.

Overington, Caroline, 'Fair share?', *The Weekend Australian Magazine*, 5–6 September 2009, pp. 15–17.

Pocock, Barbara, *The Work–Life Collision: What Work is doing to Australians and what to do about it*, Federation Press, Annandale, NSW, 2003.

Rosaldo, Michelle and Lamphere, Louise (eds), *Woman, Culture and Society*, Stanford University Press, Calif., 1974.

Rudd, Kevin, 'The global financial crisis', *The Monthly*, February 2009.

Ryan, Susan, *Catching the Waves: Life in and out of Politics*, Harper Collins, Sydney, 1999.

Sawer, Marian with Radford, Gail, *Making Women Count: A History of the Women's Electoral Lobby in Australia*, UNSW Press, Sydney, 2008.

Sutton, Peter, 'Culture Worriers' (2009) 4(5) *Australian Literary Review* 4.

The Adelaide Advertiser, 'Rob Cupid of his arrow', *The Adelaide Advertiser*, 27 August 1984.

The Age, 'Sex bill splits the opposition', Editorial, *The Age* (Melbourne), 20 September 1983.

The Canberra Times, 'Women's groups support Sex Discrimination Bill', *The Canberra Times*, 12 September 1983, p. 7.

The Courier-Mail, 'Are there men in Parliament?', *The Courier-Mail* (Brisbane), 27 September 1983, p. 13.

The Courier-Mail, 'Sex discrimination ban "a must"', *The Courier-Mail* (Brisbane), 29 September 1983, p. 15.

The Week, 'Issue of the week: the gender pay gap', *The Week*, 4 September 2009, p. 37.

Thornton, Margaret, *The Liberal Promise: Anti-Discrimination Legislation in Australia*, Oxford University Press, Melbourne, 1990.

Thornton, Margaret, 'The Seductive Allure of EEO' in Norma Grieve and Ailsa Burns (eds), *Australian Women: Contemporary Feminist Thought*, Oxford University Press, Melbourne, 1994.

Wallach Scott, Joan, 'The Sears Case' in *Gender and the Politics of History*, Columbia University Press, New York, 1988.

West Australian, 'US professor: what sexual harassment?', *West Australian* (Perth), 17 September 1983, p. 3.

Wilkinson, Richard and Pickett, Kate, *The Spirit Level: Why More Equal Societies Almost Always Do Better*, Allen Lane, London, 2009.

Legislation

Paid Parental Leave Act 2010 (Cth)

Reports and miscellaneous primary sources

Australian Council of Trade Unions, Media release launching an alliance of 135 organisations to mark Equal Pay Day, 31 August 2009.

Mitchell, Roma, Address at Monash University, 10 December 1983, State Library of South Australia, Adelaide, PRG 778/17/27.

Part III
Critiquing the SDA

5. The *Sex Discrimination Act* at 25: Reflections on the Past, Present and Future

Beth Gaze

The Sex Discrimination Act *(SDA) was adopted against strident opposition in 1984. This chapter critically analyses its effect after 25 years. The symbolic impact of prohibiting sex discrimination is highly significant, but the real impact of the Act on practices in the workforce and elsewhere appears more limited. Although formal exclusion of women has largely passed, informal practices of discrimination continue. Not only is Australia far from reaching substantive equality for women, it has moved backwards in recent years. This chapter considers what the SDA could achieve and its limits, and whether reforming the Act would move us closer to its avowed objectives of 'eliminating discrimination against persons on the ground of sex' and 'promot[ing] recognition and acceptance within the community of the principle of the equality of men and women'.*

Introduction

The Commonwealth *Sex Discrimination Act 1984* (*SDA*) turned 25 in August 2009. Has it come of age as a full-grown and effective piece of legislative regulation? Or is it instead a case of arrested development? Answering this question requires an evaluation of the effects of the *SDA* against a background of extensive social change over 25 years and persistent sex differentiation in our society. Analysing changes in large-scale social phenomena such as gender relations or workplace practices is challenging, and identifying operative causes of change from among the multitude of factors that affects these social institutions is even more difficult. Conclusive and comprehensive answers about the effects of such legislation are elusive. Hunter has argued that the *SDA* has been overtaken by social and political change, which has rendered it relatively ineffective to change things for women.[1] Thornton has noted that the courts have tended to interpret the Act to preserve current arrangements, rather than to bring about change.[2]

---

1   Rosemary Hunter, 'The Mirage of Justice: Women and the Shrinking State' (2002) 16 *Australian Feminist Law Journal* 53.

2   Margaret Thornton, 'Auditing the *Sex Discrimination Act*' in Marius Smith (ed.), *Human Rights 2004: The Year in Review*, Castan Centre for Human Rights Law, Monash University, Melbourne, 2005, p. 21.

This chapter assesses the Act's influence and argues that despite its undeniable achievements, there is cause for concern about its current and future roles, and that more than cosmetic reform is necessary. Since the Act was adopted, a generation of women has grown to maturity with its promise of equality. Over the decades, however, experience with the Act has shown that its response to sex discrimination is severely limited in vital respects and the promise of equality has not been fulfilled.

The *Sex Discrimination Act*

There is no doubt that the *SDA* was a vital legislative milestone in Australia. It was a national proclamation that sex discrimination was unacceptable throughout the country. This was a crowning achievement of the efforts of second-wave feminist activists. Although Victoria and New South Wales had legislated in 1977 to prohibit sex discrimination, and Western Australia and South Australia did so in 1984, the *SDA* first prohibited sex discrimination in the other States and Territories and federal activities.[3] It clearly precluded overt formal distinctions based on sex. Jobs could no longer be advertised for 'men and boys' or 'women and girls', with the better jobs in the former category.[4] Women could no longer be paid two-thirds of men's rates for the same work,[5] excluded from jobs or from promotion simply because they were female or dismissed from their jobs simply because they married or became pregnant. Compared with what preceded it, the Act's practical and symbolic effects were enormously significant and produced major advances in women's positions. From today's perspective, however, where formal equality has been established for three decades, it is easier to see the Act's limitations, its disappointing record in the courts and the need for further changes.

One of the most important achievements of the Act was the creation of the office of the Sex Discrimination Commissioner, which has been occupied by a series of courageous, articulate women (including the current Governor-General, Quentin

---

3   *Anti-Discrimination Act 1977* (NSW), *Equal Opportunity Act 1977* (Vic.), *Equal Opportunity Act 1984* (SA), *Equal Opportunity Act 1984* (WA). South Australia was the first state to legislate to prohibit discrimination in Australia, but its first legislation was directed only to racial discrimination; the *Prohibition of Discrimination Act 1966* (SA), which contained only criminal penalties, was replaced by the *Racial Discrimination Act 1976* (SA).
4   Susan Magarey, this volume.
5   In Australia, equal pay has traditionally been dealt with in industrial rather than equal opportunity law. Equal pay principles adopted in industrial cases in 1969 (equal pay for equal work) and 1972 (equal pay for work of equal value) were limited in scope, and further effort was required for implementation in specific areas of the labour market. Many women worked in female-dominated industries in which all employees received low pay, so women's wages remained inequitably lower than men's. Attempts to run cases on the value of women's jobs, such as nursing, were unsuccessful: Jane Innes, 'Claiming Equal Pay for Work of Equal Value: The ACTU's Comparable Worth Test Case' (1986) 4 *Law Society Journal* 52; Jane Innes, 'Equal Pay and the *Sex Discrimination Act 1984*' (1986) 11 *Legal Service Bulletin* 254.

Bryce), who have been prepared to enter sometimes hostile public debate to raise issues that need attention and to press for reform. They have kept issues of importance to women on the agenda, including sexual harassment, pregnancy discrimination, work and family conflict and the need for paid maternity leave.[6] Most have not yet received adequate social or legislative responses.

The *SDA* prohibits discrimination on the basis of sex, marital status, pregnancy and sexual harassment (not merely discrimination against women)[7] with potential pregnancy, breastfeeding and limited family responsibilities grounds added later. Such discrimination is prohibited in the areas of employment (including selection), education, provision of goods and services, accommodation, clubs and government administration. Two main types of discrimination are prohibited.[8] Direct discrimination occurs where a person is treated less favourably on the ground of sex, marital status, pregnancy or potential pregnancy than a person of a different sex in circumstances that are not materially different. Indirect discrimination occurs where a group of people of a particular sex or marital status is disadvantaged by the effect of an apparently neutral condition, requirement or practice, where that practice is not reasonable. The Act is enforced solely by private litigation. Although it contains provision for some criminal offences— for example, for advertising that indicates an intention to discriminate[9] or for victimisation[10]—there are no reported cases in which these provisions have been enforced.

Direct Discrimination and Formal Equality

The initial impact of direct sex discrimination law was illustrated by the 1980 decision in *Ansett Transport Industries v Wardley*,[11] in which the High Court

---

6   See Human Rights and Equal Opportunity Commission, *The Equal Pay Handbook*,1998; *Pregnant and Productive: It's a Right not a Privilege to Work while Pregnant*, 1999; *A Bad Business: Review of Sexual Harassment in Employment Complaints*, 2002; *A Time to Value: Proposal for a National Scheme of Paid Maternity Leave*, 2002; *Striking the Balance: Women, Men, Work and Family*, 2005; *Sexual Harassment: Serious Business*, 2008.

7   Unlike the International Convention on the Elimination of All Forms of Discrimination Against Women (CEDAW) (opened for signature on 1 March 1980, 1249 UNTS 13, entered into force on 3 September 1981), which is asymmetrical, aimed only at discrimination against women, the *SDA* can rely on Australia's obligations in relation to sex discrimination in international law only in relation to discrimination against women, and the constitutional basis of its prohibition on sex discrimination against men is unclear. See also the Australian Law Reform Commission (*Equality Before the Law: Justice For Women*, Report No. 69, Australian Law Reform Commission, Sydney, 1994), in which the majority recommendation was for an Equality Act with a symmetrical equality provision, while a minority of commissioners preferred legislation directed to equality for women.

8   *SDA*, ss 5–7C.

9   *SDA*, s. 86.

10   *SDA*, s. 94.

11   *Ansett Transport Industries (Operations) Pty Ltd v Wardley* ((1980) 142 CLR 237; [1980] HCA 8) was brought under the equivalent direct discrimination provisions of the Victorian *Equal Opportunity Act 1977*.

upheld the law's prohibition on excluding a woman from recruitment as a trainee pilot simply because she was female. After this decision, it was clear that refusing to employ a woman on the ground of sex was unlawful. Formal equality appeared to have been achieved, at least where the refusal was overtly based on sex. The decision is, however, an excellent example of the difference between a legal victory and a broad social change: nearly 30 years after Wardley's case, most of us will rarely have been on a commercial airline flight with a female pilot in charge. The absence of women pilots and captains provides the clearest evidence of the state of practical equality of opportunity in Australia now. The absence of women is reflected in innumerable positions of power and influence throughout our society despite decades of sex discrimination law. Simply removing the most formal of exclusionary practices did not dissolve barriers.

Traditional attitudes, practices and social patterns did not disappear, but found other avenues of expression. The social structures of gender, race, sexuality and ability all continued (and still continue) to affect opportunities and expectations, while the target became less overt and hence more difficult to identify. Discrimination turned out to be a stronger and more subtle phenomenon than the law had anticipated and the law a correspondingly weaker tool against it. In particular, dealing with areas of women's difference from men, such as pregnancy and the need for maternity leave, through an area of law that insists on comparative assessment leads to incoherence. Pregnancy is not merely comparable with extended sick leave for an illness, although the cases on pregnancy discrimination treat it this way in order to find a comparator for assessing whether treatment was less favourable.[12] Such a comparison is highly artificial and deprives any analysis of an adequate consideration of the contextual issues that surround discrimination based on pregnancy and having taken maternity leave. It evidences the law's inability to see women's lives except through the prism of men's experience.[13]

The courts have not seen sex discrimination laws as requiring them to pursue the social goal of equality or equity beyond the minimal level. They have insisted that the person complaining of direct discrimination has to prove that the prohibited ground was the basis of the action against her, even though

---

Ansett refused to recruit Deborah Wardley as a pilot even though her scores on intake testing were higher than those of some men who were recruited, because Mr Ansett did not want women flying his planes—asserting that passengers would not feel safe.

12   See, for example: *Howe v Qantas Airways Ltd* (2004) 188 FLR 1; [2004] FMCA 242; *Iliff v Sterling Commerce (Australia) Pty Ltd* [2007] FMCA 1960; *Fenton v Hair & Beauty Gallery Pty Ltd & Anor* [2006] FMCA 3. A woman who is ill during pregnancy would be entitled to sick leave, but pregnancy involves normal incidents that cannot necessarily be analogised to sickness—for example, the need for time off for regular medical checks of normal progress.

13   See, for example: Catharine MacKinnon, *Feminism Unmodified: Discourses on Life and Law*, Harvard University Press, Cambridge, Mass., 1987; Regina Graycar and Jenny Morgan, *The Hidden Gender of Law*, Second edition, Federation Press, Sydney, 2002.

knowledge and evidence of the actual basis of the decision or action are in most cases confined to the respondent.[14] The courts have also been influenced by two other social factors that operate as major barriers to women's equality at work: managerial prerogative (where courts can be reluctant to constrain too far the freedom of an employer to make choices) and the 'market' defence (where a respondent argues that they are acting only to provide what the market—that is, the customer—demands). Judges are often reluctant to infer that a respondent acted on a prohibited basis, unless there is clear evidence of that basis—for example, in admissions by the respondent.[15] In defence, respondents often argue that the complainant was not competent or had personality problems that contributed to the events in dispute. The personal strain of running a case in which such allegations will be raised is obvious and, along with the financial costs of running a case and the risks of ending up with an order to pay the other side's costs, is a major disincentive to bringing a claim.[16]

During the 2000s, there was discussion about the need for a more effective method of proof of direct discrimination, such as exists in many other comparable countries.[17] In Europe and the United Kingdom, for example, once a prima facie case is established, the onus of proof shifts to the respondent to show that it was not based on the prohibited ground.[18] Legislative reforms to this effect have been recommended by government inquiries,[19] but no such reform has yet occurred.

The *SDA* in the Courts

In this section, the experience of litigation under the *SDA* is reviewed from two perspectives. First, the reported cases on the *SDA* in the past 10 years are analysed to see what this indicates about the state of usage of the law. Then legal doctrine from some high-profile decisions is analysed. Strangely enough given the *SDA*'s symbolic importance, the High Court has never decided a case on its substantive provisions.[20] All the sex discrimination cases that have

14   See Neil Rees, Katherine Lindsay and Simon Rice, *Australian Anti-Discrimination Law: Text, Cases and Materials*, Federation Press, Sydney, 2008, pp. 146–55; Jonathon Hunyor, 'Skin-Deep: Proof and Inferences of Racial Discrimination in Employment' (2003) 25 *Sydney Law Review* 535; Dominique Allen, 'Reducing the Burden of Proving Discrimination in Australia' (2009) 31 *Sydney Law Review* 579.

15   *Thomson v Orica Australia Pty Ltd* (2002) 116 IR 186; [2002] FCA 939.

16   Beth Gaze and Rosemary Hunter, *Enforcing Human Rights In Australia: An Evaluation of the New Regime*, Federation Press, Sydney, (forthcoming).

17   Hunyor, 'Skin-Deep', and Allen, 'Reducing the Burden of Proving Discrimination in Australia'.

18   This is required by a European Union Directive on the Burden of Proof, Council Directive 97/80/EC (see also 98/52/EC), discussed in Rees et al., *Australian Anti-Discrimination Law*, p. 150.

19   Department of Justice, *An Equality Act for a Fairer Victoria*, Final Report, Equal Opportunity Review, Department of Justice, Government of Victoria, Melbourne, 2008, <http://www.justice.vic.gov.au/wps/wcm/connect/DOJ+Internet/Home/Your+Rights/Equal+Opportunity/>

20   The reasons for the absence of High Court decisions on the *SDA* are not clear. In contrast, there have been several High Court decisions on the *Disability Discrimination Act 1992* (Cth) (*DDA*) and the *Racial*

gone to the High Court have been appeals under State sex discrimination law: *Wardley* from Victoria, and from New South Wales, *Dao v Australia Post*, *AIS v Banovic* and *NSW v Amery*.[21] Only *Re McBain* involved the *SDA* itself.[22] In that case, the Federal Court had held that the *Infertility Treatment Act 1995* (Vic.) was inconsistent with the *SDA* and invalid to the extent of the inconsistency under Section 109 of the *Constitution*. On appeal, the High Court did not consider the *SDA*, but decided the case on grounds relating to the prerogative remedy of certiorari.[23] The cases decided on equivalent provisions in State sex discrimination laws are, however, applicable to the *SDA*, so this analysis draws on those cases and lower federal court decisions on the *SDA*.

The litigation record under the *SDA* in the lower federal courts is equivocal. Before 2000, claims under the *SDA* were heard in the Human Rights and Equal Opportunity Commission, which acted as a tribunal. Constitutional problems, however, led to the recasting of the enforcement system.[24] In 2000, enforcement of cases under the *SDA* that did not settle at conciliation was moved from a tribunal to the Federal Magistrate's Court (FMC) and the Federal Court. Less complex cases are heard in the FMC, while cases expected to run for more than two days may be heard in the Federal Court. In both courts, the losing party is usually ordered to pay the winner's costs, but in the FMC the costs scale, and therefore the risks of litigation are lower than in the Federal Court.

From 2000 to 2009, the Federal Magistrate's Court heard 46 substantive sex discrimination matters—an average of five cases each year. Of these, 12 were unsuccessful while 34 were successful. Almost all of the successful sex discrimination claims related to employment and more than half (20) involved sexual harassment claims. The damages awards have ranged from $750 to $100 000, but in only four cases was more than $25 000 compensation awarded, with the highest award being $100 000 awarded to a female civilian employee at a naval base who was sexually harassed, including rape.[25] The median damages award in the FMC was $12 000, and several cases had damages awarded in the range $1–2000. Although damages assessment is intended to be compensatory, little is given by way of general damages, which suggests that the courts regard the harms women suffer from discrimination and sexual harassment as not very serious. Since the enforcement of the Act rests on private litigation, damages awards of less than $2000 after undertaking the personal and financial risks

---

Discrimination Act 1975 (Cth) (*RDA*).

21   *Ansett Transport Industries (Operations) Pty Ltd v Wardley* (1980) 142 CLR 237; [1980] HCA 8; *Dao v Australian Postal Commission* (1987) 162 CLR 317 [1987] HCA 13; *Australian Iron & Steel Pty Ltd v Banovic* (1989) 168 CLR 165; [1989] HCA 56 ('*Banovic*'); *New South Wales v Amery* (2006) 230 CLR 174; [2006] HCA 14.

22   *Re McBain; Ex parte Australian Catholic Bishops Conference* (2002) 209 CLR 372; [2002] HCA 16.

23   Kristen Walker, 'The Bishops, the Doctor, his Patient and the Attorney-General: The Conclusion of the McBain Litigation' (2002) 30 *Federal Law Review* 507.

24   *Brandy v Human Rights & Equal Opportunity Commission* (1995) 183 CLR 245; [1995] HCA 10.

25   *Lee v Smith & Ors* [2007] FMCA 59.

inherent in litigation suggest that there is a serious problem with incentives for enforcement, especially as legal aid for *SDA* matters is very difficult to obtain.[26] When sexual harassment cases are taken out of these data, the FMC upheld 14 claims over 10 years of discrimination based on sex, pregnancy or family responsibilities. Only two of these cases involved a successful indirect discrimination claim.

Since 2000, the Federal Court has heard 14 substantive matters under the *SDA* and upheld five of them (about 36 per cent)—four of which were sexual harassment matters. In one sexual harassment case, the respondent did not appear and damages of $10 000 were awarded.[27] In the other sexual harassment cases, damages awards were $20 000,[28] $24 000[29] and, in the most recent case, $466 000, where a relatively well-paid real estate agent lost her job and was unable to work for some time.[30] The last case is, however, under appeal to the Full Federal Court at the time of writing. The other awards not only reflect a low valuation of the harms that women suffer in discrimination, they are outweighed by the risk of paying very substantial costs to the other party as well as one's own costs if Federal Court litigation is lost, leaving very little incentive to enforce the law. There was only one successful case of sex discrimination in the Federal Court in the period 2000–09, in which no damages award was made, as the outcome was negotiated between the parties after the finding of liability had been made.[31]

Since 2000, there have been 13 appeals in *SDA* matters in the Federal Court, mainly against FMC decisions. Of eight appeals brought by complainants, two have succeeded, and of five brought by respondents against a finding of liability, two were successful. In one of those appeals, the matter was remitted to the FMC for rehearing, where the sexual harassment claim was upheld again.[32] In the other appeal, the Federal Court decided that an indirect discrimination claim must fail, but upheld a family responsibilities discrimination claim.[33]

This analysis shows that in the Federal Court, only one case of (direct) sex discrimination (rather than sexual harassment) has been upheld in a contested hearing since 2000, and that was a case in which there were statements by the complainant's supervisor deploring her falling pregnant.[34] In the FMC, there

---

26   Beth Gaze and Rosemary Hunter, 'Access to Justice for Discrimination Complainants: Courts and Legal Representation' (2009) 32 *University of New South Wales Law Journal* 699.

27   *Grulke v K C Canvas Pty Ltd* [2000] FCA 1415—although the judgment does not outline the nature of the discrimination involved.

28   *Elliott v Nanda & Commonwealth* (2001) 111 FCR 240; [2001] FCA 418.

29   *Gilroy v Angelov* [2000] FCA 1775.

30   *Poniatowska v Hickinbotham* [2009] FCA 680.

31   *Thomson v Orica.*

32   *Kirkland v Wattle* [2002] FCA 145; *Wattle v Kirkland & Anor (No. 2)* [2002] FMCA 135.

33   *Commonwealth of Australia v Evans* (2004) 81 ALD 402; [2004] FCA 654.

34   *Thomson v Orica.* The presence of direct evidence of the employer's hostility towards the employee's pregnancy was important to the finding that the employer's actions were based on pregnancy. Without this

were 12 cases during this decade in which a claim of discrimination based on sex, pregnancy or family responsibilities was upheld. Only two cases involved a successful claim of indirect discrimination. For a national law on sex discrimination, which has stronger provisions in relation to indirect discrimination law than most State laws (as discussed below), there is a question as to why it has not had more use. Perhaps stronger cases might have been settled before hearing or brought in the State systems to avoid the risks of paying costs in Federal Court litigation, especially as damages awards were quite low. While larger amounts can be obtained in private or conciliated settlements, the lack of publicity and precedent means that such cases cannot serve the public interest by establishing precedents on either liability or quantum of damages that might assist the elimination of sex discrimination more broadly. Whatever the reason, these statistics raise serious concerns about the attractiveness of the *SDA* as providing a remedy for discrimination. There is a need for some research to identify whether cases are being deterred or whether they are obtaining advantageous settlements by means other than litigation. We now turn to the doctrinal decisions of the courts on sex discrimination matters.

The largest category of successful claims under the *SDA* since 2000 has been sexual harassment, followed by termination based on family responsibilities and then pregnancy discrimination.[35] In these categories, the issues of proof present less of a barrier. In sexual harassment cases, there is often a question of credibility if there were no witnesses to conduct that was alleged to have occurred, but if the complainant is found to be credible, there is no need to show the basis of the action or to identify a comparator. In family responsibilities matters, the discrimination is often directly linked to limits on the employee resulting from caring needs, so establishing the basis is less problematic. In pregnancy discrimination matters, courts have been more willing to infer pregnancy was a cause.[36] The employment consequences of losing a job during pregnancy can be very serious. Because most 'good' jobs are advertised only as full-time, many women access them by returning part-time after childbirth to their own job. Pregnancy discrimination can deprive a woman of the chance to request flexible work in her existing job. It can be impossible to get another similar job part-time after the birth, so the employment setback can have very significant long-term consequences. Recent moves to provide a right to request

---

evidence, success would have depended on whether the court was prepared to infer such a motivation.

35   Of the successful cases, the grounds involved in the Federal Court were: sexual harassment in four out of five successful cases, pregnancy-related discrimination in the other. In the FMCA, sexual harassment was the basis in 21 of the 34 successful or partly successful matters, with family responsibilities discrimination in seven and pregnancy discrimination in four cases. There is some overlap in the grounds in the FMCA cases, as some cases involved more than one of these grounds.

36   It is difficult to determine the exact extent of particular discrimination in the workforce. See the discussion of this problem in Human Rights and Equal Opportunity Commission, 'Statistics and the extent of discrimination', *Pregnant and Productive: It's a Right not a Privilege to Work while Pregnant*, Human Rights and Equal Opportunity Commission, Sydney, 1999.

flexible work could help, although some contain an inbuilt barrier by requiring a qualifying period of one year's (presumably inflexible) work before a request can be made.[37] If they are used more by women than men, employers might try to minimise or avoid employment of women they think are likely to make use of this right.

Indirect Discrimination and Equality

Wardley confirmed that direct discrimination requires that women be treated the same as men, and the law takes this to be equality.[38] Hence, once formal exclusion of women was prohibited, workforce practices moved from exclusion to treating women as if they were men. In a social and employment context designed by men for men, treating women as if they were men cannot provide genuine equality, as data on women's progress in a number of areas (discussed below) indicate. This approach is clearly contrary to the concept of equality in international conventions, which acknowledge that where women are situated differently they need different treatment.[39] Refusing to take account of pregnancy and childbirth,[40] and responsibilities for care of dependants such as children, people with disabilities and the elderly, reinforces the disadvantages experienced by the group that tends to be allocated these responsibilities— disproportionately women.

The persistence of discriminatory employment practices made it clear that sex discrimination law needed better tools to tackle covert and systemic practices, and indirect discrimination law appeared to have some promise.[41] Indirect discrimination had significant potential to expand the idea of equality that is protected by sex discrimination law by allowing challenges to broad-based practices that have the effect of disadvantaging women. There is no need to show the 'true basis' for the respondent's action, although the claimant must establish that women (or pregnant women, and so on) are disadvantaged by the practice.[42]

---

37   *Fair Work Act 2009* (Cth), s. 65(2). In contrast, the duty not to refuse unreasonably a request for flexible work in the *Equal Opportunity Act 1995* (Vic.) is not conditioned on a particular length of time in employment: see ss 13A and 14A.

38   See Regina Graycar and Jenny Morgan, 'Examining Understandings of Equality: One Step Forward, Two Steps Back?' (2004) 20 *Australian Feminist Law Journal* 23; Regina Graycar and Jenny Morgan, 'Thinking About Equality' (2004) 27 *University of New South Wales Law Journal* 833; Regina Graycar and Jenny Morgan, this volume.

39   See, for example, CEDAW, Article 4(1).

40   Although unpaid parental leave has been provided under industrial law and many employers have provided paid maternity leave voluntarily, there is no current entitlement to paid maternity leave. Government policy is to make a scheme available from 2011, but the legislation had not been passed at the time of writing.

41   Rosemary Hunter, *Indirect Discrimination in the Workplace*, Federation Press, Annandale, NSW, 1992.

42   *SDA*, ss 5(2), 6(2), 7(2), 7B and 7C.

Some advances have been made though indirect discrimination law in challenging widely accepted and facially neutral workforce practices that were not necessarily imposed intentionally to harm women, even though this was their effect. Indirect discrimination was, however, developed from the American disparate impact principle adopted by the US Supreme Court in *Griggs v Duke Power Company*[43] to deal with a test imposed by an employer whose covert aim was to continue the racial segregation of its workforce. It has been contended that the aim of indirect discrimination was merely to prevent this type of covert direct discrimination—that is, neutral practices chosen to exclude particular groups.[44] Indirect discrimination law was not really designed to deal with the much more subtle and widespread issues facing women at work, which are less obviously based in prejudice and tend to be more structural and based on widespread assumptions of naturally different gender roles and preferences. Australian anti-discrimination laws, including the *SDA*, contain no basis for limiting the scope of indirect discrimination only to situations of covert intentional discrimination, and instead appear to create an avenue to challenge any neutral social practice that has a differential impact on or disadvantages women.

The idea that the same treatment that disadvantages people with a particular attribute is discriminatory is potentially revolutionary because it offers the opportunity to challenge apparently neutral social and employment practices. Similar to the fate of direct discrimination law, however, barriers to litigation and court resistance to giving effect to the full implications of indirect discrimination mean its potential has never been realised. Practices that disadvantage are unlawful only if they are 'not reasonable' and, until 1995, the complainant had the onus of proving this negative and vague proposition, despite not having access to information on why the respondent might have imposed the requirement. The ambiguity of the limit perhaps reflects ambivalence and lack of clarity in what indirect discrimination is really intended to challenge.

The first case in the High Court, *Banovic*,[45] received a sympathetic decision that upheld a finding of indirect discrimination in the retrenchment of women from a workforce under a last-on first-off policy, where they were last on because of prior biased and discriminatory recruiting. In *Banovic*, the *SDA* required the complainants to prove that the requirement affected a higher proportion of women than of men and that the practice involved was 'not reasonable'. The issue of proportionality was complex because the composition of the workforce was biased by the previous discrimination that had made it much

---

43   401 US 424 (1971); (1971) 28 L Ed 2d 158.
44   R. Primus, 'Equal Protection and Disparate Impact: Round Three' (2003) 117 *Harvard Law Review* 493, cited by Rees et al., *Australian Anti-Discrimination Law*, pp. 120–2.
45   *Banovic*.

harder for women to get jobs than for men. The decision centred on working out statistical ratios rather than assessing the discriminatory impact of the practice. This reflects a common approach in discrimination litigation in Australia of preoccupation with technicalities rather than the substantial issues presented. While some technical legal analysis might be unavoidable, it has often been allowed to dominate interpretation of the law at the expense of its purposes.[46]

In case law in the lower courts, the interpretation of 'not reasonable' has been contentious and unpredictable, leading to conservative and narrow interpretations of indirect discrimination provisions. Although a number of cases succeed in the Human Rights and Equal Opportunity Commission on indirect discrimination, judicial decisions reviewing them for error have been variable and unpredictable and have tended to overturn tribunal decisions,[47] creating high levels of litigation risk and deterring litigation. In all three Full Federal Court judicial review (appeal) cases concerning the *SDA* decided under the pre-2000 enforcement system, the Court set aside decisions of the Human Rights and Equal Opportunity Commission in favour of a complainant on the basis that they had not established that the requirement was 'not reasonable'.[48] No such case was decided in favour of a complainant. As already noted, this is a major problem in a system that relies solely on enforcement through individual litigation.

In the early 1990s, the *SDA* was reviewed by the House of Representatives Legal and Constitutional Committee, whose report, *Half Way to Equal* (1992), identified a number of changes to improve the effectiveness of the law. The Australian Law Reform Commission's review of *Equality before the law* followed in 1994, providing further ideas for strengthening the law. Some of these ideas were implemented in reforms to the Act in 1992 and 1995, which rendered it the most advanced anti-discrimination law in Australia. Of particular importance were changing the definition of indirect discrimination to focus on practices that disadvantage members of one sex, rather than technical assessments of disproportionate impact and inability to comply, and reversing the onus of proof of 'not reasonable' in indirect discrimination, so that the respondent had to prove that its requirement or practice was reasonable.[49]

---

46   Beth Gaze, 'Context and Interpretation in Anti-Discrimination Law' (2002) 26 *Melbourne University Law Review* 325.

47   For example, Sheppard J in *Commonwealth v Human Rights and Equal Opportunity Commission* (1995) 63 FCR 74 (*Dopking No. 2*) thought all the test required was 'whether a respondent's conduct was logical and understandable', whereas this was said to set too low a standard by Sackville J in *Commonwealth Bank of Australia v Human Rights and Equal Opportunity Commission* (1997) 80 FCR 78; 150 ALR 1. See Margaret Thornton, 'The Indirection of Sex Discrimination' (1993) 12 *University of Tasmania Law Review* 88.

48   *Secretary, DFAT v Styles* (1989) 23 FCR 251; 88 ALR 621; *Commonwealth Bank of Australia v Human Rights and Equal Opportunity Commission* (1997) 80 FCR 78; 150 ALR 1; *Commonwealth of Australia v HREOC* (*Dopking No. 2*) (1995) 63 FCR 74; 133 ALR 629.

49   In addition, the amendments provided that special measures to advance women were not discriminatory (*SDA*, s. 7D).

These changes, which brought the focus of indirect discrimination onto practices that unreasonably disadvantage groups identified by sex, marital status or pregnancy, and especially reversing the onus of proof of reasonableness, were expected to make *SDA* litigation easier. Apart from a number of cases dealing with the right to return to work part-time after maternity leave (discussed below), there has, however, been little indirect discrimination litigation. Perhaps the other barriers already discussed outweighed the effect of these changes. Again, the reasons for this can only be the subject of speculation, as there is no published research or information that might provide an answer.[50] The precedents regarding 'not reasonable' could still deter litigation despite the changed onus of proof or it could be that what has to be proved is too unclear or still too onerous. The test for disadvantage requires judges to develop criteria for identifying effects that 'disadvantage' women,[51] which is a very open-textured test. In a recent interlocutory decision in a case claiming indirect discrimination under the *SDA*, the respondent mounted arguments about selection of pools for comparison in order to establish disadvantage, harking back to the approach in *Banovic*.[52] The apparent strengthening of the law could be illusory, but in the absence of case law, what the law requires is not clear.

The decision of Commissioner Elizabeth Evatt in the 1996 Human Rights and Equal Opportunity Commission case *Hickie v Hunt and Hunt*[53] showed that indirect discrimination law could sometimes provide an avenue to deal with social practices that exclude women where the decision was made by a decision maker who understood the equality issues involved. In that case, the Human Rights and Equal Opportunity Commission held that failure to support a law firm partner in undertaking part-time work as agreed following her return from maternity leave amounted to indirect discrimination. This was based on accepting that a requirement to work full-time disadvantaged women on the basis of sex, because their gender-associated primary-caring responsibilities made it more difficult for them to comply. A series of cases followed in which this argument was either accepted or rejected in some cases where employers argued that they did not offer part-time employment to anyone in their workforce and had no part-time work available.[54] As mentioned above, only two cases have been successful in this argument, and there have been no other attempts to argue indirect discrimination that have reached final judgment in *SDA* cases.

---

50   The cases and outcomes cited in Note 48 represent a serious deterrent to future litigation. See also Margaret Thornton, 'Sex Discrimination, Courts and Corporate Power' (2008) 36 *Federal Law Review* 31.

51   Ironically, this has been pointed out by the Australian Industrial Relations Commission, although never discussed by a court: *Australian Municipal, Administrative, Clerical and Services Union v Moreland City Council* PR972644 [2006] AIRC 318 at [7]. See also *Wylie v McCann Worldgroup Pty Ltd & Ors* [2009] FMCA 959 ('*Wylie*') at [85]–[88] and [100]–[104].

52   *Wylie* at [86].

53   [1998] HREOCA 8.

54   Indirect discrimination cases succeeded in *Escobar v Rainbow Printing Ltd (No. 2)* (2002) 120 IR 84; [2002] FMCA 122, and *Mayer v ANSTO* [2003] FMCA 209, but failed in *Kelly v TPG Internet* [2003] FMCA 584 and

This avenue to work flexibility is not, however, available to men because it rests on the disproportionate impact of the requirement to work full-time on women as a group. Indirect discrimination law has proved insufficient to bring about the changes needed to help women (and men) make progress towards equality at work and in caring responsibilities. The current trend is to follow the UK model of introducing specific provisions providing employees with young or disabled children a right to request flexible work and requiring employers to provide a business-based answer. Such rights had been introduced in the industrial relations system in the Australian Industrial Relations Commission's Family Provision test case of 2005,[55] but were abolished by the WorkChoices scheme that existed from 2006 to 2008, and have now been reintroduced in the *Fair Work Act 2009* (Cth).[56]

In parallel with those developments, a series of cases showed exactly how unpredictable the 'not reasonable' limit on indirect discrimination could be and how difficult it was for a complainant to establish that the employer's requirement was 'not reasonable'. The term has no defined degree and has been applied by judges almost as a matter of personal assessment. In several cases, respondents were able to challenge decisions of tribunals or lower courts that found discrimination merely by convincing an appeal court to apply a different test of 'reasonable' or to take a different view of what was reasonable on the facts as proved.[57] This level of uncertainty must produce hesitation on the part of litigants to bring claims at all, and undermines the use of indirect discrimination.

In 2008, the Senate Legal and Constitutional Affairs Committee reported on *The Effectiveness of the Commonwealth* Sex Discrimination Act 1984 *in Eliminating Discrimination and Promoting Gender Equality*.[58] The committee recommended a large number of changes that could be adopted quickly, together with a more detailed investigation into further reforms. No action has been taken, however, and the *SDA* still awaits amendment.

The most recent High Court sex discrimination decision illustrates how indirect discrimination law has proved not to be an effective method for challenging gendered social practices. In *NSW v Amery*,[59] a group of female long-term casual teachers complained of sex discrimination because their pay scale stopped at the equivalent of level eight of the 13-point pay scale available to permanent teachers. Women were disproportionately represented in the long-term casual category, because permanent teachers could be posted anywhere in the State.

Howe v Qantas Airways Ltd (2004) 188 FLR 1; [2004] FMCA 242.

55   *Family Provisions Case*—PR082005 [2005] AIRC 692.

56   *Fair Work Act 2009* (Cth), Part 2-2, Division 4: National Employment Standards.

57   See cases cited in Note 48.

58   See <http://www.aph.gov.au/Senate/committee/legcon_ctte/sex_discrim/index.htm>

59   *New South Wales v Amery* (2006) 230 CLR 174, [2006] HCA 14 (*Amery*). This case was brought under the *Anti-Discrimination Act 1977* (NSW).

To avoid such a posting for reasons of child care or their husband's job, many women who were permanent teachers reverted to casual status when they had children, and women were over-represented as long-term casuals and under-represented as permanent teachers. Their indirect sex discrimination claim was upheld by the NSW Court of Appeal, but the High Court rejected it, saying that permanent and casual teacher categories could not be regarded as one job category to which a condition—of being a permanent teacher—was applied to access the higher pay scale. Instead, they were completely different job categories because of the importance of the requirement to be redeployable.[60] This decision is further evidence of the legal system's refusal to take account of the structure of women teachers' lives, insisting that they have to conform to the male career model in order to access men's pay.

The *Amery* decision confirms that neither direct nor indirect discrimination law is sufficient to bring about the changes to the deeply embedded social and employment practices necessary for greater equality at work. The *SDA* has not limited workforce practices, conditions and expectations that are based on an assumption that the worker is free of care responsibilities. This is not equality for women and it is not surprising that the data on women's position in Australia today indicate that equality has not been achieved, and there is still a long way to go.

Women in Australia Today

Data on the position of women indicate that women in Australia are not progressing towards equality. Statistics collated by the Sex Discrimination Commissioner show, compared with other developed countries, in Australia, progress towards equality for women has been disappointing.[61] Women represent more than 50 per cent of the Australian population, but held only 29 per cent of elected positions in the 2007 Australian Parliament. Among the Australian Stock Exchange's top-200 companies, women chair only 2 per cent of boards (four boards), hold only 8.3 per cent of board directorships, only four chief executive officer positions and only 10.7 per cent of executive management positions. Although Australia is in a group of countries ranked number one for women's educational attainment, it ranks 41 for women's participation in the workforce, 17 overall in the Global Gender Gap Index and 28 in the world for women's representation in Parliament. Women are 45.1 per cent of the Australian

---

60   In addition, the distinction was found in the *Education Act 1990* (NSW), which authorised, but did not require, different pay scales: *Amery* at [73]–[83], per Gleeson CJ. Cf. Kirby J (dissenting) at [154]–[155].

61   Australian Human Rights Commission, 'Sex Discrimination Commissioner: 25th Anniversary of the *Sex Discrimination Act* (1984)', *Gender Equality Statistics*, Australian Human Rights Commission, Sydney, 1984, <http://www.hreoc.gov.au/sex_discrimination/sda_25/index.html>

workforce, and 58.9 per cent of women participate in the workforce compared with 72.1 per cent of men, but many women work part-time and casual jobs to fit in family responsibilities. Women earn 84.3 cents in the male dollar (for full-time adult ordinary-time earnings), but only 66 per cent of what men earn overall, because of their part-time status and the slight widening of the gender pay gap during the WorkChoices period from 2005 to 2008.

The Australian Human Rights Commission's recent report *Accumulating Poverty? Women's Experiences of Inequality over the Lifecycle*[62] identifies the consequences of women's systematic exclusion from economic participation by undervaluing the work that they do, and the workforce's refusal to adjust to enable women to maintain both caring work and decently paid work, and men to share responsibility for both.[63] While factors such as neo-liberalism have contributed to the lack of progress (and even regression) for women, some problems in the Act are also significant.[64] Its definitions of discrimination were weaker at the outset than those of comparable overseas laws and its enforcement depended solely on litigation by the victims of discrimination—no small matter for someone who had lost their job or endured sexual harassment at work, especially given the very limited legal aid in this area. When cases have been litigated, narrow and technical interpretations have often been adopted, especially by the higher courts, as in *Amery*, which have further weakened the law as a weapon against discrimination. In successful cases, damages have been quite low. There is limited incentive to enforce the law, and hence limited pressure through the law for change in social and workforce practices to avoid discrimination. Thus, the *SDA* appears to have had limited impact on the structural features that construct women's disadvantage.

Paradoxes of Change and Lack of Change

The result is that after 25 years of the *SDA*, workplaces still operate on the assumption that the 'normal' employee is a full-time worker with no domestic caring responsibilities or that they have someone to fulfil those responsibilities for them. Sex discrimination law has not been effective to challenge this model, which fits men's but not women's lives. The male norm at work is

---

62   Australian Human Rights Commission, *Accumulating Poverty: Women's Experiences of Inequality over the Lifecycle*, Australian Human Rights Commission, Sydney, 2009.

63   See also YWCA Australia and Women's Legal Services Australia, *NGO Report on the Implementation of the Convention on the Elimination of All Forms of Discrimination Against Women (CEDAW) in Australia*, [Shadow Report to Australia's Periodic Report to the CEDAW Committee], July 2009; and Elizabeth Broderick, Life Lines: Sex Discrimination over the Lifecycle, The Australian National University, Canberra, <http://law.anu.edu.au/coast/events/Sex_Discrim/Broderick_paper.pdf>

64   Sandra Berns, *Women Going Backwards: Law and Change in a Family Unfriendly Society*, Ashgate Aldershot, Hants, UK, 2002; and Thornton, 'Auditing the *Sex Discrimination Act*'.

further maintained through women's exposure to sexual harassment, gender pay inequity and working conditions that do not make allowances for caring responsibilities that are assumed to be women's obligations. This virtually ensures that many women will 'choose' to take the available casual and part-time, often poorly paid jobs in retail, clerical and community services, which enable them to both carry out the care responsibilities that are regarded as theirs and remain in the workforce. Women can also be forced into these areas by the process of work intensification and the move to long hours or by the casualisation and deterioration of pay and working conditions for the low paid that have occurred in the past decade.

Recent moves to allow employees to request flexible work hours to manage their care responsibilities[65] have come through the industrial law system rather than sex discrimination law. There have, however, been no initiatives to encourage men to share care responsibilities or to solve the underlying problems of gender pay inequity, sexual harassment and the male norm of the ideal worker. Paid parental leave will arrive (eventually) in 2011, but unless the underlying problems are addressed, paid parental leave without encouragement for men to take their share of responsibility for child care will simply reinforce women's responsibility for infant care and subsequent child care. In easing the work–family conflict for women, the equality laws have failed to disrupt women's assumed primary responsibility for child care.

Employment practices that disadvantage women because they do not meet stereotypical expectations, or because they have care responsibilities that might restrict their mobility or ability to work long hours, have not changed. It is hard to see how women can be equal in the workforce unless such practices are challenged.[66] Our social and economic arrangements ensure that women are poorer throughout their lives than comparable men and face poverty in much higher proportions in retirement.[67] Despite apparent advances for women in

---

65   This is one of the rights in the National Employment Standards for all employees under the *Fair Work Act 2009* (Cth) (Part 2-2, Division 4 [ss 65–6]). The 'right to request' is only a procedural, not a substantive, right— to request flexible conditions of work and to receive an answer that addresses the substance of the employer's workforce needs, not simply a blanket refusal. There is no mechanism for directly enforcing any such right, although a refusal that was discriminatory could be the subject of a discrimination complaint. A similar right in the United Kingdom has been successful, but defines the permissible grounds for refusing more clearly (see *Employment Rights Act 1996* [UK], s. 80G), and is supported by a right to complain to an employment tribunal where the employer fails to comply with the requirements of the Act (s. 80H).

66   Commentators no longer believe that the 'pipeline effect' (that women have not yet come through the system in sufficient numbers to move into senior positions) is the reason for these disparities, since they have persisted despite women's presence in substantial numbers in the workforce and professions over several decades.

67   Australian Human Rights Commission, *Accumulating Poverty*. The statistics referred to in Note 61 show that in 2007, 2.8 million women and 1.6 million men aged fifteen years and over reported not being covered by superannuation; half of all women aged between forty-five and fifty-nine have $8000 or less in superannuation; and current superannuation payouts for women are one-third of men's—$37 000 compared

the workforce, these data confirm that many women are only a relationship breakdown away from poverty—a situation that has changed very little in past centuries.

The *SDA* has not even begun to engage with the paradox that making child care easier for employed women to access simply reinforces their responsibility for it, thereby cementing their disadvantage. It is only by disrupting the gendered link to care work that improvements in conditions will be more widespread and could allow both women and men the ability to function effectively in both work and care. This is a step towards the most substantial aim—of disrupting gender-based norms as the ideal on which the system of employment rests—so that the male pattern is the norm and the female pattern the exception that falls short.

Language frames our thinking about what is possible in future. Women have, however, been largely removed from government language in Australia. Under the Howard Liberal Government (1996–2007), virtually all references in government policy and publications to women disappeared. References were made only to families and 'women's' interests were assumed to be those of their families. With the election of the Rudd Labor Government, this became a reference to 'working families'. Progress towards government recognition of the interests of women themselves (as well as the interests of men and children) is very slow, and ground that was gained during the 1980s has substantially been lost. Instead, the economic discourse of efficiency prevails.

Equality is also at risk of being overtaken and disappearing under the new discourse of human rights. Equal opportunity has been removed from the title of the Australian Human Rights Commission (previously the Human Rights and Equal Opportunity Commission) and its governing act, and the Gardner Review of Victoria's *Equal Opportunity Act* recommended that the Victorian Equal Opportunity and Human Rights Commission be renamed Human Rights Victoria. The spotlight now is on human rights, which is supposed to include equality. Equality as a collective right does not, however, necessarily sit easily with the individualist ethos of human rights and its fortunes appear to be slipping as those of human rights expand. Debate about equality in Australia— whether for women, racial or ethnic groups, Indigenous people or people with disabilities—is very limited.

---

with $110 000. At the same time, government policies direct support through superannuation subsidies to those with the highest salaries and greatest workforce connection, rather than individuals whose need is greatest (for example, through social security pensions).

Assessing the Act's Achievements: The Need for Change at the Systemic Level

In comparison with the days before the *SDA*, there have been major advances in women's position. In more recent times and compared with other developed countries, however, its achievements look more problematic. Arguably, sex discrimination law based on private enforcement has failed. While it is necessary for individuals to have an avenue to seek compensation for harms they suffer, to leave this as the sole enforcement method suggests a lack of commitment to ensuring that discrimination stops. Sex discrimination needs to be recognised as a broad social problem, not just a problem for the few individuals who recognise it and are prepared to fight for their rights. It must be tackled at a systemic level in order to change practices on a society-wide basis. The responsibility for enforcement has to be undertaken publicly and be directed towards changing systemic practices rather than solely redressing individual cases. Sex discrimination law needs better tools to tackle systemic practices that continue to disadvantage women.

Advances for women will not be possible unless change is also made possible for men in relation to the balance between work and care in their lives. Australian men are presently deprived of choice about their role in the family, with very limited access to parental leave and with strong social and employer inhibition on making less conventional choices.

Ironically, change could come through the industrial relations system rather than anti-discrimination law. *The Fair Work Act 2009* (Cth) includes provisions prohibiting discrimination at work that have the potential to virtually replace anti-discrimination laws in relation to employment discrimination. Of particular importance is that the *Fair Work Act* system includes an active and well-resourced public agency charged with enforcing the law (the Fair Work Ombudsman) and provides that litigation in the Federal Courts to enforce the 'adverse action' provisions does not attract the usual costs rules. The industrial relations system, based on collectivist ideas of employee organisations to protect and maintain rights, counterbalances the power of employers over employees, and of judges whose professional orientation is maintenance of the current system.[68] It could prove more able to address the concerns of women about the gendered nature of workforce assumptions and practices than individualised sex discrimination laws. It could, however, take some years to determine whether the potential of the new provisions will be realised.

---

68   Thornton, 'Sex Discrimination, Courts and Corporate Power' 33.

In the years since the *SDA* was adopted, we have learned a bit more about the phenomena of discrimination and prejudice. Valian has sought to explain why women's disadvantage is so difficult to alter based on the social-psychological theory of gender schemas in the cognitive processes of the individual.[69]

According to this theory, schemas are sets of expectations and assumptions that we all use every day to save ourselves from having to work things out from the beginning. They are cognitive shortcuts and include but are not limited to stereotypes and they exist below our conscious awareness. Among the most powerful are the gender schemas, which are sets of expectations that were formed and learned from our environments from birth and that are shaped by the world in which we live and the way things are done. Valian argues that gender schemas affect all of us, even those who consciously seek to end women's disadvantage. The effect of gender schemas is to create unconscious expectations that can lead to subtle and small differences in expectations and treatment of men and women that are repeated many times and that accumulate to result in large differences in overall outcomes. Valian argues that women's disadvantage is not necessarily the result of any large or egregious barriers or acts of discrimination, but instead the result of pervasive and repeated small disadvantages. This is not to deny that there are egregious violations of women's rights in Australia and elsewhere—for example, in relation to Indigenous women, family violence, and so on. Instead, this is a theory about one of the less noticeable causes of women's general disadvantage and why it is so difficult to challenge.

If gender schemas have this effect then it is difficult to see how individual legal remedies could be effective. The role of law is usually to deal with harms that are sufficiently serious to justify the cost and formality of legal intervention. Where differences in treatment are small but pervasive, they can be seen individually as trivial and not justifying legal intervention. This view makes a change of emphasis to systemic processes absolutely necessary, with a focus on changing practices and patterns that disadvantage, or on ensuring outcomes become more similar as an indication that disadvantage is not continuing, rather than identifying specific harms of sufficient degree. Focusing on sex discrimination law, which appears to be relatively ineffective in bringing about needed changes, could be an indication of the 'mesmerising' effect of general equality claims.[70] Instead of relying on a general claim to equality that is so open textured and subvertible, reformers might achieve more by focusing on the intellectual work and detailed analysis needed to push for identified changes to specific social practices.

69 Virginia Valian, *Why So Slow? The Advancement of Women*, MIT Press, Cambridge, Mass, 1998.
70 Margaret Thornton, 'Rapunzel and the Lure of Equal Citizenship' (2004) 8 *Law/Text/Culture* 231, 239.

Another argument for systemic and proactive rather than retrospective focus is that accusing a person of discrimination could be more likely to limit than to produce change, even at the individual level. It is likely to make the person feel defensive and refuse to change, because change could be seen as an admission that their practices were discriminatory. This phenomenon is often seen in response to litigation. Moving to proactive duties takes the emphasis in enforcement away from individual cases and past actions, and puts it on the systems that need to change.[71]

Comparable countries have placed much more emphasis on enforcement by public authorities, such as equality agencies, and on developing proactive requirements. For example, the United Kingdom has an equality duty that requires public sector bodies to consider women's (and other) equality issues in all policy development and service provision.[72] The UK Equality Bill 2010 has provisions for requiring employers of more than 250 staff to report on pay equity in their workforces, to provide the greatest chance of change.[73] The United States requires companies seeking government contracts to comply with affirmative action requirements (relating to minorities as well as gender) and ensure their subcontractors do so as well. Some Australian governments have used this approach in very limited areas—such as equal opportunity in briefing barristers—yet there is scope for much broader application.[74] These approaches are still in their early stages. Effective regulation requires a substantial investment in enforcement and monitoring, and there is some risk that they could become merely bureaucratic exercises or burdensome and difficult to monitor and enforce broadly.

There is another possible alternative. Norway has imposed quotas on women's board representation since the mid-2000s with success, and France is currently considering doing so. France has a quota for women's representation as political candidates. Closer to home, the ALP has had an affirmative action quota for women in winnable seats that has been highly effective in increasing women's representation in the current government. Even the Australian Stock Exchange has recently adopted a policy that requires changes to be demonstrated in women's participation on boards to avert the imposition of a quota.[75] Quotas

---

71   Belinda Smith, 'A Regulatory Analysis of the *Sex Discrimination Act 1984* (Cth): Can It Effect Equality or Only Redress Harm?' in Joanne Conaghan and Kerry Rittich (eds), *Labour Law, Work, and Family: Critical and Comparative Perspectives*, Oxford University Press, New York, 2005, p. 105.

72   Simon Rice, this volume; and Sandra Fredman, *Human Rights Transformed: Positive Rights and Positive Duties*, Oxford University Press, UK, 2008.

73   *Equality Act 2010* (UK), s. 78. Enforcement provisions for this requirement that were in the Equality Bill 2009 (UK) (cl 75), as introduced in the House of Commons, were, however, deleted in the House of Lords.

74   See, for example: Christopher McCrudden, *Buying Social Justice: Equality, Government Procurement, and Legal Change*, Oxford University Press, UK, 2007.

75   Australian Securities Exchange, *Recommendations on Diversity*, December 2009, Corporate Governance Council, Australian Securities Exchange, Sydney, <http://www.asx.com.au/about/pdf/mr_071209_asx_cgc_communique.pdf>

seem consistent with modern management approaches that concern themselves with outputs and results, rather than inputs or processes. Despite media hysteria about quotas, after 25 years, this could be the stronger alternative necessary to keep faith with the generations of women who have been promised equality but found the promise to be empty.

Conclusion

Although the *SDA* has been vital to progress, it has not been enough, and thorough legislative reform will be needed for greater progress. At 25, it has been outflanked by social change and economic ideology,[76] while media and much public discourse asserts that women are now equal. Sex discrimination law based on private enforcement has not been up to task. There is an urgent need for change, towards dealing with systemic discrimination and ensuring that public enforcement action is taken. While individuals need an avenue to seek compensation for harms they suffer, relying solely on private enforcement reflects a weak commitment to stopping discrimination. Sex discrimination needs to be recognised as a broad social and structural problem, and tackled at a systemic level. The burden of enforcement has to be undertaken publicly and be directed towards changing systemic practices rather than solely to redressing individual cases.

Although the need for reform has been recognised in recent reviews of anti-discrimination law,[77] there is no sign yet of any legislative change. Strengthening the Act's substantive provisions without addressing enforcement is unlikely to produce real social change on the wide basis needed. Systemic enforcement that does not rely on the individual affected to take action offers the best way forward for broad-based change. To maximise the chances of social change, a focus on positive duties and proactive measures that could help to counteract gender schemas and stereotyping appears most promising. After the *SDA*'s silver anniversary, more effective action is needed to keep faith with the generation of women who have been promised, but not yet allowed, equality.

---

76 Hunter, 'The Mirage of Justice'.
77 See, for example: Senate Legal and Constitutional Committee, *Report on the Effectiveness of the Commonwealth* Sex Discrimination Act 1984 *in Eliminating Discrimination and Promoting Gender Equality*, Parliament of Australia, Canberra, 2008; Department of Justice, *An Equality Act for a Fairer Victoria: Report of the Equal Opportunity Review*, Government of Victoria, Melbourne, [Gardner Review], 2008.

Bibliography

Books and articles

Allen, Dominique, 'Reducing the Burden of Proving Discrimination in Australia' (2009) 31(4) *Sydney Law Review* 579.

Berns, Sandra, *Women Going Backwards: Law and Change in a Family Unfriendly Society*, Ashgate Aldershot, Hants, UK, 2002.

Broderick, Elizabeth, Life Lines: Sex Discrimination over the Lifecycle, The Australian National University, Canberra, <http://law.anu.edu.au/coast/events/Sex_Discrim/Broderick_paper.pdf>

Conaghan, Joanne and Rittich, Kerry (eds), *Labour Law, Work, and Family: Critical and Comparative Perspectives*, Oxford University Press, New York, 2005.

Department of Justice 2008, *An Equality Act for a Fairer Victoria: Equal Opportunity Review Final Report*, Department of Justice, Government of Victoria, Melbourne, [*Gardner Report*], <http://www.justice.vic.gov.au/wps/wcm/connect/DOJ+Internet/Home/Your+Rights/Equal+Opportunity/>

Fredman, Sandra, *Human Rights Transformed: Positive Rights and Positive Duties*, Oxford University Press, UK, 2008.

Gaze, Beth, 'Context and Interpretation in Anti-Discrimination Law' (2002) 26 *Melbourne University Law Review* 325.

Gaze, Beth and Hunter, Rosemary, 'Access to Justice for Discrimination Complainants: Courts and Legal Representation' (2009) 32 *University of New South Wales Law Journal* 699.

Gaze, Beth and Hunter, Rosemary, *Enforcing Rights in Australia: An Evaluation of the New Regime*, Federation Press, Sydney, (forthcoming).

Graycar, Regina and Morgan, Jenny, *The Hidden Gender of Law*, Second edition, Federation Press, Sydney, 2002.

Graycar, Regina and Morgan, Jenny, 'Examining Understandings of Equality: One Step Forward, Two Steps Back?' (2004) 20 *Australian Feminist Law Journal* 23.

Graycar, Regina and Morgan, Jenny, 'Thinking about Equality' (2004) 27 *University of New South Wales Law Journal* 833.

Hunter, Rosemary, *Indirect Discrimination in the Workplace*, Federation Press, Annandale, NSW, 1992.

Hunter, Rosemary, 'The Mirage of Justice: Women and the Shrinking State' (2002) 16 *Australian Feminist Law Journal* 53.

Hunyor, Jonathon, 'Skin-Deep: Proof and Inferences of Racial Discrimination in Employment' (2003) 25 *Sydney Law Review* 535.

Innes, Jane, 'Claiming Equal Pay for Work of Equal Value: The ACTU's Comparable Worth Test Case' (1986) 4 *Law Society Journal* 52.

Innes, Jane, 'Equal pay and the *Sex Discrimination Act 1984*' (1986) 11 *Legal Service Bulletin* 254.

McCrudden, Christopher, *Buying Social Justice: Equality, Government Procurement, and Legal Change*, Oxford University Press, UK, 2007.

MacKinnon, Catharine, *Feminism Unmodified: Discourses on Life and Law*, Harvard University Press, Cambridge, Mass., 1987.

Primus, R., 'Equal Protection and Disparate Impact: Round Three' (2003) 117 *Harvard Law Review* 493.

Rees, Neil, Lindsay, Katherine and Rice, Simon, *Australian Anti-Discrimination Law: Text, Cases and Materials*, Federation Press, Sydney, 2008.

Smith, Belinda, 'A Regulatory Analysis of the *Sex Discrimination Act 1984* (Cth): Can It Effect Equality or Only Redress Harm?' in Joanne Conaghan and Kerry Rittich (eds), *Labour Law, Work, and Family: Critical and Comparative Perspectives*, Oxford University Press, New York, 2005.

Thornton, Margaret, 'The Indirection of Sex Discrimination' (1993) 12 *University of Tasmania Law Review* 88.

Thornton, Margaret, 'Rapunzel and the Lure of Equal Citizenship' (2004) 8 *Law/Text/Culture* 231.

Thornton, Margaret, 'Auditing the *Sex Discrimination Act*' in Marius Smith (ed.), *Human Rights 2004: The Year in Review*, Castan Centre for Human Rights Law, Monash University, Melbourne, 2005.

Thornton, Margaret, 'Sex Discrimination, Courts and Corporate Power' (2008) 36 *Federal Law Review* 31.

Valian, Virginia, *Why So Slow? The Advancement of Women*, MIT Press, Cambridge, Mass., 1998.

Walker, Kristen, 'The Bishops, the Doctor, his Patient and the Attorney-General: the Conclusion of the McBain Litigation' (2002) 30 *Federal Law Review* 507.

Legislation

Anti-Discrimination Act 1977 (NSW)

Disability Discrimination Act 1992 (Cth)

Education Act 1990 (NSW)

Employment Rights Act 1996 (UK)

Equal Opportunity Act 1977 (Vic.)

Equal Opportunity Act 1984 (SA)

Equal Opportunity Act 1984 (WA)

Equal Opportunity Act 1995 (Vic.)

Fair Work Act 2009 (Cth)

Prohibition of Discrimination Act 1966 (SA)

Racial Discrimination Act 1975 (Cth)

Racial Discrimination Act 1976 (SA)

Sex Discrimination Act 1984 (Cth)

Cases

Ansett Transport Industries (Operations) Pty Ltd v Wardley (1980) 142 CLR 237; [1980] HCA 8

Australian Iron & Steel Pty Ltd v Banovic (1989) 168 CLR 165; 1989 HCA 56

Australian Municipal, Administrative, Clerical and Services Union v Moreland City Council PR972644 [2006] AIRC 318

Brandy v Human Rights & Equal Opportunity Commission, (1995) 183 CLR 245; [1995] HCA 10

Commonwealth Bank of Australia v Human Rights and Equal Opportunity Commission (1997) 150 ALR 1; [1997] FCA 1311

Commonwealth of Australia v Evans (2004) 81 ALD 402; [2004] FCA 654

Commonwealth v Human Rights and Equal Opportunity Commission (Dopking No. 2) (1995) 63 FCR 74

Dao v Australian Postal Commission (1987) 162 CLR 317; [1987] HCA 13

Elliott v Nanda & Commonwealth (2001) 111 FCR 240; [2001] FCA 418

Escobar v Rainbow Printing Ltd (No. 2) (2002) 120 IR 84; [2002] FCMA 12

Family Provisions Case PR082005 [2005] AIRC 692

Fenton v Hair & Beauty Gallery Pty Ltd & Anor [2006] FMCA 3

Gilroy v Angelov [2000] FCA 1775

Griggs v Duke Power Co. 401 US 424 (1971); (1971) 28 L Ed 2d 158

Grulke v K C Canvas Pty Ltd [2000] FCA 1415

Hickie v Hunt and Hunt [1998] HREOCA 8

Howe v Qantas Airways Ltd (2004) 188 FLR 1; [2004] FCMA 242

Iliff v Sterling Commerce (Australia) Pty Ltd [2007] FMCA 1960

Kelly v TPG Internet [2003] FMCA 584

Kirkland v Wattle [2002] FCA 145

Lee v Smith & Ors [2007] FMCA 59

Mayer v ANSTO [2003] FMCA 209

New South Wales v Amery (2006) 230 CLR 174; [2006] HCA 14

Poniatowska v Hickinbotham [2009] FCA 680

Re McBain; Ex parte Australian Catholic Bishops Conference (2002) 209 CLR 372; [2002] HCA 16

Secretary, DFAT v Styles (1989) 23 FCR 251

Thomson v Orica Australia Pty Ltd (2002) 116 IR 186; [2002] FCA 939

Wattle v Kirkland & Anor (No. 2) [2002] FMCA 135

Wylie v McCann Worldgroup Pty Ltd & Ors [2009] FMCA 959

Reports and miscellaneous primary sources

Australian Human Rights Commission, *Accumulating Poverty: Women's Experiences of Inequality over the Lifecycle*, Australian Human Rights Commission, Sydney, 2009.

Australian Human Rights Commission, 'Sex Discrimination Commissioner: 25th Anniversary of the Sex Discrimination Act (1984)', Gender Equality Statistics, Australian Human Rights Commission, Sydney, 2009, <http://www.hreoc.gov.au/sex_discrimination/sda_25/index.html>

Australian Law Reform Commission, Equality Before the Law: Justice for Women, Report 69, Australian Law Reform Commission, Sydney, 1994.

Australian Securities Exchange, Recommendations on Diversity, Corporate Governance Council, Australian Securities Exchange, Sydney, 2009, <http://www.asx.com.au/about/pdf/mr_071209_asx_cgc_communique.pdf>

European Union, Directive on the Burden of Proof of Discrimination

Human Rights and Equal Opportunities Commission, The Equal Pay Handbook, Human Rights and Equal Opportunities Commission, Sydney, 1998.

Human Rights and Equal Opportunities Commission, Pregnant and Productive: It's a Right not a Privilege to Work while Pregnant, Human Rights and Equal Opportunities Commission, Sydney, 1999.

Human Rights and Equal Opportunities Commission, A Bad Business: Review of Sexual Harassment in Employment Complaints, Human Rights and Equal Opportunities Commission, Sydney, 2002.

Human Rights and Equal Opportunities Commission, A Time to Value: Proposal for a National Scheme of Paid Maternity Leave, Human Rights and Equal Opportunities Commission, Sydney, 2002.

Human Rights and Equal Opportunities Commission, Striking the Balance: Women, Men, Work and Family, Human Rights and Equal Opportunities Commission, Sydney, 2005.

6. The *Sex Discrimination Act:* Advancing Gender Equality and Decent Work?

Sara Charlesworth

This chapter starts with a brief overview of the main Australian regulatory measures that address sex/gender (in)equality in employment. It argues that a major constraint on the influence of the Sex Discrimination Act 1984 *(SDA) on the conditions of women's employment has been its effective separation from industrial relations law. This has made it difficult to conceive of sex discrimination as a mainstream employment issue and means that the gender equality impact of industrial relations regulation— reflected in classification structures, bargaining provisions and working-time arrangements—remains invisible. The chapter weighs up the potential of the decent work agenda first proposed by the International Labour Organisation (ILO) and the ILO's framing of gender equality as being 'at the heart of decent work' as the basis for a more effective and integrated policy and regulatory framework.*

Introduction

With the regulatory and institutional basis for regulation in the area of gender equality in employment the subject of various inquiries and of recent legislative reform, it is opportune not only to reflect on where we have been over the past 25 years but to imagine where we might go in the future.

In her chapter, Beth Gaze highlights the limited impact of the *Sex Discrimination Act 1984* (Cth) (*SDA*) on workforce practices. In this chapter, I focus more broadly on regulation in the area of paid employment. The persistence of gender inequality in employment is often seen as due to the ineffectiveness of the *SDA* and other state-based anti-discrimination laws. As set out below, however, at the federal level in Australia, there are three quite distinct approaches in employment regulation to eliminating discrimination against women. These include the use of specific sex discrimination provisions in the *SDA*, the implementation of affirmative action provisions initially in the *Affirmative Action (Equal Opportunity for Women) Act 1986* (Cth) and then in the *Equal Opportunity for Women in the Workplace Act 1999* (Cth), and the prohibition of sex and other forms of discrimination in industrial relations law. I argue that the historical separation of anti-discrimination provisions from industrial relations law and the sidelining of discrimination measures within the industrial relations jurisdiction make it difficult both to conceive of sex discrimination as a mainstream industrial relations issue and to render problematic the gender equality impact of industrial relations regulation. Further, I argue that the success of any legislative action to prevent sex discrimination and advance gender equality in employment needs an integrated regulatory and policy framework. To that end, I want to canvass the potential of the 'decent work' agenda first proposed by the International Labour Organisation (ILO) as the basis for a recasting of gender inequality as a mainstream industrial relations concern.

Gender Equality and Australian Employment Regulation

I begin by reflecting on the main regulatory strategies in Australian employment regulation for dealing with gender inequality in employment drawing on existing critiques and empirical studies.

The Anti-Discrimination Approach

While prompted by Australia's ratification of the Convention on the Elimination of All Forms of Discrimination Against Women (CEDAW), the *SDA* drew on a more formal conception of gender equality, constituting the problem it addresses as unequal opportunity measured in terms of 'less favourable' treatment where women and men are similarly situated. This comparator conception takes the male pattern of life as the norm and does not tackle deep-rooted causes of inequality, including the gender division of labour.[1]

Notwithstanding the successes of the *SDA*, which have been outlined in other chapters, particularly in the normative role it has played and in redress for individual women, close analysis of case law has highlighted the narrowness and complexity of the *SDA*'s direct and indirect discrimination provisions, which together with its individual complaints-based model and ineffectual enforcement processes have emerged as major structural problems.[2] All these problems are exacerbated by the increasingly narrow judicial interpretation of

---

1 Sylvia Walby, *Gender (In) Equality and the Future of Work*, Equal Opportunities Commission, Manchester, 2007.

2 See Rosemary Hunter, 'The Mirage of Justice: Women and the Shrinking State' (2002) 16 *Australian Feminist Law Journal* 53; Beth Gaze, 'The *Sex Discrimination Act* after Twenty Years: Achievements,

anti-discrimination statutes and of the international law on which they draw.[3] Empirical studies of the operation of the *SDA* suggest its implementation is also flawed—highlighted by growing formalism and a 'creeping legalism',[4] with a concentration on procedural fairness that ignores the power disparity between complainants and respondents, as well as a more time-consuming and less transparent conciliation process than has historically been the case in the industrial relations jurisdiction.[5] Problems with legislative awareness and enforcement have also emerged in specific areas such as sexual harassment and pregnancy discrimination.[6]

The profound changes wrought by globalisation and the deregulation of national labour markets have also contributed to newer forms of gender inequality, which were not envisaged when the *SDA* was first enacted. The move to the new economy with its reliance on 'flexible' labour has brought with it not only increased demands for women workers, particularly in the service sector, but also risk, uncertainty and underemployment for those who fall outside traditional models of employment regulation.[7] The growth of non-standard and precarious employment, individualised work relationships and the decline of union coverage and influence impact disproportionately on women, particularly where employment rights remain based on the dominant male, full-time, permanent job paradigm.[8]

Disappointments, Disillusionment and Alternatives' (2004) 19 *University of New South Wales Law Journal Forum* 57; Margaret Thornton, 'Auditing the *Sex Discrimination Act*' in Marius Smith (ed.), *Human Rights 2004: The Year in Review*, Castan Centre for Human Rights Law, Monash University, Melbourne, 2005.

3   Beth Gaze, 'Context and Interpretation in Anti-Discrimination Law' (2002) 26 *Melbourne University Law Review* 325; Belinda Smith, 'From Wardley to Purvis—How Far has Australian Anti-Discrimination Law Come in 30 Years?' (2007) *Australian Journal of Labour Law* 21.

4   Margaret Thornton, *The Liberal Promise: Anti-Discrimination Legislation in Australia*, Oxford University Press, UK, 1990.

5   Rosemary Hunter and Alice Leonard, *The Outcomes of Conciliation in Sex Discrimination Cases*, Working Paper No. 8, Centre for Employment and Labour Relations Law, Faculty of Law, The University of Melbourne, Vic., 1995; Anna Chapman, 'Discrimination Complaint-Handling in NSW: The Paradox of Informal Dispute Resolution' (2000) 22 *Sydney Law Review* 321; Sara Charlesworth, 'The Overlap of the Federal Sex Discrimination and Industrial Relations Jurisdictions: Intersections and Demarcations in Conciliation' (2003) 6 *Australian Journal of Labour Economics* 559; Thornton, 'Auditing the *Sex Discrimination Act*'.

6   Human Rights and Equal Opportunity Commission, *Sexual Harassment: Serious Business.Results of the 2008 Sexual Harassment National Telephone Survey*, Human Rights and Equal Opportunity Commission, Sydney, 2008; Paula McDonald, Sandra Backstrom and Kerriann Dear, 'Reporting Sexual Harassment: Claims and Remedies' (2008) 46 *Asia Pacific Journal of Human Resources* 173; Sara Charlesworth and Fiona Macdonald, 'The Unpaid Parental Leave Standard: What Standard?', *Refereed Proceedings of the 21st Conference of Association of Industrial Relations Academics of Australia and New Zealand*, Melbourne, 6–8 February 2008.

7   Leah Vosko, "Decent Work": The Shifting Role of the ILO and the Struggle for Global Social Justice' (2002) 2 *Global Social Policy* 19; Iain Campbell, 'Australia: Institutional Changes and Workforce Fragmentation' in Sangheon Lee and Francois Eyraud (eds), *Globalization, Flexibilization and Working Conditions in Asia and the Pacific*, Chandros Publishing, Oxford, 2008.

8   Judy Fudge and Rosemary Owens, *Precarious Work, Women and the New Economy: The Challenge to Legal Norms*, Hart Publishing, Oxford, 2006.

The Human Resource Management Approach

As outlined in earlier chapters, the positive action provisions in the original Sex Discrimination Bill were sheared off into the separate *Affirmative Action (Equal Opportunity for Women) Act 1986* (Cth) (*AAA*). Despite the potential of the original provisions to encourage action at the enterprise level, implementation of this regulation and its weakening of the *Equal Opportunity for Women in the Workplace Act 1999* (*EOWWA*) reflect what is arguably a human resource management approach to improving equal employment opportunity (EEO) for women through voluntary action by large employers. The implementation of the *AAA* and the *EOWWA* has relied on the individualised human resource management discourse of 'diversity' that implicitly undermines the regulation's mandate to address structural discrimination.[9]

In the past decade in particular, voluntary action through best practice was promoted by the Howard Government—in effect substituting for any regulatory action to improve EEO. Paid maternity leave is a case in point. The few existing studies of the impact of the *AAA/EOWWA* on organisational practice suggest there is little relationship between mandatory reporting by organisations on basic indicators and the achievement of positive organisational outcomes for women.[10] This is not surprising as compliance with the regulation is based on the submission of reports rather than action taken. Studies drawing on data from organisational reports paint a mixed picture of the impact of *AAA/EOWWA* regulation, suggesting some correlation between gender-specific human resource management strategies and EEO structures and increases of women in management positions yet little organisational action in the areas of recruitment and the promotion of women.[11] Industry-specific and organisational studies reveal little connection made between conditions of employment and EEO/diversity action with a striking lack of interaction between *AAA/EOWWA* regulation and enterprise bargaining in most large workplaces.[12]

---

9   Carol Bacchi, 'The Seesaw Effect: Down Goes Affirmative Action, Up Comes Workplace Diversity' (2000) 5 *Journal of Interdisciplinary Gender Studies* 64.

10   Alison Sheridan, 'Affirmative Action in Australia—Employment Statistics can't tell the whole Story' (1995) 10 *Women in Management Review* 26; Valarie Braithwaite, 'The Australian Government's Affirmative Action Legislation: Achieving Social Change through Human Resource Management' (1993) 15 *Law and Policy* 322; Glenda Strachan and Erica French, 'Equal Opportunity: Disentangling Promise from Achievement', *Proceedings of the Gender, Work and Organisation: 5th Biennial International Interdisciplinary Conference*, Keele University, UK, 2007, pp. 1–22.

11   Erica French, 'Approaches to Equity Management and their Relationship to Women in Management' (2001) 12 *British Journal of Management* 267; Strachan and French, 'Equal Opportunity'.

12   John Burgess and Glenda Strachan, 'Equal Employment Opportunity, Employment Restructuring and Enterprise Bargaining: Complementary or Contradictory?' (1998) 3 *Journal of Interdisciplinary Gender Studies* 23; Glenda Strachan and John Burgess, 'W(h)ither Affirmative Action Legislation in Australia?' (2000) 5 *Journal of Interdisciplinary Gender Studies* 46; Strachan and French, 'Equal Opportunity'; Sara Charlesworth, Philippa Hall and Belinda Probert, *Drivers and Contexts of Equal Employment Opportunity and Diversity Action in Australian Organisations*, RMIT Publishing, Informit E-library, Melbourne, 2005.

I believe that, apart from its limited effect on systemic discrimination within organisations, the enthusiastic promotion of a short-term business case for EEO as part of this human resource management approach to the implementation of the *AAA/EOWWA* has in fact done very real damage to the pursuit of gender equality in Australia. Its promise that advancing women is good for the business bottom line, assumes, as Sandra Fredman argues, the business interests of employers are compatible with EEO and indeed the good of the business will further the good of all.[13] The business case thus creates the space for inaction. Further, it hides the business case for unequal opportunity—reflected most tangibly in the gender pay gap—and contributes to a privileging of the rights of business over the rights of women workers to EEO both in public discourse and policy responses.

The Industrial Relations Approach

Sex discrimination was first recognised in the federal industrial relations jurisdiction in the *Industrial Relations Act 1988* (Cth) with the requirement that the Australian Industrial Relations Commission (AIRC) take account of the principles embodied in the *SDA*. In 1994, further amendments required the AIRC to ensure that labour standards met Australia's international obligations, such as those imposed under the Convention on the Elimination of All Forms of Discrimination Against Women (CEDAW).[14] The AIRC was also charged with the responsibility to help prevent and eliminate discrimination on various grounds, including on the basis of sex, sexual preference, family responsibilities and pregnancy. These amendments also opened the way for the pursuit of individual claims by employees and explicitly proscribed termination of employment on discriminatory grounds. While these provisions have contributed to important improvements in standards around carers and unpaid parental leave, they have had little practical impact on the fundamental regulation of the employment relationship, particularly in terms of classification structures, wage rates and both enterprise and individual bargaining. This is perhaps unsurprising. The past two decades have seen the erosion of the standard employment relationship (SER) with a growth of temporary and part-time work. The SER, like the 'ideal worker' norm, was based on a concept of full-time permanent waged work with regulation of its basic conditions such as working time and wages by labour law and/or collective agreement.[15] In Australia, however, as in many other developed countries, what Leah Vosko refers to as 'SER-centrism' continues to permeate the regulation of work.[16] That is, the greater the deviation from the

---

13   Sandra Fredman, *Discrimination Law*, Oxford University Press, UK, 2005, p. 25.
14   *Industrial Relations Reform Act 1993* (Cth). The amendments took effect in March 1994.
15   Gerhard Bosch, 'Towards a New Standard Employment Relationship in Western Europe?' (2004) 42 *British Journal of Industrial Relations* 617.
16   Leah Vosko, Precarious Employment and the Problem of SER-Centrism: Regulating for 'Decent Work', Paper given to the Regulating for Decent Work—Innovative Labour Regulation in a Turbulent World Conference, International Labour Organisation, Geneva, 8 July 2009.

standard employment relationship, such as the part-time and casual employment in which a large proportion of Australian women workers are engaged, the less protection there is for workers.

There is a rich vein of empirical studies on the gendered impact of industrial relations regulation on pay inequity and the failure of federal industrial relations regulation to address it,[17] on the concentration of women in precarious work,[18] on the regulatory exclusion of groups of women such as outworkers[19] and on Australia's gendered and polarised working-time regime.[20] One focus of research has been on the more limited access many women have to so-called 'family-friendly' arrangements through industrial relations mechanisms such as awards and enterprise agreements because of their location in poor-quality jobs.[21] Changes in industrial relations regulation in the past 15 years have prompted the analysis of the gendered impact of enterprise bargaining,[22] of individualised workplace agreements[23] and of the far-reaching changes introduced through the WorkChoices amendments to the *Workplace Relations Act 1996* (Cth) (*WRA*).[24]

---

17   Gillian Whitehouse, 'Recent Trends in Pay Equity: Beyond the Aggregate Statistics' (2001) 43 *Journal of Industrial Relations* 66; Alison Preston and Gillian Whitehouse, 'Gender Differences in Occupation of Employment within Australia' (2004) 7 *Australian Journal of Labour Economics* 309; Alison Preston and Therese Jefferson, 'Trends in Australia's Gender Wage Ratio' (2007) 18 *Journal of Labour and Industry* 69; Meg Smith and Michael Lyons, '2020 Vision or 1920s Myopia? Recent Developments in Gender Pay Equity in Australia' (2007) 13 *International Employment Relations Review* 27.

18   Rosemary Owens, 'Decent Work for the Contingent Workforce in the New Economy' (2002) 15 *Australian Journal of Labour Law* 209; Fudge and Owens, *Precarious Work*; Iain Campbell, Gillian Whitehouse and Janine Baxter, 'Australia: Casual Employment, Part-time Employment and the Resilience of the Male Breadwinner Model' in Leah Vosko, Martha MacDonald and Iain Campbell (eds), Gender and the Contours of Precarious Employment, Routledge, London.

19   Rosemary Owens, 'The Peripheral Worker: Women and the Legal Regulation of Outwork' in Margaret Thornton (ed.), *Public and Private: Feminist Legal Debates*, Oxford University Press, Melbourne, 1995.

20   Barbara Pocock, *The Work–Life Collision: What Work is doing to Australians and what to do about it*, Federation Press, Sydney, 2003; Campbell, 'Australia'.

21   John Buchanan and Louise Thornthwaite, *Paid Work and Parenting: Charting a New Course for Australian Families*, Australian Centre for Industrial Relations Research and Training, Sydney, 2001; Jenny Chalmers, Iain Campbell and Sara Charlesworth, 'Part-Time Work and Caring Responsibilities in Australia: Towards an Assessment of Job Quality' (2005) 15 *Labour & Industry* 41.

22   Laura Bennett, 'Women and Enterprise Bargaining: The Legal and Institutional Framework' (1994) 36 *Journal of Industrial Relations* 191; Philippa Hall and Di Fruin, 'Gender Aspects of Enterprise Bargaining: The Good, the Bad and the Ugly' in D. E. Morgan (ed.), *Dimensions of Enterprise Bargaining and Organizational Relations*, UNSW Studies in Australian Industrial Relations, No. 36, University of New South Wales, Sydney, 1994; John Burgess, Paul Keogh, Duncan Macdonald, G. H. Morgan, Glenda Strachan and Suzanne Ryan, *Enterprise Bargaining in Three Female Dominated Workplaces in the Hunter*, Employment Studies Research Paper No. 23, University of Newcastle, NSW, 1996; Sara Charlesworth, *Stretching Flexibility: Women and Working Time Arrangements in Enterprise Bargaining*, Human Rights and Equal Opportunity Commission, Sydney, 1996; Meg Smith and Peter Ewer, *The Position of Women in the National Training Reform Agenda and Enterprise Bargaining*, Department of Education, Employment and Training, Australian Government Printing Service, Canberra, 1995.

23   John Burgess, Anne Sullivan and Glenda Strachan, 'Australian Workplace Agreements, EEO and Family Friendly Arrangements in the Retail Sector' (2004) 4 *Employment Relations Record* 61.

24   Barbara Pocock, Jude Elton, Alison Preston, Sara Charlesworth, Fiona Macdonald, Marian Baird, Rae Cooper and Bradon Ellem, 'The Impact of "Work Choices" on Women in Low paid Employment in Australia: A Qualitative Analysis' (2008) 50 Journal of Industrial Relations 475; David Peetz, 'Collateral Damage: Women and the WorkChoices Battlefield' (2007) 33 *Hecate* 61.

While the lack of fit between the reality of many women's lives and industrial relations regulation and policy modelled around the 'ideal worker' has been highlighted in these studies, there remains almost a wilful blindness in the industrial relations jurisdiction to the role of classification structures, working-time provisions and enforcement in the persistence of gender inequality. Indeed, the view that discrimination in employment has little to do with such matters was highlighted by the AIRC last year, when it decided to remove the anti-discrimination clause in awards from the new 'modern awards' on the grounds that 'discrimination is the subject of legislative regulation elsewhere'.[25]

Separation of Industrial Relations and Anti-Discrimination Regulation

In Australia, there is some overlap between anti-discrimination and industrial relations provisions, and the (largely unsuccessful) pursuit of equal remuneration has occurred within the industrial relations jurisdiction. A practical and symbolic divide between two very different regulatory domains remains,[26] however, as we see in the AIRC's approach to award modernisation.

While employment remains the overwhelming area in which inquiries and formal complaints are made under the *SDA*,[27] it remains on the periphery of mainstream employment regulation in practical and policy terms and in terms of envisioning alternatives.[28] This means that sex discrimination, involving, for example, sexual harassment and pregnancy discrimination, has not been seen as a mainstream employment issue. Further, the gender equality impact of industrial relations regulation—such as the regulation of classification structures, bargaining provisions and working-time arrangements—remains invisible. As Jill Murray argues, pre-existing laws act as a constraining mechanism that limits the choices available to those with the power to shape employment laws.[29] Perhaps more importantly, they constrain our imagination as to what might be.

---

25   Australian Industrial Relations Commission, Statement of the Full Bench, 12 September 2008 [2008] AIRCFB 717, at Clause 33.

26   Charlesworth, 'The Overlap of the Federal Sex Discrimination and Industrial Relations Jurisdictions' 559.

27   Data show that in 2007–08, 87 per cent of formal complaints lodged under the *SDA* were in the area of employment. Human Rights and Equal Opportunity Commission, *Annual Report 2007–2008*, Human Rights and Equal Opportunity Commission, Sydney, 2008.

28   This is reflected in the report of the senate inquiry into the effectiveness of the *SDA*, in which the *Workplace Relations Act 1996* and the (then) Fair Work Australia Bill 2008 were referred to only in passing and not at all in any of the report's 43 recommendations, despite their relevance to many of the issues raised in the report—from workers with family responsibilities to pay inequity. Senate Standing Committee on Legal and Constitutional Affairs 2008, *Report on the Effectiveness of the Commonwealth* Sex Discrimination Act 1984 *in Eliminating Discrimination and Promoting Gender Equality*, Parliament of Australia, Canberra.

29   Jill Murray, Working Conditions Laws in an Integrating World Project: Australia, Unpublished paper prepared for the International Labour Organisation 2009.

So Where to Now?

At the current time, we are in a state of flux, both in terms of proposed and likely legislative changes and institutionally. To date, there has been only a limited government response to the relatively modest recommendations coming out of the senate inquiry into the effectiveness of the *SDA* made last year,[30] or to the more far-reaching recommendations of the 2010 report from the House of Representatives inquiry into pay equity and related matters.[31] The KPMG consultation report on the review of the *EOWWA* and its Agency for the Federal Office for Women has just been released.[32] There could be some pressure on the federal government to renovate the basic architecture of the *SDA* and the *EOWWA* and to rethink some of the links between industrial relations and anti-discrimination regulation, including positive action. The industrial relations regulatory and institutional arrangements are more settled with the enactment of the *Fair Work Act 2009* (Cth) (*FWA*). Some of the changes in the new *FWA* suggest that discrimination issues will have a more important place than before in the mainstream employment arena. The Act provides strengthened equal remuneration provisions, a low-paid enterprise bargaining stream and a potentially useful framing of discrimination as 'adverse action'. The Office of the Fair Work Ombudsman has recently set up an anti-discrimination compliance unit. Indeed, if relevant recommendations of the Senate Pay Equity Inquiry are taken up we could yet see a specialist Pay Equity Unit and a Deputy Commissioner for Pay Equity within Fair Work Australia.

Nevertheless, the continuing dominance of the male breadwinner model in the gendered architecture of the 10 National Employment Standards (NES) and draft modern awards—which together are to provide the new safety net for workers— is striking. Workers who are employed on a casual basis and/or who have less than 12 months service—workers who are more likely to be women[33]—are effectively excluded from a number of the standards. And in terms of enforcement, the *FWA* specifically prevents workers from pursing a breach of the NES rights to request flexible work arrangements and an extension of unpaid parental leave.[34]

---

30 *Sex Discrimination Amendment Bill 2010* (Cth).

31 House of Representatives Standing Committee on Employment and Workplace Relations, *Making it Fair: Pay Equity and Associated Issues related to Increasing Female Participation in the Workforce*, Commonwealth of Australia, Canberra, 2009.

32 KPMG, *Review of the* Equal Opportunity for Women in the Workplace Act 1999. *Consultation Report*, KPMG, Melbourne, 2010. The KPMG report uses a rather curious 'weighting' of submissions reporting the percentage in favour of particular changes to both the *EOWWA* and the agency that implements it, rather than engaging with the merits or substance of the arguments.

33 Australian Bureau of Statistics, *Australian Labour Market Statistics, July 2009*, Cat. No. 6105, Australian Bureau of Statistics, Canberra, 2009.

34 Sections 739(2) and 740(2) of the *Fair Work Act* provide there can be no determination of whether an employer had reasonable business grounds for refusing a request, *unless* the employer has specifically consented in an enterprise or other agreement.

In the exposure drafts of 'modern' awards, we see the reproduction of gendered working-time arrangements in male and female-dominated industries, which underpin the relatively poorer quality work available in the latter.[35]

The limited effectiveness of anti-discrimination law in addressing such entrenched structures has led in many countries to a rethinking of the traditional anti-discrimination framework with regulatory proposals for broader conceptions of equality and for positive action[36] and a more comprehensive implementation of the widely ratified CEDAW.[37] Recent renovations of equality regulation in the United Kingdom hold promise, for example, in re-conceiving gender inequality in employment in human rights terms.[38] It remains unclear, however, whether and how such conceptions will affect mainstream employment regulation or indeed its implementation at the labour market, industry and workplace levels.

A Decent Work Regulatory and Policy Framework

One innovation I believe could be fruitful is the decent work agenda first proposed by the ILO. Changes in the nature and regulation of work have led to increasing international attention to the dimensions of quality or decent work.[39] The concept of quality or decent work—which goes to the nature and content of jobs—is a broad one that has not always been gender sensitive.[40] There is, however, growing recognition of the importance of a gender analysis of job

---

35   For example, a comparison of the exposure drafts of the Metals Award (Exposure Draft of the Manufacturing and Associated Industries and Occupations Award, <http://www.airc.gov.au/awardmod/databases/metal/Modern/PR988376.doc>) and the Community Services Award (Exposure Draft of the Social, Community, Home Care and Disability Services Industry Award, <http://www.airc.gov.au/awardmod/databases/social/Exposure/social.doc>) shows the maintenance of significant differences in the span of hours provisions and access to penalty rates for work outside these hours, the rights to overtime for part-time workers, as well as more limited classification structures for the community services occupational groups.

36   Joanne Conaghan, 'Intersectionality and UK Equality Initiatives' (2007) 23 *South African Journal on Human Rights* 317; Sandra Fredman, 'Changing the Norm: Positive Duties in Equal Treatment Legislation' (2005) 12 *Maastricht Journal of European and Comparative Law* 369.

37   Rikki Holtmaat and Christa Tober, 'CEDAW and the European Union's Policy in the Field of Combating Gender Discrimination' (2005) 12 *Maastricht Journal of European and Comparative Law* 399.

38   Sandra Fredman, *Human Rights Transformed: Positive Duties and Positive Rights*, Oxford University Press, UK, 2008.

39   See, for example: Sangheon Lee, Deirdre McCann and John Messenger, *Working Time Around the World: Trends in Working Hours, Laws, and Policies in a Global Comparative Perspective*, Routledge, Oxford, 2004; Francis Green, *Demanding Work: The Paradox of Job Quality in the Affluent Economy*, Princeton University Press, NJ, 2005; Mark Smith, Brendan Burchell, Colette Fagan and Catherine O'Brien, 'Job Quality in Europe' (2008) 39 *Industrial Relations Journal* 586.

40   Francis Green describes job quality as constituted by 'the set of work features which foster the wellbeing of the worker' (see *Demanding Work*, p. 9). Green focuses on the specific aspects of a job including skill, effort (including work intensity), job control and discretion, wages and risk (in respect of both job security and health and safety). Other approaches employ a broader lens and measure aspects such as labour market status, intrinsic and extrinsic job characteristics, job satisfaction and employee wellbeing, incorporating an assessment not only of the aspects of job quality but also of the outcomes for employees (see Graham Lowe, *21st Century Job Quality: Achieving What Canadians Want*, Research Report W/37 Work and Learning, Canadian Policy Research Networks, Toronto, 2007).

quality, with a recent study indicating that gender, along with occupational status and job characteristics such as working time and sector (status and characteristics that are themselves highly gendered in the Australian context), has more influence on an individual's job quality than the country or national model in which they are situated.[41] Growing attention is also being paid to the roles of national and international mechanisms aimed at improving the conditions of work.[42] At the international institutional level, both the European Commission (EC) and the ILO have focused on the development of separate agendas around quality or decent work. The ILO's conception of decent work, which built on the ILO Declaration on Fundamental Principles and Rights at Work, was first formally elaborated in 1999 as involving

> opportunities for work that is productive and delivers a fair income, security in the workplace and social protection for families, better prospects for personal development and social integration, freedom for people to express their concerns, organize and participate in the decisions that affect their lives and equality of opportunity and treatment for all women and men.[43]

This conception of decent work offers a valuable alternative to the traditional framing of most contemporary employment regulation. It moves beyond the regulatory norm of the standard employment relationship, which excludes so many women.[44] And the attainment of gender equality has a more central and less contingent place than in the European Commission's 'more and better' jobs agenda,[45] illustrated in the ILO's 2008–09 campaign around 'gender equality at the heart of decent work'. This framing of gender equality in the context of decent work, according to the ILO,

> embraces equality of opportunity and treatment, equality of remuneration and access to safe and healthy working environments, equality in association and collective bargaining, equality in obtaining meaningful career development, maternity protection, and a balance between work and home life that is fair to both men and women.[46]

---

41 Smith et al., 'Job Quality in Europe'.

42 Vosko, 'Decent Work'; Mary Cornish, Ending Labour Market Gender Discrimination- Bringing Gender Mainstreaming into Parliamentary Laws and Institutions, Presentation to Women & Work Conference of International Parliamentary Unions, Geneva, 6 December 2007.

43 International Labour Organisation, *Decent Work: A Report of the Director-General*, 89th Session of the International Labour Organisation, Geneva, 1999.

44 Vosko, 'Decent Work'; Mary Cornish, 'Closing the Global Gender Pay Gap: Securing Justice for Women's Work' (2007) 28 *Comparative Labour Law and Policy Journal* 219.

45 Alexandra Scheele, 'Gender and the Quality of Work: An Overview of European and National Approaches' (2007) 13 *Transfer* 595.

46 International Labour Organisation, *ABC of Women Workers' Rights and Gender Equality*, Second edition, International Labour Organisation, Geneva, 2007, p. 92.

The attainment of gender equality, then, sits squarely in mainstream employment regulation. Importantly, in its inclusion of personal development and social integration, it recognises the relationship between paid work and unpaid work as critical for the realisation of gender equality. The concept of decent work thus has potential to move beyond the confines of the workplace to 'work's place' in personal, social and economic life.[47]

There are of course inherent tensions and limitations in the decent work agenda[48]—not least that in practice it is directed mainly at developing countries. In Australia, the aspirations of the decent work agenda have not yet been taken up politically. In the lengthy debates about the Fair Work Bill and about the current award modernisation process, there has been very little reference, if any, to gender equality, decent work or to related international standards.[49] There also remains some ambivalence in various articulations of the decent work agenda about the full extension of the same level of statutory entitlements, protections and benefits accorded to standard workers to *all* workers in need of protection.[50] Further, while the importance of gender equality is explicit in elaborations of the decent work agenda, to date the focus has been on gender equality *as one outcome of employment regulation* rather than as a central rationale or driver of such regulation.

Nevertheless, I think the conception of gender equality at the heart of decent work can be used as a regulatory and policy starting point for a reframing of rights to gender equality in paid work that might be translated into tangible and sustainable improvements in women's status in and experience of paid employment. Leah Vosko argues that ensuring decent work for all means developing an alternative imaginary that addresses more fully the complex interplay between employment norms, gender relations and citizenship boundaries, which sees the realisation of decent work *through* gender equality.[51] To this end, one of the key principles she proposes is 'global universal caregiving', building on Nancy Fraser's 'universal caregiver' and Eileen Applebaum's 'shared work/valued care' models. Gender equality *and* decent work thus require a redistribution of work between women and men and between the unemployed and the employed[52] and, I would add, the *under*employed.

---

47   Karl Klare, 'The Horizons of Transformative Labour and Employment Law' in Joanne Conaghan, Richard Fischl and Karl Klare (eds), *Labour Law in an Era of Globalization: Transformative Practices and Possibilities*, Oxford University Press, UK, 2004.
48   See Vosko, 'Decent Work'; Scheele, 'Gender and the Quality of Work'.
49   This is despite the Australian Council of Trade Unions (ACTU) endorsing a decent work policy for the first time at its July 2009 Congress (<http://www.actu.asn.au/Issues/DecentWork/default.aspx#>).
50   Vosko, 'Decent Work' 19, 32.
51   Vosko, Precarious Employment and the Problem of SER-Centrism.
52   Scheele, 'Gender and the Quality of Work' 595, 608.

With increasing international recognition of the limits of the so-called free market in ending discrimination, including sex discrimination, national governments are now grappling with the issue of re-regulation.[53] Indeed, the failure of current regulatory models to meet the challenge of responding to the place of paid work and of workers in the new economy underpins a wholesale rethinking not only of the role of employment regulation, but also of the gender equality project and the role of international law and institutions within it.[54] As Judy Fudge points out, the new economy with its heterogeneity and diversity need not intensify inequality and exclusion; it can also mean equality and inclusion by accommodating a range of different types of jobs and workers.[55] It is therefore timely to start assessing the potential of the decent work agenda approach as a way of moving towards a more comprehensive realisation of the CEDAW goals for gender equality—something that Caroline Lambert's chapter takes up. The challenge is to move to an integrated legislative framework, policy and practice that meet the threefold approach of CEDAW to gender equality[56]

- to achieve full equality of women before the law and in public administration

- to improve the de facto position of women

- to address the prevailing gender relations and the persistence of gender-based stereotypes.

To be successful in advancing the position of women in paid work, this multi-layered understanding of gender equality needs to be brought into the centre of the mainstream employment jurisdiction and not just left up to the *SDA* or the *EOWWA*. The ILO's decent work agenda provides the basis of a framework to achieve this. The task ahead is to identify the central elements of an Australian integrated regulatory framework that could underpin progress to greater gender equality in paid work, including recognition of life outside paid work.[57]

---

53   Cornish, Ending Labour Market Gender Discrimination.

54   See Conaghan et al., *Labour Law in an Era of Globalization*; Fredman, *Human Rights Transformed*; Belinda Smith, 'It's About Time—For a New Approach to Equality' (2008) 36 *Federal Law Review* 117; Vosko, 'Decent Work'; Rikki Holtmaat, *Catalysts for Change? Equality Bodies according to Directive 2000/43/EC*, Directorate-General for Employment, Social Affairs and Equal Opportunities, European Commission, Brussels, 2007.

55   Judy Fudge, 'Equity Bargaining in the New Economy' (2006) 8 *Just Labour* 82.

56   See Rikki Holtmaat, *Towards Different Law and Public Policy: The Significance of Article 5a CEDAW for the Elimination of Structural Gender Discrimination*, Reed Business Information, The Hague, 2004.

57   An existing gender equality policy framework that the government could extend into the domestic policy context is that which underpins the Australian Agency for International Development (AusAID) program (see <http://www.ausaid.gov.au/publications/pdf/gender_policy.pdf>). Gender equality is stated to be 'an overarching principle of Australia's aid program'. This means that 'gender equality is integral to all Australian government aid policies, programs and initiatives'. This policy framework places emphasis on gender equality outcomes including the demonstration of progress towards the improved economic status of women and equal participation in decision making and leadership. In progress towards gender equality, the framework is designed to encourage strategic and well-targeted interventions, which are informed by operating principles such as: engaging with both men and women to advance gender equality; strengthening accountability mechanisms to increase effectiveness; and collecting and analysing information to improve gender equality

Bibliography

Books and articles

Bacchi, Carol, 'The Seesaw Effect: Down Goes Affirmative Action, Up Comes Workplace Diversity' (2000) 5 *Journal of Interdisciplinary Gender Studies* 64.

Bennett, Laura, 'Women and Enterprise Bargaining: The Legal and Institutional Framework' (1994) 36 *Journal of Industrial Relations* 191.

Bosch, Gerhard, 'Towards a New Standard Employment Relationship in Western Europe?' (2004) 42 *British Journal of Industrial Relations* 617.

Braithwaite, Valerie, 'The Australian Government's Affirmative Action Legislation: Achieving Social Change through Human Resource Management' (1993) 15 *Law and Policy* 322.

Buchanan, John and Thornthwaite, Louise, *Paid Work and Parenting: Charting a New Course for Australian Families*, Australian Centre for Industrial Relations Research and Training, Sydney, 2001.

Burgess, John and Strachan, Glenda, 'Equal Employment Opportunity, Employment Restructuring and Enterprise Bargaining: Complementary or Contradictory?' (1998) 3 *Journal of Interdisciplinary Gender Studies* 23.

Burgess, John, Keogh, Paul, Macdonald, Duncan, Morgan, G. H., Strachan, Glenda and Ryan, Suzanne, *Enterprise Bargaining in Three Female Dominated Workplaces in the Hunter*, Employment Studies Research Paper No. 23, University of Newcastle, NSW, 1996.

Burgess, John, Sullivan, Anne and Strachan, Glenda, 'Australian Workplace Agreements, EEO and Family Friendly Arrangements in the Retail Sector' (2004) 4 *Employment Relations Record* 61.

Campbell, Iain, 'Australia: Institutional Changes and Workforce Fragmentation' in Sangheon Lee and Francois Eyraud (eds), *Globalization, Flexibilization and Working Conditions in Asia and the Pacific*, Chandros Publishing, Oxford, 2008.

---

results. Given the clear and unequivocal expectations Australia has of countries that receive Australian aid, it would behove the Australian Government to practice what it preaches within Australia itself. The federal government should insist that gender equality is integral to all Australian Government policies, programs and initiatives within Australia, with the appropriate mechanisms put in place to operationalise this commitment, including in employment regulation and policy.

Campbell, Iain, Whitehouse, Gillian and Baxter, Janine, 'Australia: Casual Employment, Part-time Employment and the Resilience of the Male Breadwinner Model' in Leah Vosko, Martha MacDonald and Iain Campbell (eds), Gender and the Contours of Precarious Employment, Routledge, London, 2009.

Chalmers, Jenny, Campbell, Iain and Charlesworth, Sara, 'Part-Time Work and Caring Responsibilities in Australia: Towards an Assessment of Job Quality' (2005) 15 Labour & Industry 41.

Chapman, Anna, 'Discrimination Complaint-Handling in NSW: The Paradox of Informal Dispute Resolution' (2000) 22 Sydney Law Review 321.

Charlesworth, Sara, Stretching Flexibility: Women and Working Time Arrangements in Enterprise Bargaining, Human Rights and Equal Opportunity Commission, Sydney, 1996.

Charlesworth, Sara, 'The Overlap of the Federal Sex Discrimination and Industrial Relations Jurisdictions: Intersections and Demarcations in Conciliation' (2003) 6 Australian Journal of Labor Economics 559.

Charlesworth, Sara, Hall, Philippa and Probert, Belinda, Drivers and Contexts of Equal Employment Opportunity and Diversity Action in Australian Organisations, RMIT Publishing, Informit E-library, Melbourne, 2005.

Charlesworth, Sara and Macdonald, Fiona, 'The Unpaid Parental Leave Standard: What Standard?', Refereed Proceedings of the 21st Conference of Association of Industrial Relations Academics of Australia and New Zealand, Melbourne, 6–8 February 2008.

Conaghan, Joanne, 'Intersectionality and UK Equality Initiatives' (2007) 23 South African Journal on Human Rights 317.

Conaghan, Joanne, Fischl, Richard and Klare, Karl (eds), Labour Law in an Era of Globalization: Transformative Practices and Possibilities, Oxford University Press, UK, 2004.

Cornish, Mary, 'Closing the Global Gender Pay Gap: Securing Justice for Women's Work' (2007) 28 Comparative Labour Law and Policy Journal 219.

Cornish, Mary, Ending Labour Market Gender Discrimination: Bringing Gender Mainstreaming into Parliamentary Laws and Institutions, Presentation to Women & Work Conference of International Parliamentary Unions, Geneva, 6 December 2007.

Dickens, Linda, 'The Road is Long: Thirty Years of Equality Legislation in Britain' (2007) 45 British Journal of Industrial Relations 463.

French, Erica, 'Approaches to Equity Management and their Relationship to Women in Management' (2001) 12 *British Journal of Management* 267.

French, Erica and Strachan, Glenda, 'Equal Opportunity Outcomes for Women in the Finance Industry in Australia: Evaluating the merit of EEO Plans' (2007) 45 *Asia Pacific Journal of Human Resources* 314.

Fredman, Sandra, *Discrimination Law*, Oxford University Press, UK, 2002.

Fredman, Sandra, 'Changing the Norm: Positive Duties in Equal Treatment Legislation' (2005) 12 *Maastricht Journal of European and Comparative Law* 369.

Fredman, Sandra, *Human Rights Transformed: Positive Duties and Positive Rights*, Oxford University Press, UK, 2008.

Fudge, Judy, 'Equity Bargaining in the New Economy' (2006) 8 *Just Labour* 82.

Fudge, Judy and Owens, Rosemary, *Precarious Work, Women and the New Economy: The Challenge to Legal Norms*, Hart Publishing, Oxford, 2006.

Gaze, Beth, 'The *Sex Discrimination Act* after Twenty Years: Achievements, Disappointments, Disillusionment and Alternatives' (2004) 19 *University of New South Wales Law Journal* 57.

Green, Francis, *Demanding Work: The Paradox of Job Quality in the Affluent Economy*, Princeton University Press, NJ, 2005.

Hall, Philippa and Fruin, Di, 'Gender Aspects of Enterprise Bargaining: The Good, the Bad and the Ugly' in D. E. Morgan (ed.), *Dimensions of Enterprise Bargaining and Organizational Relations*, UNSW Studies in Australian Industrial Relations No. 36, University of New South Wales, Sydney, 1994.

Holtmaat, Rikki, *Towards Different Law and Public Policy: The Significance of Article 5a CEDAW for the Elimination of Structural Gender Discrimination*, Reed Business Information, The Hague, 2004.

Holtmaat, Rikki, *Catalysts for Change? Equality bodies according to Directive 2000/43/EC*, Directorate-General for Employment, Social Affairs and Equal Opportunities, European Commission, Brussels, 2007.

Holtmaat, Rikki and Tober, Christa, 'CEDAW and the European Union's Policy in the Field of Combating Gender Discrimination' (2005) 12 *Maastricht Journal of European and Comparative Law* 399.

Hunter, Rosemary, 'The Mirage of Justice: Women and the Shrinking State' (2002) 16 *Australian Feminist Law Journal* 53.

Hunter, Rosemary and Leonard, Alice, *The Outcomes of Conciliation in Sex Discrimination Cases*, Working Paper No. 8, Centre for Employment and Labour Relations Law, Faculty of Law, University of Melbourne, Vic., 1995.

Klare, Karl, 'The Horizons of Transformative Labour and Employment Law' in Joanne Conaghan, Richard Fischl and Karl Klare (eds), *Labour Law in an Era of Globalization: Transformative Practices and Possibilities*, Oxford University Press, UK, 2004.

Lee, Sangheon, McCann, Deirdre and Messenger, John, *Working Time Around the World: Trends in Working Hours, Laws, and Policies in a Global Comparative Perspective*, Routledge, Oxford, 2004.

Lowe, Graham, *21st Century Job Quality: Achieving What Canadians Want*, Research Report W/37 Work and Learning, Canadian Policy Research Networks, Toronto, Ont, 2007.

McDonald, Paula, Backstrom, Sandra and Dear, Kerriann, 'Reporting Sexual Harassment: Claims and Remedies' (2008) 46 *Asia Pacific Journal of Human Resources* 173.

Murray, Jill, Working Conditions Laws in an Integrating World Project: Australia, Unpublished paper prepared for the International Labour Organisation, Geneva, 2009.

Owens, Rosemary, 'The Peripheral Worker: Women and the Legal Regulation of Outwork' in Margaret Thornton (ed.), *Public and Private: Feminist legal debates*, Oxford University Press, Melbourne, 1995.

Owens, Rosemary, 'Decent Work for the Contingent Workforce in the New Economy' (2002) 15 *Australian Journal of Labour Law* 209.

Peetz, David, 'Collateral Damage: Women and the WorkChoices Battlefield' (2007) 33 *Hecate* 61.

Pocock, Barbara, *The Work–Life Collision: What Work is doing to Australians and what to do about it*, Federation Press, Sydney, 2003.

Pocock, Barbara, Elton, Jude, Preston, Alison, Charlesworth, Sara, Macdonald, Fiona, Baird, Marian, Cooper, Rae and Ellem, Bradon, 'The Impact of "Work Choices" on Women in Low paid Employment in Australia: A Qualitative Analysis' (2008) 50 Journal of Industrial Relations 475.

Preston, Alison and Jefferson, Therese, 'Trends in Australia's Gender Wage Ratio' (2007) 18 *Journal of Labour and Industry* 69.

Preston, Alison and Whitehouse, Gillian, 'Gender Differences in Occupation of Employment within Australia' (2004) 7 *Australian Journal of Labour Economics* 309.

Scheele, Alexandra, 'Gender and the Quality of Work: An Overview of European and National Approaches' (2007) 13 *Transfer* 595.

Sheridan, Alison, 'Affirmative Action in Australia – Employment Statistics can't tell the Whole Story' (1995) 10 *Women in Management Review* 26.

Smith, Belinda, 'From Wardley to Purvis—How Far has Australian Anti-Discrimination Law come in 30 Years?' (2007) 21 *Australian Journal of Labour Law*.

Smith, Belinda, 'It's About Time—For a New Approach to Equality' (2008) 36 *Federal Law Review* 117.

Smith, Mark, Burchell, Brendan, Fagan, Colette and O'Brien, Catherine, 'Job Quality in Europe' (2008) 39 *Industrial Relations Journal* 586.

Smith, Meg and Ewer, Peter, *The Position of Women in the National Training Reform Agenda and Enterprise Bargaining*, Department of Education, Employment and Training, Australian Government Printing Service, Canberra, 1995.

Smith, Meg and Lyons, Michael, '2020 Vision or 1920s Myopia? Recent Developments in Gender Pay Equity in Australia' (2007) 13 *International Employment Relations Review* 27.

Strachan, Glenda and Burgess, John, 'W(h)ither Affirmative Action Legislation in Australia?' (2000) 5 *Journal of Interdisciplinary Gender Studies* 46.

Strachan, Glenda and French, Erica, 'Equal Opportunity: Disentangling Promise from Achievement', *Proceedings of the Gender, Work and Organisation: 5th Biennial International Interdisciplinary Conference*, Keele University, UK, 2007.

Thornton, Margaret, *The Liberal Promise: Anti-Discrimination Legislation in Australia*, Oxford University Press, UK, 1990.

Thornton, Margaret, 'Auditing the *Sex Discrimination Act*' in Marius Smith (ed.), *Human Rights 2004: The Year in Review*, Castan Centre for Human Rights Law, Monash University, Melbourne, 2005.

Vosko, Leah, '"Decent Work": The Shifting Role of the ILO and the Struggle for Global Social Justice' (2002) 2 *Global Social Policy* 19.

Vosko, Leah, Precarious Employment and the Problem of SER-Centrism: Regulating for "Decent Work"', Paper given to the Regulating for Decent Work—Innovative labour regulation in a turbulent world Conference, International Labour Organisation, Geneva, 8 July 2009.

Walby, Sylvia, *Gender (In)Equality and the Future of Work*, Equal Opportunities Commission, Manchester, 2007.

Whitehouse, Gillian, 'Recent Trends in Pay Equity: Beyond the Aggregate Statistics' (2001) 43 *Journal of Industrial Relations* 66.

Legislation

Fair Work Act 2009 (Cth)

Industrial Relations Reform Act 1993 (Cth)

Sex Discrimination Act 1984 (Cth)

Workplace Relations Act 1996 (Cth)

Case

Australian Industrial Relations Commission, *Award Modernisation—Statement*, 12 September, 2008, [2008] AIRCFB 717, Giudice J, Lawler VP, Watson VP, Watson SDP, Harrison SDP, Acton SDP and Smith C., <http://www.fwa.gov.au/decisionssigned/html/2008aircfb717.htm>

Reports and miscellaneous primary sources

Australian Bureau of Statistics, *Australian Labour Market Statistics, July 2009*, Cat. No. 6105, Australian Bureau of Statistics, Canberra, 2009.

European Commission, *Employment in Europe 2008*, European Communities, Luxembourg, 2008.

House of Representatives Standing Committee on Employment and Workplace Relations, *Making it Fair: Pay Equity and Associated Issues related to increasing Female Participation in the Workforce*, Commonwealth of Australia, Canberra, 2009.

Human Rights and Equal Opportunity Commission, *Annual Report 2007–2008*, Human Rights and Equal Opportunity Commission, Sydney, 2008.

Human Rights and Equal Opportunity Commission, *Sexual Harassment: Serious Business.Results of the 2008 Sexual Harassment National Telephone Survey*, Human Rights and Equal Opportunity Commission, Sydney, 2008.

International Labour Organisation, *Decent Work: A Report of the Director-General*, 89th Session of the International Labour Organisation, Geneva, 1999.

International Labour Organisation, *ABC of Women Workers' Rights and Gender Equality*, Second edition, International Labour Organisation, Geneva, 2007.

KPMG, *Review of the* Equal Opportunity for Women in the Workplace Act 1999: *Consultation Report*, KPMG, Melbourne, 2010.

Senate Standing Committee on Legal and Constitutional Affairs, *Report on the Effectiveness of the Commonwealth* Sex Discrimination Act 1984 *in Eliminating Discrimination and Promoting Gender Equality*, Parliament of Australia, Canberra, 2008.

7. Reproducing Discrimination: Promoting the Equal Sharing of Caring Work in CEDAW, at the ILO and in the *SDA*

Caroline Lambert[1]

This chapter is interested in caring work and the impact of reproductive labour on the realisation of substantive equality for women. It will examine the unique approach of the Convention on the Elimination of All Forms of Discrimination Against Women (CEDAW) to reproductive labour and the conjunction of reproductive and productive labour, as well as considering germane International Labour Organisation (ILO) conventions on workers with family responsibilities. Drawing on CEDAW and the ILO, the chapter will put forward a pentamerous schema of obligations that should be realised in Australia and examine the extent to which the Sex Discrimination Act *(SDA) achieves these obligations—in particular, the terms and conditions that reflect the needs of workers with family responsibilities in the context of the* SDA.

Introduction

The profile of Australian workplaces has changed significantly in recent years as more women have entered the workforce and more women, and some men, have sought workplaces that better respond to their combined roles as workers and carers of family members.[2] How has the *Sex Discrimination Act 1984* (Cth) (*SDA*) responded to caring work (commonly practised by women) and to what extent does the *SDA* reflect the international labour and human rights obligations that relate to this issue?

---

1   This chapter draws on an essay submitted as part of a graduate diploma in international law from the University of Melbourne and my doctoral thesis, also from the University of Melbourne.
2   Sara Charlesworth, 'Managing Work and Family in the "Shadow" of Anti-Discrimination Law' (2005) 23 *Law in Context* 88; Barbara Pocock, *The Work–Life Collision: What Work is doing to Australians and what to do about it*, Federation Press, Sydney, 2003; Don Edgar, *The War Over Work: The Future of Work and Family*, Melbourne University Press, Carlton, 2005.

This chapter is limited to a discussion of the *SDA*. I note nonetheless that anti-discrimination law is but one aspect of a broader range of legal and policy responses to the needs of workers with family responsibilities. I particularly note that the industrial relations framework, which has been central to the development of terms and conditions supportive of workers with family responsibilities,[3] falls beyond the purview of this chapter. Likewise, while international legal obligations apply to all jurisdictions—federal, State and Territory—this chapter focuses solely on the provisions of the *SDA*.

Fundamental to my analysis of the efficacy of the *SDA* in responding to caring work is an engagement with the figures of the 'ideal worker' and the 'domestic care giver'[4] in liberal legal and economic theory. Charlesworth argues that workplaces 'continue to be based on the presumption of an "ideal worker" with few domestic responsibilities, full-time work and little or no time off to care for family'.[5] The assumption of course is that the ideal worker has a corollary in the private sphere: the 'full-time carer engaged in family work of housework and childcare, whose unpaid work subsidises the paid work of the ideal worker'.[6] This dichotomy is inherently gendered, with men taking on the ideal worker role and women the domestic caregiver role—the 'mummy track'.[7]

Moreover, while the imperative of economic growth depends on maximising productive labour (which increasingly necessitates harnessing women's labour as well as men's), women who are conscripted to the productive labour market still retain their reproductive labour obligations. Pocock has suggested that while the increased labour force participation by women found a 'happy co-conspirator in a market greedy for women's labour…and enthusiastic for the spending power of women's earnings', the market and other social and political institutions were far less responsive to changing the structure and valuation of productive and reproductive labour.[8] Equally, women's labour force attachment has also been affected by pregnancy-based discrimination and maternity-based discrimination. Despite the existence of social-liberal frameworks to outlaw maternity-based discrimination and pregnancy-based discrimination, they have remained a significant part of many women's productive labour

---

3   For a discussion of the industrial relations system, see: Steve O'Neill, *Work and Family Policies as Industrial and Employment Entitlements*, Parliamentary Library, Canberra, 2004; Human Rights and Equal Opportunity Commission, *Striking the Balance: Women, Men, Work and Family*, Discussion Paper, Human Rights and Equal Opportunity Commission, Canberra, 2005, p. 3.

4   Joan Williams, *Unbending Gender: Why Work and Family Conflict and What to do About it*, Oxford University Press, UK, 2000 (cited in Charlesworth, 'Managing Work and Family in the "Shadow" of Anti-Discrimination Law' 96).

5   Ibid.

6   Joanne Conaghan, 'Women, Work and Family: A British Revolution?' in Joanne Conaghan, Michael Fisch and Karl Klare (eds), *Women, Work and Family: A British Revolution?*, Oxford University Press, UK, 2004 (cited in Charlesworth, 'Managing Work and Family in the "Shadow" of Anti-Discrimination Law').

7   Human Rights and Equal Opportunity Commission, *Striking the Balance*, p. 57.

8   Pocock, *The Work–Life Collision*, p. 8.

experiences, particularly in the private-market sphere. For example, 'business case' arguments have been accepted by courts as a legitimate rationale for maternity-based discrimination, particularly in the context of flexible work arrangements for women with childcare responsibilities (even if they are short-term responsibilities).[9]

In the first section of this chapter, I will establish the nature of obligations that inhere in the relevant international treaties. I argue that five elements can be discerned in our international legal obligations. These constitute a framework for assessing whether the *SDA* contributes to the realisation of our international legal obligations with respect to workers with family responsibilities. In particular, I will examine the terms and conditions that reflect the needs of workers with family responsibilities in the context of the *SDA*.

International Legal Framework

The focus of this section of the chapter is to inquire into the international legal approach to workers with family responsibilities. Three key treaties are analysed: CEDAW, the Maternity Leave Convention and the Workers with Family Responsibilities Convention.

Women's Labour

Rights associated with women's labour are articulated in a range of international instruments, within the UN system and also by the ILO.[10] With the exception of CEDAW and the ILO Convention on Workers with Family Responsibilities, the standards relating to women's labour have typically encompassed productive work. In considering women's experiences of productive work, international legal instruments have addressed a range of non-discrimination issues, including pay equity and conditions at work. The focus on conditions at work has provided

---

9 For example, Margaret Thornton, 'Feminism and the Changing State: The Case of Sex Discrimination (2006) 21 *Australian Feminist Studies* 158.

10 The ILO identifies the 'key gender equality conventions' to be the International Labour Organisation Equal Remuneration Convention (Number 100) (adopted 29 June 1951, ILO Document Number C100, entered into force 23 May 1953), the International Labour Organisation Discrimination Convention (Employment and Occupation) (Number 111) (adopted 25 June 1958, ILO Document Number C111, entered into force 15 June 1960), the International Labour Organisation Workers with Family Responsibilities Convention (Number 156) (adopted 23 June 1981, ILO Document Number C156, entered into force 11 August 1983) and the International Labour Organisation Maternity Protection Convention (Number 183) (adopted 15 June 2000, ILO Document Number C183, entered into force 7 February 2002) (International Labour Organisation, *Women's Employment: Global Trends and ILO Responses*, 49th Session of the Commission on the Status of Women, United Nations, New York, 2005, p. 23). CEDAW, as will be discussed, addresses the issues, as does the International Covenant on Economic, Social and Cultural Rights (ICESCR). For a review and critique of these documents, see: Valerie Oosterveld, 'Women and Employment' in Kelly Askin and Doreen Koenig (eds), *Women and International Human Rights Law*, Transnational, Ardsley, NY, 1999.

the entry point for consideration of reproductive labour issues, particularly discrimination on the basis of pregnancy or maternal responsibilities. The best-known example is the ILO Maternity Leave Convention.[11] The Convention asserts that provision for protection of pregnancy is a shared responsibility of government and society and applies to all women workers (though the definition is limited to those workers with a contractual relationship with an employer, thus excluding self-employed women or women working in family enterprises). The Convention establishes a period of not less than 14 weeks' maternity leave,[12] including a six-week compulsory minimum period of leave after the birth,[13] and provides that cash benefits, optimally provided through a compulsory social insurance scheme or public funds, should be available.[14] In instances where the cash benefits are based on previous earnings, they should not be less than two-thirds of the woman's previous earnings.[15] The Convention also provides that women returning from maternity leave are guaranteed their previous job or an equivalent position at the same rate of pay.[16] Finally, the Convention provides for breastfeeding breaks for mothers who have returned to work.[17]

Most international legal instruments have, however, struggled to articulate a notion of individual rights or state responsibilities at the point at which reproductive labour obligations have constituted an opportunity cost and have removed (predominantly) women from the productive labour sphere. The opportunity cost extends beyond lost contributions to the productive labour sphere into the loss of women from community building, leadership and political participation. The result has been that reproductive work, where there has been no intersection with the productive labour sphere, has been largely ignored by mainstream UN or ILO treaties.

A striking example of this is the general comment on work issued by the International Covenant on Economic, Social and Cultural Rights (ICESCR) Committee.[18] While it contains an excellent analysis of the role of governments and private sphere actors in ensuring workers' rights in both the public and private spheres, it does not address the issue of unpaid work (with the exception of gender-neutral discussions of forced labour). The recognition accorded to reproductive labour discrimination is confined to the context of paid labour.

---

11   The first convention on maternity was adopted by the ILO in 1919 (Convention 3), which was revised in 1952 by Convention 103, and revised again in 2000 (Convention 183).

12   Convention 183, Art. 4(1).

13   Ibid., Art. 4(4).

14   Ibid., Art. 6(8). A subsequent article introduces a progressive realisation component for economies that are insufficiently developed to support such a scheme (at Art. 7).

15   Ibid., Art. 6(3).

16   Ibid., Art. 8(2).

17   Ibid., Art. 10.

18   For example, Committee on Economic, Social and Cultural Rights, *General Comment 16, Art 3: The Equal Right of Men and Women to the Enjoyment of All Economic, Social and Cultural Rights*, UN Doc E/C 12/2005/3 (2005) (General Comment 16), para. 4.

Even this approach is limited: the general comment focuses on pregnancy-based discrimination. It ignores issues of maternity-based discrimination and eschews a discussion of family-friendly working practices.[19]

In contrast, the CEDAW Committee has consistently addressed productive and reproductive labour in its General Recommendations and in its Concluding Comments (CCs). Most strikingly, the recognition accorded to women's reproductive work by the CEDAW Committee has been unique. Underpinning the conceptualisation of reproductive and productive labour by the CEDAW Committee is their understanding of gender-based stereotypes and the obligation, established at Article 5, to reconfigure gender relations and to challenge gender-based stereotypes.[20] In order to understand the conceptualisation of reproductive and productive labour by the CEDAW Committee, I analysed recent CCs and the relevant General Recommendations.[21] I discerned three themes: views on productive labour; views on the intersection of productive labour and reproductive labour; and views on reproductive labour. In this chapter, I shall focus my analysis on the second two themes.

The Intersection of Productive Labour with Reproductive Labour

Women's participation in the productive labour force can be significantly affected by two key reproductive labour functions: pregnancy and reproductive labour responsibilities. The relevant provisions of CEDAW include the prohibition of pregnancy-based discrimination,[22] temporary special measures to protect maternity,[23] occupational health and safety provisions related to pregnancy and maternity,[24] education to increase understanding of maternity as a social function[25] and support for services that enable parents to combine family obligations.[26]

---

19 3D, *The Committee on Economic, Social and Cultural Rights: A Compilation of Trade-Related Issues*, 3D, Geneva, 2006, para. 13.

20 Committee on the Elimination of All Forms of Discrimination Against Women, *General Recommendation Number 25, on Art 4, Paragraph 1, of the Convention on the Elimination of All Forms of Discrimination Against Women, on Temporary Special Measures*, UN Doc. A/59/38, 2004 ['*CEDAW General Recommendation 25*'], paragraph 7.

21 Based on a review of reports available online (<www.bayefsky.com>), which examined the thematic analysis prepared on 'Work—Equality in the Workplace', 'Pregnancy and Maternity', 'Work—Working Conditions', and 'Work—Right to Work'.

22 Convention on the Elimination of All Forms of Discrimination Against Women, opened for signature 18 December 1979, General Assembly Resolution 34/108; UN General Assembly Official Records, 34th Session, Supplement No. 46, Art. 5(b) (entered into force 3 September 1981), Art. 11.2.a.

23 Ibid., Art. 4.2.

24 Ibid., Art. 11.1.f.

25 Ibid., Art. 5.b.

26 Ibid., Art. 11.2.c.

In focusing on the intersection of productive labour with reproductive labour, CEDAW shares some ground with the ILO Convention on Workers with Family Responsibilities in that both treaties call for governments to be more supportive of workers looking after children and immediate family members. Recommended measures include the adoption of anti-discrimination frameworks (specifically to outlaw pregnancy-based and maternity-based discrmination), education programs and childcare and family services.[27]

Reproductive Labour

The CEDAW Committee has addressed reproductive labour as a stand-alone issue in two key ways: by challenging gendered assumptions about reproductive labour and through an examination of unremunerated reproductive labour in the private sphere. The latter approach in particular has assessed the opportunity costs to women (and the small number of men) who engage in unremunerated reproductive labour.

The CEDAW Committee has articulated a more theorised approach to reproductive labour than the ILO, challenging the social values ascribed to caring labour. For example, the general recommendation on equality in marriage and family relations draws attention to the different value and regulation ascribed to human activities in the public and private spheres. The recommendation acknowledges the lesser value attached to women's labour: 'In all societies women who have traditionally performed their roles in the private or domestic sphere have long had those activities treated as inferior.'[28] The CEDAW Committee has challenged the discriminatory nature of such a practice, pointing to the necessity of these forms of labour as a means for the 'survival of society'.[29]

The value of women's reproductive labour has also been raised in the dissenting opinion of CEDAW Committee members, Morvai and Belmihoub-Zerdani, in relation to a complaint submitted under the Optional Protocol to CEDAW. In the complaint, a German woman, Mrs B.-J., disputed the terms of her divorce settlement. Mrs B.-J. was divorced by her husband after 30 years of marriage. She argued that the courts failed to mandate an adequate level of maintenance. She referred to the couple's decision that she would stay at home to raise their children, her husband's resistance to her retraining and her consequent absence from the labour market and the concomitant difficulties she had in finding work subsequent to the divorce. While the majority view of the CEDAW Committee

---

27 See ILO Workers with Family Responsibilities Convention, Articles 1, 2, 3, 4, 5 and 6. See CEDAW, Articles 2, 3 and 11.2.

28 CEDAW Committee 1994, *General Recommendation 21, on Equality in Marriage and Family Relations*, UN Document Number A/49/38 at 1, paragraph 11.

29 Ibid., para. 12.

found the complaint inadmissible—largely on technical grounds—Morvai and Belmihoub-Zerdani argued that Mrs B.-J.'s husband had 'successfully capitalised the 30 years of unremunerated work of the author', and that a different level of maintenance was mandated.[30] In effect, Morvai and Belmihoub-Zerdani sought to quantify and differently value Mrs B.-J.'s reproductive labour.

The second way the CEDAW Committee has developed an understanding of reproductive labour is in its reflections on the contours of unremunerated reproductive labour. In particular, the CEDAW Committee has considered the impact of women's unremunerated reproductive labour on women's participation in a range of public and private sphere activities. For example, one general recommendation examines the issue of unpaid women workers in rural and urban family enterprises. It identifies that by working—unpaid—in family enterprises, women are not only being denied a wage (which constitutes a form of exploitation contrary to CEDAW), they are also being denied access to social security and benefits.[31] Another General Recommendation grapples with the issue of unremunerated work and the failure of governments to address the issue in their reports. It argues that 'the measurement and quantification of the unremunerated domestic activities of women, which contribute to development in each country, will help to reveal the de facto economic role of women'.[32] This General Recommendation builds on politically negotiated agreements adopted at world conferences on women. The CEDAW Committee has affirmed this approach in a series of CCs.[33]

The CEDAW Committee's understanding of unremunerated reproductive labour has also extended to an analysis of the impacts on women's capacity to contribute to other private and public sphere activities. A recommendation on women in political and public life analyses the impact that reproductive labour has on women's political and public participation:

> [I]n all nations, the most significant factors inhibiting women's ability to participate in public life have been the cultural framework of values and

---

30   CEDAW Committee, *Report of the Committee on the Elimination of All Forms of Discrimination Against Women, Decision of the Committee on the Elimination of All Forms of Discrimination Against Women, Declaring a Communication Inadmissible under the Optional Protocol to CEDAW, Communication Number 1/2003, Ms B-J V Germany*.

31   CEDAW Committee, *General Recommendation 16, on Unpaid Women Workers in Rural and Urban Family Enterprises*, UN Document Number A/46/38, 1, United Nations, New York, 1991.

32   CEDAW Committee, *General Recommendation 17, on Measurement and Quantification of the Unremunerated Domestic Activities of Women and Their Recognition in the Gross National Product*, UN Document Number A/46/38 at 2, United Nations, New York, 1993.

33   CEDAW Committee (*Report of the Committee on the Elimination of All Forms of Discrimination Against Women, 28th and 29th Sessions*) discussing the reports received from Ukraine (at para. 294), the Czech Republic (at para. 100), Hungary (at para. 328), Albania (at para. 75), Switzerland (at para. 131), Norway (at para. 430), Slovenia (at para. 213), Japan (at para. 370), Estonia (at para. 107).

religious beliefs, the lack of services and men's failure to share the tasks associated with the organization of the household and with the care and raising of children.[34]

The recommendation argues that 'relieving women of some of the burdens of domestic work would allow them to engage more fully in the life of their community'.[35] It also notes that the economic dependence wrought by this arrangement, in addition to women's double burden of productive and reproductive work, diminishes their political independence and their capacity to fully engage in public life. The recommendation challenges the work cultures associated with public and political work, which, it asserts, manifest in long or inflexible hours. It argues that these factors also inhibit the capacity of women to contribute effectively in public and political work.[36]

International Framework to Reconcile Work–Family Responsibilities

Taken together, these conventions provide state parties with a comprehensive range of actions that should be taken to enable workers to reconcile work–family responsibilities—specifically

- prohibition of pregnancy-based discrimination in preparing for work, entering into work, participating in work and advancing at work (CEDAW and ILO Maternity Leave Convention)

- provision of paid maternity leave, for a period not less than 14 weeks, with a minimum period of six weeks (CEDAW and ILO Maternity Leave Convention for provision of paid maternity leave; ILO Maternity Leave Convention for time frame)

- terms and conditions that reflect the needs of workers with family responsibilities, including the prohibition of maternity-based discrimination (CEDAW, ILO Maternity Leave Convention [breastfeeding breaks], ILO Workers with Family Responsibilities Convention) and prohibition of family responsibilities being grounds for dismissal (ILO Workers with Family Responsibilities Convention and CEDAW)

- the promotion, development or provision of child and family care by public or private means (CEDAW and ILO Workers with Family Responsibilities Convention)

---

34   CEDAW Committee, *General Recommendation 23, on Women in Political and Public Life*, UN Document Number A/52/38/Rev 1, 61, United Nations, New York, 1997, para. 10.

35   Ibid., para. 11.

36   Ibid.

- education to challenge social, economic and cultural values on family responsibilities and the function of maternity (CEDAW and ILO Workers with Family Responsibilities Convention).

In the remainder of this chapter, I will discuss the positive and negative impacts of the *SDA* on the terms and conditions that reflect the needs of workers with family responsibilities.

Terms and Conditions that Reflect the Needs of Workers with Family Responsibilities

Legislative protection of workers with family responsibilities from discrimination has been implemented in various jurisdictions.[37] At a federal level, Article 8 of the ILO Workers with Family Responsibilities Convention, which provides that family responsibilities shall not constitute a valid reason for termination of employment,[38] was used as a basis for amending the *SDA* to incorporate limited protection for workers with family responsibilities. The legislative provision for terms and conditions that reflect the needs of workers with family responsibilities—in particular, the role of anti-discrimination law— is contentious. Employer groups argue that it is inappropriate to further expand anti-discrimination law to provide remedy for a failure to provide flexible workplace terms and conditions.[39]

The ILO Workers with Family Responsibilities Convention does not, however, simply seek to address termination of employment but seeks to obligate state parties to promote laws and policies across a range of workplace behaviours. Likewise, while operating from a paradigm of discrimination against women, CEDAW seeks to alter the 'understanding of maternity as a social function' and to foster 'recognition of the common responsibilities of men and women in the upbringing and development of their children'.[40] To this end, State and Territory legislation provides greater implementation of international legal obligations

---

37   In New South Wales, discrimination is on the basis of status as a carer; in Victoria, status as a parent or a carer; in Queensland, family responsibilities; in Western Australia, family responsibilities and family status; in Tasmania, family responsibilities; in the Australian Capital Territory, status as a parent or carer; and in the Northern Territory, parenthood. South Australia does not have provisions addressing this issue. State/ territory-based legislation is generally broader than the federal provisions, which are restricted to termination of employment.
38   ILO, Workers with Family Responsibilities Convention, Art. 8.
39   See, for example: Victorian Automobile Chamber of Commerce, Submission to the Human Rights and Equal Opportunity Commission, Striking the Balance: Women, Men, Work and Family, 2005, p. 3; Australian Industry Group, Submission: HREOC Inquiry into Paid Work and Family, 2005, p. 5; Peter Anderson, 'The *Sex Discrimination Act*: An Employer Perspective—Twenty Years On' (2004) 27 *University of New South Wales Law Journal* 905.
40   CEDAW, Art. 5.

than federal legislation, which is restricted to termination of employment. There was intent at the time that this provision be extended further in the future,[41] and the Senate Legal and Constitutional Inquiry into the efficacy of the *SDA* called for the provisions to be expanded.[42] The Rudd Government enacted legislation guaranteeing paid parental leave in 2010.[43]

While it is clear that, in a de jure sense, the *SDA* now meets the obligation to protect workers with family responsibilities from termination of employment by virtue of their family responsibilities, two questions remain. The first is whether the broader provisions on family responsibilities at the international level have been implemented, and the second is whether the judicial interpretation of the de jure provisions contributes to the de facto realisation of the obligations. In the discussion that follows, I will discuss three key issues that arise as limitations to anti-discrimination law

- the challenges of the comparator and causation in the *SDA*

- the limitations of indirect discrimination, including the reasonableness test

- the model of equality pursued.

Challenges Associated with the Comparator and Causation in the *SD* Family Responsibilities Provisions

The *SDA* (ss 7A and 14[3A]) establishes that it is discriminatory behaviour if an employer dismisses an employee with family responsibilities because of their real family responsibilities or because of characteristics that generally appertain to or are imputed to people with family responsibilities. The scope of family responsibilities is defined in Sections 4 and 4A and relates to the responsibility to 'care for or support a dependent child or immediate family member, being a spouse, adult child, parent, grandparent, grandchild or sibling of the employee or of a spouse of the employee'.[44] The Human Rights and Equal Opportunity Commission notes that the definition of a de facto spouse is limited to heterosexual relationships.[45] The judiciary has incorporated constructive dismissal into its understanding of termination of employment, which has enabled its application to a broader range of facts.[46]

---

41   John Von Doussa and Craig Lenehan, 'Barbequed or Burned? Flexibility in Work Arrangements and the *Sex Discrimination Act*' (2004) 27 *University of New South Wales Law Journal* 892, 896.
42   Senate Standing Committee on Legal and Constitutional Affairs, *Report on the Effectiveness of the Commonwealth* Sex Discrimination Act 1984 *in Eliminating Discrimination and Promoting Gender Equality*, Parliament of Australia, Canberra, 2008, Recommendations 13 and 14; see also Recommendation 30.
43   *Paid Parental Leave Act 2010* (Cth).
44   Human Rights and Equal Opportunity Commission, *Striking the Balance*, p. 83.
45   Ibid.; Von Doussa and Lenehan, 'Barbequed or Burned?' 901–3.
46   Human Rights and Equal Opportunity Commission, *Striking the Balance*, p. 85.

The case law arising from Sections 7A and 14(3A) has proved controversial for the reasoning associated with identifying the comparator group and factors of causation.[47] Within the context of the comparator, the dominance of the 'ideal worker' model has stymied decision makers. Direct discrimination requires that a comparison be made between the complainant and a 'straw group', proving that the complainant would be treated less favourably than the comparator because of family responsibilities. The difficulty has arisen in the identification of the comparator group. In *Song v Ainsworth Game Technology Group Pty Ltd*, Raphael FM found that the applicant had been constructively dismissed by reason of direct discrimination on the grounds of family responsibilities.[48] The applicant was of the view that she had negotiated an arrangement with her employer to leave work between 2.55 pm and 3.15 pm each day to move her son between kindergarten and child care. Her employer disputed the fact that she had negotiated an arrangement and directed her to work the hours as stipulated in her contract: 9 am to 5 pm with a lunchbreak from 12–12.30 pm. The applicant refused and continued to leave work between 2.55pm and 3.15pm. As a result, the employer determined that her status moved from full-time to part-time and her hours were reduced from 9 am to 3 pm, with a half-hour lunchbreak.[49] Von Doussa and Lenehan argue that, 'although not entirely clear', it seems that Raphael FM found that the comparator group included such groups of people as 'employees who need to leave the workplace to smoke or were allowed flexibility in their work hours for other reasons'.[50]

In a second case, *Evans v National Crime Authority*,[51] the applicant was the primary carer for her toddler child—a responsibility that sometimes necessitated her taking leave. She did so within the parameters of her employment agreement. Her manager was dissatisfied with her use of annual leave, carer's leave and sick leave and was reported to say that if he had known she had childcare responsibilities he would not have employed her. The manager's dissatisfaction was manifested in a poor performance review and shortened contract extensions.[52] Raphael FM found that the applicant had been constructively dismissed on the basis of both sex and family responsibilities.[53] Von Doussa and Lenehan argue that Driver FM (this should be Raphael FM) 'correctly identified the comparator as being an employee who took leave within her or his entitlements for reasons unrelated to family responsibilities'.[54]

---

47 Von Doussa and Lenehan, 'Barbequed or Burned?'.
48 *Song v Ainsworth Game Technology Pty Ltd* (2002) FMCA 31 (*Song*) [76].
49 Ibid.
50 Von Doussa and Lenehan, 'Barbequed or Burned?' 898.
51 *Evans v National Crime Authority* (2003) FMCA 375 (*Evans*).
52 Ibid., [88], [93].
53 Ibid., [106]–[108].
54 Von Doussa and Lenehan, 'Barbequed or Burned?' 898.

Two issues arise. First, Von Dousa and Lenehan argue that the logic in Raphael's finding of the comparator was undermined by his acknowledgment that the respondent had a negative attitude to part-time work of any variety, regardless of motivation. Given the test established for assessment of disadvantage, it is open to suggest that the respondent would have rejected a request for part-time work from any employee.[55] Von Doussa and Lenehan argue that the approach taken by Raphael (not Driver) is more satisfactory and, subject to caveats, could provide the basis for working fathers to challenge refusal to countenance part-time work.[56] The second issue relates to Raphael FM's seeming identification of the comparator group as including those who require flexible work arrangements to accommodate smoking. The issue arose because it appears the company had a policy of allowing workers to take 20-minute smoking breaks. Thus, in identifying comparator groups within the workplace, it was open to Raphael FM to draw on such a group. Nonetheless, the identification of this group as a comparator points to the challenges of the comparator requirement. The family responsibilities provisions seek to address endemic and structural discrimination against a particular group of people in our community, who—workforce participation figures suggest—are regularly discriminated against in the context of full-time employment.[57] The comparator element requires that this level of discrimination be assessed against an alternative group, smokers, who do not seem to experience the same level of discrimination in seeking full-time employment, though they are increasingly being required to smoke further and further away from their desks.

Finally, and briefly, Von Doussa and Lenehan argue, citing Song and Escobar,[58] that case law has demonstrated challenges associated with the concept of causation in family responsibility claims. They suggest that there is very often a lack of clarity around refusals to envisage flexible work practices and that this could pose 'difficulties in the terms of causation'.[59]

Limitations of Indirect Discrimination

Given the limitations inherent in the restriction of family responsibilities provisions to direct discrimination,[60] the Human Rights and Equal Opportunity Commission notes that

---

55 Ibid., 899.
56 Ibid., 900.
57 Pocock, *The Work–Life Collision*, p. 34.
58 In this case, an employee was found to have been discriminated against on the basis of family responsibilities and sex when she sought to return to work part-time at the conclusion of her maternity leave, was denied and had her employment terminated. *Escobar v Rainbow Printing Pty Ltd (No. 2)* (2002) FMCA 122 (*Escobar*) [36].
59 Von Doussa and Lenehan, 'Barbequed or Burned?' 900.
60 Human Rights and Equal Opportunity Commission, *Striking the Balance*, p. 83.

rather than relying on the limited family responsibilities provisions, many women complainants are using the sex and pregnancy discrimination provisions of the SDA to pursue allegations of workplace failure to accommodate family responsibilities. In particular, the indirect sex and pregnancy discrimination provisions of the SDA have proved useful to complainants.[61]

Sections 5(2) and 7(B1) are the relevant provisions in the *SDA*, defining indirect discrimination and the reasonableness test, respectively. Several cases are germane:[62]*Hickie v Hunt and Hunt,*[63]*Mayer v Australian Nuclear Science and Technology Organisation,*[64]*Escobar v Rainbow Printing Pty Ltd,*[65]*Howe v Qantas Airways Ltd*[66] and *Kelly v TPG Internet Pty Ltd.*[67] These cases have explored the principle that women returning to work after maternity leave should be able to negotiate flexible terms that enable them to maintain a workforce attachment and meet family care responsibilities. A central component of the cases has been the judicial notice that far more women than men seek part-time work to enable them to care for young children. Thus, in *Hickie*, refusal to provide for part-time work arrangements constituted indirect discrimination on the basis of sex.[68] In *Hickie*, Commissioner Evatt asserted that it was 'general knowledge that women are far more likely than men to require at least some periods of part-time work during their career, and in particular a period of part-time work after maternity leave in order to meet family responsibilities'.[69]

This statement has become the authoritative articulation of the issue. In *Mayer*, Driver FM drew on *Hickie* in finding that the applicant had experienced indirect sex discrimination on the basis that she was denied available part-time work, which would have enabled her to reconcile work and family responsibilities.[70] In *Howe*, however, a more limited approach was taken. While Driver FM found that the respondent had subjected the applicant to pregnancy-based discrimination in failing to allow her to access sick leave when pregnancy stopped her from

---

61   Ibid., p. 85.
62   Given the focus of this chapter on federal anti-discrimination law, several relevant cases from State/Territory jurisdictions have been excluded from discussion. The most important of these relate to the litigation of Ms Schou against the State of Victoria. For excellent articles on the issues raised and implications, please see: Therese MacDermott and Rosemary Owens, 'Recent Cases: Equality and Flexibility for Workers with Family Responsibilities: A Troubled Union?' (2000) 13 *Australian Journal of Labour Law* 20; Beth Gaze, 'Context and Interpretation in Anti-Discrimination Law' (2002) 26 *Melbourne University Law Review* 325; Fiona Knowles, 'Misdirection for Indirect Discrimination' (2004) 17 *Australian Journal of Labour Law* 1; Margaret Thornton, 'Feminism and the Changing State' (2006) 21 *Australian Feminist Studies* 151.
63   *Hickie v Hunt & Hunt* [1998] HREOCA 8 (*Hickie*).
64   *Mayer v Australian Nuclear Science and Technology Organisation* (2003) FMCA 209 (*Mayer*).
65   *Escobar*.
66   *Howe v Qantas Airways Lt*, (2004) FMCA 242 (*Howe*).
67   *Kelly v TPG Internet Pty Ltd* (2003) FMCA 584 (*Kelly*).
68   *Hickie* [6.17.12].
69   Ibid. [6.17.10].
70   *Mayer* [75].

flying, he dismissed the claim that the respondent's refusal to provide the applicant part-time work at the previous level constituted constructive dismissal on the grounds of indirect sex discrimination.[71] Nonetheless, he did assert that

> family responsibilities is not necessarily a characteristic appertaining generally to women. The point is that the present state of Australian society shows that women are the dominant caregivers to young children. While that position remains (and it may well change over time) s5(2) of the SDA operates to protect women against indirect sex discrimination in the performance of that care giving role.[72]

Nonetheless, as shall be discussed below, Driver FM still dismissed the application for indirect discrimination on the basis that the respondent did not impose a condition of full-time work and was unable to offer part-time work at the previous level because of conditions established in the enterprise bargaining agreement.[73] In *Kelly*, Raphael FM argued that a part-time return to work after maternity leave was a benefit rather than a condition or requirement.[74] This judgment has been distinguished subsequently by Driver FM in *Howe* and caution has been expressed by lawyers and academic publications as to its veracity.[75] The question of whether the *SDA* provides for a part-time return to work from maternity leave on the basis of family responsibilities remains unresolved.

Finally, recourse to the claim of indirect discrimination necessitates engagement with the reasonableness test. Von Doussa and Lenehan suggest that the reasonableness test has constituted a less significant barrier at the federal level than State levels.[76] At the federal level, *Mayer* upheld the validity of business needs in the reasonableness test, as, to a certain extent, did *Howe*.[77] Nonetheless, the significant detriment that the reasonableness test has caused in the *Schou* cases in Victoria suggests quite major limitations to the anti-discrimination framework in the context of family responsibilities.[78]

Equality Models

One of the most significant challenges that arises in the context of the family responsibilities cases is the model of equality that is being promoted through

---

71   *Howe* [100], [113].
72   Ibid. [118].
73   Ibid. [131].
74   *Kelly* [82].
75   *Howe*; Freehills, *Employee Relations Bulletin: Pregnancy Prohibits Promotion*, Freehills, Melbourne, 2004; Von Doussa and Lenehan, 'Barbequed or Burned?'.
76   Von Doussa and Lenehan, 'Barbequed or Burned?' 903.
77   *Mayer*; *Howe*.
78   See references at Note 62.

the decisions and the legislative provisions. Two issues arise: first, the reliance (touched on above) of indirect sex discrimination claims on formal equality in promoting the view that women are the primary care givers. Second, the promotion of a formal model of equality in the line of reasoning associated with the test of reasonableness.

The CEDAW Committee has asserted, very strongly, that a formal equality approach will not satisfy the realisation of CEDAW obligations: identical treatment will not suffice, rather biological, social and cultural constructions of difference must be addressed along with a contextual consideration of the gender differences so as to ensure that measures go 'towards a real transformation of opportunities, institutions and systems so that they are no longer grounded in historically determined male paradigms of power and life patterns'.[79] This, combined with the CEDAW obligations in challenging the gendered representation of family responsibilities, results in a clear expectation that for substantive equality to be achieved laws, policies and programs will need to transform social relations. In their review of court cases on family responsibilities under the indirect sex discrimination provisions of the *SDA*, Von Doussa and Lenehan note, however, that there could be some limitation to the legal reasoning.[80] The reliance on Evatt's articulation of sex discrimination on the basis of women's familial responsibilities has the potential to harden community and judicial perceptions that women are the 'natural' providers of care for small children.[81] The Human Rights and Equal Opportunity Commission concurs and notes that '[t]ogether with workplace cultures that may discourage men from claiming a better balance between their paid work and family responsibilities, this failure of the federal anti-discrimination framework effectively locks men into the breadwinner model'.[82]

While the indirect discrimination provisions of the *SDA* are commonly understood to be working towards the achievement of substantive equality, in this instance they contribute to the perpetuation of particular ideas about natural caring capacities of women over men. They therefore do not meet the measure of substantive equality established in the CEDAW General Recommendation on Temporary Special Measures.

The second issue that arises relates to the model of equality being pursued in some of the findings around reasonableness. In *Howe*, Driver FM asserted that the facts did not support a finding of indirect discrimination. In the absence of part-time work at the level at which she had previously been employed, the applicant chose to take a demotion because the lower position provided her

79   CEDAW Committee, 'General Recommendation 25', paras 8, 10.
80   Von Doussa and Lenehan, 'Barbequed or Burned?' 901.
81   Ibid.
82   Human Rights and Equal Opportunity Commission, *Striking the Balance*, p. 86.

with increased flexibility. Rather than acknowledging the invidiousness of the decision the applicant was forced to make, Driver FM asserts that 'the applicant has chosen to characterise that transfer as a "demotion" but, if it was, it was a demotion that the applicant sought and was granted in order to give her the flexibility she needed to provide care for her young second child'.[83]

It is not beyond the realms of interpretation to infer from this that Driver FM is of the view that the quality of a woman's workforce attachment is of little relevance as long as her workforce attachment is maintained. He seems to suggest that having satisfying work that will contribute to progression rather than regression in a career is to be sacrificed at the altar of family responsibilities. A similar view is propounded in *Mayer*, where business needs were used by the respondent, and accepted by Driver FM, as a reason for denying that the applicant could have returned to work in her former position. The possibility of a flexible workplace response—for example, a job-sharing situation—was rejected by Dr Carr and Driver FM asserted that 'his views are certainly reasonable' in this regard.[84] Both these views undermine the transformation of workplace culture to one that would contribute to the realisation of the substantive equality objective of CEDAW. In this respect, the figures of the 'ideal worker' and 'domestic care giver' are not so much challenged as reinscribed.

From the discussion above, it can be seen that, at a federal level, provisions on family responsibilities and indirect sex discrimination have begun to contribute to the implementation of the ILO Workers with Family Responsibilities obligations on more flexible workplace practices. Nonetheless, limitations to the grounds for complaint and requirements to identify a comparator group, challenges with causation and the indirect sex discrimination approach along with the prevalence of a formal model of equality all negatively impact on the full realisation of the ILO and CEDAW obligations to transform work practices to better respond to the needs of workers with family responsibilities.

Conclusion

What conclusions can be drawn from this discussion about the contribution of sex discrimination law to the implementation in Australia of international legal obligations relating to workers with family responsibilities? To what extent does the *SDA* contribute to the implementation of international legal obligations pertaining to the terms and conditions that reflect the needs of workers with family responsibilities, including the prohibition of maternity-based discrimination and prohibition of family responsibilities being grounds

---

83   *Howe* [131].
84   *Mayer* [66].

for dismissal? As noted, the *SDA* proscribes direct discrimination on the basis of family responsibilities in the context of termination of employment. The indirect sex discrimination provisions of the *SDA* have also been interpreted to provide remedies against workplace practices that have discriminated against female workers with family responsibilities. A legal lacuna remains, however, for male workers with family responsibilities, and at one level the provisions in the *SDA* in fact contribute to the perpetuation of women as the primary care givers and a model of formal as opposed to substantive equality. In addition, the failure to enact broader provisions in the context of family responsibilities (that is, to extend them beyond termination of employment and direct discrimination) has limited the de jure implementation of the international obligations. Similar challenges to those described in relation to pregnancy-based discrimination exist in the context of the de facto realisation of the rights. As the federal government considers its response to the senate inquiry into the efficacy of the *SDA*, it would do well to remedy the shortcomings of the *SDA* for workers with family responsibilities.

Bibliography

Books and articles

3D, *The Committee on Economic, Social and Cultural Rights: A Compilation of Trade-Related Issues*, 3D, Geneva, 2006.

Anderson, Peter, 'The *Sex Discrimination Act*: An Employer Perspective— Twenty Years On' (2004) 27 *University of New South Wales Law Journal* 905.

Charlesworth, Sara, 'Managing Work and Family in the "Shadow" of Anti-Discrimination Law' (2005) 23 *Law in Context* 88.

Conaghan, Joanne, 'Women, Work and Family: A British Revolution?' in Joanne Conaghan, Michael Fisch and Karl Klare (eds), *Women, Work and Family: A British Revolution?*, Oxford University Press, UK, 2004.

Edgar, Don, *The War Over Work: The Future of Work and Family*, Melbourne University Press, Carlton, 2005.

Gaze, Beth, 'Context and Interpretation in Anti-Discrimination Law' (2002) 26 *Melbourne University Law Review* 325.

Knowles, Fiona, 'Misdirection for Indirect Discrimination' (2004) 17 *Australian Journal of Labour Law* 185.

MacDermott, Therese and Owens, Rosemary, 'Equality and Flexibility for Workers with Family Responsibilities: A Troubled Union?' (2000) 13 *Australian Journal of Labour Law* 278.

O'Neill, Steve, *Work and Family Policies as Industrial and Employment Entitlements*, Parliamentary Library, Canberra, 2004.

Oosterveld, Valerie, 'Women and Employment' in Kelly Askin and Doreen Koenig (eds), *Women and International Human Rights Law*, Transnational, Ardsley, NY, 1999.

Pocock, Barbara, *The Work–Life Collision: What Work is doing to Australians and what to do about it*, Federation Press, Sydney, 2003.

Thornton, Margaret, 'Feminism and the Changing State: The Case of Sex Discrimination' (2006) 21 *Australian Feminist Studies* 151.

Von Doussa, John and Lenehan, Craig, 'Barbequed or Burned? Flexibility in Work Arrangements and the *Sex Discrimination Act*' (2004) 27 *University of New South Wales Law Journal* 892.

Williams, Joan, *Unbending Gender: Why Work and Family Conflict and What to Do About It*, Oxford University Press, UK, 2000.

Legislation

Paid Parental Leave Act 2010 (Cth)

Sex Discrimination Act 1984 (Cth)

Cases

Escobar v Rainbow Printing Pty Ltd (No. 2) (2002) FMCA 122

Evans v National Crime Authority (2003) FMCA 375

Hickie v Hunt & Hunt (1998) 92-910 EOC

Howe v Qantas Airways Ltd (2004) FMCA 242

Kelly v TPG Internet Pty Ltd (2003) FMCA 584

Mayer v Australian Nuclear Science and Technology Organisation (2003) FMCA 20.

Song v Ainsworth Game Technology Pty Ltd (2002) FMCA 31

Reports and miscellaneous primary sources

Australian Industry Group, Submission: HREOC Inquiry into Paid Work and Family, 2005, <http://www.humanrights.gov.au/sex_discrimination/publication/strikingbalance/submissions/>

Committee on Economic, Social and Cultural Rights, *General Comment 16, Art 3: The Equal Right of Men and Women to the Enjoyment of All Economic, Social and Cultural Rights*, UN Doc E/C 12/2005/3, United Nations, New York, 2005.

Committee on the Elimination of All Forms of Discrimination Against Women, *General Recommendation 16, on Unpaid Women Workers in Rural and Urban Family Enterprises*, UN Document Number A/46/38, United Nations, New York, 1991.

Committee on the Elimination of All Forms of Discrimination Against Women, *General Recommendation 17, on Measurement and Quantification of the Unremunerated Domestic Activities of Women and Their Recognition in the Gross National Product*, UN Document Number A/46/38, United Nations, New York, 1993.

Committee on the Elimination of All Forms of Discrimination Against Women, *General Recommendation 21, on Equality in Marriage and Family Relations*, UN Document Number A/49/38, United Nations, New York, 1994.

Committee on the Elimination of All Forms of Discrimination Against Women, *General Recommendation 23, on Women in Political and Public Life*, UN Document Number A/52/38/Rev 1, United Nations, New York, 1997.

Committee on the Elimination of All Forms of Discrimination Against Women, *Report of the Committee on the Elimination of All Forms of Discrimination Against Women, Decision of the Committee on the Elimination of All Forms of Discrimination Against Women, Declaring a Communication Inadmissible under the Optional Protocol to CEDAW*, Communication Number 1/2003, *Ms B-J v Germany*, United Nations, New York, 2003.

Committee on the Elimination of All Forms of Discrimination Against Women, *General Recommendation Number 25, on Art 4, Paragraph 1, of the Convention on the Elimination of All Forms of Discrimination Against Women, on Temporary Special Measures*, UN Doc. A/59/38, United Nations, New York, 2004.

Convention on the Elimination of All Forms of Discrimination Against Women, Opened for signature 18 December 1979, General Assembly Resolution

34/108, UN General Assembly Official Records, 34th Session, Supplement No. 46, Art. 5(b) (entered into force 3 September 1981), United Nations, New York.

Freehills, *Employee Relations Bulletin: Pregnancy Prohibits Promotion*, Freehills, Melbourne, 2004.

Human Rights and Equal Opportunity Commission, *Striking the Balance: Women, Men, Work and Family*, Discussion Paper, Human Rights and Equal Opportunity Commission, Sydney, 2005.

International Labour Organisation, Equal Remuneration Convention 100, Adopted 29 June 1951, ILO Document Number C100, Entered into force 23 May 1953, International Labour Organisation, Geneva, 1951.

International Labour Organisation, Discrimination Convention (Employment and Occupation) 111, Adopted 25 June 1958, ILO Document Number C111, Entered into force 15 June 1960, International Labour Organisation, Geneva, 1958.

International Labour Organisation, Workers with Family Responsibilities Convention 156, Adopted 23 June 1981, ILO Document Number C156, Entered into force 11 August 1983, International Labour Organisation, Geneva, 1981.

International Labour Organisation, Maternity Protection Convention 183, Adopted 15 June 2000, ILO Document Number C183, Entered into force 7 February 2002, International Labour Organisation, Geneva, 2002.

International Labour Organisation, *Women's Employment: Global Trends and ILO Responses*, 49th Session of the Commission on the Status of Women, United Nations, New York, 2005.

Senate Standing Committee on Legal and Constitutional Affairs, *Report on the Effectiveness of the Commonwealth* Sex Discrimination Act 1984 *in Eliminating Discrimination and Promoting Gender Equality*, Parliament of Australia, Canberra, 2008.

Victorian Automobile Chamber of Commerce, Submission to the Human Rights and Equal Opportunity Commission: Striking the Balance: Women, Men, Work and Family, <http://www.humanrights.gov.au/sex_discrimination/publication/strikingbalance/submissions/>

Part IV
Equivocations of Equality

8. Equality Unmodified?

Reg Graycar and Jenny Morgan[1]

This chapter examines a recent suggestion by the Senate Standing Committee on Legal and Constitutional Affairs in its Report on the Effectiveness of the Commonwealth *Sex Discrimination Act 1984* in Eliminating Discrimination and Promoting Gender Equality *that it might be timely to consider redrafting Commonwealth discrimination laws so that—unlike the current situation, where there are separate acts for each of the various forms of discrimination (for example, sex, race, age, disability)—there is instead one piece of legislation: an Equality Act. Does this proposal have any potential to enhance women's equality in Australia? Might it more readily address problems of intersectionality—the fact that women have a race, a sexuality—a multiplicity of identities that operates differently at different times and in different contexts? Would such an approach encourage a move beyond the complaints-based focus of traditional discrimination laws? We conclude by raising questions about the processes by, and the fora within, which these issues have been debated.*

Introduction

When we were asked to speak at the conference out of which this collection arises, it was suggested we speak on the proposal that Australia should consider the enactment of an 'Equality Act'.[2] In doing so, we reflect on a previous proposal to introduce an Equality Act, and the central importance of defining what we mean by equality. We then go on to consider the one aspect of Australia's equal opportunity laws that is explicitly gendered: the *Equal Opportunity for Women in the Workplace Act 1999* (Cth) (previously the *Affirmative Action (Equal Opportunity for Women) Act 1986* (Cth)). Towards the end of our chapter, we raise questions about the processes of law reform by asking who or which body might be the most appropriate to consider any proposal to introduce a broad-based 'Equality Act.

---

1   We are indebted to the Australian Research Council for supporting our research on law reform processes, 'Changing Law/s, Changing Communities'. Thanks also to Laura Barnett who worked with us on this project, and also to Beth Goldblatt..

2   Senate Standing Committee on Legal and Constitutional Affairs, *Report on the Inquiry into the Effectiveness of the Commonwealth* Sex Discrimination Act 1984 *in Eliminating Discrimination and Promoting Gender Equality*, Parliament of Australia, Canberra, 2008, Recommendation 43, <http://www.aph.gov.au/Senate/committee/legcon_ctte/sex_discrim/report/report.pdf>

An Equality Act for the 1990s?

In the early 1990s, we were part-time commissioners of the Australian Law Reform Commission (ALRC) (with Hilary Charlesworth) on its reference on *Equality Before the Law*.[3] While the term 'sex equality' was not used in the title, it was clear from the terms of reference and from the way the inquiry proceeded that the reference concerned equality before the law *for women*.[4] As

---

3   Australian Law Reform Commission, *Equality Before the Law: Justice for Women*, Report 69, Australian Law Reform Commission, Sydney, 1994, Part I, <http://www.austlii.edu.au/au/other/alrc/publications/reports/69part1/ALRC69part1.pdf>; Australian Law Reform Commission, *Equality Before the Law: Women's Equality*, Report 69, Australian Law Reform Commission, Sydney, 1994, Part II, <http://www.austlii.edu.au/au/other/alrc/publications/reports/69part2/ALRC69part2.pdf> See also Australian Law Reform Commission, *Women's Access to the Legal System (Interim Report)*, Report No. 67, Australian Law Reform Commission, Sydney, 1994, <http://www.austlii.edu.au/au/other/alrc/publications/reports/67/>

4   The terms of reference were as follows: 'I, MICHAEL JOHN DUFFY, Attorney-General of Australia, HAVING REGARD TO:

(a) the principle of equality before the law;

(b) Australia's obligations under international law, including under articles 2 and 26 of the International Covenant on Civil and Political Rights to ensure the equal right of men and women to the enjoyment of all civil and political rights set forth in that Covenant and to the equal protection of the law; and the Convention on the Elimination of All Forms of Discrimination Against Women in pursuance of section 6 of the *Law Reform Commission Act 1973*, HEREBY REFER to the Law Reform Commission the following matters:

(a) whether any changes should be made to any laws made by, or by the authority of, the Parliament of the Commonwealth of Australia, including laws of the Territories so made, and any other laws, including laws of the Territories, that the Parliament has power to amend or repeal;

(b) whether any additional laws should be made within the legislative power of the Commonwealth to effect change to the unwritten laws of Australia;

(c) whether any changes should be made to the ways these laws are applied in courts and tribunals exercising Commonwealth jurisdiction;

(d) the appropriate legislative approach to reforming that law; and

(e) any non-legislative approach so as to remove any unjustifiable discriminatory effects of those laws on or of their application to women with a view to ensuring their full equality before the law.

IN PERFORMING its functions in relation to the Reference, the Commission shall:

(i) consult widely amongst the Australian community and with relevant bodies, and particularly with the Human Rights and Equal Opportunity Commission, the Affirmative Action Agency and the Sex Discrimination Commissioner;

(ii) consider & report on Australian community attitudes on difficulties associated with gender bias as it relates to women;

(iii) in recognition of work already undertaken, have regard to all relevant reports, including:

• the National Strategy on Violence Against Women prepared by the National Committee on Violence Against Women;

• the Report of the Joint Select Committee on Certain Aspects of the Operation and Interpretation of the *Family Law Act 1975*;

• the Report of the House of Representatives Standing Committee on Legal and Constitutional Affairs on its Inquiry into Equal Opportunity and Equal Status for Women in Australia, particularly as it relates to the *Sex Discrimination Act 1984*;

• the Australian Law Reform Commission's Report No 57 on *Multiculturalism and the Law*;

• the Australian Law Reform Commission's Report No 39 on *Matrimonial Property*; and

• the Review of the *Affirmative Action (Equal Employment Opportunity for Women) Act 1986* by the Affirmative Action Agency; and

(iv) consider and report on the relevant law of any other country.

one of its final recommendations in *Equality Before the Law: Women's Equality*, the majority of the commission recommended that an equality provision— either in the *Constitution* or (much more likely) a statutory provision in ordinary legislation—an Equality Act, should enshrine equality for women and men.[5] We (that is, the two of us and Hilary Charlesworth) agreed generally with the idea that there should be an Equality Act that was independent of, and separate from, the *Sex Discrimination Act 1984* (Cth) (*SDA*), which is, in effect, a complaint-based Act. We dissented, however, and published a 'minority view' in which we argued that any new equality legislation should apply for the benefit of women only.[6] We had a number of reasons for taking that position.

First, we argued that it was essential to identify clearly what was the problem or 'mischief' that such legislation was designed to respond to. Specifically, our concern was the needs of people who suffer inequality in the legal system because of their sex. While the term 'gender' is often used loosely, in fact, when we talk about a gender issue, we are almost invariably talking about women (just as when we talk about race we are referring to those who are racialised as other: non-Anglo). So 'gender disadvantage' is just a gender-neutral way of describing the concept of 'women's inequality'. It is women, rather than men, who experience gender disadvantage. This is not to suggest that men do not suffer discrimination or disadvantage in the legal system—far from it—but in most circumstances that is going to occur because of some factor such as their race, their class or their sexuality, not solely because they are men. We took the view that only if the problem of women's lack of equality in law is recognised by name in the title and body of the legislation would we be able to label the problem accurately and only if we did that, would it be capable of being properly addressed.

Second, we argued that the central issue in gender equality is the power imbalance between women and men, rather than mere differences between them. For that reason, we saw an *Equality for Women* Act, rather than an *Equality for Gender-Neutral Persons* Act, as most consistent with a subordination or disadvantage approach to equality.[7] That is, the issue is not whether men and women are different and should be treated differently, or the same and treated in the same way legally, but rather the focus should be on the relative distribution of power between women and men. An Act that on its face dealt with equality for women was more likely to recognise such power imbalances.

---

5   Australian Law Reform Commission, *Equality Before the Law: Justice for Women*, Recommendation 4.

6   Australian Law Reform Commission, *Equality Before the Law: Women's Equality*, Chapter 16.

7   This approach is most frequently attributed to Catharine MacKinnon (see her, *Feminism Unmodified: Discourses on Life and Law*, Harvard University Press, Cambridge, Mass., 1987, especially Chapter 3). For some discussion of different approaches to equality, see: Regina Graycar and Jenny Morgan, *The Hidden Gender of Law*, Second edition, Federation Press, Sydney, 2002, Chapter 3.

An approach that focused on women was also, we argued, consistent with our international obligations. Specifically, the *SDA* was enacted as Australia's implementation of the Convention on the Elimination of All Forms of Discrimination Against Women (CEDAW), a treaty concerned with discrimination against women (not with discrimination against men). This was spelled out clearly by Justice Spender in *Aldridge v Booth*, where His Honour rejected a challenge to the validity of the sexual harassment provisions of the *SDA*. It was argued that to the extent that the express statutory prohibition of sexual harassment addressed only sexual harassment of women, the legislation did not implement Article 15(1) of the Convention, which provides that 'States Parties shall accord to women equality with men before the law'. Spender J stated:

> To give effect to the Convention, the legislation must be directed at the elimination of discrimination against women. Legislation which was directed at the elimination of discrimination generally could not fairly be characterised as legislation 'giving effect to the Convention'. The argument of the respondents assumes that one cannot promote the exercise and enjoyment of rights 'on the basis of equality with men' by prohibiting discrimination against women. There is implicit in this argument a necessity for a legislative prohibition of sexual harassment of men to be in existence.
>
> I reject this argument. It would seriously restrict the operation of the Convention, and its implementation. It puts an unwarranted premium on the existence of legislation, which may or may not reflect the true position in fact.
>
> If this argument of the respondent be right, legislation prohibiting the killing of young girls would be inconsistent and contrary to the terms of the Convention, unless there was in existence legislation prohibiting the killing of young boys, even though, in fact, the killing of young girls was widespread, and the killing of young boys non-existent or rare.
>
> The fact that the legislation, as having effect by s 9(10), does not address sexual harassment of men in the workplace is irrelevant, in my view, to the question of whether the Act gives effect to the Convention.[8]

In any event, the current *SDA*, despite being passed in pursuance of Australia's ratification of CEDAW, does not preclude men from bringing general claims of sex discrimination—something they have tended to do with some frequency.[9]

---

8   *Aldridge v Booth* (1988) 80 ALR 1, 17–18.
9   See the discussion of cases such as the notorious challenge brought by Dr Proudfoot (*Proudfoot v ACT Board of Health* (1992) EOC 92-417) in Graycar and Morgan, *The Hidden Gender of Law*, Chapter 3.

Indeed, this led to our fourth argument. A further disadvantage we saw in a gender-neutral Act that applies equally to women and men was that it would perhaps encourage further legal challenges to women-only programs or services that were designed to address some of the well-documented legal disadvantages experienced by women.

An Equality Act in 2010?

We would have to concede that part of the reason we recommended a women-only equality guarantee in 1994 was that, like good academics, we wanted to provoke debate. A women-only Act, however, probably was not politically feasible then, and it probably is not now. There is nonetheless a live proposal on the table (from the Senate Standing Committee on Legal and Constitutional Affairs)[10] suggesting that there be an inquiry into an Equality Act for Australia.

There seems little reason to think that if we did get such an Act—whether it was constitutional or statutory—it would recognise on its face only those who are disadvantaged on the grounds of race, sexual orientation, and so on. If there is to be equality legislation, it would almost certainly protect the interests of heterosexuals as much as gay men and lesbians, white Anglo-Celtic Australians as well as Asian Australians, men as well as women. In our view, such an approach fails to identify who it is that is suffering disadvantage.

It was for this reason that, when working on the ALRC inquiry, we considered it essential to provide a definition—or what might perhaps be better described as a methodology—for determining whether equality rights have been infringed, to enable us to move beyond mere formal equality. In a recommendation that was endorsed by the whole commission, we recommended (drawing on some of the early equality jurisprudence of the Supreme Court of Canada)[11] that:

> **In assessing whether a law, policy, program, practice or decision is inconsistent with equality in law regard must be had to**

- the historical and current social, economic and legal inequalities experienced on the ground of gender [race, sexual orientation, and so on]

---

10   Senate Standing Committee on Legal and Constitutional Affairs, *Report of the Inquiry into the Effectiveness of the Commonwealth* Sex Discrimination Act 1984 *in Eliminating Discrimination and Promoting Gender Equality*, Recommendation 43.

11   The commission referred in particular to *Law Society of British Columbia v Andrews* [1989] 1 SCR 143. In this case, the Supreme Court first set out its substantive view of 'equality'—a view subsequently reaffirmed in a number of cases. See, for example: *Law v Canada (Minister for Employment and Immigration)* [1999] 1 SCR 497; *Symes v Canada* [1993] 4 SCR 695; *Egan v Canada* [1995] 2 SCR 513; *Miron v Trudel* [1995] 2 SCR 418; *Thibaudeau v Canada* [1995] 2 SCR 627; *Eldrige v British Columbia (Attorney General)* [1997] 3 SCR 624; and *Vriend v Alberta* [1998] 1 SCR 493.

- the historical and current practices of the body challenged and the extent to which those practices have contributed to or perpetuate the inequalities experienced

- the history of the rule or practice being challenged.[12]

The provision of a method by which to approach the issue of equality provides some chance of ensuring that the court dealing with a challenge to a particular program, including one enacted for the benefit of women, does not merely apply a formal equality approach but rather assesses whether there is 'equality' in context. So, for example, in order to decide whether there has been a violation of an equality guarantee in the context of women-only health services, it would not be possible to say merely that there are no men-only health services and therefore women-only services must go. Instead, there would need to be an examination of, say, women's disadvantage in the health field, the aims and bona fides of the organisation providing the service, an analysis of why the service was introduced, and so on, before it could be decided whether equality had, in the particular context, been promoted or denied.[13]

Would Having a Single Equality Act Address any of these Concerns?

Would having a single Equality Act address any of these concerns? Once again, drawing on our academic backgrounds, the answer is—like the answer to almost every question in law school—'it depends'. Before we could even attempt an answer, we would need to untangle what the proposal for a single Equality Act really involves. It could mean one of two things, or a combination thereof. At one end is the complaints-handling aspect: the equality law is there to enable an individual to complain about discrimination (the current main role of both federal and State anti-discrimination laws). A proposed single Equality Act could mean that we should simply follow the approach of Australia's States and put all our discrimination law grounds into one omnibus Act.[14] At the other end of the spectrum of possibilities is the introduction or promotion of a positive or proactive right to equality. This has been little explored in Australia, with the exception of the 1980s affirmative action legislation, now renamed the *Equal Opportunity for Women in the Workplace Act 1999* (Cth) (*EOWWA*). As we were

---

12   Australian Law Reform Commission, *Equality Before the Law: Women's Equality*, Recommendation 4.5.
13   Contrast with *Proudfoot v ACT Board of Health* (1992) EOC 92-417.
14   See *Anti-Discrimination Act 1977* (NSW); *Anti-Discrimination Act 1991* (Qld); *Equal Opportunity Act 1984* (SA); *Anti-Discrimination Act 1998* (Tas.); *Equal Opportunity Act 1995* (Vic.); *Equal Opportunity Act 1984* (WA).

reminded by Margaret Thornton and others at the conference, the language of affirmative action appears to have disappeared from public discourse. We will consider these different possibilities in turn.

One Act for Complaints

The first possibility would involve the creation of an omnibus complaint-handling Act—that is, merging the *SDA*, the *Racial Discrimination Act 1975* (Cth), the *Disability Discrimination Act 1992* (Cth) and the *Age Discrimination Act 2004* (Cth), and perhaps adding new grounds not currently included such as religion or trade union activity. One possible advantage of such a move is arguably to ensure that the best aspect(s) of each piece of legislation is used (for example, it is sometimes suggested that there should be a general prohibition against sex discrimination, as there is in relation to race discrimination.[15] Of course, any such attempt to enhance each of the Acts could be done by way of simple legislative amendment, without the need for an omnibus Act. Such an approach would be consistent with the Australian Human Rights Commission's submission to the senate committee inquiry in which it argued that there should be some immediate changes to the *SDA* and a more thoroughgoing review later.[16]

Intersectionality

Perhaps the strongest argument presented for combining the Acts is that, theoretically at least, it should make the issue of intersectionality easier to deal with.[17] That is, if all the grounds are in the one Act, it might be argued that it is easier to recognise that a woman has both a gender and a race, and might well be discriminated against in particular ways, because she is, say, an Indigenous woman. This was certainly the view taken by a number of those who made submissions to the senate committee.[18] Others, however, appeared more sceptical.[19] After all, we do have the perfect experiment, with all State legislation currently including multiple grounds in the one piece of legislation. There are, however, few examples of litigation in fact raising multiple grounds. Moreover, surely a complaint that raised issues of intersectionality could be—

---

15   See *Racial Discrimination Act 1975* (Cth), s. 9.
16   Australian Human Rights and Equal Opportunity Commission, Submission 69 to the Senate Standing Committee on Legal and Constitutional Affairs, 1 September 2008, Chapter 6, <http://www.aph.gov.au/Senate/committee/legcon_ctte/sex_discrim/submissions/sub69.pdf> The AHRC's recommendations for immediate change to the *SDA* include reforming the definition of indirect discrimination, specifying breastfeeding as a separate protected ground and increasing protection on the grounds of family and carer responsibility, and strengthening sexual harassment laws.
17   For a discussion of intersectionality, see Graycar and Morgan, *The Hidden Gender of Law*, pp. 48–55.
18   See, for example: submissions by Women's Lawyers' Association of New South Wales and Australian Women Lawyers, National Association of Community Legal Centres, Women's Legal Services Australia, Australian Council of Trade Unions and the Human Rights Law Resource Centre.
19   See, for example: submissions by UNIFEM and Margaret Thornton.

and arguably already is—dealt with administratively by the Australian Human Rights Commission (AHRC), to try to ensure that all aspects of the complaint are addressed.

It could be instead that what is needed is a change in thinking rather than a change in legislation in order to deal effectively with intersectional discrimination. As such, it seems unlikely that a mere inclusion of all grounds in the one Act would contribute much, if anything, to that change of thinking.

As for possible downsides, it is also possible, as a number of submissions to the senate inquiry noted,[20] that the inclusion of all grounds in the one Act could lead to a reduced focus on any one—and here of course we are especially concerned about gender. Margaret Thornton, for example, referred to the fact that a single omnibus Act would be likely to mean treating 'all forms of discrimination as the same',[21] which could lead to a 'distorting effect'.[22] So, beyond the administrative convenience of addressing a series of new grounds in one Act, we are at the least sceptical about whether a single complaints-handling Act will add much.

Separation of Complaints Handling and Broader Equality Mission

When the ALRC proposed an Equality Act, it was in the context of the continued existence of the *SDA*. That is, an Equality Act was not meant to replace the *SDA*, but rather was intended to operate separately and independently of that Act. This would have had the effect of having an agency such as in New South Wales, the Anti-Discrimination Board, or the Australian Human Rights Commission continue to deal with individual complaints, but other enforcement of equality rights would be done in a different way and/or by a different agency. There is some consideration of this sort of model in the most recent review of the Victorian *Equal Opportunity Act*: the *Gardner Report*.[23] In this report, Julian Gardner, former Victorian Public Advocate, suggested that a 'proactive and strategic approach towards compliance' might conflict with the need for the Equal Opportunity and Human Rights Commission (Vic.) to appear to be impartial, as is required for its dispute-resolution function.[24] Arguably, the

---

20   Ibid.
21   Senate Standing Committee on Legal and Constitutional Affairs, *Report on the Inquiry into the Effectiveness of the Commonwealth Sex Discrimination Act 1984 in Eliminating Discrimination and Promoting Gender Equality*, p. 44.
22   Margaret Thornton, Testimony before the Senate Standing Committee on Legal and Constitutional Affairs, 11 September 2008, *Hansard*, p. 44.
23   Julian Gardner, *An Equality Act for a Fairer Victoria: Equal Opportunity Review Final Report*, June 2008, Department of Justice, Government of Victoria, Melbourne, [*Gardner Report*], <http://www.justice.vic.gov.au/wps/wcm/connect/DOJ+Internet/home/your+rights/equal+opportunity/>
24   'The Act does not clearly empower the Commission to take a more proactive and strategic approach towards compliance. Further, the exercise of proactive powers under the current Act could create potential conflicts of interest with the Commission's complaint handling function. This may compromise the perception of impartiality' (ibid., p. 43).

AHRC, with its capacity to, say, intervene in cases that raise human rights issues, has either breached its impartiality obligation or negotiated it successfully. In any event, it could be that to advocate (gender) equality effectively, regardless of any perception of 'bias', it would be useful to separate out complaints handling from other functions. Such a division might allow a greater focus on education, research, determining and advocating for 'equality-achieving' best practice, strategic pursuit of bad practice, review of legislation and other practices and policies, and the identification and remediation of systemic inequality. That is, an Equality Act could be a good move but in addition to, not in substitution for, the *SDA*, the *Racial Discrimination Act*, the *Disability Discrimination Act*, and so on. We return below to the concern about perceptions of bias that could arise if an equality body has more than one function.

Positive Duties

As has been noted, one of the central concerns when we proposed an Equality Act was the definition of equality. We have in the previous section considered that one possible way of moving towards 'equality' legislation is to place all the grounds of discrimination into one Act, as the States currently do. Such a proposal does not, however, necessarily touch on the basic understanding of equality. Another option is to propose a positive duty to ensure equality. Without clear attention to what is meant by equality, however, that proposal also raises questions about the extent to which, if at all, it takes us beyond a constrained equality of opportunity scenario.

As we mentioned above, however, Australia has—and has had for 23 years— legislation that might be seen as embodying a more proactive approach to equality: the *Equal Opportunity for Women in the Workplace Act 1999* (Cth) (*EOWWA*), or as it was formerly known, the *Affirmative Action (Equal Employment Opportunity for Women) Act 1986* (Cth). Currently, that Act covers some 20–25 per cent of employees, provides an obligation on private employers of more than 100 people to report progress on various employment matters and has as its sanction public reporting/reporting in Parliament of non-compliant organisations. Such organisations are also not eligible for government contracts for the supply of goods and services.

This legislation, too, is currently under review, by the Department of Families, Housing, Community Services and Indigenous Affairs (FaHCSIA), at the request of the minister.[25] As part of that review, KPMG was asked to conduct a consultation that included

---

25   KPMG, *Office for Women, Department of Families, Housing, Community Services and Indigenous Affairs, Review of the* Equal Opportunity for Women in the Workplace Act 1999 *Consultation Report*, January 2010, KPMG, Melbourne [hereafter, *Review*]. The terms of reference of that review are to: 'examine the contribution that the EOWW Act has made to increasing women's employment opportunities and advancing women's

- the release of an Issues Paper and a call for public submissions

- individual interviews with key stakeholders

- roundtables in capital cities across Australia with key stakeholders

- a survey of reporting organisations under the *EOWWA*

- a survey of employees.[26]

This report became available in January 2010. Some of the limitations of the *EOWWA* are obvious, but the particular contribution of the report for our purposes is first of all the identification of more finely grained and up-to-date critiques, but perhaps even more importantly suggestions for change to the legislation. These two aspects are canvassed in some detail below.

Clearly there are limitations on the powers of the Equal Opportunity for Women in the Workplace Agency (EOWA). The Act excludes government agencies and 'small' employers from its purview.[27] What the KPMG report makes clear, however, is the large number of organisations that do not bother to report at all. The EOWA, in its submission to KPMG, estimates that there are some 13 000 organisations employing 100 or more people and only some 8500 have identified themselves to the EOWA.[28] That is, some 4500 eligible organisations have not submitted themselves to scrutiny and are thus not subject to even the very soft forms of enforcement contained in the legislation. In short, in addition to the specifically excluded government and 'small' employers, these 4500 organisations remain unidentified, are not on any list of non-compliant organisations and therefore remain eligible for government contracts.

In addition, the EOWA cannot, for example, begin an investigation of an organisation of its own motion.[29] It undertakes community education, awards 'Employer of Choice' designation to selected organisations (111 in 2009) and has

---

equality in the workplace; examine the role that the EOWW Act and the EOWA [the Equal Opportunity for Women in the Workplace Agency] have in gathering and reporting on workplace data; consider the effectiveness of the existing legislation and arrangements in delivering equal opportunity for women; provide advice on practical ways in which the equal opportunity for women framework could be improved to deliver better outcomes for Australian women; consider opportunities to reduce the cost of existing regulation and/or ways to ensure that any new legislation is cost-effective and well-targeted; consider the EOWW Act and EOWA within the framework of existing and proposed human rights and proposed human rights and workplace-related legislation, policy and administration, with a view to maximising complementarity and reducing overlap; and have regard to the effects of the EOWW Act, or any proposed recommendations resulting from this review, on social inclusion, the economy, the labour market, business competitiveness and the general wellbeing of the Australian community' (p. 1).

26   Ibid., pp. 1–2. The key stakeholders were identified or at least approved by FaHCSIA (p. i).

27   Interestingly, 37 per cent of submissions to the KPMG consultation thought the coverage of the act was inadequate—usually proposing increasing the coverage to smaller and governmental organisations. Only one submission proposed reducing the coverage of the act (ibid., p. 47 [5.1.1]). It appears that there was less consensus in roundtable discussions (ibid., pp. 79–80 [7.1.4]).

28   Ibid., at 3.1.1.

29   Ibid., p. 13 [3.1.2].

as its 'flagship event' the annual Business Achievement Awards.[30] Interestingly, a number of those who made submissions to the KPMG consultation felt that these awards were on occasion given to organisations that in fact had serious problems in relation to the employment of women.[31] More generally, it was suggested that data collection from those employers who do comply was inadequate—for example, there was a lack of data on the 'industry pay differential between men and women',[32] the data on Indigenous women[33] and women with disabilities were also inadequate, as were the data on available child care in the area.[34] More broadly, a number of submissions to KPMG argued that the Act, and the agency, did not adequately focus on outcomes; the provision of data seemed to be enough.[35]

'A recurring theme arising from the consultations was that reporting [the reporting currently required under the Act] was process, rather than outcomes, driven and, overall, largely ineffective in improving employment outcomes for women.'[36]

And, according to the EOWA, itself:

> Flexibility that was built into the 1999 Act has created uncertainty among employers about the standards to be applied to both their equal opportunity programs (ie, their analysis, actions and evaluations) and to their reporting. This uncertainty has been reflected in employers' reports and has often meant that the Agency may not have a clear basis for evaluating many programs.[37]

Indeed, some 21 per cent of public submissions to KPMG argued for the inclusion of numerical targets in organisations' plans—a view also strongly supported in roundtable discussions.[38] Government, expert individuals and community organisations were the strongest advocates for setting targets.[39] It is worth noting that while the Australian Chamber of Commerce and Industry opposed the introduction of targets—'employers resist their workplaces being used' to engineer social attitudes or to experiment with policy that is ahead

---

30 Ibid., p. 17 [3.1.4].
31 Ibid., p. 55 [5.1.5]. Anne Summers is quoted as saying that there was a need 'to end the charade of government giving awards to companies that are barely compliant (and sometimes in breach) of even the watered-down legislation that currently exists' (ibid., p. 114 [7.2.3]).
32 Ibid., p. 30 [4.1.2].
33 See also Aileen Moreton-Robinson, 'Masking Gender and Exalting Race: Indigenous Women and Commonwealth Employment Policies' (1992) 15 *Australian Feminist Studies* 5.
34 KPMG, *Review*, pp. 30, 31 [4.1.2]. This is further elucidated at pp. 48–9 [5.1.2].
35 See for example: ibid., p. 31 [4.1.2].
36 Ibid., p. 50 [5.1.3].
37 Ibid., p. 51 [5.1.3].
38 Ibid., p. 69 [6.2.5]. As KPMG notes, this proposition was also contested by some respondents—for example, the Australian Chamber of Commerce. (See also pp. 87–94 [7.1.6]).
39 Ibid., p. 88 [7.1.6].

of community attitudes'[40]—other private employers were, like government and expert individuals, in favour, as 'focusing efforts'.[41] So, one industry submission, quoted by KPMG, said:

> The absence of adequate and appropriate targets and benchmarks linked to an enforcement regime allows organisations to be seen to make progress, when the reality is otherwise...our preferred model would be the establishment of voluntary targets for organisations (eg, specific year-on-year improvements in female representation at leadership and senior leadership levels).[42]

There was less industry support for mandatory quotas set by government, though strong union and academic support for such initiatives.[43]

Current sanctions available to the EOWA were, unsurprisingly, also viewed as inadequate, with 34 per cent of submissions indicating penalties were inadequate.[44] Others suggested that 'non-compliance' should cover those who had 'failed to make any improvements for women in their organisation',[45] and not just inadequate or no reporting.[46] Other proposals for improvement included strong support for compliance auditing, perhaps in conjunction with the Fair Work Ombudsman, and restricting access to government grants for non-compliant organisations;[47] additionally, a public league table of the top-200 and bottom-200 companies was proposed.[48]

So, do proposals for the development of a proactive equality obligation indicate that we are simply arguing for a return to the 1980s (perhaps complete with shoulder pads)? We think it is clear that we are not just returning to the 1980s; while progress in achieving gender equality in the workplace has been frustratingly slow, we should be at least marginally heartened by some of the changes in attitude towards 'affirmative action'—for example, the very widespread support manifest in the KPMG report for what in the 1980s would have been seen as radical proposals.

---

40   Ibid., p. 91 [7.1.6].

41   Ibid.

42   Ibid.

43   Ibid., pp. 92–3 [7.1.6].

44   Ibid., p. 53 [5.1.4].

45   Ibid., p. 72 [6.3.3] and p. 97 [7.1.7].

46   See Part IV of the *EOWWA*. Further information about sanctions for non-compliance and current lists of non-compliant organisations are available on the Equal Opportunity for Women in the Workplace Agency's web site ('Sanctions for Not Complying': <http://www.eowa.gov.au/Reporting_And_Compliance/ Complying_with_the_Act/Sanctions_for_not_Complying.asp>). See also Sara Charlesworth's chapter in this collection.

47   KPMG, *Review*, pp. 97 and 101 [7.1.7].

48   Ibid., p. 105 [7.2.1]. A continuing role for the EOWA in education and an increased role in leading relevant research were also discussed and supported (pp. 107–11), as well as the development of stronger links with industry (pp. 111–12 [7.2.2]). It was also suggested that financial incentives through the tax system should be pursued (pp. 119–20 [7.3.1]).

A Focus on 'Out-Groups'?

Sandra Fredman has argued that a 'more nuanced approach to the aims of a proactive model goes beyond the opportunity-results conceptual framework'. In her view:

> [I]t should break the cycle of disadvantage associated with out-groups. Second, it should promote respect for the equal dignity and worth of all, thereby redressing stigma, stereotyping, humiliation and violence because of membership of an out-group. Third, it should entail an accommodation and positive affirmation and celebration of identity within community, and finally, it should facilitate full participation in society.[49]

Like Fredman, we see the need to focus on 'out-groups'—that is, we see Fredman's approach as appearing to want to recognise disadvantage. We do acknowledge, as Charlesworth points out elsewhere in this volume, that recognition has often occurred, especially since the 1999 amendments to the *EOWWA*, within the confines of a limited human resource management framework.[50] The explicit recognition of disadvantage even within the current legislation, is, however, the reason why we think that positive duties might have more in common with our affirmative action legislation than is apparent from our Act's current limited scope. That is, the key aspect of affirmative action/equal employment opportunity legislation is that it does at least recognise who it is—between women and men—who is disadvantaged in the workplace. In the context of addressing continued gender inequality, we question whether there is a need for new 'equality' legislation focused on positive duties, rather than a need to vigorously pursue the renewal and revitalisation of the extant gendered legislation—the *EOWWA*—that we already have (and have had since the 1980s).

Some Reflections on Law Reform Process(es)

We want to conclude by looking at issues about the process of law reform in relation to achieving a more effective recognition of equality rights.

Just about every form of law reform body or process has been used in the drafting and review of discrimination and/or equality legislation. There have

---

49   Sandra Fredman, 'Changing the Norm: Positive Duties in Equal Treatment' (2005) 12(4) *Maastricht Journal of European and Comparative Law* 369, 377.

50   See also Carol Bacchi, 'The Seesaw Effect: Down Goes Affirmative Action, Up Comes Workplace Diversity' (2000) 5 *Journal of Interdisciplinary Gender Studies* 64.

been Private Members Bills,[51] government bills,[52] parliamentary inquiries,[53] ALRC inquiries,[54] inquiries under the auspices of the AHRC or equivalent[55] and review by a private consulting firm.[56] At the State level, we have had law reform commission inquiries,[57] stand-alone inquiries[58] and parliamentary inquiries,[59] among others. It is not possible, at least in this context, to make a comprehensive assessment of where, when and how each of these bodies might be best placed to consider and propose reforms.[60] We do, however, want to raise some specific questions about 'expertise'.

It should be recalled that while we were asked to comment on the proposed single 'Equality Act', the Senate is not in fact proposing that such legislation should be enacted. Rather, it is a proposal that an inquiry be undertaken by the AHRC into whether a single Equality Act is a good idea. In turn, the AHRC's submission to the National Human Rights Consultation suggests that it was not the appropriate body to undertake the task, arguing it had a 'vested interest' and that the ALRC was a more appropriate body (with perhaps the AHRC acting in an advisory capacity).[61] Why the ALRC, we ask? Perhaps it seemed appropriate because of the work we have talked about earlier that the ALRC undertook on an Equality Act? As we are only too aware, however, that was a very long time ago. We are not so convinced that the ALRC—a generalist law reform body—is the appropriate body. Although the commission completed the Equality Before the Law Inquiry in record time, generally, the ALRC conducts very lengthy inquiries—in both time and page numbers.[62] Additionally, can we

---

51   For example, Senator Susan Ryan introduced a Private Members Bill in 1981 aimed at implementing the provisions of CEDAW. Although the Bill was ultimately unsuccessful, it did go on to become the government-sponsored *SDA* and the *Affirmative Action (Equal Employment Opportunity for Women) Act*.

52   For example, the *SDA* and the *Affirmative Action (Equal Employment Opportunity for Women) Act*.

53   For example, the 1992 House of Representatives Standing Committee on Legal and Constitutional Affairs' inquiry, *Half Way to Equal: Report of the Inquiry into Equal Opportunity and Equal Status for Women in Australia*; and the 2008 Senate Standing Committee on Legal and Constitutional Affairs' Inquiry into the Effectiveness of the Commonwealth Sex Discrimination Act 1984 in Eliminating Discrimination and Promoting Gender Equality.

54   For example, the ALRC's 1994 inquiry, Equality Before the Law.

55   For example, the Human Rights and Equal Opportunity Commission's 1992 study, *Report on Review of Permanent Exemptions under the* Sex Discrimination Act 1984, Human Rights and Equal Opportunity Commission, Sydney.

56   For example, the current review of the *EOWWA* being undertaken by KPMG under the auspices of the Australian Government Office for Women, discussed above.

57   For example, the NSW Law Reform Commission's 1999 Review of the *Anti-Discrimination Act 1977*.

58   For example, the 2008 Gardner Review in Victoria.

59   For example, the Victorian Parliament's Scrutiny of Acts and Regulations Committee's continuing inquiry into exceptions and exemptions in the *Equal Opportunity Act 1995*.

60   Laura Barnett, The Process of Law Reform: In Search of Indicators for Success, Paper prepared as part of ARC-funded project on law reform (forthcoming; on file with the authors).

61   Australian Human Rights Commission, Submission to the National Human Rights Consultation, June 2009, pp. 91–2, <http://www.hreoc.gov.au/legal/submissions/2009/200906_NHRC_complete.pdf>

62   In a speech given in October 2008, the Special Minister of State described the ALRC's privacy report as follows: 'There are 295 recommendations for reform in the ALRC's three volume, 74 Chapter, 4.8 kg report' (see <http://www.smos.gov.au/speeches/2008/sp_20081002.html>). He might have added that the report contained 2694 pages.

assume it would have the necessary expertise? Of course, this can be met by the appointment of commissioners and/or consultants with relevant expertise. As we know, however, the wheels of government can be slow and, notwithstanding a very short reporting deadline, it was not until at least halfway through the reference that a part-time commissioner was appointed to the ALRC's current inquiry into domestic violence laws.[63]

Moreover, there seems to be a tendency to assume that expertise is inherently partial; certainly, in our experience, expertise in issues of gender equality is often associated with a lack of impartiality, as has been well documented by our colleague Hilary Astor.[64] In an article published in 1997, Astor reflected on an experience she had at an Australian law teachers' conference. She had given a paper, using a storytelling method, to raise the issue of violence in mediation. The paper was at a general plenary session (that is, not in a session on 'gender' or 'violence' or even an interest group on 'mediation'). She told the fictitious story of Elizabeth, a lawyer, who was severely beaten by her husband, whom she finally left after his violence had caused her to miscarry. Astor asked the audience to reflect on whether Elizabeth might end up in mediation in the resolution of her dispute with her husband about property and the children and how she might fare in a mediation process, given the history of the violence.

The second part of Astor's paper reflects on the audience's reaction to it. All through morning tea, which immediately followed the presentation, people were speculating on who 'Elizabeth' *really* was. One legal academic announced that he knew Elizabeth: he had taught her. Others simply assumed the story was autobiographical. Someone else claimed that the paper was unlike others at the conference: 'It was emotional! The author must have a barrow to push—perhaps she is talking about herself.'[65] Astor reflected on this experience as follows:

> One does wonder whether, when an academic gives a paper on bankruptcy, there is speculation about whether that academic has personal experience of bankruptcy. Or whether, if one used a storytelling method to illustrate the dilemmas faced by a bankrupt in the legal system,

---

63   This study was referred to the ALRC in July 2009 and its final report and recommendations are expected by July 2010. The terms of reference require the commission to consider the interaction in practice of State and Territory family/domestic violence and child protection laws with the *Family Law Act* and relevant Commonwealth, State and Territory criminal laws; and the impact of inconsistent interpretation or application of laws in cases of sexual assault occurring in a family/domestic violence context, including rules of evidence, on victims of such violence and to consider what, if any, improvements could be made to relevant legal frameworks to protect the safety of women and their children.

64   Hilary Astor, 'Elizabeth's Story: Mediation Violence and the Legal Academy' (1997) 2 *Flinders Journal of Law Reform* 13, discussed in Regina Graycar, 'Claire L'Heureux-Dubé: Reflections from Down Under' in Elizabeth Sheehy (ed.), *Adding Feminism to Law: The Contributions of Justice Claire L'Heureux-Dubé*, Irwin Law, Toronto, 2004, pp. 96–7.

65   Astor, 'Elizabeth's Story' 27.

one would be seen as pushing a 'barrow'. Speculations that Elizabeth's story was polemic motivated by autobiography are disturbing in that they do not do justice to the issues raised.[66]

This phenomenon, which seems to extend to all manner of issues relating to gender or equality, was also described by Canadian law professor Christine Boyle many years ago when she highlighted a description of herself (a feminist) in a program as having been placed 'under the heading of "Legal Scholarship for a Cause", while a male tax lawyer spoke under the heading "Conventional Legal Research"'.[67] One of us was once part of a broad group of highly experienced researchers who applied for a government consultancy contract that involved violence against women. We were told that we had not been successful in our tender because our expertise in that field meant that we were 'too close to the issue'. This is why we believe it important to draw attention to this tendency to presume that knowledge of gender equality issues, rather than demonstrating expertise, in fact indicates some lack of partiality. We would do well to ask the same questions of bodies that specialise in tax or corporations: are they ever considered inappropriate as reviewers or researchers of those issues because they are 'too close to the issue'?

So, let us return to why the Australian Human Rights Commission said it was not the appropriate body. It commented that 'the inquiry would inevitably need to examine the powers, functions and institutional arrangements of the commission itself'[68] and that, 'as the federal body responsible for receiving, investigating and conciliating discrimination complaints, the Commission is an integral component of the anti-discrimination regulatory system'.[69]

As if that was self-explanatory, it went on to say: 'An independent body such as the Australian Law Reform Commission (ALRC) would be a more appropriate choice as *it would not be as vulnerable to criticism of having a vested interest in the outcome of the inquiry*' (emphasis added).[70]

Let us try to unpack this a little. It could be said that the AHRC does have a vested interest in, say, the continuing existence of specialist commissioners; people might lose their jobs if these were abolished and someone might suggest they would be reluctant to recommend that. Is that really enough of a reason for it to decline to undertake an inquiry in a field in which it is the agency with appropriate expertise?

---

66   Ibid., 29.
67   Christine Boyle, 'Sexual Assault and the Feminist Judge' (1986) 1 *Canadian Journal of Women and the Law* 93, 102, n. 39.
68   Australian Human Rights Commission, Submission to the National Human Rights Consultation, p. 92.
69   Ibid.
70   Ibid.

We surely want those who are expert in understanding and indeed promoting equality to undertake an inquiry rather than, without intending any offence to law reform bodies, a body whose expertise is as a generalist legal reform body. This area of equality is too important to be left to non-specialists and we need to address directly this tendency to associate independence with *not* having particular expertise.

There are other possibilities for undertaking such a review and there are many models that could be explored. One possibility would be a stand-alone ad-hoc body established for this purpose and advised by the AHRC. This is not a completely foreign or new idea to this area. In the early 1980s, the Working Party on Affirmative Action Legislation consisted of a mix of politicians, representatives of employers, trade unions and women's organisations. We realise we are in a different era, with different needs—there is not quite the premium on getting politicians to be able to move beyond the notion that the *SDA* and affirmative action meant the end of the family, the death of merit and the grossest interference with business prerogative that anyone had ever imagined (as anyone as old as us will remember).[71] And the politicians this time around have had a substantial input already, via the senate inquiry itself. Another possible model is the recent National Council on Violence Against Women—comprising a range of representatives from around the country. Perhaps a group made up of some representatives from the AHRC and other stakeholders—for example, the Women's Electoral Lobby (WEL), union-based feminists, employers, and so on, but dominated by and chaired by non-AHRC people—would be a suitable group to work out fully the implications of an Equality Act.

Conclusion?

It is interesting to reflect on the difference in having this conference now, compared with a similar conference, say, three years ago. Then, we were at the height of neo-liberalism and neo-conservatism. Now there appears to have been a shift in thinking about what we can expect from governments with the advent of the Rudd Government. While we could hardly describe Kevin Rudd as a radical, the government has certainly been prodigious in setting up inquiries (though perhaps less so at delivering on their recommendations).

We need to keep on the agenda a focus on what we mean by equality and also to remember that while a lot has changed since the early days of the *SDA* and affirmative action legislation, much has stayed the same. We seem to be still having a debate that was fully discussed in the early 1990s and has not progressed much since then.

---

71   And as discussed by Chris Ronalds and Susan Ryan, in this volume.

Bibliography

Books and articles

Astor, Hilary, 'Elizabeth's Story: Mediation Violence and the Legal Academy' (1997) 2 *Flinders Journal of Law Reform* 13.

Bacchi, Carol, 'The Seesaw Effect: Down Goes Affirmative Action, Up Comes Workplace Diversity' (2000) 5 *Journal of Interdisciplinary Gender Studies* 64.

Barnett, Laura, The Process of Law Reform: In Search of Indicators for Success, Paper prepared as part of ARC-funded project on law reform (forthcoming; on file with the authors).

Boyle, Christine, 'Sexual Assault and the Feminist Judge' (1986) 1 *Canadian Journal of Women and the Law* 93.

Fredman, Sandra, 'Changing the Norm: Positive Duties in Equal Treatment' (2005) 12(4) *Maastricht Journal of European and Comparative Law* 369.

Graycar, Regina, 'Claire L'Heureux-Dubé: Reflections from Down Under' in Elizabeth Sheehy (ed.), *Adding Feminism to Law: The Contributions of Justice Claire L'Heureux-Dubé*, Irwin Law, Toronto, 2004.

Graycar, Regina and Morgan, Jenny, *The Hidden Gender of Law*, Second edition, Federation Press, Sydney, 2002.

MacKinnon, Catharine, *Feminism Unmodified: Discourses on Life and Law*, Harvard University Press, Cambridge, Mass., 1987.

Moreton-Robinson, Aileen, 'Masking Gender and Exalting Race: Indigenous Women and Commonwealth Employment Policies' (1992) 15 *Australian Feminist Studies* 5.

Legislation

Affirmative Action (Equal Employment Opportunity for Women) Act 1986 (Cth)

Anti-Discrimination Act 1977 (NSW)

Anti-Discrimination Act 1991 (Qld)

Anti-Discrimination Act 1998 (Tas.)

Equal Opportunity Act 1984 (SA)

Equal Opportunity Act 1984 (WA)

Equal Opportunity Act 1995 (Vic.)

Equal Opportunity for Women in the Workplace Act 1999 (Cth)

Racial Discrimination Act 1975 (Cth)

Sex Discrimination Act 1984 (Cth)

Cases

Aldridge v Booth (1988) 80 ALR 1

Egan v Canada [1995] 2 SCR 513

Eldrige v British Columbia (Attorney General) [1997] 3 SCR 624

Law Society of British Columbia et al. v Andrews et al. [1989] 1 SCR 143

Law v Canada (Minister for Employment and Immigration) [1999] 1 SCR 497

Miron v Trudel [1995] 2 SCR 418

Proudfoot v ACT Board of Health (1992) EOC 92-417

Symes v Canada [1993] 4 SCR 695

Thibaudeau v Canada [1995] 2 SCR 627

Vriend v Alberta [1998] 1 SCR 493

Reports and miscellaneous primary sources

Australian Human Rights and Equal Opportunity Commission, Submission 69 to the Senate Standing Committee on Legal and Constitutional Affairs, 1 September 2008, <http://www.aph.gov.au/Senate/committee/legcon_ctte/sex_discrim/submissions/sub69.pdf>

Australian Human Rights Commission, Submission to the National Human Rights Consultation, June 2009, pp. 91–2, <http://www.hreoc.gov.au/legal/submissions/2009/200906_NHRC_complete.pdf>

Australian Law Reform Commission, *Women's Access to the Legal System (Interim Report)*, Report No. 67, Australian Law Reform Commission, Sydney, 1994 <http://www.austlii.edu.au/au/other/alrc/publications/reports/67>

Australian Law Reform Commission, *Equality Before the Law: Justice for Women*, Report 69, Part I, Australian Law Reform Commission, Sydney, 1994, <http://www.austlii.edu.au/au/other/alrc/publications/reports/69part1/ALRC69part1.pdf>

Australian Law Reform Commission, *Equality Before the Law: Women's Equality*, Report 69, Part II, Australian Law Reform Commission, Sydney, 1994, <http://www.austlii.edu.au/au/other/alrc/publications/reports/69part2/ALRC69part2.pdf>

Australian Law Reform Commission, Family Violence Inquiry, Australian Law Reform Commission, Sydney, 2009, <http://www.alrc.gov.au/inquiries/current/family-violence/about.html>

Department of Justice, *An Equality Act for a Fairer Victoria: Equal Opportunity Review Final Report*, June 2008, Department of Justice, Government of Victoria, Melbourne, [*Gardner Report*], <http://www.justice.vic.gov.au/wps/wcm/connect/DOJ+Internet/home/your+rights/equal+opportunity/>

House of Representatives Standing Committee on Legal and Constitutional Affairs Inquiry, *Half Way to Equal: Report of the Inquiry into Equal Opportunity and Equal Status for Women in Australia*, Australian Government Printer, Canberra, 1992.

Human Rights and Equal Opportunity Commission, *Report on Review of Permanent Exemptions under the* Sex Discrimination Act 1984, Human Rights and Equal Opportunity Commission, Sydney, 1992.

KPMG, *Office for Women, Department of Families, Housing, Community Services and Indigenous Affairs, Review of the* Equal Opportunity for Women in the Workplace Act 1999 *Consultation Report*, January 2010, KPMG, Melbourne.

New South Wales Law Reform Commission, *Review of the* Anti-Discrimination Act 1977, New South Wales Law Reform Commission, Sydney, 1999.

Scrutiny of Acts and Regulations (SARC) Committee, *Exceptions and Exemptions to the* Equal Opportunity Act 1995—*Final Report*, 56th Parliament, State of Victoria, Government Printer for the State of Victoria, Melbourne, 2009.

Senate Standing Committee on Legal and Constitutional Affairs, *Report on the Inquiry into the Effectiveness of the Commonwealth* Sex Discrimination Act 1984 *in Eliminating Discrimination and Promoting Gender Equality*, Parliament of Australia, Canberra, 2008, <http://www.aph.gov.au/Senate/committee/legcon_ctte/sex_discrim/report/report.pdf>

Submissions by Women's Lawyers' Association of New South Wales and Australian Women Lawyers, National Association of Community Legal Centres, Women's Legal Services Australia, Australian Council of Trade Unions, the Human Rights Law Resource Centre, UNIFEM and Margaret Thornton to Senate Standing Committee on Legal and Constitutional Affairs, Inquiry into the Effectiveness of the Commonwealth *Sex Discrimination Act 1984* in Eliminating Discrimination and Promoting Gender Equality, December 2008, Parliament of Australia, Canberra.

Thornton, Margaret, Testimony before the Senate Standing Committee on Legal and Constitutional Affairs, 11 September 2008, *Hansard*, p. 44.

9. And Which 'Equality Act' Would that Be?

Simon Rice[1]

In 2008, an Australian senate committee report recommended a public inquiry into the merits of a national Equality Act, to harmonise existing federal anti-discrimination acts and to legislate for a positive equality duty along the lines of such a duty in the United Kingdom. The Australian Government has since announced a 'streamlining' exercise for federal anti-discrimination law, but has made no mention of an equality duty. I review the history of calls for an Equality Act in Australia and the process by which the United Kingdom has arrived at its own Equality Act. I propose that any Australian Equality Act is an advance on established methods of pursuing equality only if it enacts a positive equality duty, and I identify lessons for Australia arising from the extensive UK process of reform.

Introduction

In 2008, a review of the *Sex Discrimination Act 1984* (Cth) (*SDA*) recommended an inquiry 'to examine the merits of replacing the existing federal anti-discrimination acts with a single Equality Act'.[2] Submissions to the Senate Standing Committee on Legal and Constitutional Affairs canvassed different ways one can think of an 'Equality Act', and it is unclear what particular idea of an Equality Act the committee had in mind in its recommendation.[3]

The idea of an Equality Act in Australia risks going the way of the idea of 'access to justice', where the term is a rallying cry and goal for many interests, from many perspectives, without clearly having one meaning that can survive a public policy debate intact. In this chapter, I survey different 'Equality Acts— real and proposed—and attempt to 'untangle what the [the senate committee's]

---

1 I was ably assisted by research carried out by Tiffany Henderson.
2 Senate Standing Committee on Legal and Constitutional Affairs, *Report on the Effectiveness of the Commonwealth* Sex Discrimination Act 1984 *in Eliminating Discrimination and Promoting Gender Equality*, Parliament of Australia, Canberra, 2008.
3 The lack of clarity could be of little moment since the federal government, in its response to the Senate Standing Committee's report in May 2010, ignored completely the 'Equality Act' recommendation: *Government Response to Senate Standing Committee on Legal and Constitutional Affairs Effectiveness of the Commonwealth* Sex Discrimination Act 1984 *in Eliminating Discrimination and Promoting Gender Equality*, 6 May 2010, Commonwealth of Australia, Canberra.

proposal for a single Equality Act actually involves'.[4] I suggest that to have real meaning, an Equality Act is more than just another complaints-based remedial statute, but that following the spirit, though not the letter, of the *Equality Act 2010* (UK), it legislates for a positive equality duty.

The first of the 'Equality Acts' I review is the one proposed by the Australian Law Reform Commission (ALRC) in 1994. I characterise it as, effectively, a 'third-generation' form of equality law, dependent on individuals challenging offending conduct in much the same way as in all Australia's current anti-discrimination laws. Drawing on our experience of those anti-discrimination laws to date, I note various reasons why this approach to redressing inequality is unlikely to succeed, concluding that what the ALRC had in mind is not what we now need in Australia, if ever it was a good idea.

Second, I review the 'Equality Act' proposed by the senate committee in 2008, in which I identify two distinct proposals. One is to 'harmonise' Australia's four federal anti-discrimination laws and one, less obviously stated, is to introduce a positive equality duty. The duty that is envisaged seems to be along the lines of a duty that has been in place in the United Kingdom under its anti-discrimination laws for some years, but which, at the time of the senate committee inquiry, was in the Equality Bill 2008 (UK); in April 2010, that Bill became the *Equality Act 2010* (UK). In the course of considering the senate committee's 'harmonising' proposal, I comment, without enthusiasm, on the more recently announced 'streamlining' of Australia's four federal anti-discrimination laws for 'deregulatory' reasons.

I then look at the lengthy and substantial process that led to the passage of the UK *Equality Act*, and at the terms and scope of its positive equality duty. There are lessons in this for Australia, principally in relation to the process for arriving at a well-considered, contemporary and widely accepted approach to pursuing equality through legislation, which I set out subsequently. At the same time, I consider what the content of a positive equality duty in Australia might be. I conclude by suggesting that if ever Australia is to have an Equality Act that delivers positive equality, it will require a strength and vision of political leadership that we currently lack.

The ALRC's 'Equality Act'

In 1993, in anticipation of the tenth anniversary of the passage of the *SDA*, the then Commonwealth Attorney-General, Michael Duffy, asked the ALRC to investigate what steps should be taken 'so as to remove any unjustifiable

---

4   Reg Graycar and Jenny Morgan, this volume.

discriminatory effects of [Commonwealth] laws on or of their application to women with a view to ensuring their full equality before the law'.[5] At the outset, the reference was limited to equality 'before the law'; the ALRC, looking in particular at the *SDA*, recognised that it 'will be unable to address fully issues of women's inequality'.[6]

The ALRC assessed the adequacy of the *SDA* and found it wanting, saying that[7]

- the *SDA* addresses only individual acts of discrimination within specified fields of activity for which a person may make a complaint

- it has a limited understanding of equality; it does not take account of the historical and contextual framework of disadvantage

- it is unable to address the issue of violence against women as discrimination other than within the framework of sexual harassment

- it is unable to challenge directly gender bias or systemic discrimination in the content of the law

- it concentrates on the treatment of individuals rather than the effects of laws

- it cannot strike down rules or laws

- it exempts areas from its operation

- its protection is activated only by making a complaint.

Reflecting many of the submissions it received, the ALRC's response to the limitations of the *SDA* was to recommend—in terms drawn from the Canadian experience under its Charter of Rights and Freedoms[8]—a legislative guarantee of 'equality before the law, equality under the law, equal protection of the law, equal benefit of the law, and the full and equal enjoyment of human rights and fundamental freedoms'.[9] This legislative guarantee was the ALRC's Equality Act.

Following the Canadian experience of a constitutional equality right operating alongside, and not instead of, existing sex discrimination legislation, the ALRC's proposed Equality Act was to be a national human rights standard, obliging government to ensure that its conduct resulted in equality to women, while anti-discrimination laws would continue to set local standards, obliging both public and private actors to treat women equally. Importantly, the ALRC's Equality Act was premised on an adversarial mechanism that would enable women (and men) to mount a legal challenge against law or conduct that operated with unequal effect; as the ALRC said: 'An Equality Act would ensure that women's rights

---

5   Australian Law Reform Commission, *Equality Before the Law: Justice for Women*, Report No. 69, Australian Law Reform Commission, Sydney, 1994, Part I, p. xv.

6   Ibid., Part II [4.5].

7   Ibid. (endnotes omitted).

8   Ibid., Part II [4.20].

9   Ibid., Part I, Rec. 4.3.

are fully acknowledged and protected in law. It would be *a means by which women could challenge laws, procedures and practices* that create or perpetuate inequality. It would affect the interpretation and development of the common law' (emphasis added).[10]

Although aspects of the ALRC's reports were implemented,[11] the proposed Equality Act did not eventuate. In hindsight, that might not have been a bad thing—not because nothing more needed to be done to address discrimination against women, but because the ALRC's Equality Act would have been only more of the same approach that had, and has, proved to be of limited effectiveness.

Negative Duties

I should explain what I mean by 'more of the same approach'. It is true that the ALRC's Equality Act would have been different from the *SDA* and, on the *SDA's* twentieth anniversary, Gaze proposed, as an alternative to the *SDA*, legislation 'perhaps modelled on the Equality Act proposed by the Australian Law Reform Commission'.[12] The difference would have been in declaring equality before the law, rather than merely proscribing 'a narrow band of discrimination and promot[ing] a limited form of equality'.[13] Women would have had access to a much wider range of claims—significantly, for example, in relation to discriminatory legislation[14] and 'acts of government and the performance of public functions, powers and duties';[15] it would not have been bound by the 'closed' categorisation of types of discrimination that characterises Australia's anti-discrimination legislation.[16]

What would have been the same was the legislative model, premised on individual complaint as the means of identifying and remedying offending conduct, whether that conduct offended a technical definition of discrimination or a broader concept of equality. The ALRC, for example, described the protection offered by its Equality Act as 'a declaration or an injunction from a court and…the ordinary range of administrative law remedies'.[17] Even when the ALRC could see past the making of an order 'striking down laws or actions', it

---

10   Ibid., Part II [4.1].
11   Australian Law Reform Commission, *Summary: Equality Before the Law (ALRC Reports 67 & 69)*, Australian Law Reform Commission, Sydney, <www.alrc.gov.au/inquiries/title/summary_alrc67&69.htm>
12   Beth Gaze, 'The *Sex Discrimination Act* after Twenty Years: Achievements, Disappointments, Disillusionment and Alternatives' (2004) 27(3) *University of New South Wales Law Journal* 914, 921.
13   Belinda Smith, 'Models of Anti-Discrimination Laws – Does Canada offer any Lessons for the Reform of Australia's Laws?' in Deirdre Howard-Wagner (ed.), *'W(h)ither Human Rights?' Proceedings of the 25th Annual Conference of the Law and Society Association of Australia and New Zealand*, 2008, p. 1.
14   Gaze, 'The *Sex Discrimination Act* After Twenty Years' 917.
15   Australian Law Reform Commission, *Equality Before the Law*, Part II [4.21].
16   Smith, 'Models of Anti-Discrimination Laws', p. 3.
17   Australian Law Reform Commission, *Equality Before the Law*, Part II [4.21]; [5.24]–[5.32].

remained within the adversarial sphere of making orders against a wrongdoer (granting 'appropriate relief' to parties)[18] and anticipated only a broader form of injunctive order, which could require a party who has 'violated' the equality right to take some positive action.[19]

Put simply, the ALRC's Equality Act was, in its conception of the manner in which legislation operates to achieve social change, 'modelled on the negative duties and the individualistic, adversarial approach of [so-called] third-generation…legislation, rather than the fourth-generation positive duties and affirmative action legislation'.[20] Discussion of an Equality Act, in this chapter and in 2010 generally, is discussion of the merits of such 'fourth-generation' legislation, not of the 'old' approach of the ALRC's Equality Act.

In Australia,[21] as in the United Kingdom, 'there can be no doubt that the third generation legislation [for example, the *SDA*]…has broken down many barriers for individuals in their search for jobs, housing and services, and…[has] driven underground those overt expressions of discrimination that were current 25 years ago'.[22] It is also true to say, however—perhaps even more so in the federated jurisdiction that is Australia rather than is the case in the United Kingdom—that third-generation anti-discrimination legislation such as the *SDA* is unable to overcome structural barriers that entrench inequality, because 'it adopts a fragmented, inconsistent and incoherent approach to different manifestations of inequality of opportunity'.[23]

Even as a means of awarding an individual remedy, let alone as legislation for social reform, the individual complaint model for addressing discrimination is excessively demanding of a litigant. Conceptually, a complainant must first fit themselves into a category that is defined precisely and exclusively according to a personal attribute (without accommodating intersectional or 'multiple grounds' claims),[24] and then must fit the circumstances they complain of into a 'rigid, complex and artificial'[25] statutory definition of discrimination. The latter requirement can be contrasted with the more accessible and accommodating approach in Canadian anti-discrimination law.[26]

---

18 Ibid., Part II [5.33].

19 Ibid.

20 Bob Hepple, Mary Coussey and Tufyal Choudhury, *Equality, A New Framework: Report of the Independent Review of the Enforcement of UK Anti-Discrimination Legislation*, Hart Publishing, Oxford, 2000, p. 7.

21 Gaze, 'The *Sex Discrimination Act* After Twenty years' 915.

22 Hepple et al., *Equality, A New Framework*, p. 14.

23 Ibid., p. 19.

24 Senate Standing Committee on Legal and Constitutional Affairs, *Report on the Effectiveness of the Commonwealth Sex Discrimination Act 1984 in Eliminating Discrimination and Promoting Gender Equality*, [4.50]–[4.56]; and see Thornton, and Graycar and Morgan, this volume.

25 *IW v City of Perth* (1997) 191 CLR 1, 12, per Brennan CJ and McHugh J.

26 Smith, 'Models of Anti-Discrimination Laws'. For a critique of 'categories' of discrimination under Canada's discrimination laws, see: Nitya Iyer, 'Categorical Denials: Equality Rights and the Shaping of Social Identity' (1993–94) 19 *Queen's Law Journal* 179.

If a complainant can fit within the definitional constraints, they must then pursue a remedy in an adversarial environment. They are complaining of discrimination precisely because they are the less powerful of two parties, yet they must gather and maintain the resources—money, time, expertise, resilience—to meet technical legal requirements to hold the more powerful party accountable. Resources aside, the technical aspects of proving discrimination are a significant obstacle, such as the burden of proof,[27] the standard of proof,[28] the comparator test for direct discrimination[29] and the requirements to prove indirect discrimination such as identifying a condition and addressing the reasonableness test.[30]

Reliance on the Courts

At the time that the ALRC proposed its version of an Equality Act, there was reason enough to question whether faith should be placed in legislatures and courts to facilitate, let alone embrace, the aims of the Equality Act that was envisaged. In the years since, however, we have been given further reason to hesitate before relying on either institution to advance human rights guarantees.

Parliaments in Australia have shown little courage or leadership in enacting human rights legislation[31] and have at times been quick to enact otherwise.[32] The conduct of federal, State and Territory parliaments in relation to proposed human rights acts and charters has shown that on the rare occasions that they volunteer to have their conduct bound by human rights standards, those standards are expressed in terms that are both conditional and avoidable. In

---

27   Senate Standing Committee on Legal and Constitutional Affairs, *Report on the Effectiveness of the Commonwealth* Sex Discrimination Act 1984 *in Eliminating Discrimination and Promoting Gender Equality*, [6.46]–[6.51], Rec. 22. See Jonathon Hunyor, 'Skin-Deep: Proof and Inferences of Racial Discrimination in Employment' (2003) 25 *Sydney Law Review* 535.

28   See Loretta de Plevitz, 'The *Briginshaw* "Standard of Proof" in Anti-Discrimination Law: "Pointing with a Wavering Finger"' (2003) 27(2) *Melbourne University Law Review* 308.

29   Senate Standing Committee on Legal and Constitutional Affairs, *Report on the Effectiveness of the Commonwealth* Sex Discrimination Act 1984 *in Eliminating Discrimination and Promoting Gender Equality*, [3.15]–[3.22], Rec. 5.

30   Ibid., [3.27]–[3.34], Rec. 6.

31   Examples include: the journey in South Australia from the Equal Opportunity (Miscellaneous) Amendment Bill 2006 to the *Equal Opportunity (Miscellaneous) Amendment Act 200*9; the *Government Response to the Productivity Commission's Review of the* Disability Discrimination Act 1992, January 2005 (<www.ag.gov.au/PCDDA>); the failure of the Tasmanian Government to act on the recommendations in Tasmania Law Reform Institute (*A Charter of Rights for Tasmania*, Report No. 10, October 2007, Tasmania Law Reform Institute, Hobart) and the failure of the West Australian Government to act on the recommendations in *Report of the Consultation Committee for a Proposed WA Human Rights Act* (November 2007); and the explicit refusal of the federal government (Attorney-General Hon. Robert McClelland MP, Launch of Australia's Human Rights Framework, Address to the National Press Club of Australia, Canberra, 21 April 2010) to act on Recommendations 17–31 of the Commonwealth of Australia (*National Human Rights Consultation Report*, Commonwealth of Australia, Canberra, 2009, [*Brennan Report*]).

32   For example, *Anti-Discrimination Amendment (Drug Addiction) Act 2002* removing discrimination protection for people whose disability is due to addiction to a prohibited drug and, to the same effect, the Disability Discrimination Amendment Bill 2003 (Cth); the Sex Discrimination Amendment (Teaching Profession) Bill 2004 (Cth) to allow sex discrimination 'in order to redress a gender imbalance [in favour of women] in teaching'; the Human Rights Legislation Amendment Bill (No. 2) 1998 to allow the Attorney-General to veto court intervention by the Australian Human Rights Commission.

the Australian Capital Territory, for example, failure to table a compatibility statement for a bill or to report on a human rights issue raised by a bill does not invalidate a law[33]—and similarly in Victoria for failure to table a compatibility statement.[34]

A further reason to baulk at a complaint-based remedial model for addressing inequality is that it is dependent on courts and tribunals. Courts and tribunals of course have no institutional obligation to promote human rights, although they do have an obligation to prefer 'a construction that would promote the purpose or object underlying the Act...to a construction that would not promote that purpose or object'.[35] As Gaze has recounted in some detail, this obligation is too often overlooked:

> Australian judges have generally approached interpretation of anti-discrimination statutes as being similar in kind to other statutes: a matter of giving effect to the words...[the] subject matter has not been seen as a basis for any different approach to interpretation...
>
> In interpreting anti-discrimination legislation...it is rare for judges to consider the policy or concepts underlying these laws. On the occasions on which the High Court has discussed the purpose of anti-discrimination laws, it has unambiguously stated that they are remedial and should receive a beneficial construction...However, at the same time, the Court has found reasons for adopting a narrow approach to the interpretation of specific terms in the legislation...which has been followed with such wholeheartedness by some lower courts that one Federal Court judge has said:[36]
>
> It is not appropriate to consider the question of reasonableness [in indirect discrimination] by commencing first with a view that human rights and discrimination legislation should be liberally construed. Nor is it correct to approach the meaning of reasonableness informed by the objects and purposes of the Act.
>
> As a result, Australian judges most often give a literal or a narrow reading of specific provisions or terms they are construing, using only textual methods to reach a decision. In this process, some very narrow and technical distinctions have been introduced, making success more difficult for complainants and discouraging the bringing of actions.[37]

---

33 *Human Rights Act 2004* (ACT), s. 38.

34 *Charter of Human Rights and Responsibilities Act 2006* (Vic.), s. 28.

35 For example, *Acts Interpretation Act 1901* (Cth), s. 15AA.

36 *Commonwealth Bank of Australia v Human Rights and Equal Opportunity Commission* (1997) 80 FCR 78, 88 per Davies J, relying on Brennan CJ and McHugh J in *IW v City of Perth* (1997) 191 CLR 1, 15.

37 Beth Gaze, 'Context and Interpretation in Anti-Discrimination Law' (2002) 26 *Melbourne University Law Review* 325, 332–3 (some references omitted).

Australia has a long history of relying on adversarial litigation under anti-discrimination legislation to achieve the aim of equality, and the conduct of the courts in giving effect to this aim has been dispiriting. The High Court's anti-discrimination jurisprudence is a sad example of the failure to have regard to the aims of the legislation, and other superior courts have been little better. They have been highly technical and out of touch with the spirit of the legislation, overturning decisions of trial courts and tribunals because of disagreement over the meaning and the application of the statutory provisions without regard to aims and purpose.

Rees et al. point out that '[t]he sheer regularity with which appellate courts have overturned decisions in favour of complainants has generated a passionate response from Kirby J, on three separate occasions'.[38] In *IW v City of Perth*, in dissent, Kirby J said:

> Courts grappling with the novel concepts and objectives of [anti-discrimination] legislation quite frequently complain about the difficulties which they are called upon to resolve. They warn against 'misdirected' litigation which seeks to impose upon such legislation 'a traffic it was not designed to bear' [citing *Waters v Public Transport Corporation*, (1991) HCA 49; (1991) 173 CLR 349 at 372].

> ...unless courts are willing to give such legislation the beneficial construction often talked about, it seems likely that the legislation will continue to misfire.[39]

In *X v Commonwealth*, Kirby J began his dissent in resigned exasperation—'Once again, this Court has before it an appeal which concerns the operation of anti-discrimination legislation'—and went on to say with some drama:

> [T]his [case] again demonstrates [that] the field of anti-discrimination law is littered with the wounded who appear to present the problem of discrimination which the law was designed to prevent and redress but who, following closer judicial analysis of the legislation, fail to hold on to the relief originally granted to them.[40]

In *NSW v Amery*, Kirby J—again in dissent—was palpably annoyed: 'This case joins a series, unbroken in the past decade, in which this Court has decided appeals unfavourably to claimants for relief under anti-discrimination and equal opportunity legislation.' After giving an account of earlier High Court cases

---

38   Neil Rees, Katherine Lindsay and Simon Rice, *Anti-Discrimination Law in Australia*, Federation Press, Sydney, 2008, p. 30.
39   [1997] HCA 30; 191 CLR 1, 52.
40   [1999] HCA 63; 200 CLR 177, 211.

that 'reflected the beneficial interpretation of the laws in question', citing, for example, *Mabo v Queensland (No. 2)*, Kirby J said resignedly: 'The wheel has turned.'[41]

Elsewhere in this volume, Belinda Smith has compared the approaches to anti-discrimination law taken by courts in Canada and Australia. She suggests that the 'narrow, technical approach' taken by the Australian High Court is referrable to the prescriptive and equally narrow and technical approach in the drafting of Australia anti-discrimination statutes.[42] It could be that if, as Smith proposes, the legislation is rewritten appropriately, the courts will feel they are more able to pursue and develop its beneficial aims, but for the moment they cannot be relied on to behave in that way.

Litigating for Equality

Graycar and Morgan observe that 'engagement in test case litigation…is not a major site of feminist engagement in Australia, unlike in Canada'.[43] Advocates for women's equality in Canada have, however, had more to work with than have advocates in Australia; the Canadian Charter of Rights and Freedoms offers a constitutional guarantee of equality, just as the ALRC proposed working towards with its legislative guarantee in an Equality Act. Graycar and Morgan's account of Canadian litigation refers principally to the renowned women's rights advocacy organisation Legal Education and Action Fund (LEAF), which began its existence on the same day that the delayed equality provisions of the Canadian Charter began operation.[44] While there are heroic tales of test case litigation in Canada and the United States under an equality right, there are many more unrecorded and familiar tales of litigants who have been defeated by cost and delay, of principles clouded and rulings reversed by the vagaries of judicial opinion and of repeat players not learning—or not caring about—the lessons that an adverse finding in litigation is supposed to teach them.

LEAF's commitment to litigation as a strategy for achieving social change has been assessed, and its effectiveness qualified, by LEAF itself[45] and by commentators.[46] To the extent that test case litigation is an attractive strategy, Graycar and Morgan have reservations about attempting to replicate LEAF's

---

41   *New South Wales v Amery* [2006] HCA 14; (2006) 230 CLR 174, 200.

42   Belinda Smith, this volume.

43   Regina Graycar and Jenny Morgan, 'Law Reform: What's In It For Women?' (2005) 23 *Windsor Yearbook on Access to Justice* 393, n. 2.

44   Lynn Smith, 'Equality' in Nasreen Rajab-Budlender and Steven Budlender (eds), *Judges in Conversation: Landmark Human Rights Cases of the Twentieth Century*, JUTA, Cape Town, 2009, p. 37.

45   Melina Buckley (ed.), *Transforming Women's Future: A Guide to Equality Rights Theory and Action*, West Coast Women's Legal Education and Action Fund, Vancouver, BC, 2001.

46   Sherene Razack, 'The Women's Legal Education and Action Fund' in Frederick Lee Morton (ed.), *Law, Politics, and the Judicial Process in Canada*, University of Calgary Press, Alberta, 2002, p. 316.

litigation campaigning in an Australian context.[47] Galligan and Morton have observed that in Australia, despite there being 'a large number of rights-protection organizations in Australia…[m]ost do not use "test case" litigation as a strategy for advancing their rights goals', and '[t]here has not been a court-based rights revolution'.[48] Consistently with LEAF's reassessment of test case litigation as a strategy, Galligan and Morton report that the Public Interest Advocacy Centre, for example, 'has shifted its…tactics away from straight litigation to an integrated approach to public interest advocacy that combines litigation, policy development and education and training'.

Galligan and Morton point out that in Australia '[t]here is no dedicated test-case funding program as in Canada'—presumably a reference to the Court Challenges Program of Canada, a national non-profit organisation, which, until it was closed in 2006, funded test cases that advanced language and equality rights in the Canadian Charter of Rights and Freedoms.[49] And although they are wrong to say that the Australian Human Rights Commission 'is barred by statute from initiating test cases on its own',[50] it is true to say that the commission is not empowered to initiate litigation[51] and that is a significant limitation on what prospects there might be for the strategic use of anti-discrimination legislation in Australia.

The utility of test case litigation as a means of achieving social change is constantly under debate;[52] a small sample of the literature runs from early reservations within the American Council for Civil Liberties[53] and a review of the use of the strategy in the US 'war on poverty'[54] to an analysis of test cases for

---

47   Regina Graycar and Jenny Morgan, 'A Quarter Century of Feminism in Law: Back to the Future?' (1999) 24 *Alternative Law Journal* 117, 119.

48   Brian Galligan and Fred Morton, Australian Rights Protection, Paper presented to the Australasian Political Studies Association Conference, University of Adelaide, 29 September – 1 October 2004, p. 9. Cf., for example, the 'Test case litigation program' administered by the Australian Taxation Office, which funds litigation 'to develop legal precedent [to] provide guiding principles' on the operation of tax provisions (<http://www.ato.gov.au>).

49   Court Challenges Program of Canada (<http://www.ccppcj.ca/e/ccp.shtml>).

50   Galligan and Morton, Australian Rights Protection, p. 12.

51   See *Australian Human Rights Commission Act 1986* (Cth), ss 10A, 11 and 13.

52   Referring to 'a lively debate about the role and efficacy of…"test case litigation"', Dianne Martin (*A Seamless Approach to Service Delivery in Legal Aid: Fulfilling a Promise or Maintaining a Myth?*, Department of Justice Canada, Ottawa, 2002,) refers at note 95 to: Amy Bartholomew and Alan Hunt, 'What's wrong with Rights?' (1991) 9 *University of Minnesota Law School Journal* 1; Stephen Brickey and Elizabeth Comack, 'The Role of Law in Social Transformation: Is a Jurisprudence of Insurgency Possible?' (1987) 2 *Canadian Journal of Law and Society* 97; Gwen Brodsky and Shelagh Day, *Canadian Charter Equality Rights for Women: One Step Forward or Two Steps Back?*, Canadian Advisory Council on the Status of Women, Ottawa 1989; Board of Directors, Parkdale Community Legal Services, 'Poverty Law and Community Legal Clinics: A View From Parkdale Community Legal Services' (1997) 35 *Osgoode Hall Law Journal* 595.

53   Stephen Halpern, 'Assessing the Litigative Role of ACLU Chapters' (1972) 4(2) *Policy Studies Journal* 157.

54   Martha Davis, *Brutal Need: Lawyers and the Welfare Rights Movement, 1960–1973*, Yale University Press, New Haven, Conn, 1993.

child protection[55] and a reflection in light of an unsuccessful Canadian Charter case in relation to same-sex relationships.[56] There is widespread sympathy for Rhode's claim that 'test case litigation [is not an] effective means of addressing the structural sources of poverty. Routine cases deal with symptoms not causes… and courtroom victories are seldom significant or enduring without a political base to support them.'[57]

Effectiveness

Differently from assessing whether anti-discrimination laws 'work' in a procedural sense,[58] we have little understanding of whether and how anti-discrimination laws, through the consistent and accumulating decisions of liability in individual discrimination cases, result in broader understanding of the aims of the legislation, and in consequent changes in behaviour.[59]

An interesting empirical study was conducted in Australia to determine whether and how conventional 'third-generation' or 'negative' anti-discrimination legislation affected employer behaviour in the recruitment process.[60] The short answer to the question was that 'the anti-discrimination legislation does not appear to be particularly significant or relevant for employers…[that] discrimination at the recruitment and selection stages is still very common, and that anti-discrimination legislation has only had a limited effect'.[61] Employers in the sample 'indicated that they are able to "find a way around" the legislation'.[62] These research results contrast starkly with, for example, the 'significant impact' of fourth-generation positive equality measures in Northern Ireland.[63]

---

55   Bruce Hafen, 'Exploring Test Cases in Child Advocacy: Review of Robert H. Mnookin *In the Interest of Children, Advocacy Law Reform and Public Policy*' (1986–87) 100 *Harvard Law Review* 435.

56   Jody Freeman, 'Defining Family in *Mossop v DSS*: The Challenge of Anti-Essentialism and Interactive Discrimination for Human Rights Litigation' (1994) 44 *University of Toronto Law Journal* 41.

57   Deborah L. Rhode, *Access to Justice*, Oxford University Press, UK, 2004, p. 110.

58   For example, technical issues such as burden and standard of proof, and so on. See: Dominique Allen, Reforming Australia's Anti-Discrimination Legislation: Individual Complaints, The Equality Commission and Tackling Discrimination, Doctoral thesis, University of Melbourne, Vic., 2009.

59   For an overview of theories of legislative failure, see: Edward Rubin, 'The Conceptual Explanation for Legislative Failure; review of Noga Morag Levine, *Chasing the Wind: Regulating Air Pollution in the Common Law State*' (2005) 30 *Law and Social Inquiry* 583.

60   Lynne Bennington and Ruth Wein, 'Anti-Discrimination Legislation in Australia: Fair, Effective, Efficient or Irrelevant?' (2000) 21 *International Journal of Manpower* 21. For an economic analysis of employers' evasion of discrimination obligations, see: Shelly Lundberg, 'The Enforcement of Equal Opportunity Laws Under Imperfect Information: Affirmative Action and Alternatives' (1991) 106 *Quarterly Journal of Business and Economics* 309. For a study of enforcement of discrimination law by the US Equal Employment Opportunity Commission, see: Lenahan O'Connell, 'Investigators at Work: How Bureaucratic and Legal Constraints Influence the Enforcement of Discrimination Law' (1991) 51 *Public Administration Review* 123.

61   Bennington and Wein, 'Anti-Discrimination Legislation in Australia'.

62   Ibid.

63   Hepple et al., *Equality, A New Framework*, pp. 67–9.

So, the general challenges of litigating, the poor record of Australian courts in developing anti-discrimination legislation consistently with its beneficial aims, the mixed success of litigating equality guarantees in countries such as Canada and the uncertain effectiveness of 'negative' legislation together augur badly for a plan to achieve social change that is premised, as the ALRC's Equality Act was, on the success and influence of adversarial litigation.

The Senate Committee's Equality Act

In Chapter 4 of its 2008 report on the *SDA*, the senate committee asked the question, 'An Equality Act?' Its deliberations in answering that question make it clear that its conception of an Equality Act is one that consolidates the four existing and concurrent anti-discrimination acts—an exercise commonly referred to as 'harmonisation'.

Harmonisation

The senate committee canvassed a number of submissions, which proposed consolidating the four existing federal anti-discrimination laws into one. Australian Women Lawyers, for example, 'submitted that replacing the existing separate pieces of federal anti-discrimination legislation with a single Equality Act would be a more effective mechanism for dealing with intersecting forms of discrimination';[64] the National Association of Community Legal Centres proposed that 'a single Act would provide a means of harmonising the processes for promoting equality, addressing systemic discrimination and inequality, and dealing with individual complaints';[65] and the Law Council said that 'to have all of the relevant anti-discrimination provisions in one Act at a federal level would certainly make the process much easier for applicants, respondents and practitioners because there is not a consistency in the terms of all of the federal acts'.[66]

Towards achieving this harmonisation, the Australian Human Rights Commission[67] (AHRC) suggested an inquiry to examine 'incorporating the Sex Discrimination Act with other federal discrimination laws, such as the

---

64 Senate Standing Committee on Legal and Constitutional Affairs, *Report on the Effectiveness of the Commonwealth* Sex Discrimination Act 1984 *in Eliminating Discrimination and Promoting Gender Equality*, [4.57].
65 Ibid. [4.58].
66 Ibid. [4.59].
67 The Human Rights and Equal Opportunity Commission (HREOC) as it then was.

Disability Discrimination Act, into one piece of legislation'. This would lead to 'a considered view on whether having a single federal equality act is indeed preferable to the current situation of separate federal acts'.[68]

Against submissions such as these, Margaret Thornton cautioned against 'a so-called omnibus act':

> One of the problems with a so-called omnibus act having a whole range of grounds within the legislation—sex, race, sexuality, age, disability and so on—is that they end up being treated as mirror images of the other. That, I think, can have a distorting effect. We see this happen with State acts, which do follow the omnibus model. I suppose it is both a strength and a weakness of the federal legislation that it has adopted a different model of having the discrete pieces of legislation so that one is not necessarily seen as a mirror image of the other.[69]

Nevertheless, it is clear that in Chapter 4 of its report the senate committee had in mind an 'omnibus' Equality Act that would be a considered consolidation of the existing four federal anti-discrimination laws, and it recommended that the Australian Human Rights Commission 'conduct a public inquiry to examine the merits of replacing the existing federal anti-discrimination acts with a single Equality Act'.[70] In making this recommendation:

> The committee accepts the evidence it received that a clear deficiency of the existing Act and other federal anti-discrimination legislation is its inability to deal with claims of discrimination on intersecting grounds. The committee believes there is some merit in the proposal to address this difficulty by replacing the existing anti-discrimination acts with a single Equality Act.[71]

'Streamlining' the Federal Laws

In April 2010, the federal government announced the 'streamlining' of the four federal anti-discrimination statutes into 'one single comprehensive law'.[72] It seems that the senate committee's harmonisation recommendation will be acted on, although the announcement did not refer to the senate committee and

---

68 Senate Standing Committee on Legal and Constitutional Affairs, *Report on the Effectiveness of the Commonwealth Sex Discrimination Act 1984 in Eliminating Discrimination and Promoting Gender Equality*, [4.62].
69 Ibid. [4.60].
70 Ibid., Rec. 43.
71 Ibid. [11.48].
72 Attorney-General Hon. Robert McClelland MP and Minister for Finance and Deregulation Hon. Lindsay Tanner MP, Reform of Anti-discrimination Legislation, Media release, 21 April 2010, Parliament House, Canberra; Commonwealth of Australia, *Australia's Human Rights Framework*, Commonwealth of Australia, Canberra, 2010, p. 9.

the process does not obviously intend enhancing coverage and protection of anti-discrimination laws, which was the reason behind the senate committee's recommendation. From the little that has been announced, the exercise will produce an omnibus statute, not to enhance protection against discrimination, but to 'reduce the regulatory burden and drive greater efficiencies and improved productivity outcomes by reducing compliance costs for individual and business particularly small business'.[73]

It seems that consolidation of the current four federal anti-discrimination laws into a single 'omnibus' law will be an exercise in technical legal reform, amending problematic provisions and harmonising inconsistent provisions of the four federal anti-discrimination acts. The 'deregulatory' terms of the intended process suggest it is unlikely that there will be any new prescribed personal attributes as grounds for unlawful conduct,[74] although the federal government's subsequent response to the senate committee's report did say that '[f]urther consultation on additional grounds of discrimination will be undertaken as part of the consolidation project'.[75]

Such an omnibus act (and it would not appear to warrant the name 'Equality Act') would reform practice and procedure and, for as long as Australia relies on the complaints-based approach of its current federal anti-discrimination laws, the need for such technical reform is becoming vital. Current anti-discrimination laws—federal, State and Territory—risk losing integrity and respect as their unprincipled diversity increasingly creates confusion, and imposes costs on the private, public and business communities. The laws are poorly worded or dysfunctional and differences among the various statutes are confusing and unprincipled.[76] Some of the differences are historical, some are policy based and some are simply inexplicable. The situation certainly invites an attempt at streamlining, if not 'harmony', although to harmonise anti-discrimination laws nationally would be a herculean task.

Elsewhere in this volume, Graycar and Morgan have set out a number of reasons for being wary of attempting an 'omnibus' solution to these inconsistencies, and I noted above Thornton's warning to the senate committee. Harmonisation of anti-discrimination statutes was, however, a principal reason for the UK *Equality Act 2010*, which I discuss in more detail below, and there were

---

73   McClelland and Tanner, Reform of Anti-Discrimination Legislation.
74   See Senate Standing Committee on Legal and Constitutional Affairs, *Report on the Effectiveness of the Commonwealth* Sex Discrimination Act 1984 *in Eliminating Discrimination and Promoting Gender Equality*, Rec. 43—referring to the possibility of sexual orientation and gender identity as additional grounds.
75   Commonwealth of Australia, *Government Response to Senate Standing Committee on Legal and Constitutional Affairs Report on the Effectiveness of the Commonwealth* Sex Discrimination Act 1984 *in Eliminating Discrimination and Promoting Gender Equality*.
76   See Rees et al., *Anti-Discrimination Law in Australia* [5.1.5.4]–[5.1.5.11].

concerns there too about the difficulty of the task.[77] Certainly, the process of consolidation will be difficult, because it will force provisions for the protection of four very different personal attributes into one legislative regime when there are reasons to maintain some of those differences. The risk that consolidation will result in different provisions being resolved at the level of the lowest common denominator is heightened by the ominous 'deregulatory' rationale for the exercise.

I describe below the extensive process of consultation and expert advice that resulted in the United Kingdom's *Equality Act* and, most relevantly for the technical process of consolidating legislation, the Discrimination Law Review, *A Framework for Fairness*.[78] The McClelland/Tanner media release does not promise such a process. Instead, the government will go straight to developing 'exposure draft legislation as the basis for consultation',[79] obviating the opportunity for any public deliberation about theory, philosophy or principle that might be resolved before words are put on paper. The dominant principle seems to have been decided: deregulate and reduce the burden of compliance. If a reduced compliance burden is the goal, there is no need to consult; the best way to achieve this would be to repeal anti-discrimination laws. That is a fanciful prospect, one would hope, but it is consistent with the fact that the streamlining exercise seems not to be motivated by reasons such as the pursuit of equality, recognition of the right to non-discrimination, respect for human rights or protection of marginalised groups.

The government appears unconcerned to inquire into, for example, how to reduce the burden of proof or, more substantially, to inquire into the fundamental conceptual issues that were the subject of deep and extensive deliberation in the United Kingdom, such as the meaning and type of equality goal, the extent and nature of the harm that is being addressed and the continuing usefulness of reactive, negative, third-generation anti-discrimination laws.

A Positive Equality Duty?

Separately from its discussion of an Equality Act in Chapter 4, the senate committee considered in Chapter 9 proposals for legislating a 'positive duty to promote equality'. The senate committee canvassed submissions from the Equal

---

77   See Robin Allen, A Single Equality Act: Patchwork of Promise, Paper presented at Equal Protection, Working for a Single Equality Act Conference convened by Justice, National Aids Trust and the Trades Union Congress, 12 May 2003.

78   *A Framework for Fairness: Proposals for a Single Equality Bill for Great Britain* (<http://www.equalities. gov.uk/PDF/DLRConsultation.pdf>). For a critique of the consultation paper's 'radical shift of regulatory philosophy in equality legislation', see Christopher McCrudden, 'Equality and Reflexive Regulation: A Response to the Discrimination Law Review's Consultative Paper (2007) 36 *Industrial Law Journal* 25.

79   McClelland and Tanner, Reform of Anti-Discrimination Legislation.

Opportunity Commission of Western Australia,[80] Women's Health Victoria[81] and the WA Equal Opportunity Commission,[82] which recommended amending the *SDA* to impose a positive duty on public organisations to eliminate discrimination and harassment and to promote equality—similar to the approach taken in the United Kingdom under what is now the *Equality Act 2010* (UK).

The idea of a positive duty characterises the fourth generation of equality legislation. The attraction of a positive duty is that it gets in first; it is preventive rather than remedial. While anti-discrimination laws allow inequality to continue—including in the conduct of the state—until it is challenged, a positive duty attempts to achieve equality by requiring conduct, not by punishing misconduct.[83]

Under a positive duty, a person's right to equality is championed by the state, which sets out what is required to be done to realise the right. This is in clear contrast with the current remedial approach, where the state merely enables a person to claim a right to equality by calling someone to account for their conduct. The fourth-generation equality laws are 'based on a positive duty to promote equality rather than simply to refrain from discriminating'.[84]

Fredman identifies this shift in emphasis—from restraining conduct to requiring conduct—as following from the growing awareness that duties of restraint are ineffective in addressing discrimination and inequality.[85] The foreword to the *Discrimination Law Review Consultation Paper* in the United Kingdom spells out transition from third to fourth generation:

> We have reached a situation where we want our institutions to work in a way which prevents unfairness happening in the first place, rather than addressing it after the event through litigation by individuals—though without removing any rights to seek redress where any discrimination has occurred. Getting it right in the first place is better for individuals, for business and for public administration.[86]

---

80 Senate Standing Committee on Legal and Constitutional Affairs, *Report on the Effectiveness of the Commonwealth Sex Discrimination Act 1984 in Eliminating Discrimination and Promoting Gender Equality*, [9.2].

81 Ibid. [9.4–9.6].

82 Ibid., Submission 57.

83 See Hepple et al., *Equality, A New Framework*, pp. 59–65; Sandra Fredman, *Human Rights Transformed: Positive Rights and Positive Duties*, Oxford University Press, UK, 2008. For a useful overview of legislation with positive equality duties and references, see: Gabrielle Szabo, *Mainstreaming Equality in the ACT: An Equality Duty for the ACT* Discrimination Act, ACT Human Rights Commission, Canberra, 2008.

84 Sandra Fredman, 'Combating Racism with Human Rights' in Sandra Fredman (ed.), *Discrimination and Human Rights: The Case of Racism*, Oxford University Press, UK, 2001, p. 27; and see Anita Mackay, 'Recent Developments in Sexual Harassment Law: Towards a New Model' (2009) 14 *Deakin Law Review* 189, 204–5.

85 Fredman, *Human Rights Transformed*, p. 175. Fredman is a champion of the idea of positive equality duties and has written about them extensively, in detail and with enthusiasm: see bibliography.

86 Ruth Kelly, 'Foreword', in *A Framework for Fairness*, p. 7.

From an international human rights perspective, Article 3 of the International Covenant on Civil and Political Rights obliges states to 'ensure the equal right of men and women to the enjoyment of all civil and political rights set forth in the present Covenant'. In its General Comment 28, the UN Human Rights Committee considers that the meaning of Article 3 focuses on 'the important impact of this article on the enjoyment by women of the human rights protected under the Covenant',[87] and says that '[t]he State party must not only adopt measures of protection, *but also positive measures* in all areas so as to achieve the effective and equal empowerment of women' (emphasis added).[88]

In her submission, Belinda Smith pointed out to the senate committee that Canada and the United Kingdom, with anti-discrimination regimes analogous to Australia's, had supplemented their 'negative anti-discrimination law system—an individual, complaint based, human rights based mechanism—[with] a positive duty that supplements [that mechanism]'.[89] She noted the positive duties imposed by the *Equal Opportunity for Women in the Workplace Act 1999* (Cth) (*EOWWA*), but described them as 'a very mild, soft process' in contrast with stronger obligations under the *Equality Act 2006* (UK).[90] In her submission to the senate committee, Sara Charlesworth agreed with Smith that the existing duties of private sector employers under the *EOWWA* are inadequate,[91] and suggested that the mooted positive duty to promote equality be imposed on private as well as public sector employers.[92] She invoked the oft-cited example of 'a statutory requirement on private sector employers in Northern Ireland to monitor and report on their equality practices in relation to the employment of Catholics',[93] saying that 'these duties have been effective in improving the employment profile of Catholics'.[94]

The senate committee received a collaborative submission from leading women's organisations and women's equity specialists,[95] which provided an extensive explanation of the equality duty in the United Kingdom and argued strongly for such a duty. The Australian Council of Trade Unions (ACTU) supported a positive duty to eliminate discrimination applicable to the public and private

---

87   United Nations Human Rights Committee, *General Comment No. 28: Equality of Rights between Men and Women (Article 3)*, 29 March 2000, CCPR/C/21/Rev 1/Add 10 [1], United Nations, New York.

88   Ibid. [3].

89   Senate Standing Committee on Legal and Constitutional Affairs, *Report on the Effectiveness of the Commonwealth Sex Discrimination Act 1984 in Eliminating Discrimination and Promoting Gender Equality*, [9.3].

90   Ibid. [9.7].

91   Ibid. [9.9].

92   Ibid. [9.8].

93   See Hepple et al., *Equality, A New Framework*, pp. 67–9.

94   Senate Standing Committee on Legal and Constitutional Affairs, *Report on the Effectiveness of the Commonwealth Sex Discrimination Act 1984 in Eliminating Discrimination and Promoting Gender Equality*, [9.10].

95   Ibid., Submission 60.

sectors,[96] and the Australian Human Rights Commission supported amending the *SDA* to impose a positive duty to eliminate sex discrimination similar to the approach taken in relation to standards for disability discrimination under the *Disability Discrimination Act 1992* (Cth).[97]

Opposition came from the Australian Chamber of Commerce and Industry, which protested that '[t]he difficulty for employers is knowing exactly what their legal obligation is and how to comply with it. If there is a general amorphous obligation on employers, particularly vicarious liability, it would be very difficult for the employer to ensure that they comply with it',[98] and that

> compulsory plans and the like are simply additional costs to small businesses, additional regulatory burdens…They will simply become an exercise in compliance and will not contribute to further cultural change and awareness and diversity and the like, but will also be potentially resented because they cost money or will be quite narrowly complied with and put away…it is a far more powerful notion to see a more diverse workplace, to see a more diverse [range] of people in work and the benefits they provide in your company and in your peer companies and to hear personal stories of successes.[99]

The extent to which the senate committee was looking ahead to a positive equality duty is unclear. The possibility that such a duty was in their contemplation can only be inferred from its having canvassed the issue of positive duties in Chapter 9, where it said, for example, 'it would be worthwhile considering the creation of broad positive duties: to promote equality and remove discrimination [and] to take reasonable steps to avoid sexual harassment'.[100] The senate committee referred specifically to the UK *Equality Act* as 'a useful model which could be adopted and applied either to public sector organisations or to both the public and private sector',[101] and as an add-on to Recommendation 43, said: 'The inquiry…should also consider…what additional mechanisms Commonwealth law should adopt in order to most effectively promote equality.'[102]

In considering 'additional mechanisms', the senate committee had in mind what it called the 'more innovative approaches to addressing discrimination both overseas and in our own states and territories'.[103] This was being generous to the States and Territories. There is little that is innovative in their approach to

---

96   Ibid. [9.11].
97   Ibid. [9.12].
98   Ibid. [9.16].
99   Ibid. [9.17].
100   Ibid. [11.9].
101   Ibid. [11.94].
102   Ibid., Rec. 43.
103   Ibid. [11.110].

addressing discrimination; the legislation is invariably of the 'third-generation' approach to addressing inequality. What differences exist between the anti-discrimination legislation of the States and Territories on the one hand, and the federal anti-discrimination statutes on the other, are variations on a persistent theme of individual remedial measures for unlawful conduct. Some of those variations are of interest—such as a different test for discrimination in the Australian Capital Territory and Victoria,[104] a prohibition against vilifying women in Tasmania,[105] absolute proscription in Queensland of sexual harassment without limit to an area of activity[106] and protection against 'ethno-religious' discrimination in New South Wales[107]—but they are not the 'innovative approaches to addressing discrimination' that the senate committee was looking for. Only the standards under the *Disability Discrimination Act (DDA)*[108] are a real step away from the 'if you keep scolding them they'll eventually learn' approach to eliminating discriminatory behaviour, which characterises Australian anti-discrimination law.[109] The standards have not, however, been replicated in other legislation—not even the subsequent federal anti-discrimination statute: the *Age Discrimination Act 2004*.

It would seem, therefore, that as well as the technical reforms that go towards 'harmonisation' and an omnibus anti-discrimination statute, the senate committee's report does anticipate positive duties as 'additional mechanisms Commonwealth law should adopt in order to most effectively promote equality' along the lines of positive duties legislation in the United Kingdom to which the senate committee was referred by many of the submissions.

The federal government's response to the senate committee's recommendation pointedly makes no comment on 'additional mechanisms', saying only that the recommendation has been 'noted'.[110] As the government's earlier 'streamlining' announcement does not refer to the possibility of a positive equality duty, it seems the government has no interest in considering new ways of achieving equality through legislative measures—welcome news no doubt to the Australian Chamber of Commerce and Industry in light of its submissions to the senate committee.

---

104 *Discrimination Act 1991* (ACT), s 8(1)(a) and *Equal Opportunity Act 2010* (Vic.), s 8(1), where mere unfavourable treatment is sufficient and there is no need for 'less' favourable treatment.

105 *Anti-Discrimination Act 1998* (Tas.), s. 17(1).

106 *Anti-Discrimination Act 1991* (Qld), s. 118.

107 Definition of 'race', *Anti-Discrimination Act 1977* (NSW), s. 4.

108 *Disability Discrimination Act 1992* (Cth), Part 2, Division 2A.

109 For an overview of Australia's anti-discrimination regime, see Belinda Smith, 'Australian Anti-Discrimination Laws—Framework, Developments and Issues' in Hiroya Nakakubo and Takashi Araki (eds), *New Developments in Employment Discrimination Law*, Kluwer Law International, London, 2008, pp. 115–46.

110 Commonwealth of Australia, *Government Response to Senate Standing Committee on Legal and Constitutional Affairs Report on the Effectiveness of the Commonwealth* Sex Discrimination Act 1984 *in Eliminating Discrimination and Promoting Gender Equality*.

Enacting an Equality Act in the United Kingdom

The British Labour Government went to the 2005 election with a policy to enact an Equality Bill. The Equality Bill was to

> simplify the law which, over the last four decades, has become complex and difficult to navigate. Nine major pieces of legislation and around 100 statutory instruments will be replaced by a single Act written in plain English to make it easier for individuals and employers to understand their legal rights and obligations.[111]

As well, the Bill would 'put a new duty on public bodies, government and local councils to consider how to reduce socio-economic inequalities'.[112] These became the 'two main purposes' of the government's 2009 Equality Bill: 'to harmonise discrimination law, and to strengthen the law to support progress on equality.'[113]

Background Inquiries

The UK Government's reform process can be traced to the independent report in 2000, *Equality: A New Framework*,[114] conducted by the University of Cambridge Centre for Public Law and the Judge Institute of Management Studies, and funded by the Joseph Rowntree Charitable Trust, the Nuffield Foundation and Organizational Resources Counselors Incorporated. It was described as the 'brainchild of Anthony (Lord) Lester, whose enthusiasm, guidance and unfailing support' is credited with making the review happen at all.[115] The report was 'supported by a series of papers written by commentators of the first rank'[116] and by an advisory panel and a panel of experts. It made 53 recommendations— the first of which was that '[t]here should be a single Equality Act in Britain'. Anticipating the *Equality Act* that eventuated, Recommendation 7 was that '[a] nti-discrimination measures should be augmented by positive duties to promote equality which do not depend upon proof by individuals'.

In 2000, at the beginning of the United Kingdom's journey to an Equality Act, Lester describes a situation in the United Kingdom that is very like that in Australia in 2010:

---

111 UK Labour Party, *Labour Policies: Equality*, Labour Party, London, <http://www.labour.org.uk/ Equalities>
112 Ibid.
113 UK Parliament, *Explanatory Notes: Equality Bill 2009 (UK), Bill as introduced (incorporating side-by-side Explanatory Notes). Volume I*, Bill 85 08-09, (27 April 2009), Parliament of the United Kingdom, London, [10], <http://www.publications.parliament.uk/pa/cm200809/cmbills/085/voli/09085i.i-ii.html>
114 Hepple et al., *Equality, A New Framework*.
115 Ibid., 'Acknowledgements'.
116 Allen, Reforming Australia's Anti-Discrimination Legislation, p. 5.

[The anti-discrimination] legislation is now outdated, and there is a really pressing need for reform to make the law comprehensive, consistent, effective, and user-friendly. During the quarter century since its enactment, the limits and defects of the legislation have become more and more apparent, and the passing of each new measure has added to the incoherence and opaqueness...[Equality] Commissions and other[s] have repeatedly called for the reform of this tangled web of legislation...[b]ut successive Governments have failed to heed their recommendations, preferring instead to make limited and piecemeal changes. The defective state of the law helps no-one except lawyers.[117]

The momentum created by the independent review led to reports from two concurrent public inquiries. One was The Equalities Review—a 'root and branch review to investigate the causes of persistent discrimination and inequality in British society'[118]—which produced the report *Fairness and Freedom*.[119] The other was the Discrimination Law Review, which produced a consultation paper, *A Framework for Fairness*.[120]

The Equalities Review tackled the conceptual and practical issue of 'equality' and, based on data, expert evidence, commissioned empirical research, consultations, stakeholder discussions and personal narratives,[121] it set out 10 steps to greater equality,[122] and criteria against which progress should be measured.[123]

The Discrimination Law Review consulted on 'proposals for a Single Equality Bill for Great Britain',[124] meeting with general audiences in regional public events, with specialist audiences on age discrimination and public sector duties, and with stakeholders and interest groups.[125] The scope of the Discrimination Law Review anticipated the three principal parts of what became the *Equality Act 2010* (UK): first, 'harmonising and simplifying the law',[126] which included

---

117   Hepple et al., *Equality, A New Framework*, 'Preface'.
118   UK Cabinet Office, Background information on the Equalities Review, <http://archive.cabinetoffice.gov.uk/equalitiesreview/background.html>
119   UK Government, *Fairness and Freedom: The Final Report of the Equalities Review*, Government of the United Kingdom, London, 2007, <http://archive.cabinetoffice.gov.uk/equalitiesreview/upload/assets/www.theequalitiesreview.org.uk/equality_review.pdf>
120   UK Government Discrimination Law Review, *A Framework for Fairness—The Equality Bill*, June 2008, Consultation Paper, Government of the United Kingdom, London. For a critique of the consultation paper's 'radical shift of regulatory philosophy in equality legislation', see McCrudden, 'Equality and Reflexive Regulation'.
121   UK Government, *Fairness and Freedom*, Annexure D.
122   Ibid., pp. 10–11, Ch. 5.
123   Ibid., p. 11, Ch. 5.
124   Ibid., p. 3.
125   UK Government, *The Equality Bill—Government Response to the Consultation*, June 2008, Government of the United Kingdom, London, p. 14 [1.6]–[1.7], <http://www.equalities.gov.uk/pdf/EqBillGovResponse.pdf>
126   UK Government, *Fairness and Freedom*, p. 16.

simplifying and standardising definitions and tests in discrimination law, and simplifying and harmonising exceptions; second, 'making the law more effective',[127] which included simplifying the existing public sector equality duties in a single duty; and third, 'modernising the law',[128] which included adding and extending protected grounds such as age, gender reassignment and maternity, extending protection to new areas such as private clubs and expanding the grounds for protection from harassment.

In its response to the Discrimination Law Review,[129] the government announced its intention to introduce an Equality Bill, informed by the Discrimination Law Review and the Equalities Review, and by an analysis of disadvantage set out by the Government Equalities Office, *A Fairer Future—The Equality Bill and other Action to make Equality a Reality*.[130] Among the many stark conclusions the data in *A Fairer Future* pointed to were that without the restructuring of discrimination law as proposed in the Equality Bill, 'the pay gap between men and women in the UK will not close until 2085; and it will take almost 100 years for people from ethnic minorities to get the same job prospects as white people'.[131]

Complementing its response, the government published its proposal for an Equality Bill, *Framework for a Fairer Future—The Equality Bill*,[132] to 'strengthen protection, advance equality and declutter the law'.[133]

The *Equality Act 2010* (UK)

The Equality Bill was in the British Parliament for a few days short of a year. It was introduced in the House of Commons on 24 April 2009 and was debated and refined in 20 sittings of the Public Bill Committee. On 2 December, the Bill was reported to the House and the motion that it be read a third time was passed 338 votes to eight. This degree of support is significant in light of concerns that a change in government in the United Kingdom in the 2010 elections could lead to repeal, or at least to obstruction, of the *Equality Act*. In the House of Lords, the Bill was scrutinised at six committee sittings and was returned to the House of Commons on 23 March 2010 with proposed amendments. The House of Commons accepted the amendments and passed the Bill on 6 April;

---

127   Ibid.
128   Ibid.
129   UK Government, *The Equality Bill—Government Response to the Consultation.*
130   UK Government Equalities Office, *A Fairer Future—The Equality Bill and other Action to make Equality a Reality*, June 2008, Government of the United Kingdom, London, <http://www.equalities.gov.uk/pdf/ NEWGEO_FairerFuture_may09_acc.pdf>
131   Ibid., p. 6.
132   UK Government, *Framework for a Fairer Future—The Equality Bill*, June 2008, Government of the United Kingdom, London, <http://www.equalities.gov.uk/PDF/FrameworkforaFairerFuture.pdf>
133   Ibid., p. 8.

the *Equality Act 2010* (UK) received the Royal Assent on 8 April 2010.[134] While some provisions began on assent, most of the Act will begin at the discretion of the government.[135] This too is significant, as the government elected in the 2010 elections is under no obligation to put the UK *Equality Act* into operation.

The UK *Equality Act* is an omnibus act of the sort anticipated by the Australian senate committee in its review of the *SDA* and now the subject of the federal government's streamlining process. It repeals and replaces the whole of the *Equal Pay Act 1970*, the *Sex Discrimination Acts 1975* and *1986*, the *Race Relations Act 1976* and the *Disability Discrimination Act 1995*, and various Employment Equality Regulations relating to, for example, religion and belief, sexual orientation and age,[136] and leaves intact so much of the *Equality Act 2006* as relates to the *Constitution* and the operation of the Equality and Human Rights Commission.

As an illustration of its 'omnibus' nature, the UK *Equality Act* makes common provision for what it calls 'particular strands of discrimination',[137] which are discrimination 'because of' age, disability, gender reassignment, marriage and civil partnership, race, religion or belief, sex and sexual orientation. As well, the Act deals with harassing conduct 'related to' age, disability, gender reassignment, race, religion or belief, sex and sexual orientation[138] and victimisation.[139]

More than merely consolidating different anti-discrimination statues into one, however, the UK *Equality Act 2010* legislates to impose a positive equality duty.

The Equality Duty in the UK *Equality Act*

The statement of a positive duty in the UK *Equality Act* is a very tentative one. It is not a guarantee of equality. In parliamentary debates on the UK Equality Bill 2009, Lynne Featherstone, a Liberal Democrat, thought that 'the Government could have taken a more radical perspective and extended the commitment to equality beyond the Bill, with an overarching equality guarantee'.[140]

The duty in Section 149 of the *Equality Act* is called a 'Public sector equality duty' and is limited in its operation to public sector actors. A public authority must, in the exercise of its functions, have due regard to the need to

---

134 *Equality Act 2010* (UK).
135 Ibid., s. 216(3).
136 Ibid., Schedule 27.
137 Ibid., s. 25.
138 Ibid., s. 26.
139 Ibid., s. 27.
140 *Hansard*, House of Commons, 11 May 2009, Column 577.

- eliminate discrimination, harassment, victimisation and any other conduct that is prohibited by or under the Act

- advance equality of opportunity between people who share a relevant protected characteristic and people who do not share it

- foster good relations between people who share a relevant protected characteristic and people who do not share it.

A duty to 'have due regard' is weak. As early as 2001, Fredman described as 'disturbingly vague' the then new duty in the *Race Relations Act 1976* (UK) to 'have regard to the need…to promote equality of opportunity'.[141] Fredman repeated the concern in 2008, when commenting on a similar duty ('have due regard') introduced to the *Sex Discrimination Act 1975* (UK).[142] In their submission to both the Equality Review and the Discrimination Law Review, Fredman and Spencer made the point again and—after describing the limitations of a duty to 'have due regard'—they proposed instead a duty to 'take such steps as are necessary and proportionate to eliminate discrimination and to achieve the progressive realisation of equality (as defined)'.[143]

The extent of the duty 'to have regard' (whether 'due' or not) has been left in the hands of the courts—a legislative drafting decision by which the Parliament has effectively opted to entrust the courts with the full development of its reforms. Commenting on the duty in the *Race Relations Act*, Fredman said:[144]

> [I]t only requires the authority to 'pay due regard'…This means that the duty is only breached by a failure to 'properly consider whether there was any potential discrimination' [citing *R (Elias) v. Secretary of State for Defence, Commission for Racial Equality* [2005] EWHC 1435]. If, after considering these matters, the authority adopts precisely the same scheme, it would have done so after having due regard to the obligations under the statute and therefore discharged its duty. Nor is the duty breached if an authority forms the view on proper grounds that there is no issue of unlawful discrimination which could sensibly be said to arise.

The nature of the duty was explained more recently, in 2009, by the UK Court of Appeal in *Domb v The London Borough of Hammersmith and Fulham*.[145] The

---

141 Sandra Fredman, 'Equality: A New Generation' (2001) 30 *Industrial Law Journal* 145, 146, 168.
142 Sandra Fredman, 'Reforming Equal Pay Laws' (2008) 37 *Industrial Law Journal* 193, 214. A duty in the same terms was introduced by the *Disability Discrimination Act 1992* (Cth), s. 49A.
143 Sandra Fredman and Sarah Spencer, Delivering Equality: Towards an Outcome-Focused Positive Duty, Submission to the Cabinet Office Equality Review and to the Discrimination Law Review, June 2006.
144 Fredman, 'Reforming Equal Pay Laws', p. 214.
145 *Domb, Sobral and Bushiwa v The London Borough of Hammersmith and Fulham, and The Equality and Human Rights Commission* [2009] EWCA Civ 941.

burden of the duty is not onerous: 'there is no statutory duty to carry out a formal impact assessment…the duty is to have due regard, not to achieve results or to refer in terms to the duty…due regard does not exclude paying regard to countervailing factors, but is "the regard that is appropriate in all the circumstances".'[146] More positively, however, 'the test of whether a decision maker has had due regard is a test of the substance of the matter, not of mere form or box-ticking…the duty must be performed with vigour and with an open mind'.[147]

The Meaning of 'Equality' in the UK *Equality Act*

The object of the duty is 'equality' and there are many ways in which equality can be characterised. Fredman suggests a range of equality principles that might drive the imposition of a duty, such as formal equality, equality of outcomes and equality of opportunity, and three equality aims that a duty might be directed towards: 'removal of stigma, redistribution [and] accommodation.'[148] She would agree with Graycar and Morgan's observation in this volume that to propose a duty 'does not necessarily touch upon the basic understanding of equality' and that 'without clear attention to what is meant by equality', the new provisions could be limited only to equality of opportunity.

The UK Equalities Review canvassed some ways of seeing equality: equality of process, which it described as ensuring that people are treated in the same manner in any given situation; equality of worth (according each individual equal respect); equality of outcome (aiming for equal wealth or the same educational attainment); and equality of opportunity (ensuring that circumstances beyond an individual's control should not undermine the opportunity an individual has to thrive).[149] The review observed that

> in the real world, outcomes are dependent on opportunities and opportunities on outcomes. If your family is poor, your educational potential is less likely to be realised; and if your educational achievement is lower, you are likely to earn less. But it is central to our terms of reference to focus on outcomes and, in particular, what will reduce the gap between those who enjoy the best life chances and those who suffer the worst.[150]

---

146 *Domb, Sobral and Bushiwa* [52], per Lord Justice Rix.
147 Ibid.
148 Fredman, 'Combating Racism with Human Rights', p. 29.
149 UK Government, *Fairness and Freedom*, pp. 14–15.
150 Ibid., p. 15.

This led the review to a definition that 'attempts to accommodate the rigorous testing of the intellectual, but also strives to be meaningful and practical to everyone':

> An equal society protects and promotes equal, real freedom and substantive opportunity to live in the ways people value and would choose, so that everyone can flourish. An equal society recognises people's different needs, situations and goals and removes the barriers that limit what people can do and can be.[151]

The long title of the *Equality Act* describes the Act as one concerned with 'reducing socio-economic inequalities' and 'increas[ing] equality of opportunity'. It does not define equality or socioeconomic inequality and relies on two strategies: the longstanding 'negative' approach of prohibiting conduct on prescribed characteristics in prescribed areas of activity[152] and the more recent 'positive' approach of imposing a duty to act to eliminate, or at least reduce, inequality.[153]

Lessons for Australia from the United Kingdom

Without gainsaying the issues for creating omnibus legislation that Thornton[154] and Graycar and Morgan[155] have warned of, the UK *Equality Act* shows that it is possible to roll into one statute separate concurrent statutes that prohibit characteristic-based discrimination. The federal government's proposed streamlining exercise will be the test of that—although the UK reform exercise was driven by a commitment to enhancing protection, not to reducing the compliance burden.

The UK *Equality Act* shows as well that it can make sense to complement the negative prohibitions on conduct that offend equality by imposing a positive duty that promotes equality—although the federal government's response to the senate committee inquiry makes clear that a positive equality duty is not within its contemplation.

Process

The obvious lessons for Australia from the recent UK experience are of process. As the extensive collaborative submission to the senate committee said of the reform exercise in the United Kingdom: 'By embracing a three-year process the

---

151 Ibid., pp. 6, 16.
152 *Equality Act 2010* (UK), Parts 2–10, 14, 15.
153 Ibid., Parts 1, 11, 12, 13.
154 Thornton, Testimony before the Senate Standing Committee on Legal and Constitutional Affairs, [4–60].
155 Graycar and Morgan, this volume.

Government has been able to bring people along.'[156] Even this simple lesson of 'bringing people along' seems lost on the federal government, which has announced only that it 'intends to develop exposure draft legislation as the basis for consultation with stakeholders and the public'.[157]

Of the many important lessons in process from the UK experience, one is that if a government shows no interest in improving protection against discriminatory conduct then non-government actors, perhaps led by committed (and well-connected) champions, need to make the issue one of public importance, as Lord Lester's independent review in the United Kingdom did.

Another lesson—harder to emulate but vital to achieving measures that will work—is that the analysis of current inadequacy and the proposals for reform need to be informed by extensive research such as statistical and survey data, expert advice and extensive consultation. The UK *Equality Act* is the culmination of a reform process that was based on sophisticated research and widespread consultation. The Equalities Review, for example, commissioned surveys, studies and advice from various expert academics, research centres and consultancies on issues such as the history of equality for different groups in the past 60 years, personal testimonies and case studies on people's lived experiences of inequality, prejudice and discrimination, equality issues for children and families, gay, lesbian, transgender and transsexual people's experiences of inequality, employment disadvantages of different social groups, prejudice in Britain and public attitudes to equality, tools with which to tackle prejudice and a framework for measuring inequality.[158]

A refinement to this emphasis on research is that it needs to be undertaken with an explicit desire to pursue the same social policy goal of equality as was the subject of the inadequate regime, but to find better means of doing so. Lester's independent review, for example, engaged in a 'profound study of what is wrong with existing laws', with the aim of establishing 'what could be done to develop an accessible legislative framework…to promote equal opportunities'.[159] When the UK Government began responding to the momentum established by the independent report, it established the Discrimination Law Review in a similar spirit—'to consider the opportunities for creating a clearer and more streamlined discrimination legislative framework which produces better outcomes for those who currently experience disadvantage'.[160]

---

156 Senate Standing Committee on Legal and Constitutional Affairs, *Report on the Effectiveness of the Commonwealth* Sex Discrimination Act 1984 *in Eliminating Discrimination and Promoting Gender Equality*, Submission 60, p. 37.
157 McClelland and Tanner, Reform of Anti-Discrimination Legislation.
158 UK Government, *Fairness and Freedom*, pp. 148–50.
159 Hepple et al., *Equality, A New Framework*, 'Preface'.
160 UK Government, *A Framework for Fairness*, p. 3.

The tone of the reform process in the United Kingdom was established from the outset. It was not motivated principally by a desire to reduce the burden of compliance. More fundamentally, it did not revisit a commitment to eliminating inequality. I contrast this with an approach that would treat the reform process as one that, even only impliedly, reopens for discussion the merits of a discrimination legislative framework at all—and of state intervention designed to achieve equality. Such an invitation does seem implicit in the proposed federal streamlining process, which invites those who need to comply with anti-discrimination laws to say how the burden of doing so could be reduced; as I suggested above, the best way to achieve this would be, if not wholly to repeal anti-discrimination laws, then to significantly reduce their strength and scope.

A further lesson is that the discussion of reform needs to be informed by a theoretical conception of the equality aims that are being perused. From the independent review[161] and the Equalities Review[162] through to the government's proposal for an Equality Bill,[163] discussion in the United Kingdom centred consistently on two conceptions of equality—equality of recognition and equality of opportunity—which manifested in the *Equality Act* as, respectively, the continuing prohibitions against discriminatory conduct and the imposition of positive duties. This exercise of clearly conceptualising the equality goals again seems outside the contemplation of the proposed Australian federal streamlining process.

An important issue of process is who will conduct the necessary review, and how. Elsewhere in this volume, Graycar and Morgan make a strong case for the work to be done by experts such as are to be found at the Australian Human Rights Commission. Certainly, the UK process shows the benefit of extensive contribution by a wide range of experts in discrimination theory, philosophy, law, practice, comparative studies, research and lived experience, who participated in processes that were run within departments and by independent bodies. There is no sign of this extensive, deep and thoughtful approach in the 'streamlining' exercise announced by the federal government in April 2010, in which a 'Better Regulation Ministerial Partnership' will consult on already-drafted legislation with a predetermined deregulatory goal.

The Content of a Positive Equality Duty in Australia

The UK process for achieving an *Equality Act* that both harmonises negative provisions and establishes positive duties is attractive. The result of the process

---

161 Hepple et al., *Equality, A New Framework*.
162 UK Government, *Fairness and Freedom*.
163 UK Government, *Framework for a Fairer Future*.

is less appealing—at least in the formulation of the positive duty: the UK *Equality Act* requires only the vague standard of 'having due regard' to certain matters, and requires it only of public authorities.

Neither the senate committee nor the submissions to it turned their mind to how such a duty ought to be framed. If we are to admire the UK process that achieved an *Equality Act*—and I think we ought—then we must be careful at the same time not to unthinkingly accept the result of that process. The point that the UK *Equality Act* arrived at after its political gestation ought not be the point at which Australia begins its own deliberations.

Smith cautioned that Australia needs to take account of local considerations in working out how best to implement positive duties, but did not spell out those considerations.[164] I suggest some considerations here.

One that comes to mind is the Australian judiciary's persistently technical and curmudgeonly approach to the beneficial aims of discrimination legislation, which I noted above. This suggests to me that a detailed prescriptive statutory duty is desirable, leaving the courts with a limited interpretative role. While Smith suggests that with less prescriptive legislation the courts could be less technical and more inclined to give effect to the beneficial aims of anti-discrimination legislation,[165] I am not as confident. Indeed, I am inclined to think that the legislative terms of the duty ought to be quite prescriptive—effectively codified—if it is to withstand the unsympathetic approach the Australian courts have been inclined to take to anti-discrimination legislation.

A local consideration is the constitutional limitation on the effective scope of a positive duty imposed by federal legislation on public actors, given the extent of services provided by the States. The Commonwealth is likely to have power to require government actors, whether Commonwealth or State, to give effect to an equality right, although there would be some limitations on the extent of that power.[166]

Another consideration—a favourable one—is the well-entrenched acceptance in the Australian public sector of merits review and judicial review of decisions, a process that lies at the heart of the justiciability of a positive equality duty.

There was little discussion in the United Kingdom about whether the equality duty under the UK *Equality Act* would operate in the private sphere. As Smith

---

164   Belinda Smith, 'It's about Time—For a New Regulatory Approach to Equality' (2008) 36 *Federal Law Review* 117, 138.
165   Smith, 'Models of Anti-Discrimination Laws'.
166   I am grateful to my colleague James Stellios for advice on this point.

points out,[167] the independent report in the United Kingdom did not limit the proposed positive duty to public authorities,[168] and Fredman has criticised the fact that the duty in the United Kingdom is limited in that way.[169] There could and should be, however, a good discussion of that possibility in Australia, where the established history of anti-discrimination laws operating in both public and private spheres suggests that we need not be coy about expecting private actors to comply with an equality duty.[170]

The concurrent operation in the Australian Capital Territory and in Victoria of human rights legislation is not a relevant consideration—at least not one that militates against an Equality Act. As the UK experience shows, an Equality Act that imposes positive duties is conceptually separate from a human rights act or charter. Whatever right to equality is provided for in a human rights law, the active and prescriptive imposition of an equality duty is a related but separate exercise. The *Victorian Equal Opportunity Review Report*, for example, explains the concurrent operation of the proposed positive duty with the duty under Section 38 of the Charter on a public authority to give effect to human rights.[171]

Existing Positive Duties in Australia

Before the passage in Victoria of a new *Equal Opportunity Act* in 2010, the few existing positive equality duties in Australia were limited to employment— and largely to public sector employment—although Mackay makes the point that complying with a positive equality duty in Australia would 'not involve a radical departure from what many employers are already doing to avoid vicarious liability' (for negligence).[172]

The best-known explicit positive equality duty in Australia is in the *EOWWA*, which was the subject of submissions to and discussion by the senate committee, noted above.[173] There is consensus that the *EOWWA* needs considerable strengthening, but its scope would never be so wide as to obviate the desirability of a general equality duty, as Graycar and Morgan suggest elsewhere in this volume.

---

167   Belinda Smith, Positive Equality Duties (UK), Paper presented at The Future of Australian Anti-Discrimination Law Workshop, University of Melbourne Law School, Melbourne, 15 November 2007.

168   Hepple et al., *Equality, A New Framework*, Rec. 7.

169   Fredman, 'Reforming Equal Pay Laws' 214.

170   See Szabo, *Mainstreaming Equality in the ACT*, pp. 37–8.

171   Department of Justice, *An Equality Act for a Fairer Victoria: Equal Opportunity Review Final Report*, Department of Justice, Government of Victoria, Melbourne, June 2008, p. 80.

172   Mackay, 'Recent Developments in Sexual Harassment Law' 206.

173   Senate Standing Committee on Legal and Constitutional Affairs, *Report on the Effectiveness of the Commonwealth Sex Discrimination Act 1984 in Eliminating Discrimination and Promoting Gender Equality*, [9.7]–[9.9].

Similar positive duties exist under legislation covering Australian government employees, under legislation in New South Wales and Queensland, and under policy in Western Australia.[174] A type of positive duty exists under the disability standards in the *Disability Discrimination Act 1992* (Cth), also noted above. By way of international example, there are legislated positive duties in like jurisdictions such as Northern Ireland,[175] South Africa,[176] Canada[177] and the United States.[178]

The Victorian *Equal Opportunity Act 2010* was passed by the Victorian Parliament on 15 April 2010 and most of its provisions will begin on 1 August 2011 if they are not proclaimed to start before then.[179] It implements many of the two inquiries that preceded it,[180] including that '[t]he Act should contain a duty to eliminate discrimination as far as possible'.[181] Section 14 of the Act very closely follows the recommendation: 'A person must take reasonable and proportionate measures to eliminate...discrimination, sexual harassment and victimisation as far as possible.' The review report recommended that the duty apply in both public and private spheres[182]—and that, too, is just what the new Victorian *Equal Opportunity Act* does. An alleged breach of the duty can be the subject of investigation, inquiry and report by the Victorian Equal Opportunity and Human Rights Commission.[183]

Conclusion: The Best Next Step

Positive duties are an innovative and necessary conception of an Equality Act, to move beyond the 'third-generation' reactive and negative legislative response to discrimination and towards an active approach to achieving equality. There is, however, a real question of whether there will ever be such an Equality Act in Australia.

---

174 See Szabo (*Mainstreaming Equality in the ACT*, Part 2 and Appendix A), citing: *Pubic Service Act 1999* (Cth); *Equal Employment Opportunity (Commonwealth Authorities) Act 1987* (Cth); *Anti-Discrimination Act 1977* (NSW), Part 9A; *Equal Opportunity in Employment Act 1992* (Qld); WA Equal Opportunity Commission, *Policy Framework for Substantive Equality*, 2004.

175 *Northern Ireland Act 1998* (UK) (s. 75 and Schedule 9), relating to public authorities, and the *Fair Employment and Treatment (NI) Order 1998* ('FETO'; previously the *Fair Employment Act 1976*).

176 *Employment Equity Act 1998* (South Africa); *Promotion of Equality and Prevention of Unfair Discrimination Act 2000* (South Africa), s. 5.

177 *Employment Equity Act 1995* (Can.).

178 *Executive Order 11246 of Sept. 24, 1965—Equal employment opportunity* (US).

179 *Equal Opportunity Act 2010* (Vic.), s. 2(5).

180 Scrutiny of Acts and Regulations Committee (SARC), *Exceptions and Exemptions to the Equal Opportunity Act 1995—Final Report*, Government of Victoria, Melbourne, 2009; *An Equality Act for a Fairer Victoria*.

181 *An Equality Act for a Fairer Victoria*, Rec. 9, p. 41.

182 Ibid.

183 *Equal Opportunity Act 2010* (Vic.), s. 15(4), Part 9.

I would like to be hopeful that the *Equal Opportunity Act 2010* (Vic.) will pave the way for a national equality duty, but it is hard to see this happening. First, there is the dispiriting failure of successive federal governments to follow the examples of the Australian Capital Territory and Victoria of legislating to establish human rights standards for public conduct. The current federal Labor Government continues to avoid committing itself to passing legislation that would commit its own legislation and conduct to human rights compliance.[184] And there is the very limited, perhaps even diminishing, vision of anti-discrimination protection in either the federal government's announcement of a deregulatory streamlining process or its very limited response to the senate committee's report.

The travesty is that when dealing with anti-discrimination legislation, federal governments choose to respond to the demands of those who do not need protection, rather than taking the initiative to help those who do. With exceptions from time to time and place to place, our governments' policies for the past 15 years or so have tended both to support under-regulated free-market activity and to pander to the shrill and shifting demands of media news and opinion. There will be no equality law at all without public leadership—and that is what we face in Australia.

Strategic activists will perhaps be able to make out a low-compliance, regulation-lite 'business case' for a positive equality duty. Even then, however, they face a battle to overcome government vulnerability to lobbies that are as intent now as they were when opposing the *Sex Discrimination Act* 25 years ago[185] on preserving the power and privilege they have accrued from social inequality.

Bibliography

Books and articles

Allen, Dominique, Reforming Australia's Anti-Discrimination Legislation: Individual Complaints, the Equality Commission and Tackling Discrimination, Doctoral thesis, University of Melbourne, Vic., 2009.

Allen, Robin, A Single Equality Act: Patchwork of Promise, Paper presented at Equal Protection, Working for a Single Equality Act Conference convened by Justice, National Aids Trust and the Trades Union Congress, 12 May 2003.

---

184 McClelland (Launch of Australia's Human Rights Framework) declining to act on Recommendations 17–31 of the National Human Rights Consultation Committee (*National Human Rights Consultation Report*, Commonwealth of Australia, Canberra, 2009).

185 Marian Sawer, this volume.

Australian Taxation Office, *Test Case Litigation Program*, Australian Taxation Office, Canberra, 2010.

Bennington, Lynne and Wein, Ruth, 'Anti-discrimination Legislation in Australia: Fair, Effective, Efficient or Irrelevant?' *(2000) 21 International Journal of Manpower* 21.

Buckley, Melinda (ed.), *Transforming Women's Future: A Guide to Equality Rights Theory and Action*, West Coast Women's Legal Education and Action Fund, Vancouver, BC, 2001.

Davis, Martha, *Brutal Need: Lawyers and the Welfare Rights Movement, 1960–1973*, Yale University Press, New Haven, Conn., 1993.

de Plevitz, Loretta, 'The *Briginshaw* "Standard of Proof" in Anti-Discrimination Law: "Pointing with a Wavering Finger"' (2003) 27(2) *Melbourne University Law Review* 308.

Fredman, Sandra, 'Combating Racism with Human Rights' in Sandra Fredman (ed.), *Discrimination and Human Rights: The Case of Racism*, Oxford University Press, UK, 2001.

Fredman, Sandra, 'Equality: A New Generation' (2001) 30 *Industrial Law Journal* 145.

Fredman, Sandra, *Human Rights Transformed: Positive Rights and Positive Duties*, Oxford University Press, UK, 2008.

Fredman, Sandra, 'Reforming Equal Pay Laws' (2008) 37 *Industrial Law Journal* 193.

Freeman, Jody, 'Defining Family in *Mossop v DSS*: The Challenge of Anti-Essentialism and Interactive Discrimination for Human Rights Litigation' (1994) 44 *University of Toronto Law Journal* 41.

Galligan, Brian and Morton, Fred, Australian Rights Protection, Paper presented to the Australasian Political Studies Association Conference, University of Adelaide, 29 September – 1 October 2004.

Gaze, Beth, 'Context and Interpretation in Anti-Discrimination Law' (2002) 26 *Melbourne University Law Review* 325.

Gaze, Beth, 'The *Sex Discrimination Act* after Twenty Years: Achievements, Disappointments, Disillusionment and Alternatives' *(2004) 27(3) University of New South Wales Law Journal* 914.

Graycar, Regina and Morgan, Jenny, 'A Quarter Century of Feminism in Law: Back to the Future?' (1999) 24 *Alternative Law Journal* 117.

Graycar, Regina and Morgan, Jenny, 'Law Reform: What's In It For Women?' *(2005) 23 Windsor Yearbook on Access to Justice* 393.

Hafen, Bruce, 'Exploring Test Cases in Child Advocacy: Review of Robert H Mnookin *In the Interest of Children, Advocacy law Reform and Public Policy*' (1986–87) 100 *Harvard Law Review* 435.

Halpern, Steffen, 'Assessing the Litigative Role of ACLU Chapters' (1972) 4(2) *Policy Studies Journal* 157.

Hepple, Bob, Coussey, Mary and Choudhury, Tufyal, *Equality, A New Framework: Report of the Independent Review of The Enforcement of UK Anti-Discrimination Legislation*, Hart Publishing, Oxford, 2000.

Hunyor, Jonathon, 'Skin-Deep: Proof and Inferences of Racial Discrimination in Employment' (2003) *25 Sydney Law Review* 535.

Iyer, Nitya, 'Categorical Denials: Equality Rights and the Shaping of Social Identity' (1993–94) 19 *Queen's Law Journal* 179.

Lundberg, Shelly, 'The Enforcement of Equal Opportunity Laws Under Imperfect Information: Affirmative Action and Alternatives' (1991) 106 *Quarterly Journal of Business and Economics* 309.

McClelland, Robert, Launch of Australia's Human Rights Framework, Address to the National Press Club of Australia, Canberra, 21 April 2010.

McClelland, Robert and Tanner, Lindsay, Reform of Anti-discrimination Legislation, Media release, 21 April 2010, Parliament House, Canberra.

McCrudden, Christopher, 'Equality and Reflexive Regulation: A Response to the Discrimination Law Review's Consultative Paper (2007) 36 *Industrial Law Journal* 25.

Mackay, Anita, 'Recent Developments in Sexual Harassment Law: Towards a New Model' (2009) 14 *Deakin Law Review* 189.

Martin, Dianne, *A Seamless Approach to Service Delivery in Legal Aid: Fulfilling a Promise or Maintaining a Myth?*, Department of Justice, Ottawa, 2002.

O'Connell, Lenahan, 'Investigators at Work: How Bureaucratic and Legal Constraints Influence the Enforcement of Discrimination Law' (1991) 51 *Public Administration Review* 123.

Razack, Sherene, 'The Women's Legal Education and Action Fund' in Frederick Lee Morton (ed.), *Law, Politics, and the Judicial Process in Canada*, University of Calgary Press, Alberta, 2002.

Rees, Neil, Lindsay, Katherine and Rice, Simon, *Anti-Discrimination Law in Australia*, Federation Press, Sydney, 2008.

Rhode, Deborah L., *Access to Justice*, Oxford University Press, UK, 2004.

Rubin, Edward, 'The Conceptual Explanation for Legislative Failure; Review of Noga Morag Levine, *Chasing the Wind: Regulating Air Pollution in the Common Law State*' (2005) 30 *Law and Social Inquiry* 583.

Smith, Belinda, Positive Equality Duties (UK), Paper presented at The Future of Australian Anti-Discrimination Law Workshop, University of Melbourne Law School, Melbourne, 15 November 2007.

Smith, Belinda, 'Australian Anti-Discrimination Laws—Framework, Developments and Issues' in Hiroya Nakakubo and Takashi Araki (eds), *New Developments in Employment Discrimination Law*, Kluwer Law International, London, 2008.

Smith, Belinda, 'It's About Time—For a New Regulatory Approach to Equality' *(2008) 36 Federal Law Review* 117.

Smith, Belinda, Models of Anti-Discrimination Laws – Does Canada offer any Lessons for the Reform of Australia's Laws?, Paper to Law and Society Association Australia and New Zealand Conference, 10–12 December 2008.

Smith, Lynn, 'Equality' in Nasreen Rajab-Budlender and Steven Budlender (eds), *Judges in Conversation: Landmark Human Rights Cases of the Twentieth Century*, JUTA, Cape Town, 2009.

Szabo, Gabrielle, *Mainstreaming Equality in the ACT: An Equality Duty for the ACT* Discrimination Act, ACT Human Rights Commission, Canberra, 2008.

Legislation

Acts Interpretation Act 1901 (Cth)

Anti-Discrimination Act 1977 (NSW)

Anti-Discrimination Act 1991 (Qld)

Anti-Discrimination Act 1998 (Tas.)

Anti-Discrimination Amendment (Drug Addiction) Act 2002 (NSW)

Australian Human Rights Commission Act 1986 (Cth)

Charter of Human Rights and Responsibilities Act 2006 (Vic.)

Charter of Rights and Freedoms 1985 (Can.)

Civil Rights Act Executive Order 11246 of Sept. 24, 1965—Equal employment opportunity (US)

Disability Discrimination Act 1992 (Cth)

Discrimination Act 1991 (ACT)

Employment Equity Act 1995 (Can.)

Employment Equity Act 1998 (South Africa)

Equal Opportunity Act 2010 (Vic.)

Equal Opportunity (Miscellaneous) Amendment Act 2009 (SA)

Equality Act 2010 (UK)

Fair Employment and Treatment Order 1998 (Northern Ireland)

Human Rights Act 2004 (ACT)

Northern Ireland Act 1998 (UK)

Promotion of Equality and Prevention of Unfair Discrimination Act 2000 (South Africa)

Cases

Commonwealth Bank of Australia v Human Rights and Equal Opportunity Commission (1997) 80 FLR 88

Domb, Sobral and Bushiwa v the London Borough of Hammersmith and Fulham, and the Equality and Human Rights Commission [2009] EWCA Civ 941

IW v City of Perth (1997) 191 CLR 1

New South Wales v Amery [2006] HCA 14; (2006) 230 CLR 174

X v Commonwealth [1999] HCA 63; 200 CLR 177

Reports and miscellaneous primary sources

Australian Government, *Government Response to the Productivity Commission's Review of the* Disability Discrimination Act 1992, January 2005, Commonwealth of Australia, Canberra.

Australian Government , *Government Response to Senate Standing Committee on Legal and Constitutional Affairs' Review of the Effectiveness of the Commonwealth* Sex Discrimination Act 1984 *in Eliminating Discrimination and Promoting Gender Equality*, 6 May 2010, Commonwealth of Australia, Canberra.

Australian Government, *Australia's Human Rights Framework*, Commonwealth of Australia, Canberra, 2010.

Australian Law Reform Commission, *Equality Before the Law: Justice for Women*, Report No. 69, Australian Law Reform Commission, Sydney, 1994, Pts I & II.

Australian Law Reform Commission, *Summary: Equality Before the Law (ALRC Reports 67 & 69)*, Australian Law Reform Commission, Sydney, 2010.

Collaborative submission from leading women's organisations and women's equity specialists, Submission 60 to Senate Standing Committee on Legal and Constitutional Affairs Effectiveness of the Commonwealth *Sex Discrimination Act 1984* in Eliminating Discrimination and Promoting Gender Equality, Commonwealth of Australia, Canberra.

Consultation Committee for a Proposed WA Human Rights Act, *Report of the Consultation Committee for a Proposed WA Human Rights Act*, November 2007.

Court Challenges Program of Canada 2010

Department of Justice, *An Equality Act for a Fairer Victoria: Equal Opportunity Review Final Report*, June 2008, Department of Justice, Government of Victoria, Melbourne [*Gardner Report*].

Discrimination Law Review (UK), *A Framework for Fairness: Proposals for a Single Equality Bill for Great Britain*, Consultation Paper, Government of the United Kingdom, London, 2007.

Fredman, Sandra and Spencer, Sarah, Delivering Equality: Towards an Outcome-Focused Positive Duty, Submission to the Cabinet Office Equality Review and to the Discrimination Law Review, June, London, 2006.

Hansard, House of Commons, 11 May 2009.

National Human Rights Consultation Committee, *National Human Rights Consultation Report*, Commonwealth of Australia, Canberra, 2009.

Scrutiny of Acts and Regulations Committee (SARC), *Exceptions and Exemptions to the* Equal Opportunity Act 1995—*Final Report*, State of Victoria, Melbourne, 2009.

Senate Standing Committee on Legal and Constitutional Affairs, *Report on the Effectiveness of the Commonwealth* Sex Discrimination Act 1984 *in Eliminating Discrimination and Promoting Gender Equality*, Parliament of Australia, Canberra, 2008.

Tasmania Law Reform Institute, *A Charter of Rights for Tasmania*, Report No. 10, October 2007, Tasmania Law Reform Institute, Hobart.

UK Cabinet Office, *Background Information on the Equalities Review*, Cabinet Office, Government of the United Kingdom, London, 2007.

UK Equalities Review, *Fairness and Freedom: The Final Report of the Equalities Review*, Government of the United Kingdom, London, 2007.

UK Government, *The Equality Bill—Government Response to the Consultation*, June 2008, Government of the United Kingdom, London.

UK Government Discrimination Law Review, *Framework for a Fairer Future— The Equality Bill*, June 2008, Government of the United Kingdom, London.

UK Government Equalities Office, *A Fairer Future—The Equality Bill and Other Action to make Equality a Reality*, June 2008, Government of the United Kingdom, London.

UK Labour Party, *Labour Policies: Equality*, Labour Party, London, 2010.

UK Parliament, *Explanatory Notes: Equality Bill 2009 (UK), Bill as introduced (incorporating side-by-side Explanatory Notes)*—volume I, Bill 85 08-09 (27 April 2009), Parliament of the United Kingdom, London.

UN Human Rights Committee, *General Comment No. 28: Equality of Rights between Men and Women (Article 3)*, 29/03/2000, CCPR/C/21/Rev 1/Add 10, United Nations, New York.

10. Rethinking the *Sex Discrimination Act*: Does Canada's Experience Suggest we Should give our Judges a Greater Role?

Belinda Smith

It is not uncommon to hear laments about how Australian judges have failed to progress or have even undermined gender equality by providing conservative or technical interpretations of anti-discrimination legislation and reinforcing merely a formal notion of equality. A comparison of Australian and Canadian anti-discrimination statutes suggests, however, that the way in which Australian anti-discrimination laws have been drafted both reflects and possibly reinforces a very limited role for our judiciary in mediating value conflicts and addressing complex social problems such as inequality. The open-textured drafting style of Canadian human rights statutes and the advent of the Charter of Rights and Freedoms have given the Canadian courts the power and legitimacy to develop more interesting and effective approaches to equality and discrimination than judges in Australia, who have highly prescriptive legislation that reflects and reinforces a strict separation of powers and narrow judicial role. This raises the question: should we give our judges a greater role?

Introduction

Seeking to understand how the *Sex Discrimination Act 1984* (Cth) (*SDA*) has operated in the past 25 years and why it has not achieved all we might have wished of it, this contribution compares the Act with equivalent legislation in Canada and contrasts the approaches taken by each nation's judiciary in interpreting this legislation. This comparison prompts the question: should Australian judges be given a greater role in determining what constitutes discrimination and what is meant by 'equality'?

At first glance, Canada's anti-discrimination laws do not appear to differ greatly from Australia's, apart from the important constitutional backdrop of Canada's Charter of Rights and Freedoms. The regulatory frameworks for anti-discrimination laws look similar: a statutory prohibition on discrimination on particular grounds, such as sex, in particular fields such as employment, enforceable by an individual complaints mechanism, through the courts.[1] A comparison of the central element of anti-discrimination laws, however—namely, the definition of discrimination—reflects three features that fundamentally distinguish the Canadian model from Australia's. The most striking difference is the legislative drafting approach and specifically the level of detail provided in the legislation; the Canadian Acts prohibit discrimination, but do not in fact define this term—in stark contrast with the prescriptive formulations found in Australia. With less prescription from the legislature, Canadian courts are thereby allocated much greater scope for identifying and shaping the meaning of discrimination and the vision of equality. Australia's compulsory conciliation model also means few discrimination matters reach the courts for determination.

Having been given scope to identify and address inequality issues, the Canadian judiciary has transparently engaged with this complex problem, developing sophisticated jurisprudence and shaping equality debates. And it is here, in the jurisprudence of the Canadian courts, that we find a second significant difference: an explicit acknowledgment that the kind of equality sought is substantive, not merely formal equality.[2] I question whether the absence of much opportunity for judicial debate in Australia about equality and inclusion has undermined the development of public awareness and commitment to human rights.

Finally, in the struggle to give meaning and effect to the notion of substantive equality, the Supreme Court of Canada in the case of *British Columbia (Public Service Employee Relations Commission) v BCGSEU* [1999] 3 SCR 3 (known as *Meiorin*, after the applicant) significantly revised the definition of discrimination to create a unified test that covers direct and indirect discrimination and includes both procedural and substantive components. This provides a mechanism that could promote the institutional transformation necessary for addressing inequality in a sustainable and legitimate way.

The limited role given to Australian courts reflects a very traditional notion of the separation of governmental powers that denies the judiciary a legitimate role in mediating value conflicts and shaping public norms. It also *reinforces* this limited judicial role, as judges, lacking a wider mandate, choose narrow and technical interpretations under the guise of fulfilling parliamentary intent; the limited discretion given by the legislature is exercised in a conservative way by the courts responding to a traditional notion of the judicial role. In this way, the drafting of anti-discrimination laws has constrained the development of progressive equality jurisprudence, a sophisticated understanding of discrimination generally and public equality norms.

---

1   This comparison does not deal comprehensively with employment equity legislation.
2   See 'Judicial Approaches to Discrimination' below.

To explore these ideas, I will first outline what powers each nation's government has given to its judiciary under their respective anti-discrimination laws and what this suggests about different conceptions of the separation of powers. In the subsequent section, I examine what each judiciary has done with this power and implications for the development of human rights rules and norms, concluding with a provocative suggestion that Australian judges should be given a greater role in addressing inequality.

What Powers Have the Courts Been Given?

In all fields of human endeavour that we seek to regulate by law there are issues of normative ambiguity. In respect of the twin notions of discrimination and inequality, this ambiguity is substantial. In the face of a lack of clear consensus about what behaviour is appropriate and what behaviour is wrong, a simple prohibition will be ineffective. Any such legal prohibition needs elaboration—traditional, legislative or judicial—to provide guidance to those governed by the law.

There is a range of regulatory models for proscribing discrimination and dealing with this ambiguity. One way to categorise the different models is on a continuum from 'open' to 'closed' in respect of the definition of the discrimination that is prohibited.[3] In an open model, discrimination is very generally defined, leaving it largely up to the courts to determine what behaviour constitutes discrimination and when, if ever, discrimination is justified or permissible. The alternative model is a closed one in which prohibited discrimination is carefully and precisely defined, leaving less discretion to the courts.

Attempts by Canada and Australia to address inequality through anti-discrimination laws reflect the open and closed models, respectively. I argue that the use of these two different models indicates a fundamental difference in these nations' understanding of the appropriate role for their courts in addressing complex social problems such as inequality.

A typical Canadian equality law prohibits discrimination in employment in the following way:

Discrimination in employment

13 (1) A person must not

---

3   Aalt Heringa, 'Standards of Review for Discrimination: The Scope of Review by the Courts' in Titia Loenen and Peter Rodrigues (eds), *Non-Discrimination Law: Comparative Perspectives*, Kluwer Law, The Hague, 1999, pp. 25–37.

(a) refuse to employ or refuse to continue to employ a person, or

(b) discriminate against a person regarding employment or any term or condition of employment

because of the race, colour, ancestry, place of origin, political belief, religion, marital status, family status, physical or mental disability, sex, sexual orientation or age of that person or because that person has been convicted of a criminal or summary conviction offence that is unrelated to the employment or to the intended employment of that person.

…(4) Subsections (1) and (2) do not apply with respect to a refusal, limitation, specification or preference based on a bona fide occupational requirement.[4]

What is notable is that there is no definition of discrimination in the legislation. This single, short section contains the discrimination prohibition, across all grounds including race, sex and disability, and a general exception, but the official role of defining discrimination in Canada is given to the judiciary. Much discretion is given to the courts to determine the nature of discrimination, the meaning of 'bona fide requirement' and the onus in respect of this element, and to then apply these rules. With this scope for interpretation, the courts are invited and even required to establish principles and, importantly, also to revise them over time as society changes. The legislature provides the prompt or mandate and then allows the court to do what it supposedly does well in a common-law legal system: develop rules on a case-by-case basis, attuned to the specific details of each parties' circumstances, and occasionally articulate overarching principles, factors and tests.[5]

In drafting Australian laws, a number of contributors have pointed out the range and intensity of constraints faced in trying to get the *SDA* enacted. What is clear is that in comparison with the Canadian drafting, the Australian legislation reflects a significantly more closed model, attempting to precisely define a formula for discrimination, on specific grounds in specific areas and with specific exceptions. The legislated definition of sex discrimination in the *SDA*, for instance, provides:

---

4   *Human Rights Code*, RSBC 1996, c 210.
5   Michael Kirby (*Judicial Activism: Authority, Principle and Policy in the Judicial Method*, Hamlyn Lecture Series, Sweet & Maxwell, London, 2004, pp. 90–1)—referring to the common law as a garden tended to by judges who occasionally perform 'horticultural activism' when they attempt to clean up a section of law.

5 Sex discrimination

(1) For the purposes of this Act, a person (in this subsection referred to as the *discriminator*) discriminates against another person (in this subsection referred to as the *aggrieved person*) on the ground of the sex of the aggrieved person if, by reason of:

(a) the sex of the aggrieved person;

(b) a characteristic that appertains generally to persons of the sex of the aggrieved person; or

(c) a characteristic that is generally imputed to persons of the sex of the aggrieved person;

the discriminator treats the aggrieved person less favourably than, in circumstances that are the same or are not materially different, the discriminator treats or would treat a person of the opposite sex.

(1A) To avoid doubt, breastfeeding (including the act of expressing milk) is a characteristic that appertains generally to women.

(2) For the purposes of this Act, a person (the *discriminator*) discriminates against another person (the *aggrieved person*) on the ground of the sex of the aggrieved person if the discriminator imposes, or proposes to impose, a condition, requirement or practice that has, or is likely to have, the effect of disadvantaging persons of the same sex as the aggrieved person.

(3) This section has effect subject to sections 7B and 7D.

What is immediately obvious is that the Australian legislature has chosen to define discrimination and its exceptions—and in some detail. Following a relatively standard format for Australian anti-discrimination law, the prohibitions are then set out in separate sections covering various fields, followed by specific exceptions. Different definitions of discrimination in respect of race, disability and age are set out in three other pieces of Australian federal legislation,[6] along with different prohibitions and exceptions. So, in the federal sphere alone, there are four different definitions of discrimination, four different sets of prohibitions and four different sets of exceptions. Such differences would be tolerable if they reflected legislative efforts to tailor each Act to the particular circumstances of the disadvantaged group it was serving, but there is little evidence of this.

---

6   *Disability Discrimination Act 1992* (Cth) (*DDA*) (ss 5–6), *Racial Discrimination Act 1975* (Cth) (*RDA*) (ss 8–9), *Age Discrimination Act 2004* (Cth) (*ADA*) (ss 14–16).

Building into the definition the distinction between direct and indirect discrimination is partly historical. By the time Australia enacted its first anti-discrimination laws, in the 1970s, US courts had already developed the distinction in *Griggs v Duke Power*. The UK Government had picked up this distinction and sought to codify it by enacting legislation that specifically defined discrimination as direct and indirect. The Australian Government and the Australian States, in designing their anti-discrimination laws, adopted the UK model, including the dichotomous definition.[7]

Greater specificity can, in some cases, provide greater certainty and clarity, and legislation can be more accessible than case law. Certainty, clarity and accessibility are desirable for users of the law, as compliance and norm development depend at least in part on parties knowing and understanding their obligations and rights. In this case, however, in seeking to codify discrimination, the statute has been made significantly more detailed, but arguably no clearer. One member of the High Court of Australia asserted that in defining 'discrimination in this manner language has been employed which is both complex and obscure and productive of further disputation'.[8] This drafting has not provided certainty, clarity or accessibility.

Setting such detail into legislation had the effect of establishing a model in Australia of parliamentary prescription over judicial discretion. The prescriptive and formulaic drafting of anti-discrimination law suggests three things: first, a belief that equality can be reduced to a formula of words applicable across fields, context and time. It suggests or assumes that discrimination is amenable to clear and precise definition. Inequality is, however, too complex to capture in a single formula, as demonstrated by the decades of reformulations undertaken by the Canadian Supreme Court in search of the right rule for discrimination.[9] While not exactly a command-and-control form of regulation,[10] the Australian model contains elements of this approach of seeking to set a clear standard, the breach of which is assessed post-facto and subject to sanction. As Susan Sturm has argued persuasively, this rule-based approach can work to address blatant and intentional discrimination that contradicts a clear norm, but will not be able to capture more subtle and complex forms of bias that are embedded in social practices and structures.[11]

---

7   The *RDA* is peculiar because its open wording parallels the international convention underpinning it. The drafters were motivated to ensure that this first federal anti-discrimination Act was a constitutionally valid exercise of the external affairs power.

8   *IW v City of Perth* (1997) 191 CLR 1, 137 per Gummow J referring to the *Equal Opportunity Act 1984* (WA).

9   See 'Judicial Approaches to Discrimination', below.

10   Belinda Smith, 'A Regulatory Analysis of the *Sex Discrimination Act 1984* (Cth): Can it Effect Equality or Only Redress Harm?' in Christopher Arup, Peter Gahan, John Howe, Richard Johnstone, Richard Mitchell and Anthony O'Donnell (eds), *Labour Law and Labour Market Regulation*, Federation Press, Sydney, 2006.

11   Susan Sturm, 'Second Generation Employment Discrimination: A Structural Approach' (2001) 101 *Columbia Law Review* 458.

Second, including detail, such as direct and indirect conceptions of discrimination, could have seemed smart and progressive at the time as it was an attempt to codify jurisprudential developments from other jurisdictions;[12] however, it placed on the legislature the burden of identifying future developments in law and practice and updating the legislation in a timely way. As other contributors have noted, there have been a number of key amendments made to the *SDA* since its enactment, but many calls for law reform have also gone unheeded. This reflects the difficulties faced by an elected body in updating protections for disadvantaged groups.

Finally, the message that this prescriptive Australian drafting sends is that the legislature is the (only) appropriate body to design solutions to such social problems and the judiciary's role is merely to apply the formula. The subtext is that we, the legislature, not only have made the value judgments in identifying the undesirable behaviour to be regulated but also have taken the next step of capturing this in a code or formula for the courts to apply. Of course, in Australia the courts are given very little chance even to apply the *SDA* and other anti-discrimination legislation because of the compulsory conciliation model. The limited traditional conception of judicial function conflicts with the now relatively well-accepted view that judges do more than declare the law and cannot adjudicate mechanically; the indeterminacy of language and legal authority means that there are always 'leeways for choice'.[13] Yet, as I argue more fully in the next section, at least the High Court of Australia has accepted and used this limited conception of its role to adopt very narrow, technical and formalistic interpretations.[14]

Almost without exception, legal regulatory initiatives either establish or assume a judicial role in the regulatory framework. This prompts descriptive questions about the nature of the role assigned to the judiciary, normative questions about whether the judiciary should be performing the particular role and pragmatic questions of how effective the judiciary is in performing the role.

These questions about the nature, appropriateness and effectiveness of the roles given to courts under anti-discrimination laws echo a central debate that emerged in Australia's recent National Human Rights Consultation.[15] The opponents of any bill or charter of rights being introduced focused primarily on how such an instrument would give the judiciary greater power and an inappropriate role, and this risked upsetting the (supposedly effective) workings of Australian

---

12   See 'Judicial Approaches to Discrimination', below.

13   Julius Stone, *Social Dimensions of Law and Justice*, Maitland Publications, Sydney, 1966, pp. 649–50.

14   See, for example: *Purvis v New South Wales (Dept of Education and Training)* (2003) 217 CLR 92 (*Purvis*) (direct discrimination); *New South Wales (Dept of Education) v Amery* (2006) 226 ALR 196 (*Amery*) (indirect discrimination).

15   Commonwealth of Australia, *National Human Rights Consultation Report*, Attorney-General's Department, Canberra, 2009 [*Brennan Report*].

governance and democracy. Parliament, as an elected body, was characterised as the only institution that has a democratic mandate to mediate or regulate public disputes about social, economic and political issues (which would include human rights). The basic corollary was that the judiciary should not play more than a limited interpretative role in democracy because it is not elected.

In essence, this position reflects a majoritarian notion of democracy. It also overestimates both the representativeness and the power of the legislature and underestimates the dominance of the executive. Are policy decisions about human rights really developed and debated by the legislature or presented by the cabinet for limited debate and voting? Are the myriad details contained in legislative instruments such as regulations effectively scrutinised by the legislature or do time, expertise and other resource limitations render this infeasible? Are there effective mechanisms in place for limiting executive power and holding the executive accountable for breaches of human rights? The answers to these questions suggest a legitimate and vital role for the judiciary in promoting and sustaining democracy, as all other democracies have concluded by enacting either statutory or constitutional bills of rights that give the judiciary a role to scrutinise and evaluate government action.

Some opposition to greater judicial discretion is based on concerns about Australian courts not being sufficiently representative of the diverse citizenry to be able to appreciate fully the experience of discrimination.[16] Lack of diversity on the Australian Bench is undeniable.[17] This should, however, further strengthen the case for reform of judicial selection and training, rather than a limitation on their role that denies the important role—both symbolic and instrumental—that the judiciary already plays. All judges have the potential to make law under a common-law legal system and denial of this was described by Justice Kirby as the 'noble lie' in his controversial Hamlyn Lectures in 2003.[18] The High Court of Australia already has significant power in being the highest court of the land and being able to decide legislative validity under the *Commonwealth Constitution*.[19] Australian judges already hold positions of power and exercise discretion; they clearly have less discretion than their Canadian counterparts but failure to acknowledge the discretion that does exist is problematic.

---

16   See, for example: Beth Gaze, 'Context and Interpretation in Anti-Discrimination Law' (2002) 26 *University of Melbourne Law Review* 325.

17   See, for example: George Williams, 'High Court Appointments: The Need for Reform' (2008) 30 *Sydney Law Review* 16.

18   Kirby, *Judicial Activism*, p. 11.

19   While not explicitly stated, it is well accepted that the High Court of Australia has power to strike down federal legislation if it determines that the Federal Parliament has exceeded its limited legislative capacity under Sections 51 or 52 of the *Constitution*, and it may declare invalid State legislation to the extent it is inconsistent with federal law under Section 109.

Few issues are as normatively contested as equality. Entrusting the Canadian courts to determine the definition of discrimination and thereby the test of whether an equality norm has been breached reflects an acceptance that the judiciary has a legitimate role to play in mediating conflicting public values and shaping public norms.[20] The courts were given this role under the constitutional Charter of Rights and Freedoms (1982)[21] (and, before that, a more limited role under the statutory Bill of Rights in 1960),[22] which allocated to the judiciary a right to evaluate government action, including legislative action, against a list of human rights. In this context, the judicial role granted under anti-discrimination or human rights statutes would not have been unusual or controversial.

The Honourable Claire L'Heureux-Dubé described the role of the equality provision in the Charter in the following way:

> The year 2005 marks the twentieth anniversary of section 15 of the Charter. It celebrates a generation of constitutional protection for equality rights in Canada. In this time, the Charter has become deeply engrained in the Canadian consciousness and identity. It provides a language for and expresses aspirations for how Canadians view their relationships with the state and with each other. *It fundamentally shapes the meaning of Canadian democracy.*[23]

In this sense, the constitutional equality framework reflects and reinforces a substantive and central role for the judiciary in Canadian democracy—a role that is replicated under human rights codes and that contrasts starkly with the more limited Australian judicial role.

Having been granted these different powers, how have the judges used them?

Judicial Approaches to Discrimination

There is no single understanding of equality, not even among equality advocates. The concept has been used extensively to animate movements for social change over time, but it has been used in a myriad different ways. Rosemary Hunter notes:

---

20   To some extent, as with international instruments, this highly general drafting could reflect a lack of consensus in the Parliament and a compromise of leaving elaboration to other institutions.

21   Canadian Charter of Rights and Freedoms, Part 1 of the *Constitution Act, 1982*, being Schedule B of the *Canada Act, 1982* (UK), c 11 (note that the equality provision came into effect in 1985).

22   Canadian Bill of Rights, SC 1960. Note that the Bill of Rights was a statutory charter and the judiciary had no power under it to invalidate legislation.

23   Claire L'Heureux-Dubé, 'Preface' in Fay Faraday, Margaret Denike and M. Kate Stephenson (eds), *Making Equality Rights Real: Securing Substantive equality under the Charter*, Irwin Law, Toronto, 2006, p. 3 (emphasis added).

> [A]rguments about equality are…bedeviled by varying—and competing—conceptions of what is actually included in the term 'equality', with feminist and liberal theorists having advanced a panoply of arguments as to the most useful, desirable or defensible content of the concept. These have included the notions of formal and substantive equality…parité, equality of opportunity, equality of results or outcome, equality of condition, equality of power, recognition of differences, social equivalence, anti-subordination, an equal minimum threshold enjoyment of capabilities, equal concern, complex equality, and 'equal protection of the imaginary domain'.[24]

Legislation to prevent discrimination is expressly intended to promote equality and hence anti-discrimination litigation has been a major site for judicial consideration of the concept of equality. The definition of discrimination depends on the concept of equality that underpins it and is central to the operation and effect of anti-discrimination laws in a number of ways. The definition is the characterisation of the problem and determines the nature of the right to be free of discrimination. If discrimination is defined too narrowly—to cover only conscious or intentional conduct based on prejudice, for instance—it will operate to address only a narrow band of discrimination and promote a limited form of equality. If the definition is too complex or difficult to prove, the law will be less enforceable and thus less effective at changing behaviour. Importantly, the way in which discrimination is defined also determines whether duty holders—employers, educators, service providers, and so on—are required merely to refrain from using prejudice and assumption or are required to do something proactive to promote inclusion and participation of traditionally excluded groups. In this way, the definition allocates responsibility for change and draws lines between different types of discrimination and required responses.

Canadian Courts: Rules and Roles

The Supreme Court of Canada has not shied away from the difficult question of defining discrimination. With the grant of power and nod of legitimacy under the human rights codes, the Court has entered the fray, openly and transparently struggling to define discrimination and thereby articulate a vision of equality. In case after case, the Court has attempted to frame a rule that would apply across grounds and fields and circumstances. Along the way, it has invoked extensive commentary for its successes and failures in this endeavour.[25] What is notable,

---

24   Rosemary Hunter, 'Introduction: Feminism and Equality' in Rosemary Hunter (ed.), *Rethinking Equality Projects in Law: Feminist Challenges*, Hart Publishing, Portland, Ore., 2008, pp. 2–3 (references removed).
25   Recent examples of collections on equality jurisprudence under the Charter are: Sheila McIntyre and Sandra Rodgers (eds), *Diminishing Returns: Inequality and the Canadian Charter of Rights and Freedoms,*

however, and noticeably different to Australia,[26] is the fact that the judiciary in this quest has engaged openly with academic scholarship and public debate, through judgments[27] and extra-curial writings.[28]

So, how have the Canadian courts interpreted discrimination under their general prohibitions? In seeking to understand the nature of discrimination, the starting point usually is the notion of direct discrimination or different treatment. This is premised on a notion of formal equality or 'treating likes alike' and covers blanket and blatant kinds of discrimination, such as 'women need not apply'. The challenge for courts faced with open or general prohibitions such as the Canadian ones has, however, been to decide whether and how other forms of discrimination are to be prohibited. An alternative form of discrimination is one that results not from such category-based distinctions, but from the unfair, disproportionate *impact* of apparently neutral rules. The classic example is a minimum height requirement for a job that does not single out women for different treatment but would disproportionately exclude them. This 'indirect' form of discrimination would not be covered by a narrow definition or interpretation that merely required the same treatment of similarly situated individuals.

The Canadian courts, following on from the American judgment of *Griggs v Duke Power*[29] in 1971, extended their initial interpretation of discrimination to include this adverse impact or indirect form of discrimination in the 1985 case of *O'Malley*.[30] Importantly, in this same case, the Court determined that the burden for establishing whether the discriminatory conduct or standard was justifiable—and thus not unlawful—was to be borne by the employer or respondent.[31] This dichotomous and two-stage definition was thus established by the courts under Canadian human rights law:

> The conventional approach to applying human rights legislation in the workplace requires the tribunal to decide at the outset into which of two categories the case falls: (1) 'direct discrimination', where the standard

---

LexisNexis, Markham, Ontario, 2006; Faraday et al., *Making Equality Rights Real*.

26 Former Justice of the High Court of Australia Michael Kirby represents an exception in this regard, as he was prolific in his extra-curial writings and presentations and regularly referred to academic scholarship and international jurisprudence in his judgments (<http://www.michaelkirby.com.au>).

27 Reference to academic scholarship within judgments is common. See, for example: *British Columbia (Public Service Employee Relations Commission) v BCGSEU* [1999] 3 SCR 3 (*Meiorin*), McLachlin J at [34], [41], [49], citing extensively Shelagh Day and Gwen Brodsky, 'The Duty to Accommodate: Who Will Benefit?' (1996) 75 *Canadian Bar Review* 433; extensive list of authors cited in *R v Kapp* 2008 SCC 41, McLachlin CJ and Abella J at [22].

28 For example, L'Heureux-Dubé, 'Preface'; Claire L'Heureux-Dubé, 'Conversations on Equality' (1999) 26 *Manitoba Law Journal* 273; Beverley McLachlin, 'Equality: The Most Difficult Right' (2001) 14 *Supreme Court Law Review* (2d)17.

29 *Griggs v Duke Power Co* 401 US 424 (1971).

30 *Ontario Human Rights Commission and O'Malley v Simpsons-Sears Ltd* [1985] 2 SCR 536 (*O'Malley*).

31 Ibid.

is discriminatory on its face, or (2) 'adverse effect discrimination', where the facially neutral standard discriminates in effect: Ontario Human Rights Commission and O'Malley v. Simpsons-Sears Ltd., [1985] 2 S.C.R. 536...at p. 551, per McIntyre J. If a prima facie case of either form of discrimination is established, the burden shifts to the employer to justify it.[32]

While the Australian legislation embedded the dichotomous definition—covering different treatment and adverse impact—it is the second stage, and specifically the shifting of burden to the respondent, that is the first point of difference between the Canadian and Australian definitions. As noted below, generally the respondent in Australia has borne little more than a minimal evidentiary burden in anti-discrimination litigation.

It is critical to reflect on the constitutional backdrop of these cases. While it was the open model that allowed the Canadian Supreme Court to develop and revise the interpretation of discrimination under the human rights statutes, this does not necessarily explain its willingness to do so in this progressive way. It is probably undeniable that the constitutional role given to the judiciary—first under the Bill of Rights and then the Charter—to interpret equality provisions and evaluate governmental action against equality rights has profoundly influenced the role it has played in interpreting human rights codes.

The granting of the power in itself represents a vote of legitimacy that could have influenced the way in which the power was exercised but there is still a distinction between the granting of a power and what a court is willing and able to do with it. The broader understanding of a legitimate judicial role and possibly also the capacity, values and interests of specific judicial members would have also influenced how the power was wielded.[33]

The Charter jurisprudence has clearly influenced statutory human rights jurisprudence and vice versa, and this started early in the life of the Charter. Building on the identification of adverse impact discrimination and shifting burden in the 1985 statutory case of *O'Malley*, the Court expressly articulated a commitment to substantive equality in the first Charter equality case in 1989. This commitment was recently summarised by Chief Justice McLachlin and Abella J, in *R. v Kapp*:

> [14] Nearly 20 years have passed since the Court handed down its first s. 15 decision in the case of Andrews v. Law Society of British Columbia...

---

32   *Meiorin* [1999] 3 SCR 3, 19.
33   See Kim Brooks (ed.), *Justice Bertha Wilson: One Woman's Difference*, UBC Press, Vancouver, 2009.

[1989] 1 S.C.R. 143. Andrews set the template for this Court's commitment to substantive equality—a template which subsequent decisions have enriched but never abandoned.

[15] Substantive equality, as contrasted with formal equality, is grounded in the idea that: 'The promotion of equality entails the promotion of a society in which all are secure in the knowledge that they are recognized at law as human beings equally deserving of concern, respect and consideration': *Andrews*, at p. 171, *per* McIntyre J., for the majority on the s. 15 issue. Pointing out that the concept of equality does not necessarily mean identical treatment and that the formal 'like treatment' model of discrimination may in fact produce inequality, McIntyre J. stated (at p. 165):

> To approach the ideal of full equality before and under the law— and in human affairs an approach is all that can be expected—the main consideration must be the impact of the law on the individual or the group concerned. Recognizing that there will always be an infinite variety of personal characteristics, capacities, entitlements and merits among those subject to a law, there must be accorded, as nearly as may be possible, an equality of benefit and protection and no more of the restrictions, penalties or burdens imposed upon one than another. In other words, the admittedly unattainable ideal should be that a law expressed to bind all should not because of irrelevant personal differences have a more burdensome or less beneficial impact on one than another.

While acknowledging that equality is an inherently comparative concept (p. 164), McIntyre J. warned against a sterile similarly situated test focussed on treating 'likes' alike. An insistence on substantive equality has remained central to the Court's approach to equality claims.[34]

Over the years, the courts struggled to develop a principled definition of discrimination that would be effective in promoting substantive equality. In 1999, the Supreme Court of Canada took the opportunity in the case of Tawney Meiorin[35] to review and overhaul the test of discrimination in the statutory human rights context. The Meiorin case was one of sex discrimination in the employment of firefighters, but set a precedent for anti-discrimination cases generally in Canada. Meiorin challenged a fitness test imposed by her employer, arguing that it was discriminatory because it disproportionately impacted on women and did not reflect the real needs of the job—a job she had successfully held for two years before undergoing the test. The Court reviewed the traditional

---

34   *R. v Kapp* [2008] 2 SCR 483.
35   *Meiorin* [1999] 3 SCR 3.

distinction between direct and indirect discrimination and rejected it, replacing it with a unified test. Under the two-stage process that the Court retained, once the claimant establishes that the rule or treatment is prima facie discriminatory, the burden falls on the respondent to prove in defence that the standard is a bona fide operational requirement. The fundamental change came in the formulation of how a respondent employer could prove or justify a standard. Starting with the presumption that the legislature intended to promote substantive equality, not merely formal equality, the unanimous Court stated:

> An employer may justify the impugned standard by establishing on the balance of probabilities:
>
> 1. that the employer adopted the standard for a purpose rationally connected to the performance of the job;
>
> 2. that the employer adopted the particular standard in an honest and good faith belief that it was necessary to the fulfilment of that legitimate work related purpose;
>
> 3. that the standard is reasonably necessary to the accomplishment of that legitimate work-related purpose. To show that the standard is reasonably necessary, it must be demonstrated that it is impossible to accommodate individual employees sharing the characteristics of the claimant without imposing undue hardship upon the employer.[36]

This test has objective elements in respect of the job (1), subjective elements to capture intentional discrimination (2) and a built-in acknowledgment that substantive equality could require some adjustments or accommodation by the employer as well as the employee (3). It allows for an examination of both the employer's purpose and the means of achieving the purpose, and builds in an obligation to design workplace standards in a way that is inclusive:

> Employers designing workplace standards owe an obligation to be aware of both the differences between individuals, and differences that characterize groups of individuals. They must build conceptions of equality into workplace standards. By enacting human rights statutes and providing that they are applicable to the workplace, the legislatures have determined that the standards governing the performance of work should be designed to reflect all members of society, in so far as this is reasonably possible. Courts and tribunals must bear this in mind when confronted with a claim of employment-related discrimination. To the extent that a standard unnecessarily fails to reflect the differences among individuals, it runs afoul of the prohibitions contained in the

---

36   Ibid. [54].

various human rights statutes and must be replaced. *The standard itself is required to provide for individual accommodation, if reasonably possible.* A standard that allows for such accommodation may be only slightly different from the existing standard but it is a different standard nonetheless.[37]

Demonstrating cognisance of the need to provide guidance on how the test would apply, the Court even listed practical steps:

Some of the important questions that may be asked in the course of the analysis include:

(a) Has the employer investigated alternative approaches that do not have a discriminatory effect, such as individual testing against a more individually sensitive standard?

(b) If alternative standards were investigated and found to be capable of fulfilling the employer's purpose, why were they not implemented?

(c) Is it necessary to have all employees meet the single standard for the employer to accomplish its legitimate purpose or could standards reflective of group or individual differences and capabilities be established?

(d) Is there a way to do the job that is less discriminatory while still accomplishing the employer's legitimate purpose?

(e) Is the standard properly designed to ensure that the desired qualification is met without placing an undue burden on those to whom the standard applies?

(f) Have other parties who are obliged to assist in the search for possible accommodation fulfilled their roles?[38]

The case has been welcomed by leading Canadian equality experts. Judy Fudge and Hester Lessard described it as 'groundbreaking' because it is

the Court's most emphatic and clear endorsement of a substantive approach to discrimination and equality cases that recognizes that equality is more than treating like case alike (formal equality) and, thus, requires attention to how social norms, social practices and institutions create and reinforce advantage and disadvantage.[39]

---

37   Ibid. [68] (emphasis added).
38   Ibid. [65].
39   Judy Fudge and Hester Lessard, Challenging Norms and Creating Precedents: The Tale of a Woman Firefighter in the Forests of British Columbia, Unpublished ms, University of Victoria, British Columbia, 2009, p. 1.

Similarly, Colleen Sheppard characterised it as providing 'significant and positive contributions to human rights'[40] because it 'reinforces the importance of redressing systemic inequalities that result in exclusion and prejudice through institutional transformation and not merely by individual special treatment'.[41]

For Australian observers, *Meiorin* provides an example of a sophisticated judicial understanding of equality that contrasts starkly with the approach taken by Australian courts, outlined below.

Australian Contrasts

In the first decade or so of Australian anti-discrimination laws the courts seriously grappled not only with the detailed wording of the Acts, but also with the purpose and underlying principles. As other contributors have noted, at that time, the legislation was considered radical and even the limited discretion given to the courts under the prescriptive drafting model was used by the High Court to articulate some tentative but significant steps in promoting equality.

The year 1992, however, represented a turning point in the judiciary's foray into human rights. It was the year in which the High Court issued its most important human rights judgment to date. This was the landmark native title judgment in *Mabo*, acknowledging that Australia was not *terra nullius* on English settlement in 1788 and granting (limited) native title rights to Indigenous Australians after more than a century of denial.[42] This judgment unleashed on the Court a barrage of strident, venomous attacks for its 'inappropriate' judicial activism. Notably, the Attorney-General did not respond to or moderate these attacks in defence of the Court, thereby reinforcing the message that it was not up to the judiciary to engage in such fundamental public policy issues.

More recently, the record of the courts in affording and promoting human rights has been far more constrained, as summarised pointedly by Justice Kirby in a 2006 (dissenting) judgment:

> 86. This case joins a series, unbroken in the past decade, in which this Court has decided appeals unfavourably to claimants for relief under anti-discrimination and equal opportunity legislation.

---

40   Colleen Sheppard, 'Of Forest Fires and Systemic Discrimination: A Review of *British Columbia (Public Service Employee Relations Commission) v BCGSEU*' (2001) 46 *McGill Law Journal* 533, 535.

41   Ibid. 558.

42   *Mabo v Queensland (No. 1)* (1989) 166 CLR 186. The *RDA* played an important part in this litigation, allowing the High Court to invalidate legislation enacted by Queensland that sought retrospectively to abolish native title.

87. It was not always so. In the early days of State and federal anti-discrimination legislation, this Court, by its approach to questions of validity and application, upheld those laws and gave them a meaning that rendered them effective...Few cases that now reach this Court are unarguable. The Court's successive conclusions in these cases reflected the beneficial interpretation of the laws in question, ensuring they would achieve their large social objectives...

88. The wheel has turned. In no decision of this Court in the past decade concerned with anti-discrimination laws, federal or State, has a party claiming relief on a ground of discrimination succeeded. If the decision in the courts below was unfavourable to the claimants, it was affirmed. If it was favourable, it was reversed.

89. This is what occurred [in *IW v City of Perth, Qantas Airways Limited v Christie, X v The Commonwealth, Purvis v New South Wales.*] In each of these cases, the Court produced a finding unfavourable to the complainant. The differences in the Court's present approach to anti-discrimination legislation may lie in considerations of approach. That possibility is lent further support by the outcome of the present appeal.[43]

The two most recent High Court cases on discrimination serve to illustrate the narrow, technical approach taken by the Court. The last case of direct discrimination determined by the High Court was *Purvis v New South Wales (Dept of Education and Training).*[44] A student with multiple disabilities was expelled from a school because of antisocial and aggressive behaviour, which was a manifestation of his disability. The student brought a claim of direct discrimination, arguing that in being expelled because of his behaviour he had been treated differently to non-disabled students. Instead of the focus being on whether the school had done enough to enable this student to participate (and meet its other obligations to staff and students), the question for the Court became a highly technical and artificial one about the comparator: with whom should the student be compared—a non-disabled student who was well behaved or one who shared the same behavioural problems? The Court chose the latter and found that the school had not discriminated because it treated this disabled student the same as it would treat all students *who behaved the same way*. Notably absent from this litigation was a focus on the human right of the student to participate equally in education.

As noted above, the Australian legislation embeds a dichotomous definition of discrimination—encompassing both direct and indirect. In litigating a

---

43   *Amery* [2006] HCA 14 [86]–[89].
44   *Purvis* (2003) 217 CLR 92.

discrimination case under Australian law, an applicant must specify which kind of discrimination they plead. In the case of *Purvis*, only direct discrimination was argued. Without a specific exception or general justification provision, the Court was not able to assess whether the behavioural requirements imposed by the school were reasonable or whether the school was justified in suspending the student. Seemingly driven by the result of avoiding a finding of wrong against the school or acknowledging the deficiencies of legislative drafting, the Court, however, followed a tortuous path of reasoning that denied the student a remedy, set an extraordinarily narrow national precedent and thereby undermined the development of human rights norms.

The *Purvis* approach means that the prohibition on direct discrimination merely requires employers and education providers to 'treat likes alike' and, importantly, lets the employer or school decide who is like whom.[45] Direct discrimination provisions do not prevent employers (education providers, and so on) from using criteria that very closely connect or overlap with traits that are supposedly protected by the anti-discrimination laws. For example, while an employer may be prohibited from applying a blanket exclusion of women, *direct* discrimination provisions allow the employer to choose the candidate who can work 24/7, can do overtime on short notice, will not take extended leave, will not take their entitlement to carer's leave, can pass a fitness test based on male physiology or any other criteria that could have a gendered element but is not expressly 'sex'.

Further, under direct discrimination actions, such criteria are not subjected to any evaluation of legitimacy or connectedness to the job and there is no obligation to provide reasonable accommodation.[46] The *Purvis* decision removes the criteria from judicial scrutiny and makes clear that reasonable adjustments are not required in determining whether there has been direct discrimination.[47]

In making this decision, the Court clarified and reinforced a stark distinction between direct and indirect discrimination. The artificiality and complexity of the distinction between these categories are particularly problematic given that in Australia it is victims alone who must prove breaches of anti-discrimination laws, without even the benefit of a shifting burden of proof in most cases.

The indirect discrimination provisions are still available to challenge standards or criteria, but with all the uncertainty and burden-of-proof barriers that indirect discrimination provisions entail. Until recently, most federal and

---

45   Belinda Smith, 'From *Wardley* to *Purvis*— How Far has Australian Anti-Discrimination Law Come in 30 Years?' (2008) 21 *Australian Journal of Labour Law* 3.

46   Note: a limited duty to provide reasonable accommodation was recently introduced in respect of disability, first under the Disability Standards for Education (2005) and more generally under the *Disability Discrimination Amendment (Education Standards) Act 2005* (Cth).

47   At least not under the *SDA*; recent amendments to the *DDA* insert such a requirement.

State anti-discrimination statutes formulated indirect discrimination in similar terms. This formulation required applicants to prove four points for an indirect discrimination claim: 1) that a requirement or condition had been imposed; 2) with which the applicant could not or did not comply; 3) with which a substantially higher proportion of people without the applicant's gender/disability/race were able to comply; and, importantly, 4) that the requirement or condition was 'not reasonable' in all the circumstances.[48] The High Court's most recent pronouncement on indirect discrimination further illustrates the Court's uneasiness with the role of mediating public values and engaging in real debates about human rights.

In the case of *Amery*,[49] the Court was asked to determine whether the payment of casual teachers at a rate lower than permanently engaged teachers, regardless of experience and competence, constituted indirect sex discrimination under the *Anti-Discrimination Act 1977* (NSW) because it impacted disproportionately on female teachers who were not able to comply with the permanency requirement (as it required consent to be posted to any school in the State). The pay rates had been set by an industrial tribunal and later a collective agreement, but both of these instruments set minimum rather than real pay rates and compliance with such instruments was no longer an explicit defence to discrimination. It became an implicit defence, however, with the Court refusing to enter into the industrial arena to scrutinise the appropriateness or reasonableness of the rates of pay. Rather than assess the 'reasonableness' of the different pay structures for casuals and permanents—an exercise that would have led the Court into unfamiliar territory traditionally left to industrial relations tribunals—the Court avoided the substantive issue by focusing on a technical question of whether the respondent had imposed a 'requirement or condition'. Ultimately, it held that there was no permanency requirement imposed on 'teachers'; there were separate categories of teachers—casuals and permanents—and, since the applicants were engaged as casuals, permanency was simply not relevant.[50] In doing so, the Court ignored or sidestepped well-established precedents in which these terms had been widely interpreted, generally shifting the focus onto the issue of reasonableness. Even the *SDA* definition—which is more advantageous for claimants because the respondent bears the onus in respect of reasonableness—would not have helped here because the court entirely avoided the question of reasonableness. This case is a clear example of how the separation of discrimination laws and industrial relations laws, discussed by

---

48   Note reforms for the *SDA* and the *ADA* and recent changes to the *DDA*.
49   *Amery* [2006] HCA 14.
50   Ibid. [71]–[82] per Gummow, Hayne and Crennan JJ (with whom Gleeson CJ and Callinan J concurred on orders).

Sara Charlesworth in her contribution, has made it difficult to challenge the gender equality dimension of employment practices and classifications, such as 'casual'.

These precedents make discrimination litigation even more complex and significantly limit the progressive potential of Australian anti-discrimination laws, including the *SDA*. The *Purvis* precedent serves to narrow the scope of direct discrimination to the limited cases of prejudice and assumption, requiring applicants who wish to challenge the standard itself rather than merely its application to argue an indirect discrimination claim. The *Amery* precedent makes clear that even under the indirect discrimination provisions, the courts are unwilling to engage in the analysis required to assess the reasonableness of a standard that has been proven to impact disproportionately.

Was the Court hamstrung by the closed-model legislation and the poor definitions it had to work with? Clearly, it was constrained; the absence of a general obligation to provide reasonable accommodation for the protected classes and the absence of any burden-shifting mechanism left the applicants in both the *Purvis* and the *Amery* cases with an onerous burden. The majority judges in *Purvis* were able to conclude that the absence of an obligation to provide reasonable accommodation in the Australian *Disability Discrimination Act 1992* meant the Act was focused on equality of treatment rather than substantive equality—justifying the narrow approach taken. This narrow approach had previously been taken by the Federal Court in respect of the *SDA*[51] and was, in effect, affirmed by *Purvis*.

In both the *Purvis* and the *Amery* case, however, dissenting judges[52] illustrated that alternative, progressive interpretations were available, drawing support from the objects clauses,[53] legislative direction to take a purposive approach to interpretation,[54] academic scholarship,[55] domestic jurisprudence and the legislation's international law underpinnings.[56] In doing so, however, Kirby J demonstrated once again that his view of the judicial role is significantly different and wider than the views of many of his judicial peers.

In taking a conservative line, the Court has in the past decade denied or obscured the limited discretion it has been granted, (mis)characterising its position as merely performing statutory interpretation and fulfilling parliamentary intent.[57]

---

51 *Thomson v Orica Australia Pty Ltd*, [2002] FCA 939.
52 Kirby J, joined in *Purvis* (2003) 217 CLR 92 by McHugh J .
53 McHugh and Kirby JJ, *Purvis* (2003) 217 CLR 92 [44].
54 *Acts Interpretation Act 1901* (Cth).
55 For example: McHugh and Kirby JJ, *Purvis* (2003) 217 CLR 92 [17], [44], [67] fn21; fnn 33, 39.
56 For example: ibid. [44].
57 Margaret Thornton, 'Disabling Discrimination Legislation: The High Court and Judicial Activism' (2009) 15 *Australian Journal of Human Rights* 1.

It has necessarily still made value judgments in adjudication, but conservative choices are less apparently value judgments because of the inherent invisibility of dominant norms.[58]

Lessons for Australia?

From an Australian perspective, the *Meiorin* definition adopted by Canada provides ideas that should be considered. It has at least four advantages over the Australian legal tests of direct and indirect discrimination, outlined above. First, it starts from a goal of substantive equality and this is reflected in the requirement to provide reasonable accommodation not merely the same treatment, which elicits only formal equality. Second, the onus in litigation for establishing that reasonable accommodation has been provided is on the potential discriminator, reflecting and reinforcing a more public and collective responsibility for promoting equality. Third, the *Meiorin* development sees the bifurcated test of direct and indirect discrimination abandoned for a unified test, thereby eliminating the need to spend resources arguing over an artificial distinction. Finally, the definition of discrimination and the embedded obligation to provide reasonable accommodation have both substantive and procedural components, requiring employers for instance to examine their selection criteria and investigate less exclusionary alternatives.[59] The test ensures that the criteria used to select (and exclude) employees or applicants are subjected to some assessment of legitimacy in light of the goals of equality laws. Importantly, the Canadian test also allows for an assessment of the reasonableness of the means by which an employer seeks to achieve its goals and into this is built a limited obligation on employers to accommodate difference or make reasonable adjustments to the extent of undue hardship.

Meiorin might not be 'the' answer, but it does have these advantages over the Australian rules. It is arguable that it emerged in the Canadian jurisprudence as an evolutionary step—possible only because the courts were given wide discretion (and litigants were given correspondingly wide scope for creative arguments about the meaning of equality and discrimination). The Supreme Court of Canada—at least in the past 20 or so years—has been prepared to engage publicly in the hard question of defining discrimination and developing legal rules that promote substantive equality.

Australian anti-discrimination law jurisprudence indicates that limiting the judicial role can simply lead to unmanageable complexity as judges, faced with

---

58   Martha Minow, *Making All the Difference: Inclusion, Exclusion, and American Law*, Cornell University Press, Ithaca, NY, 1990.
59   Sheppard, 'Of Forest Fires and Systemic Discrimination'.

facts that pose real questions of normative ambiguity, are permitted and even encouraged to perform legal contortions to answer the question rather than given scope to develop appropriate principles and mechanisms for promoting problem solving. By issuing conservative and technical interpretations of anti-discrimination statutes, the courts have reinforced a simplistic formal conception of equality, which requires little of institutions and those who currently benefit from dominant norms and leaves those who are marginalised to conform or carry the burden of social change.[60]

In exploring legal reforms of the *SDA*, I suggest that we need to consider changing not merely the legislative prescription but also the prescriptiveness of the model and thereby the role of the judiciary. Rewriting the definitions without taking a look at the bigger picture of what role judges could (and should?) play might help to update the test but leaves a regulatory framework that is still ill equipped to evolve over time.

Bibliography

Books and articles

Brooks, Kim (ed.), *Justice Bertha Wilson: One Woman's Difference*, UBC Press, Vancouver, 2009.

Day, Shelagh and Brodsky, Gwen, 'The Duty to Accommodate: Who Will Benefit?' (1996) 75 *Canadian Bar Review* 433.

Faraday, Fay, Denike, Margaret and Stephenson, M. Kate (eds), *Making Equality Rights Real: Securing Substantive Equality under the Charter*, Irwin Law, Toronto, 2006.

Fudge, Judy and Lessard, Hester, Challenging Norms and Creating Precedents: The Tale of a Woman Firefighter in the Forests of British Columbia, Unpublished ms, University of Victoria, British Columbia, 2009.

Gaze, Beth, 'Context and Interpretation in Anti-Discrimination Law' (2002) 26 *University of Melbourne Law Review* 325.

Heringa, Aalt, 'Standards of Review for Discrimination: The Scope of Review by the Courts' in Titia Loenen and Peter Rodrigues (eds), *Non-Discrimination Law: Comparative Perspectives*, Kluwer Law, The Hague, 1999.

---

60 Margaret Thornton, 'Sex Discrimination, Courts and Corporate Power' (2008) 36 *Federal Law Review* 31.

Hunter, Rosemary, 'Introduction: Feminism and Equality' in Rosemary Hunter (ed.), *Rethinking Equality Projects in Law: Feminist challenges*, Hart Publishing, Portland, Ore., 2008.

Kirby, Michael, 'Julius Stone and the High Court of Australia' (1997) 20 *University of New South Wales Law Journal* 239.

Kirby, Michael, *Judicial Activism: Authority, Principle and Policy in the Judicial Method*, Hamlyn Lecture Series, Sweet & Maxwell, London, 2004.

L'Heureux-Dubé, Claire, 'Conversations on Equality' (1999) 26 *Manitoba Law Journal* 27.

L'Heureux-Dubé, Claire, 'Preface' in Fay Faraday, Margaret Denike and M. Kate Stephenson (eds), *Making Equality Rights Real: Securing Substantive Equality under the Charter*, Irwin Law, Toronto, 2006.

McIntyre, Sheila and Rodgers, Sandra (eds), *Diminishing Returns: Inequality and the Canadian Charter of Rights and Freedoms*, LexisNexis, Markham, Ontario, 2006.

McLachlin, Beverley, 'Equality: The Most Difficult Right' (2001) 14 *Supreme Court Law Review* (2d) 17.

Minow, Martha, *Making All the Difference: Inclusion, Exclusion, and American Law*, Cornell University Press, Ithaca, NY, 1990.

Sheppard, Colleen, 'Of Forest Fires and Systemic Discrimination: A Review of *British Columbia (Public Service Employee Relations Commission) v BCGSEU*' (2001) 46 *McGill Law Journal* 533.

Smith, Belinda, 'A Regulatory Analysis of the *Sex Discrimination Act 1984* (Cth): Can it Effect Equality or only Redress Harm?' in Christopher Arup, Peter Gahan, John Howe, Richard Johnstone, Richard Mitchell and Anthony O'Donnell (eds), *Labour Law and Labour Market Regulation*, Federation Press, Sydney, 2006.

Smith, Belinda, 'From Wardley to Purvis— How Far has Australian Anti-Discrimination Law Come in 30 Years?' (2008) 21 *Australian Journal of Labour Law* 3.

Stone, Julius, *Social Dimensions of Law and Justice*, Maitland Publications, Sydney, 1966.

Sturm, Susan, 'Second Generation Employment Discrimination: A Structural Approach' (2001) 101 *Columbia Law Review* 458.

Thornton, Margaret, 'Sex Discrimination, Courts and Corporate Power' (2008) 36 *Federal Law Review* 31.

Thornton, Margaret, 'Disabling Discrimination Legislation: The High Court and Judicial Activism' (2009) 15 *Australian Journal of Human Rights* 1.

Williams, George, 'High Court Appointments: The Need for Reform' (2008) 30 *Sydney Law Review* 16.

Legislation

Age Discrimination Act 2004 (Cth)

Acts Interpretation Act 1901 (Cth)

Canadian Bill of Rights, SC 1960

Canadian Charter of Rights and Freedoms, Part 1 of the *Constitution Act, 1982*, being Schedule B of the *Canada Act, 1982* (UK), 1982, c 11

Disability Discrimination Amendment (Education Standards) Act 2005 (Cth)

Disability Discrimination Act 1992 (Cth)

Human Rights Code, RSBC 1996, c 210

Racial Discrimination Act 1975 (Cth)

Sex Discrimination Act 1984 (Cth)

Cases

British Columbia (Public Service Employee Relations Commission) v BCGSEU [1999] 3 SCR 3 (*Meiorin*)

Griggs v Duke Power Co 401 US 424 (1971)

IW v City of Perth (1997) 191 CLR 1

Mabo v Queensland (No. 1) (1989) 166 CLR 186

Mabo v Queensland (No. 2) (1992) 175 CLR 1

New South Wales Department of Education v Amery (2006) 226 ALR 196

Ontario Human Rights Commission and O'Malley v Simpsons-Sears Ltd [1985] 2 SCR 536

Purvis v New South Wales (Dept of Education and Training) (2003) 217 CLR 92

R. v Kapp 2008 SCC 41

Thomson v Orica Australia Pty Ltd [2002] FCA 939

Report

Commonwealth of Australia, *National Human Rights Consultation Report*, Attorney-General's Department, Canberra, 2009 [*Brennan Report*].

11. Equality as a Basic Human Right: Choice and Responsibility

Archana Parashar

Drawing on post-structural theory, this chapter argues for a re-conceptualisation of the role of the judge in equality jurisprudence. It suggests a closer link between choice and responsibility, which would require revising conventional theories of judicial reasoning. The approach would allow the illusory distance between the decision maker and the decision to be bridged. The chapter concludes by drawing attention to the transformative potential of legal education for training law students as independent and ethical thinkers who firmly grasp the relationship between choice and responsibility.

Introduction

The recent senate review of the *Sex Discrimination Act 1984* (Cth) (*SDA*) became the occasion for asking whether the legislation is adequate for the task of eliminating discrimination and promoting gender equality.[1] The Senate, however, did not ask the initial question of how the aims of the *SDA* might be ascertained and how we would measure its effectiveness. These are recurring questions in legal scholarship and as yet remain unresolved. In this chapter, instead of focusing on measuring the effectiveness in quantitative terms, I propose to focus on the normative effect and the aim of anti-discrimination legislation.

There is robust discussion in legal scholarship about whether law can be a means of intentional and progressive social change. A related stream of thought questions whether legislation is required or effective for achieving social change and suggests instead that education is a better tool of social transformation. I take these as non-issues for this chapter because, everything else notwithstanding, the normative effect of legislation is undeniable. Therefore, as a starting point, I wish to address the narrower issue of what kind of equality legislation the

---

1   Standing Committee on Legal and Constitutional Affairs, *Report on the Effectiveness of the Commonwealth Sex Discrimination Act 1984 in Eliminating Discrimination and Promoting Gender Equality*, Parliament of Australia, Canberra, 2008, <http://www.aph.gov.au/Senate/committee/legcon_ctte/sex_discrim/report/index.htm>

law should aim for. In the senate committee review of the *SDA*, this issue was framed in part as whether we need an Equality Act.[2] There were arguments on both sides and the recommendation was for a further, wider inquiry. The following argument is my effort to identify some of the issues that must be a part of the debate about the design and scope of an Equality Act.

The initial question of what concept of equality should be pursued in legislation is answered in part by asking why equality is desired. It is uncontroversial that the demand of equality is a manifestation of the desire for non-discrimination/fairness/dignity of every human being. Legislation that will capture these aspirations best will not be in limited-scope legislation such as the current *SDA*. An Equality Act can serve as the shorthand way of describing the human rights aim of the legislation. That said, the real legislative formula remains to be developed. Moreover, there is always a large gap between the aims and their realisation and it is reasonable to expect that the Equality Act would be no different in this regard.

Therefore, it is necessary to address two separate issues: the design of the legislative provisions and the interpretation and application of these provisions. In brief, I wish to argue that it is important to formulate the legislative provisions as clearly and succinctly as possible, but however perfect the legislative formulations are, they will nevertheless be interpreted by the judiciary. Therefore, focusing merely on designing better legislative provisions is an insufficient remedy for the identified shortcomings of the law. Instead, it is essential that we also address the jurisprudential theories of how the courts can and should interpret these provisions. Therefore the two tasks—that is, design of the legislation and re-conceptualisation of the judicial role—require simultaneous attention.

My main aim in this chapter is to analyse the shortcomings of the extant literature on the nature of judicial role and argue for the re-conceptualisation of the task of judicial interpretation. In part, this re-conceptualisation of the judicial role is supported by the post-structural theories of the constructed nature of all knowledge, but I wish to extend these insights. I wish to argue that the links between judicial choice and responsibility should be the central focus of the jurisprudence of equality.

I begin with a brief discussion of the desirable design of an Equality Act. I argue that equality should be conceptualised as a basic human right. This is, however, merely to set the context for the subsequent argument about the judicial role. This is followed by an analysis of the debates about the appropriate role of the judiciary in implementing legislation. I argue that the conventional

---

2   I will not analyse the merits of the submissions made or the eventual recommendations because my main aim in this chapter is to move beyond the issue of designing appropriate legislative provisions.

theories about the nature of judicial reasoning need to be revised in order to pin the responsibility on the individual judge for choosing an appropriate interpretation. This is necessary to bridge the illusory distance between the decision maker and the decision and for the anti-discrimination legislation to fulfil the promise of achieving substantial equality. To achieve such change in the conventions of theorising, it is necessary that legal education develops the critical and self-reflective capacities of thinkers.

Legislative Definition of Equality

An extensive philosophical literature on the concept of equality already exists but this is not the focus of my chapter.[3] Sex equality debates extended these original arguments about equality to women, but feminist thinkers are also the ones who have problematised the concept of equality more than any other group of thinkers. Perhaps unsurprisingly this abundance of discussion has not as yet brought a resolution to the meaning of equality that everyone can agree on. In the contemporary debates about conceptualising equality there is, however, a big difference from the early feminist efforts when the struggle was to gain acceptance for the concept of gender justice itself.[4] In the contemporary context, it is widely accepted that inequalities of sex, race, age, sexuality, ability, and so on, are all illegitimate and the debates now are more about which strategies to use to eradicate them.[5] For example, Squires says that what it means is that gender equality advocates are expected to pursue gender equality within a wider equalities framework with attention given to the intersection of various axes of inequalities. This concern is more accurately described as a concern with diversity.[6]

This shift in the conceptualisation of equality is to an extent a function of the advent of the post-structural method of analysis and thus also carries the tendency to valorize diversity. The broadening of the concept of gender equality goes hand in hand with a reluctance to rank in importance various kinds of discrimination. It is also impossible logically to argue for directed social change as no concept of justice or fairness can be justified. I believe that the relativism

---

3   For a comprehensive discussion, see: Wojciech Sadurski, *Equality and Legitimacy*, Oxford University Press, New York, 2008. See also: Amartya Sen, *Inequality Re-Examined*, Oxford University Press, UK, 1992.

4   For a discussion of legal debates on gender equality, see: Rosemary Hunter (ed.), *Rethinking Equality Projects in Law: Feminist Challenges*, Hart Publishing, Portland, Ore., 2008.

5   For a wide-ranging discussion on this topic, see: Katherine M. Franke, 'The Central Mistake of Sex Discrimination Law: The Disaggregation of Sex from Gender' (1995–96) 144 *University of Pennsylvania Law Review* 1.

6   Judith Squires (*The New Politics of Gender Equality*, Palgrave Macmillan, Basingstoke, UK, 2007, p. 16); but she also points out the danger of losing the focus on gender equality. See also: Michele Moody-Adams, 'Reclaiming the Ideal of Equality' in Barbara S. Andrew, Jean Keller and Lisa H. Schwartzman (eds), *Feminist Interventions in Ethics and Politics*, Rowman and Littlefield Publishers, Oxford, 2005.

of this way of thinking can be logical but it is not essential.[7] Since all concepts of equality are equally constructed in discourse, rather than treating them all as equally relevant, the focus must be to explain why one construct is to be preferred over another and what are the consequences of such choices.

Anti-discrimination law is a manifestation of the aspiration that law should help in achieving a fair society,[8] although it is one that is very regularly defeated by the judiciary. The more common and plausible response to this problematic outcome is that the legislative definition of non-discrimination or equality should be changed. This suggested course of action, however, *assumes* that legislative drafting can fix the problem. There are many problems in this suggestion but even if, for argument's sake, this explanation is accepted, changing the definition nevertheless requires a prior articulation of what is or should be the aim of the legislation. Without being cynical, the desire to be fair can be seen as an uncontroversial aspiration and with that starting point it is easy to argue that equality should be given a substantive rather than a formal content in the legislation. One way of proceeding is to conceptualise equality as a basic human right.

The Human Rights Model for Equality

I draw on the literature on the US *Equal Rights Amendment* (*ERA*) to argue that we require an overarching principle that discrimination is unacceptable and this can best be achieved by a constitutional guarantee of equality as a fundamental or human right.[9] The main issue here is not whether such a human right should be a constitutional or legislative guarantee. Rather the debates about a constitutional equality right serve to focus attention on the scope or the extent of such a right. A merging of the concepts of non-discrimination and equality is necessary for conceptualising equality as a human right.[10] Therefore we need legislation that guarantees equality, and such an equality right can

---

7   There is extensive discussion in the literature about directed social change in the light of post-structural analyses. For an introduction, see: Nancy Fraser, *Justice Interruptus: Critical Reflections on the 'Postsocialist' Condition*, Routledge, New York, 1997; Jodi Dean (ed.), *Feminism and the New Democracy: Resisting the Political*, Sage, London, 1997.

8   Christopher McCrudden (ed.), *Anti-Discrimination Law*, Dartmouth Ashgate, Aldershot, UK, 2004, pp. xi–xxxii. See also, for a discussion in the context of racial discrimination but with an argument that is extendable to all bases of discrimination that more than formal equality is desirable in anti-discrimination jurisprudence: Tracy E. Higgins and Laura A. Rosenbury, 'Agency, Equality and Anti-Discrimination Law' (1999–2000) 85 *Cornell Law Review* 1194.

9   For a comprehensive review of issues, see: Martha Davis, 'The Equal Rights Amendment: Then and Now' (2008) 17(3) *Columbia Journal of Gender and Law* 419.

10   This is a fairly common idea in the literature. See, for example: Ruth Colker, 'Anti-Subordination Above All: Sex, Race and Equality Protection' (1986) 61 *New York University Law Review* 1003. See also: Australian Law Reform Commission, *Equality Before the Law: Women's Equality*, Report No. 69, Australian Law Reform Commission, Sydney, 1994, Part II.

operate as akin to a constitutional guarantee and thus broaden the scope of the right to include both state policies and individuals' actions. More importantly, it will be a blanket guarantee rather than picking and choosing which grounds of discrimination are to be proscribed—but admittedly with a drawback of reduced visibility for gender as a separate ground.[11]

Some of the objections to the *ERA* are a good indicator of the importance of such a norm. The objections are particularly instructive in that they identify the areas that the opponents of the *ERA* do not want to be covered by the equality guarantee. For example, the opponents of the *ERA* did not wish equality to govern the organisation of the military, marriage or other issues of privacy, including abortion and homosexuality.[12] As we now know, over time, greater public acceptance of the principle of non-discrimination on some of these grounds has come about.[13] Discrimination on the other remaining grounds continues to persist, however, and to be justified. The point is that the rationales for discrimination on particular grounds continue to be as arbitrary as ever despite the increased acceptance of the non-discrimination principles. It is in this context that the introduction of an Equality Act has the potential to create a normative force for treating *all* discrimination as suspect or unjustifiable.

Australia has a protracted history of unsuccessful efforts to introduce a constitutional bill of rights and the current move to introduce one as a statutory measure is the most recent 'compromise' development.[14] Given this shift in focus of the human rights movement, it might be argued that any proposed Equality Act can be part of such human rights legislation and there is no need for separate legislation. While there is an overlap between the human rights discourse and the demand for equality, there are important reasons for treating equality as a distinct issue for the time being. It is important to remember that the traditional scope of human rights has been different from the demand for equality. In human rights discourse, it is more a case of upholding equality of various identified rights described as fundamental or human rights. Treating equality itself as a human right requires a conceptual shift but it is a necessary shift if genuine non-discrimination is the legislative goal. This goal can be better

---

11   See also Margaret Thornton's observations in her submission to the Senate Standing Committee on Legal and Constitutional Affairs (*Report on the Effectiveness of the Commonwealth* Sex Discrimination Act 1984 *in Eliminating Discrimination and Promoting Gender Equality*, Ch. 4, para. 4.60).

12   Jane J. Mansbridge, *Why We Lost the ERA*, University of Chicago Press, Ill, 1986.

13   See also Barbara Sullivan ('Sex Equality and the Australian Body Politic' in S. Watson [ed.], *Playing the State*, Allen & Unwin, Sydney, 1990) for an account of the enactment of the *SDA* and the compromises made to appease the opponents who feared, inter alia, that the Act would encourage women to give up their roles as wives and mothers.

14   Gilbert and Tobin Centre of Public Law, *History of Charters of Human Rights in Australia*, <http://www.gtcentre.unsw.edu.au/Resources/cohr/historyChartersofHumanRights.asp>. It has, however, met with stiff opposition; see Claire Chaffey, 'Human Rights Proposal Still Afloat', *Lawyers Weekly*, 22 February 2010, Lexis Nexis, <http://www.lawyersweekly.com.au/blogs/top_stories/archive/2010/02/22/human-rights-proposal-still-afloat.aspx>

achieved through a stand-alone Equality Act. Therefore, the design of such equality legislation must be overarching like a constitutional guarantee but it must be embodied in separate legislation.[15]

In making this proposal for conceptualising equality as a basic human right, I am fully aware that human rights are not a panacea where other legal rights have well-documented shortcomings.[16] Nevertheless, as argued by various minority scholars, legal rights are critiqued primarily by privileged scholars. With all their shortcomings, legal rights are still valued and pursued by the relatively more oppressed minorities in the same liberal and developed societies that produce the most trenchant critique of rights. Moreover, as argued by Lacey, rights are not transcendent or objective but are a product of contestations and they can be seen as 'an emergent critical force within modern societies' and 'as a framework within which new political ideas can be articulated'.[17] The critiques of law and rights in particular operate to demonstrate the contingency of our normative concepts, including the concepts of rights, justice and equality; and by implication indicate that these concepts can be redefined in radically different ways.[18]

It is in keeping with the post-structural insights about construction of knowledge that legal analysis needs to focus on the specific sites of construction of meaning and, in common-law jurisdictions, this site is pre-eminently judicial interpretations of precedents and statutory provisions. Therefore, the main focus of the rest of my argument is on how such reconstruction of the concept of equality might happen.

Judicial Interpretation and Responsibility

The legal literature on assessing the anti-discrimination laws and judicial pronouncements is replete with analyses suggesting interpretations that are plausible and desirable but very often are not the ones adopted by judges.[19] There is a wide gap between the ideal and the real and, despite the exhortations

---

15   The relative merits of constitutional versus legislative measures are an important but separate topic and one outside the scope of the present chapter.

16   Shelley Wright, 'Human Rights and Women's Rights' in K. E. Mahoney and P. Mahoney (eds), *Human Rights in the Twenty-First Century*, M. Nijhoff, Dordrecht, Boston, 1993. See also: Didi Herman, 'Beyond the Rights Debate' (1993) 2 *Social and Legal Studies* 25.

17   Nicola Lacey, 'Feminist Legal Theory and the Rights of Women' in Karen Knop (ed.), *Gender and Human Rights*, Academy of European Law, Oxford University Press, UK, 2004, p. 42.

18   Ibid., p. 45.

19   For an incisive critique of the decisions under the *SDA*, see: Margaret Thornton, 'Sex Discrimination, Courts and Corporate Power' (2008) 36 *Federal Law Review* 31. For an analysis of decisions under the *Racial Discrimination Act*, see: Jonathan Hunyor, 'Skin-Deep: Proof and Inferences of Racial Discrimination in Employment' (2003) 25 *Sydney Law Review* 535. See also: Beth Gaze, 'Context and Interpretation in Anti-Discrimination Laws' (2002) 26(2) *Melbourne University Law Review* 325.

of scholars, judges mostly seem unable to do anything about it.[20] While everyone else seems to be able to understand equality as symbolising fairness or non-arbitrariness, legal scholars and judges, in particular, tie themselves in knots about interpreting what would be an appropriate meaning of equality. My argument is that a genuine rethinking of legal equality requires a deconstruction of the contemporary methods of legal interpretation. What I mean by this is best illustrated with the help of the story of the *SDA* since its enactment.[21]

All liberal legal systems gain legitimacy by claiming to uphold the fundamental principle of equality. The *SDA*, as with all other anti-discrimination laws, was enacted as recognition of the inadequacy of the formal equality guarantee of liberal legal systems. That is, even though liberal legal systems are premised on the equality of all legal subjects, feminists successfully illustrated the relevance of gender differences in legal discourse and the disadvantages in law suffered by women, despite the assumption that legal standards are neutral. As a result, the *SDA* was enacted to rectify this flaw in formal legal equality but once enacted it ended up being interpreted as a guarantee of formal equality.[22] Why the judges are unable to see the absurdity of this situation is hard to explain—except by deconstructing the mechanism of judicial/legal reasoning. The importance of focusing on the concept of legal reasoning is evident furthermore in that the specialised tribunals set up under anti-discrimination laws have failed to establish new ways of interpreting the non-discrimination/equality guarantees. The specialised tribunals set up to administer anti-discrimination laws have not managed to replace the dominant methods of legal reasoning primarily because it is their place in the hierarchy of the courts that makes them ineffective especially since the higher courts do not feel the need to focus on the nature of their task.[23]

---

20   This is also evidenced by the regular reversing of lower court decisions by the Australian High Court in discrimination complaints, as discussed by Thornton in 'Sex Discrimination, Courts and Corporate Power'.

21   See, for a comprehensive analysis, Margaret Thornton, *The Liberal Promise: Anti-Discrimination Legislation in Australia*, Oxford University Press, Melbourne, 1990.

22   There is some difference of opinion on this issue, as in Australia the *SDA* as well as most other anti-discrimination laws use gender-neutral language. The courts have without fail interpreted this as a guarantee of formal equality. Many commentators on these laws as well accept that the laws were enacted to guarantee formal equality; see: Thornton, 'Sex Discrimination, Courts and Corporate Power'; Beth Gaze, ' The *Sex Discrimination Act* After Twenty Years: Achievements, Disillusionments and Alternatives' (2004) 27(3) *UNSW Law Journal* 914. I prefer the interpretation put forward by Sadurski, however, that it is up to the courts to conceptualise discrimination on the basis of the effect of any classification rather than on the fact of classification per se: Wojciech Sadurski, 'Equality Before the Law: A Conceptual Analysis' (1986) 60 *Australian Law Journal* 131.

23   Institutional design is a relevant avenue for exploring possibilities of making anti-discrimination law a means of achieving substantive equality but it is outside the scope of this discussion. It is for the same reason that I am not discussing the merits of changing the regulatory regime of these laws. See Belinda Smith, 'It's About Time for a New Regulatory Approach to Equality' (2008) 36 *Federal Law Review* 117.

There is much literature suggesting avenues of making anti-discrimination laws deliver on their promise of equality.[24] As far as I have been able to ascertain, however, there is not anything written on re-conceptualising the category of judicial reasoning as one way of proceeding. It is not my intention to attribute *mala fides* to the judges; rather I am more inclined to ask why it is so. What is it about being a superior-court judge that prevents one from seeing the discrimination in the alleged situation? Moreover, what can be done to make the enterprise of interpretation a socially responsible one? These are the very questions usually silenced by the mainstream jurisprudential insistence on claiming that

- the judicial task is one of applying the law

- professional reasoning is different from ordinary reasoning

- institutional role responsibility is separate from personal responsibility.

These claims of conventional jurisprudence create the possibility of deflecting attention from the choice or discretion exercised by the judges in every instance of interpretation. Recognising this is an initial step towards conceptualising the judicial act of interpretation in a manner that emphasises choice and thus the agency of the judges in attributing meaning to legal rules. Once the element of choice is acknowledged, the responsibility for that choice becomes inevitable, for it follows that judges would strive for socially just outcomes if they were the ones exercising choice.

Judicial Task as One of Applying the Law

It is an article of faith in jurisprudence to conceptualise the judicial task as one of applying the law or more specifically as one of not making the law. While the mainstream jurisprudential writings give extensive reasons for a conception of judicial authority as constrained reasoning—otherwise described as legal reasoning[25]—it is also true that critical theorists have demonstrated the extensive discretion that judges exercise and in doing so are inevitably influenced by an array of extra-legal factors. Moreover, the nature of language and how it operates form the core of post-structural analyses that explain how interpretation requires attributing meaning. The obvious conclusions of such analyses challenge the conventional view of legal reasoning that invokes the

---

24   See, for an argument that private contract law is able to yield better results than public equality laws: Belinda Smith and Joellen Riley, 'Family Friendly Work Practices and the Law' (2004) 26 *Sydney Law Review* 395.

25   This is one of the extensively discussed issues in conventional jurisprudence scholarship, but it is not my main concern here. I have analysed some of these issues in my chapter 'Responsibility for Legal Knowledge' in Amita Dhanda and Archana Parashar (eds), *Decolonisation of Legal Knowledge*, Routledge, Delhi, 2009, p. 178.

separation-of-powers doctrine, the desirability of democratic control of legal policy and a particular understanding of how language operates. This critical legal literature has its own set of shortcomings but the more important issue for now is that despite such extensive critical scholarship the dominant view about the nature of the judicial task remains unchanged. Therefore it is necessary to focus on how—by using which legal concepts—the mainstream legal scholars as well as judges in particular manage to steer clear of this literature and thus help maintain the hegemony of the conventional view that legal reasoning is a special kind of reasoning.

I argue that it is the particular conception of legal reasoning, the idea that judges 'apply' the law and that there is a division of authority between the legislature and the judiciary, which enables the mainstream thinking to persist. One important consequence of this conception of legal reasoning is that it distances the decision maker from their decision because it is not 'their' decision. As a consequence, judges, when interpreting anti-discrimination laws, can dissociate themselves from the consequences of their interpretation. Moreover, if the judges fail to uphold justice or fairness as the guiding principle in their judgments, they are permitted or even encouraged to do so by the prevailing orthodoxy that they are simply applying an already existing law.

Such a conception of the judicial role is also a logical extension of the positivist understanding of law that dissociates law and morality. The legislators can but are not compelled to create a just or fair law, but if they have failed to do so the judge must remain agnostic. Thus, there is no possibility of expecting the judges to strive for just or fair results as they are 'constrained' by law and not free to pursue their own preferences. Although there is abundant evidence that there is no pre-constituted law waiting to be discovered and applied by the judges,[26] the mainstream jurists object that any other conception of the judicial task will 'give' judges too much power.

There are two different issues that arise out of this insistence of the mainstream jurisprudential view of the judicial task: the claim that it is necessary to maintain the legitimacy of judicial authority and that otherwise the judges will have unlimited power. Although it is undeniable that law and judges require continued legitimacy, it can be better achieved by ensuring that judges engage in interpretations that strive to achieve justice. One way of proceeding is to focus on the fact that the judges are making choices and deploying their expertise, intelligence, good conscience and so on to make reasonable decisions and not saying so does not change the facts. Second, the gains made by artificially constraining judges are lesser than the loss of opportunity to engage the judges

---

26   For a classical contrast, see the difference between the arguments of Stanley Fish and Dworkin in the discussion below.

in striving for justice and fairness in the law. If it could be openly acknowledged that judges exercise discretion in interpreting legal rules, one could then focus on how best to do so.[27]

It is difficult, however, to acknowledge that judges exercise discretion in every task of interpretation because it raises the question of why the judges can be entrusted with this authority. Or put differently, what is the basis of judicial authority? This is an unstated and unresolved issue of contemporary jurisprudence.[28] The earlier common-law understanding of law and the conception of the judicial task were complementary in so far as common law was seen as the expression of natural reason and the judges who were confined to applying this law were thus upholding the fair and just natural law. With the contemporary positivist understanding of law, however, the same confidence in the judge's capacity is sought to be achieved by the concept of 'constraint'— that is, the judge is not free to do whatever. The judge is bound by the law. The problem of course is that the law as enacted by the Parliament is now anything at all (that has the correct pedigree). The fiction of the democratic control of Parliament does nothing to ensure that laws made are just laws.[29] It is in this context that insisting on the constrained role of the judge writes out the possibility of any aspiration for justice or fairness in law.

In the meantime, judges engaged in 'applying' the law nevertheless have to choose between at least two interpretations of the same law. It thus becomes problematic to assert that judges have no more to do than 'apply' whatever the legislature enacts. Dworkin has tried valiantly to rescue the legitimacy of judicial authority by postulating that judges are constrained in exercising their discretion and therefore can be trusted to uphold the law rather than create it anew.[30] The law so upheld is a combination of rules and principles and the judges are the final authority on what weight to give to any principle. The obvious problem with this conception of the judicial task is that there is no way of knowing which principles are relevant and what weight they will carry before the judge decides. In this conception of the judicial task, the judge remains the ultimate arbiter of meaning, exercising choice but this time with the dubious guarantee that the law constrains the judge.

---

27   As I have argued above, however, merely changing the legislative formula is not enough. I therefore differ from the argument made by Belinda Smith in this volume.

28   For a comparative study discussing the more conventional issues, see: Maur Cappelletti, 'Who Watches the Watchmen? A Comparative Study of Judicial Responsibility' (1983) 31 *American Journal of Comparative Law* 1. For an interesting discussion, see: Michel Rosenfeld, 'Deconstruction and Legal Interpretation: Conflict, Indeterminacy and the Temptations of the New Legal Formalism' in Drucilla Cornell, Michel Rosenfeld and David Gray Carlson (eds), *Deconstruction and the Possibility of Justice*, Routledge, New York, 1992, p. 152.

29   Even though a theoretical possibility exists of legislatures creating perfect laws, it does not detract from the following argument.

30   Ronald Dworkin, *Law's Empire*, Harvard University Press, Cambridge, Mass., 1986.

I do not know of any satisfactory resolution of this problem as the critical theorists' answers are equally even if differently problematic, as analysed below.

Critical Theorists and the Basis of Judicial Authority

With slight variations, all post-structural critiques point out that knowledge is constituted and in turn constitutes reality. That being the case, how law is constituted becomes the initial question for such theories. Even though these analyses are of law in general, their primary focus invariably is on the judicial pronouncements. Moreover, all of these theorists seem to be mesmerised by the desire to disprove the claims of law as being about fairness, equity or its objective and principled nature. As examples of this kind of analysis, one has only to point to the extant literature that explicates the power of law as the 'force of law' or the 'racism of law', and so on.[31] It is not in doubt that such analyses are a necessary challenge to the mainstream view of the law as being about fairness or justice, but neither is it enough to stop here. Any analyses that show how law is the very means of oppression and discrimination but stop there are deterministic. They do not leave any avenue to explore whether law could also be the means of achieving non-discrimination.

At the very least, this kind of analysis makes the status quo look inevitable. The effect of this kind of theorising is as exclusionary and debilitating as that of the mainstream theorising it was meant to critique. Surely post-structural scholars must accept responsibility for their analyses—that all meanings are relative and contingent and that it is nonsensical to talk about law's role in bringing about social change or justice; they are legitimising the continuation of a status quo that is less than ideal, fair or just. The common response of critical theorists that the function of critique is not to provide alternatives is simply not good enough because critique for the sake of critique is only self-serving for the critics.

Moreover, this is a problematic outcome even for the post-structuralists because contrary to the tenets of post-structuralism, it provides an essentialist answer as it makes the law appear as if it was a pre-discursive object and one with an invariable content and effect of oppression. Even though in a stream of post-structural analysis, it is acknowledged that no law is pre-discursive and the mechanisms of oppression in law are ever changing, the overall import of such analyses still remains that law is oppressive rather than emancipatory. This predominant message of post-structural theories in turn helps avoid focusing on the question of why it is that law cannot be emancipatory.

---

31 See, for example: Peter Fitzpatrick (ed.), *Nationalism, Racism and the Rule of Law*, Dartmouth, Brookfield, UK, 1995.

For instance, this is illustrated well in the analysis of law provided by Stanley Fish.[32] He sees the judge as free to attribute meaning to the rules of law, as all rules are texts waiting to be interpreted. This is because he insists that any critique of institutional practices depends on invoking an essentialist view that pure knowledge or truth is possible and accessible. It is against this claimed objective standard that the critics argue that institutional practices are problematic. If, however, all knowledge is historically contingent, there is no basis for suggesting that such an ahistorical or universal standard is available as the measure of criticism. It follows in the argument of Fish that dominant perspectives can be explained but not replaced with supposedly neutral or objective views. Importantly, Fish does not concern himself with the issue of how to replace a problematic or dominant perspective with a more desirable, even if contingent perspective, and it is this choice made by Fish and other critical theorists that makes a post-structural analysis unsuitable for connecting law and justice/fairness/non-discrimination.

In conclusion, the relativism of most post-structural analyses of the judicial task is no more convincing than the mainstream claim that it is principled. The arguments, respectively, of Stanley Fish and Ronald Dworkin to me exemplify the shortcomings of both ways of thinking. Thus, all contemporary analyses of law are neglecting a central issue: that any meaning is attributed, created, attached. If so, those involved in such construction must take the responsibility for their choices. That there is a choice in any formulation about the nature of law must become the starting point of any analysis.

Choice and Responsibility

It is not possible or desirable to go back to a pre-post-structural way of understanding the construction of meaning but we definitely need to move beyond what Foster describes as the postmodernism of reaction to a postmodernism of resistance.[33] I understand this to mean that there is a need to extend the post-structural insight about the constructed nature of knowledge but more importantly to link it with the responsibility of those 'doing' the construction. Legal scholars are not only responsible for providing post-structural analyses of law that demonstrate the indeterminacy of meaning, they also must acknowledge their power to attribute meanings.

---

32   For this analysis, I rely on Stanley Fish, 'Anti-Professionalism' (1985) 7 *Cardozo Law Review* 645. Drucilla Cornell ('Time, Deconstruction, and the Challenge to Legal Positivism: The Call for Judicial Responsibility' (1990) 2 *Yale Journal of Law and Humanities* 267) challenges this view of Fish's.

33   Hal Foster, 'Postmodernism: A Preface' in Hal Foster (ed.), *The Anti-Aesthetic: Essays on Postmodern Culture*, Bay Press, Port Townsend, Wash., 1983, p. xii.

There is an undeniable nexus between the institutional location of the thinkers and the authority attributed or accorded to their views. The very fact that not all theorists or analyses are equally influential is cause for asking how certain readings are accepted as authoritative while others are marginalised and ignored. It is not simply a function of the merit of an argument. In some ways, the mainstream legal scholarship that manages to ignore post-structural insights is exhibiting this very nexus between knowledge and power that such scholarship is so good at postulating. More specifically, the post-structural way of thinking requires us to focus on how interpretation is a matter of attaching meaning and always involves making choices. This fact of making choices is effectively obscured in legal scholarship and thus the responsibility for the consequences flowing from those choices does not attach to the decision maker. In the next section, I analyse how responsibility is conceptualised in legal scholarship.

The concept of responsibility is used in various disciplines other than law and it has different meanings than in the discipline of law.[34] Cane has argued, and I agree, that the concepts of responsibility play an important role in both law and morality, yet philosophers pay little attention to the legal versions of the concept. A careful study of the legal concept of responsibility and legal practices associated with it could, however, be useful to understand responsibility in general.[35]

The ideas of responsibility and legal philosophy have a long connection, but a very cursory survey of legal scholarship on the concept of responsibility shows that most of the writers are engaged in discussing when the law does or should attach responsibility to a legal subject. Primarily these discussions relate to the individual's responsibility in criminal law; responsibility in civil law is discussed to a lesser extent.[36] What I found missing was any discussion of the responsibility of lawmakers and more particularly of judges for their views. Here I focus only on the lack of scholarly attention to the responsibility of judges. No doubt this is because of the prevalent conventions about the judicial role that these responsibilities are not their own but decisions necessitated by the conventions of legal reasoning that they, as professionals, have to follow. As discussed above, however, there are serious problems with this view and I am helped by Cane, who has argued that the distinction between law and morality also enables us to draw some contrasts between 'moral reasoning' and 'legal reasoning' as techniques for generating normative conclusions about

---

34   Peter Cane, *Responsibility in Law and Morality*, Hart Publishing, Oxford, 2002, p. 1.
35   Ibid., pp. 2–3.
36   For a good review of this literature, see: Nicola Lacey, 'Responsibility and Modernity in Criminal Law' (2001) 9(3) *Journal of Political Philosophy* 249.

responsibility.[37] Once it is acknowledged that normative conclusions about legal reasoning follow from the particular concept of legal reasoning, it must be possible to argue for re-conceptualising legal reasoning.

I will discuss this point in the context of the analysis of law and responsibility provided by Veitch.[38] He has argued eloquently that judges are not held responsible in their individual capacity because they are acting in the role of the judge. The institutional role of the judge is created precisely so that disputes are decided by reference to the law rather than by reference to the values of the judge as the individual decision maker. Veitch makes this argument as an aspect of his broader argument that law, by design, and not incidentally, dissociates the legal actor from the responsibility for human suffering. The legal norms define what injury is and also define by exclusion that which may be damage but not injury. Thus, suffering caused by the former (damage) is, legally speaking, legitimate. The legal actor's responsibility is transferred to the legal norm and it is the norm that decides when there is an obligation or responsibility. As long as the legal actor is conforming to the legal norm, he or she is guiltless because responsibility stops with fulfilling the legal obligation.[39] This is an effect of legal categorisation compartmentalising responsibility, so that the legal actor, the judge, is only a conduit of legal authority.[40] The judge is not personally responsible for the judgment as it is the state of law that is responsible; it is the decision's legal reasoning, and not the reasoning of the actual person, that must do the work of justifying the outcome.

Veitch goes on to argue that even if the judges have discretion, they are merely the mouthpieces of the law and their personal views are, legally speaking, irrelevant. According to Veitch, this is the reason why the judge is not personally responsible because legal responsibility in accordance with the law and the legal role is non-responsibility for the person.[41] The role usurps the autonomy of the person because when it comes to human beings acting in legal roles, there is only one living person who can act and if the law determines what the right action is the person cannot independently decide otherwise.

At one level, this is a persuasive analysis but I wish to extend it by asking what exactly does it mean to say that the 'law' determines what the right action

---

37   Cane, *Responsibility in Law and Morality*, p. 3.
38   Scott Veitch, *Law and Irresponsibility: On the Legitimation of Human Suffering*, Routledge, Oxford, 2007, p. 85 ff. His argument is impressively detailed and tightly constructed. It is not possible to do justice to its nuances in this short formulation, but I do believe that it leads to an essentialist view of law.
39   Ibid., p. 87.
40   Earlier in his argument, Veitch has explained that responsibilities are organised as role responsibilities— that is, 'action according to a set rule or role is itself blameless'; the role responsibility thus segregates responsibility for the role from the consequences—to act according to a set rule or role is itself blameless (ibid., p. 48).
41   Ibid., p. 88.

is? If this were a straightforward matter, there would be no occasion for the issue to come before the judge. The very existence of the judge is an indication that 'the law' is not unambiguous and an exercise of judgment is required to ascertain what the 'law' is. To hold otherwise, moreover, goes against all the post-structural insights about the nature of meaning and how interpretation is attributing meaning to terms and concepts. It also goes against the obvious fact that 'not only the wording of the positive law makes up the positive law in force at the time; there is also the interpretive practice of the time'.[42] The judge necessarily has to exercise a choice in deciding what 'the law' in any particular instance demands. Once this determination is made, however, the judge is not free to disregard the law, as Veitch persuasively argues. The institutional role to that extent usurps individual autonomy. This last step, however, in no way dispenses with the need to attribute meaning to 'the law' in the first instance. It is by focusing on this prior issue that it becomes clear that judges have to exercise choice in deciding the meaning of the terms used in law.

Conceptually also it needs to be acknowledged that the task of interpretation is a matter of exercising judgment rather than merely performing a mechanical task. Even in the mainstream conception, the judges are choosing an interpretation but they are able to distance themselves from the determinations in the name of their professional responsibility to act according to law rather than acting according to their personal values.

This argument can be easily illustrated in the context of anti-discrimination legislation and the interpretations adopted by judges at various levels of the judicial system. For example, in the case of *Purvis*,[43] the judge who cannot understand the disruptive behaviour of the child as an aspect of his disability is no more objective or correct than the judge who sees it otherwise. It is, therefore, not a simple matter of the law determining what the 'right action' is and the judge implementing that. Whether the action of the school is in accordance with the law or not is the very issue that the judge must decide. And to do this the judge must first ascertain what the law demands. The interpretation is

---

42   Robert Alexy, 'A Defence of Radbruch's Formula' in David Disenhaus (ed.), *Recrafting the Rule of Law: The Limits of Legal Order*, Hart Publishing, Oxford, 1999, p. 21.

43   *Purvis v NSW Department of Education and Training* (2003) 217 CLR 92. This case related to Daniel Hoggan, who had an intellectual disability that resulted in him being aggressive and violent at times. The school suspended and eventually excluded him. His foster father, Mr Purvis, brought a case of disability discrimination against the school, invoking the *Disability Discrimination Act 1992* (Cth). The dispute went through various levels of the courts and finally the High Court dismissed his application. The majority of judges held that the protection against discrimination on the basis of disability does not extend to functional limitations that may result from the condition. For doctrinal analysis, see: Susan Roberts, 'The Inequality of Treating Unequals Equally: The Future of Direct Discrimination Under the *Disability Discrimination Act 1992* (Cth)?' (2005) 45 *AIAL Forum* 20.

that of the judge and it is for the judge to choose which interpretative practice to adopt. Whether one describes it as role responsibility, institutional role or anything else, it is ultimately a task that demands an exercise of choice.

Moreover, this exercise of choice is a matter of judgment and I would like to argue that the judges, in deciding whether a practice is discriminatory or not, are as aware of the demands of justice and fairness as the next person. Their seeming inability to name the unfair or unjust practice as 'discrimination' is due not so much to particular understandings of equality and discrimination but to a large extent is a function of being able to distance themselves from 'their' decisions in the name of upholding the law.

If, however, it is argued that the conception of the judicial act in this chapter seems to free the judge of any constraint and therefore has the potential to lead to an unfettered exercise of power, the solution for that problem lies in conceptualising the exercise of authority in a responsible and meaningful manner rather than trying to constrain the judge artificially. A conception of legal reasoning that is more conducive to acknowledging the choices made by judges in interpretation can have a definite advantage. I take support for this view from Alexy, who has argued in a different context that the mere availability of a concept of law—whether positivist or anti-positivist—can have a bearing on the lawmakers' behaviour. Similarly, the availability of a conception of legal reasoning that focuses on the reasonableness or fairness of choices made can create the conditions for judges to adopt interpretations that connect law with justice.[44]

The difference between this conception and that of Dworkin lies in making the judge accountable for their choice of interpretation. The judge would no longer be the ultimate and inscrutable arbiter of the meaning of any rule of law. Instead, they would need to justify their choice in terms of its discriminatory or non-discriminatory effect. This conception of the judicial role is also in accordance with the post-structural analysis, as, unlike the mainstream theorists, the post-structural theorists explain any judgment as an effect of judicial choice. It extends the post-structural insight, however, in that it demands of the judges that they will exercise their judgment in a responsible manner. Working with this conception of the judicial task, if judges give an interpretation of an anti-discrimination rule that denies or diminishes the human dignity of the complainant, it would be incumbent on them to explain the choice of that interpretation. Importantly, such an explanation would no longer be of the kind that absolves the judge of the responsibility to reach a fair/just/non-discriminatory solution.

---

44   Alexy, 'A Defence of Radbruch's Formula', pp. 31–2.

In another context, Postema has argued persuasively that there is a distinction between the professional responsibility and the responsibility of a layperson, but the professional nevertheless has the responsibility to act in a moral way.[45] He relies on Aristotle's concept of practical judgment to argue that judgment is neither a matter of simply applying general rules to particular cases nor a matter of mere intuition. Rather it is that in judgment general principles and particularities of a case both come into play. General principles provide the broader framework and a target but not the final outcome. The ultimate decision takes into account the particular circumstances and resolves the conflict of values. Thus, morality is not merely a matter of getting things right but of relating to people in a special and specifically human way. Professionals have to act in specifically moral ways but what can be done is to conceptualise this moral responsibility in a broader sense. This professional responsibility can be linked to understanding the professional role as not a fixed role. A 'recourse role' conception of the professional role allows for the possibility that such a role requires 'the agent not only to act according to what he perceives to be the explicit duties of the role in a narrow sense, but also to carry out those duties in keeping with the functional objectives of the role'.[46]

Functional Objectives of the Role of the Judge

The fact that so many judges cannot see the wrongness of discrimination in the actions of the respondents is not an indication of their lack of moral values. Rather it is a function of a lack of agreement about the functional objectives of the role of judges—that is, whether they are constrained or free to exercise their judgment. The freedom to exercise discretion is not, however, synonymous with unfettered freedom because, if as argued above there is no 'law' pre-existing the determination made by the judge, it seems obvious that in a disputed case the judge has to ascertain the meaning of the law, in the form of a rule or concept. Thus, a legal rule that says that less favourable treatment on the basis of disability is prohibited at the very least requires the judge to decide whether a particular conduct constitutes less favourable treatment. That is, what the law demands is the very issue in dispute and it is only the judge who has the authority to decide. The contemporary judicial practices *give the judge an option* to focus on the technical aspects rather than the substantive outcomes

---

45   He makes his argument with regard to lawyers, but I think it is equally applicable to the actions of judges. See Gerald Postema, 'Moral Responsibility in Professional Ethics' (1980) 55 *New York University Law Review* 63, esp. at 68.

46   Ibid., 83.

of the matter. If, however, the interpretative practice demanded a focus on the substantive outcome of the interpretation, it would make for the possibility of judges making more realistic determinations.

In a slightly different context, Judith Butler's argument about gender as 'performative'[47] needs to be invoked in the context of law as well. 'Law' is not a natural category; it is constructed and, when judges, among others, engage in interpretation of any rule they are attributing meaning to that rule or concept. Similarly, when scholars explain the nature of law, they too are conceptualising rather than describing a pre-existing reality. A theory of judicial task that conceives the judge as personally responsible for their decision would make it inevitable that the judge does not formulate the dispute in technical terms. If the judges could make this understanding of law their starting point it is possible to imagine that discrimination issues would be resolved to achieve genuine non-oppression. For example, the dispute in the case of *Purvis*[48] or of *Amery*,[49] if decided under this conception of the judicial task, could have had a very different outcome.

In the case of *Amery*, a group of women claimed that they performed the same tasks as the permanent teachers but were paid less because they were employed as long-term casual teachers. They framed their claim as one of indirect discrimination under the *Anti-Discrimination Act 1977* (NSW) (*ADA*). They argued that the employer made it a condition of work that the teachers had to be employed as permanent staff before they could access the higher pay scales. The long-term casual teachers claimed that they were unable to meet this condition because of the gendered expectations imposed on them as women that they would give priority to family responsibilities.

The majority in the High Court, however, found that the casual employment was not a 'condition of employment' imposed by the employer and therefore the *ADA* was not relevant. Therefore, the issue of whether the different pay scales were discriminatory did not even arise for judicial consideration. At the same time, however, there is nothing in the judgments of the majority that could be classified as incorrect technically. The most that the commentators can say is that the judges should have defined the requirement of permanent employment as a 'condition' imposed by the employer and thus bring the case under the purview of the *ADA*.[50] In the contemporary conventions of legal reasoning, however, judges are able to focus on whether the situation is covered by the

---

47   Judith Butler, *Gender Trouble: Feminism and the Subversion of Identity*, Routledge, New York, 1999.
48   (2003) 217 CLR 92.
49   *NSW v Amery* (2006) 226 ALR 196.
50   See, for example, K. Lee Adams, 'Defining Away Discrimination' (2006) 19 *Australian Journal of Labour Law* 263. Her assessment that the High Court failed to deconstruct the assumptions of normalcy and objectivity and thus equality is fine but it does not provide any reason for hoping that the judges will act differently the next time around. See also Thornton, 'Sex Discrimination, Courts and Corporate Power'.

relevant legislation. Since in their understanding it is not within the purview of the legislation, it becomes irrelevant to consider whether the employment arrangements are unfair for women with family responsibilities. That is, the *ADA* has a limited scope.

It is of course a truism that the judges can give relief only if the relevant law is applicable. Whether the law is applicable or not itself requires, however, a more nuanced understanding of their responsibility. If the same judges were to operate in a milieu of equality as fairness and judges' responsibility to reach a non-discriminatory outcome, they could not avoid having to explain why it is acceptable for casual teachers—most of whom are women—to be paid less when they are doing the same work as the permanent teachers. Moreover, judges trained to achieve a fair outcome would be able to argue that the choice of permanent or casual employment is not a real choice but an effect of gender hierarchy that the anti-discrimination laws are meant to address.

Similarly, I suggest that if the majority judges in *Purvis* had the option of distancing themselves from the judgment made, they would indeed be compelled to make a more reasonable or fairer judgment. The majority judges in this instance were able to say that the school was entitled to exclude a boy with intellectual disabilities as the basis of its decision was discrimination on the ground not of disability, but of his disruptive behaviour. The bifurcation between the disability and the behaviour of the person is breathtakingly ingenious but the more important issue here is that the judges were able or were permitted by the conventions of legal reasoning to focus on the technicalities.

Now I am not suggesting that the complainant will always be correct and the respondent wrong, but I am arguing for an acknowledgment that there are at least two interpretations and the judge has to choose between them. Since there is no compulsion to choose one interpretation over another, as exemplified in the different judgments of the majority and the minority, it must be obligatory on the judges to explain their choice in terms of substantive outcomes. If a judge in *Purvis* holds that the school can exclude the student, they must explain why it is not discrimination. The reasoning in the present judgment that the ground of exclusion is not covered by the legislation is a technical reason, which does not deny that the action of the school will disadvantage the student. Instead it avoids the issue of disadvantage or unfairness of the action altogether. It is perfectly understandable that the school has to manage a difficult situation and might not have the resources to do so. If, however, the problem was identified thus many avenues could be explored to find solutions taking into account the interests of both parties. But if the problem is written out of existence—as done by the majority in the High Court—nothing more remains to be done. The difficulties related to disability are privatised and the state and its institutions absolve themselves of any responsibility by relying on technicalities.

It is in this sense that Veitch is right that the compartmentalisation of legal tasks absolves the judge of the responsibility for the outcome of a decision. Does this mean that it is futile to expect justice from the law and the judges? If yes, is this not a deterministic analysis that portrays law as inherently incapable of delivering justice? How could it be otherwise?

One way out of this dead end is to acknowledge that the judge has to exercise choice in the pursuit of justice or fairness. It has to be the pursuit of these ideals and not the pretended neutrality that provides the legitimation of judicial authority. It is however, not simply a matter of making these ideals the legislative standard that the judges have to apply.[51] Rather, it must be the requirement of the judicial role that the judges are the pursuers of justice. Justice according to which definition, one could ask? It is easier to answer this question negatively and say that it is certainly not according to the 'neutrality of the judge' standard. It necessarily means that the judge has to articulate and justify their choice of interpretation as fair or just. The emphasis is on 'justify' and in my opinion this responsibility can be discharged only if we move away from the fiction of constraint on the exercise of discretion.[52] Such a move will not be a licence for relativism in the sense that a judge is free to be totally arbitrary or idiosyncratic. The constraint in this conception of the judicial task comes from the judge's responsibility for pursuing justice or fairness. It also does not allow judges to distance themselves from the consequence of the decision and thus pins the responsibility of the consequences of the decision on the person making the choice. The disjuncture between role responsibility and personal responsibility is thus avoided but the person occupying the role of the judge cannot leave their morals at home! Undoubtedly, in a morally pluralistic society there would be inevitable disagreements about which morals are worth enforcing through the judiciary. This is an important issue but it is not one resolved by either relying on the fiction of constraint or giving in to the relativism of post-structural views. In the present context, the accountability of the judge for the interpretation chosen is the best guarantee of non-arbitrariness.

---

51 For example, suppose the conventions of legal reasoning demanded that in anti-discrimination actions the outcome should be geared to integrating the complainant in a particular setting (for example, the mainstream school in *Purvis*). It will still fall on the judge to determine what may be classified as adequate integration. The only certainty that the judge will be sympathetic to the complainant's disadvantage can come from the judge taking personal responsibility for the consequences flowing from their decision.

52 As argued by formalists as well as by natural-law theorists—in particular, those such as Dworkin. See, for example: R. M. Dworkin, 'Is Law a System of Rules' in R. M. Dworkin (ed.), *The Philosophy of Law*, Oxford University Press, UK, 1977.

Conclusion

The obvious question of course is how can this view of the judicial task be made the mainstream view? It is not simply a matter of theoretically re-conceptualising the judicial role. Such ideas need to be adopted by the legal professionals and thinkers alike. I have critiqued above the analyses that expect judges to change their ways simply because the scholars 'show' them the shortcomings of their views. The same criticism would apply to the expectation that the theorists will change their conceptions of legal reasoning because of critics' arguments.

Therefore, for this re-conceptualisation to succeed, the transformative potential of legal education needs to be deployed. New ways of theorising the connections between ideas and responsibility for the consequences flowing from those ideas will only ever come from the young legal scholars trained to be independent thinking agents. If combined with a sufficiently broad-based legal education, this conception has the potential for connecting law and justice in a principled as well as practical manner.

Therefore, we need to refocus on the transformative potential of knowledge and especially of education, as it is the site where knowledge is produced and disseminated. I use legal education as my particular focus but the argument is wider in its scope and extendable to education in general. It is necessary to combine the post-structural insights about the constructed nature of knowledge and the responsibility of scholars for their views.

Just as I have argued above about judicial responsibility, so too it can be expected that the theorists are accountable for the consequences flowing from their critiques. For this to happen, it is necessary to create the possibility and the capacities for critical thinking in the students. The idea of critical thinking is paid lip-service to in the burgeoning legal education literature,[53] but I argue that genuine critical thinking requires an appreciation that ideas are formulated by thinkers who always come from a particular perspective. The insight that objective knowledge is not possible has to be associated with the further acknowledgment that the particular perspective adopted by a thinker needs to be justified. Whether the theorist convinces the readers or not involves them

---

53   Legal education as a topic has generated extensive scholarship but I will not review it here. My point is, however, illustrated well by the Australian Universities Teaching Committee report that chronicles the extreme diversity of practices in Australian law school curricula. Diversity in itself is not the problem but the fact that there is no systematic attempt at articulating how critical capacities of students can be developed in university training. See Richard Johnstone and Sumitra Vignaendra, *Learning Outcomes and Curriculum Development in Law: A Report commissioned by the Australian Universities Teaching Committee (AUTC)*, Commonwealth of Australia, Canberra, 2003.

(us) in legitimising ideas. Therefore, the single most important aspect of training critical thinkers is that students (and thus the future professionals) learn to ask how ideas are normalised and legitimised.[54]

The acknowledgment by each one of us must follow that when we accept ideas and theories we are active agents in the process of 'creating' authoritative knowledge. Such critical thinkers who can capture their agency in the legitimation of ideas will of necessity also understand their role in making and unmaking social structures.[55] Once the individual thinker is thus implicated in making sense of the social structures it should become that much harder for the theorists to propose ideas that leave out of the theory the responsibility of the thinker. That is, if the thinker is not simply describing the surrounding reality but also partly 'constitutes' it then it is logical to expect that the injustices of the contemporary arrangements ought not be allowed to go on unchecked. Otherwise those 'constituting' such arrangements as inevitable are complicit in perpetuating them. If all that the theorists can do is establish the inevitable nature of contemporary societies, it is another way of being determinists.[56] Critique for the sake of critique can only be self-serving for the scholars.[57] Therefore, ethical responsibility can and ought to be inculcated as an integral aspect of education as it follows directly from the contemporary theories of knowledge.

In legal education, integrating legal theory in the entire curriculum is one possible way of inculcating critical thinking capacities of students.[58] To achieve this aim, however, it is crucial that students are engaged in analysing a broad spectrum of theoretical ideas.[59] That is, unless the students of law are trained to critique every idea and recognise their own agency in legitimising particular ideas, they are simply going to reproduce the authoritative knowledge that they are taught. It matters very little that what counts as authoritative could now be in the post-structural genre. Generating the capacity for the self-reflexivity

---

54   The enormity of this task is undeniable and the institutional obstructions are well analysed by Margaret Thornton 'Gothic Horror in the Legal Academy' (2005) 14(2) *Social and Legal Studies* 267.

55   I take this idea from Henry Giroux, 'Pedagogy of the Depressed: Beyond the New Politics of Cynicism' (2001) 28(3) *College Literature* 1, 14–15.

56   Cornel West, 'On Fox and Lears's *The Culture of Consumption*', *Prophetic Fragments*, Africa World Press, Lawrenceville, NJ, 1988.

57   Joel Pfister, *Critique for What: Cultural Studies, American Studies, Left Studies*, Paradigm Publishers, London, 2006.

58   I have developed this argument in greater detail in Archana Parashar and Vijaya Nagarajan, 'An Empowering Experience: Repositioning Critical Thinking Skills in the Law Curriculum' (2006) 10 *Southern Cross Law Review* 219. See also: Amita Dhanda, 'The Power of One: the Law Teacher in the Academy' in Amita Dhanda and Archana Parashar (eds), *Decolonisation of Legal Knowledge*, Routledge, Delhi, 2009.

59   A further difficulty, however, is that in legal education the inclusion of any theory is already a contentious issue and to argue for the inclusion of diverse streams is that much more difficult. See: Ian Duncanson, 'Legal Education and the Possibility of Critique: An Australian Perspective' (1993) 8 *Canadian Journal of Law and Society* p. 59. For an example of the debates, see also the articles in the special issue of *Sydney Law Review* (vol. 26 [2004]).

of thinkers in accepting or rejecting ideas is the logical basis of connecting responsibility with agency. These students are the legal thinkers of tomorrow and if equipped to think for themselves they will be the authors of a responsible jurisprudence of equality.

Bibliography

Books and articles

Adams, K. Lee, 'Defining Away Discrimination' (2006) 19 *Australian Journal of Labour Laws* 263.

Alexy, Robert, 'A Defence of Radbruch's Formula' in David Disenhaus (ed.), *Recrafting the Rule of Law: The Limits of Legal Order*, Hart Publishing, Oxford, 1999.

Butler, Judith, *Gender Trouble: Feminism and the Subversion of Identity*, Routledge, New York, 1999.

Cane, Peter, *Responsibility in Law and Morality*, Hart Publishing, Oxford, 2002.

Cappelletti, Maur, 'Who Watches the Watchmen? A Comparative Study of Judicial Responsibility' (1983) 31 *American Journal of Comparative Law* 1.

Chaffey, Claire, 'Human rights proposal still afloat', *Lawyers Weekly*, 22 February 2010, LexisNexis, <http://www.lawyersweekly.com.au/blogs/top_stories/archive/2010/02/22/human-rights-proposal-still-afloat.aspx>

Colker, Ruth, 'Anti-Subordination Above All: Sex, Race and Equality Protection' (1986) 61 *New York University Law Review* 1003.

Cornell, Drucilla, 'Time, Deconstruction, and the Challenge to Legal Positivism: The Call for Judicial Responsibility' (1990) 2 *Yale Journal of Law and Humanities* 267.

Davis, Martha, 'The Equal Rights Amendment: Then and Now' (2008) 17(3) *Columbia Journal of Gender and Law* 419.

Dean, Jodi (ed.), *Feminism and the New Democracy: Resisting the Political*, Sage, London, 1997.

Dhanda, Amita, 'The Power of One: the Law Teacher in the Academy' in Amita Dhanda and Archana Parashar (eds), *Decolonisation of Legal Knowledge*, Routledge, Delhi, 2009.

Duncanson, Ian, 'Legal Education and the Possibility of Critique: An Australian Perspective' (1993) 8 *Canadian Journal of Law and Society* 59.

Dworkin, Ronald, 'Is Law a System of Rules' in R. M. Dworkin (ed.), *The Philosophy of Law*, Oxford University Press, UK, 1977.

Dworkin, Ronald, *Law's Empire*, Harvard University Press, Cambridge, Mass., 1986.

Fish, Stanley, 'Anti-Professionalism' (1985) 7 *Cardozo Law Review* 645.

Fitzpatrick, Peter (ed.), *Nationalism, Racism and the Rule of Law*, Dartmouth, Brookfield, UK, 1995.

Foster, Hal (ed.), *The Anti-Aesthetic: Essays on Postmodern Culture*, Bay Press, Port Townsend, Wash., 1983.

Franke, Katherine M., 'The Central Mistake of Sex Discrimination Law: The Disaggregation of Sex From Gender' (1995–96) 144 *University of Pennsylvania Law Review* 1.

Fraser, Nancy, *Justice Interruptus: Critical Reflections on the 'Postsocialist' Condition*, Routledge, New York, 1997.

Gaze, Beth, 'Context and Interpretation in Anti-Discrimination Laws' (2002) 26(2) *Melbourne University Law Review* 325.

Gaze, Beth, 'The *Sex Discrimination Act* After Twenty Years: Achievements, Disillusionments and Alternatives' (2004) 27(3) *UNSW Law Journal* 914.

Gilbert and Tobin Centre of Public Law, *History of Charters of Human Rights in Australia*, University of New South Wales, Sydney, <http://www.gtcentre. unsw.edu.au/Resources/cohr/historyChartersofHumanRights.asp>

Giroux, Henry, 'Pedagogy of the Depressed: Beyond the New Politics of Cynicism' (2001) 28(3) *College Literature* 1.

Herman, Didi, 'Beyond the Rights Debate' (1993) 2 *Social and Legal Studies* 25.

Higgins, Tracy E. and Rosenbury, Laura A., 'Agency, Equality and Anti-Discrimination Law' (1999–2000) 85 *Cornell Law Review* 1194.

Hunter, Rosemary (ed.), *Rethinking Equality Projects in Law: Feminist Challenges*, Hart Publishing, Oxford and Portland, Ore., 2008.

Hunyor, Jonathon, 'Skin-Deep: Proof and Inferences of Racial Discrimination in Employment' (2003) 25 *Sydney Law Review* 535.

Lacey, Nicola, 'Responsibility and Modernity in Criminal Law' (2001) 9(3) *Journal of Political Philosophy* 249.

Lacey, Nicola, 'Feminist Legal Theory and the Rights of Women' in Karen Knop (ed.), *Gender and Human Rights*, Academy of European Law, Oxford University Press, UK, 2004.

McCrudden, Christopher (ed.), *Anti-Discrimination Law*, Dartmouth/Ashgate, Aldershot, UK, 2004.

Mansbridge, Jane J., *Why We Lost the ERA*, University of Chicago Press, Ill., 1986.

Moody-Adams, Michele, 'Reclaiming the Ideal of Equality' in Barbara S. Andrew, Jean Keller and Lisa H. Schwartzman (eds), *Feminist Interventions in Ethics and Politics*, Rowman and Littlefield Publishers, Oxford, 2005.

Parashar, Archana, 'Responsibility for Legal Knowledge' in Amita Dhanda and Archana Parashar (eds), *Decolonisation of Legal Knowledge*, Routledge, Delhi, 2009.

Parashar, Archana and Nagarajan, Vijaya, 'An Empowering Experience: Repositioning Critical Thinking Skills in the Law Curriculum' (2006) 10 *Southern Cross Law Review* 219.

Pfister, Joel, *Critique for What: Cultural Studies, American Studies, Left Studies*, Paradigm Publishers, London, 2006.

Postema, Gerald, 'Moral Responsibility in Professional Ethics' (1980) 55 *New York University Law Review* 63.

Roberts, Susan, 'The Inequality of Treating Unequals Equally: The Future of Direct Discrimination Under the *Disability Discrimination Act 1992* (Cth)?' (2005) 45 *AIAL Forum* 20.

Rosenfeld, Michel, 'Deconstruction and Legal Interpretation: Conflict, Indeterminacy and the Temptations of the New Legal Formalism' in Drucilla Cornell, Michel Rosenfeld and David Gray Carlson (eds), *Deconstruction and the Possibility of Justice*, Routledge, New York, 1992, p. 152.

Sadurski, Wojciech, 'Equality Before the Law: A conceptual Analysis' (1986) 60 *Australian Law Journal* 131.

Sadurski, Wojciech, *Equality and Legitimacy*, Oxford University Press, New York, 2008.

Sen, Amartya, *Inequality Reexamined*, Oxford University Press, UK, 1992.

Smith, Belinda, 'It's About Time for a New Regulatory Approach to Equality' (2008) 36 *Federal Law Review* 117.

Smith, Belinda and Riley, Joellen, 'Family Friendly Work Practices and the Law' (2004) 26 *Sydney Law Review* 395.

Squires, Judith, *The New Politics of Gender Equality*, Palgrave Macmillan, Basingstoke, UK, 2007.

Sullivan, Barbara, 'Sex Equality and the Australian Body Politic' in S. Watson (ed.), *Playing the State*, Allen & Unwin, Sydney, 1990.

Thornton, Margaret, *The Liberal Promise: Anti-Discrimination Legislation in Australia*, Oxford University Press, Melbourne, 1990.

Thornton, Margaret, 'Gothic Horror in the Legal Academy' (2005) 14(2) *Social and Legal Studies* 267.

Thornton, Margaret, 'Sex Discrimination, Courts and Corporate Power' (2008) 36 *Federal Law Review*, 31.

Veitch, Scott, *Law and Irresponsibility: On the Legitimation of Human Suffering*, Routledge, Oxford, 2007.

West, Cornel, 'On Fox and Lears's *The Culture of Consumption*', *Prophetic Fragments*, Africa World Press, Lawrenceville, NJ, 1988.

Wright, Shelley, 'Human Rights and Women's Rights' in K. E. Mahoney and P. Mahoney (eds), *Human Rights in the Twenty-First Century*, M. Nijhoff, Dordrecht, Boston, 1993.

Legislation

Anti-Discrimination Act 1977 (NSW)

Disability Discrimination Act 1992 (Cth)

Sex Discrimination Act 1984 (Cth)

Cases

NSW v Amery (2006) 226 ALR 196

Purvis v NSW Department of Education and Training (2003) 217 CLR 92

Reports and miscellaneous primary sources

Australian Law Reform Commission, *Equality Before the Law: Women's Equality*, Report No. 69, Australian Law Reform Commission, Sydney, 1994, Part II.

Johnstone, Richard and Vignaendra, Sumitra, *Learning Outcomes and Curriculum Development in Law: A Report commissioned by the Australian Universities Teaching Committee (AUTC)*, Commonwealth of Australia, Canberra, 2003.

Senate Standing Committee on Legal and Constitutional Affairs, *Report on the Effectiveness of the Commonwealth* Sex Discrimination Act 1984 *in Eliminating Discrimination and Promoting Gender Equality*, Parliament of Australia, Canberra, 2008, <http://www.aph.gov.au/Senate/committee/legcon_ctte/sex_discrim/report/index.htm>

Part V
Women's Rights as Human Rights

12. Raising Women Up: Analysing Australian Advocacy for Women's Rights under International and Domestic Law

Susan Harris Rimmer[1]

On the twentieth anniversary of the Sex Discrimination Act *(SDA), Elizabeth Evatt stated that Australia was 'falling short on women's rights'. Earlier in her UN role, she had said: 'Ultimately we have to be judged not by our highest ambitions and achievements, but by our ability to raise from the lowest level those whose needs...are greatest. That is the way I would like Australia, and every other country, to be judged in the United Nations.' This chapter reviews progress in Australia in the past five years according to Evatt's criteria, and celebrates the role of Australians in creating multilevel strategies to 'raise up' Australian women by improving their lives and realise their rights. The issues are analysed through a biographical lens. I examine the crucial role of Evatt, Andrew Byrnes, Jane Connors and Helen L'Orange (in the development of the UN Declaration on the Elimination of All Forms of Violence Against Women). The argument is that domestic reform and engagement with the UN system can be a mutually enriching experience, although the Australian women's movement has not always been effective in joining together international and domestic expertise and debates.*

Introduction

In 2004, to mark the twentieth anniversary of the passage of the *Sex Discrimination Act 1984* (Cth) (*SDA*), Elizabeth Evatt made a speech in Melbourne titled 'Falling Short on Women's Rights'.[2] She argued that Australian law was falling short of its obligations under the UN Convention on the Elimination of All Forms of Discrimination Against Women (CEDAW)[3] and other international instruments

---

1   Many thanks for feedback on this chapter from participants at the SDA twenty-fifth anniversary conference. My gratitude goes to Margaret Thornton for her initiative in holding the conference and in producing this volume. Many thanks go to interviewees, Hilary Charlesworth and Anne Summers, for their comments.

2   Elizabeth Evatt, 'Falling short on Women's Rights: Mis-Matches Between *SDA* and the International Regime' in Marius Smith (ed.), *Human Rights 2004: The Year in Review*, Castan Centre for Human Rights Law, Monash University, Melbourne, 2005.

3   GA res. 34/180, 34 UN GAOR Supp (No. 46) at 193, UN Doc A/34/46; 1249 UNTS 13; 19 ILM 33 (1980).

to provide equality rights and non-discrimination safeguards for women. A decade earlier, in her role as chairwoman of the CEDAW Committee, Evatt had set a test for success in this regard: 'Ultimately we have to be judged not by our highest ambitions and achievements, but by our ability to raise from the lowest level those whose needs…are greatest. That is the way I would like Australia, and every other country, to be judged in the United Nations.'[4]

This chapter reviews progress in Australia in the past five years according to Evatt's criteria, to see whether Australia has progressed in meeting its international obligations regarding the goal of gender equality. Evatt identified that the *SDA* was 'mismatched' with CEDAW due to its imperfect and partial conception of equality and lack of methods to address structural disadvantage and power redistribution.[5] The issue of intimate partner and family violence offers a prism through which to observe changes in the way international standards are employed in domestic debates about women's rights in the past quarter-century. Gender equality issues have often fallen by the wayside of wider human rights battles.

I employ the methodology of focusing on the biographies of prominent advocates to offer a way of analysing progression and regression over time. I examine the crucial role of Australians such as Evatt (in the development of CEDAW analysis), Andrew Byrnes and Jane Connors (in the development of the Optional Protocol to CEDAW) and Helen L'Orange (in the development of the UN Declaration on the Elimination of All Forms of Violence Against Women). My argument is that domestic reform and engagement with the UN system can be a mutually enriching experience. The stories of my protagonists demonstrate some common themes. These individuals were innovative in their use of the international system and created multilevel strategies at particular political moments, bolstered by a domestic emphasis on feminist representation in domestic policy machinery (especially Australia's unique 'femocracy')[6] to realise the rights of women, including Australian women. Their experience has some commonality: the importance of qualities such as patience and determination; the key role of good gender analysis as opposed to general gender awareness; and the importance of strategic thinking, especially in relation to finding combinations of key expertise and political leadership, with an eye to the improvement of the machinery of decision making. These stories of leadership at the international level should be documented, especially as the feminist movement in Australia

---

4   Australian Human Rights Commission (AHRC) and the Australian Government Office for Women (OfW), *Women of the World: Know Your International Human Rights*, Australian Government, Canberra, 2008, p. 12, <http://www.fahcsia.gov.au/sa/women/pubs/govtint/know_int_humrights/Documents/cedaw_ed_pack.pdf>
5   Evatt, 'Falling Short', p. 58.
6   See further: Marian Sawer, *Femocrats and Ecorats: Women's Policy Machinery in Australia, Canada and New Zealand*, United Nations Research Institute for Social Development, Geneva, 1996.

undergoes generational change. Australian advocates for women's rights should continue to use UN processes as a tool, with detailed knowledge of the United Nations' limitations in achieving transformative change.

Using this biographical lens demonstrates, however, that despite some conceptual progress at the international level, certain issues—particularly violence towards Indigenous women and girls—have been extremely resistant to reform. Some domestic debates have lagged behind comparable nations, such as that on paid maternity leave. The misalignment between the scope of CEDAW and the narrow limits of the *SDA* has become more apparent over time. Also, it is clear that in 2010 many features of Australia's once impressive gender policy architecture that could drive domestic reforms and therefore inspire international innovation have been dismantled. How, then, can we re-energise the synergy between international innovation and systemic reform for gender equality at the domestic level? How can the UN human rights system be rendered vital and accessible and, above all, useful as a method to 'raise up' the rights of Australian women, in solidarity with women globally? One avenue might be the innovative approach taken by Australian non-governmental organisations (NGOs) in relying on extensive community consultation in the production of NGO reports to the CEDAW Committee, the Commission for the Status of Women and follow-up meetings to the Beijing Women's Conference. Generally though, the Australian women's movement has not always been efficient in joining together international and domestic expertise and debates.[7]

Women's Rights at the United Nations

The most wide-ranging of the international human rights treaties devoted to women is CEDAW, adopted by the UN General Assembly in 1979 and now with 186 state parties (but with many states making serious reservations to certain provisions).

Australia signed CEDAW at a special signing ceremony in Copenhagen at the UN World Conference for the Decade of Women on 17 July 1980, sending a strong delegation of experts led by Robert Ellicott (Minister for Home Affairs in the Fraser Government).[8] The treaty then entered into force in September 1981. After a long consultation period with the States and Territories, Australia ratified the treaty on 28 July 1983, but made some reservations,[9] such as on

---

7   This can be attributed at least in part to the continuing damage done to the women's sector by de-funding and 'gag' clauses, and continuing secretariat reform. See further: Marian Sawer, 'Disappearing Tricks' (2008) 27(3) *Dialogue: Academy of the Social Sciences in Australia* 4, 6.

8   AHRC and OfW, *Women of the World*.

9   Including the 'federalism' declaration Australian makes to most international treaties. Australian practice is to make a short 'federal declaration' on ratification of treaties where it is intended that the States will

- maternity leave: 'The Government of Australia advises that it is not at present in a position to take the measures required by Article 11(2) to introduce maternity leave with pay or with comparable social benefits throughout Australia'

- defence personnel: 'The Government of Australia advises that it does not accept the application of the Convention in so far as it would require alteration of Defence Force policy which excludes women from combat duties'.[10]

Even with these reservations, Australia's ratification of CEDAW became part of the intense domestic and partisan debates that affected the passage of the *SDA*, as set out elsewhere in this book by Thornton and Luker.

The Convention contains a broad definition of discrimination in Article 1, covering both equality of opportunity (formal equality) and equality of outcome (de facto or substantive equality):

> [D]iscrimination against women violates the principles of equality of rights and respect for human dignity, is an obstacle to the participation of women, on equal terms with men, in the political, social, economic and cultural life of their countries, hampers the growth of the prosperity of society and the family and makes more difficult the full development of the potentialities of women in the service of their countries and of humanity.

The Convention requires states to take legal and other measures to ensure the practical realisation of the principle of sex equality (Article 2). The Convention covers a broad range of areas where state parties must work to eliminate discrimination, including political and public life (Article 7), international organisations (Article 8), education (Article 10), employment (Article 11), health care (Article 12), financial credit (Article 13b), cultural life (Article 13c), the rural sector (Article 14), the law (Article 15) and marriage (Article 16). Hilary Charlesworth notes that this

> wide coverage means the Women's Convention transcends the traditional divide between civil and political rights and economic, social and cultural

---

play a role in implementing the treaty. The CEDAW reservation follows the sample declaration attached to the *Principles and Procedures for Commonwealth–State Consultation on Treaties*: 'Australia has a Federal Constitutional System in which Legislative, Executive and Judicial Powers are shared or distributed between the Commonwealth and the Constituent States. The implementation of the Treaty throughout Australia will be effected by the Commonwealth State and Territory Authorities having regard to their respective constitutional powers and arrangements concerning their exercise.'

10   This is the current text. On 30 August 2000, with effect from that date, Australia withdrew that part of the reservation which read: 'The Government of Australia advises that it does not accept the application of the Convention in so far as it would require alteration of Defence Force policy which excludes women from combat and combat-related duties. The Government of Australia is reviewing this policy so as to more closely define "combat" and "combat-related" duties.'

rights, illustrated by the separate development of the International Covenant on Economic, Social and Cultural Rights (ICESCR) and the International Covenant on Civil and Political Rights (ICCPR). [11]

This is a key point of difference with the *SDA*, which focuses primarily on participation in the formal paid workforce, rather than other aspects of the life cycle.

CEDAW allows for progressive realisation but requires results in securing substantive gender equality under Article 2a. Notably, Article 4 allows for affirmative action, in the form of temporary special measures designed to accelerate de facto equality such as quotas in employment, education, financial services and politics to overcome historical barriers. The core organising principles of CEDAW are therefore equality, non-discrimination and state obligation. [12] CEDAW, notably, obliges governments to take proactive measures to prevent sexual stereotyping and address violations of its terms.

In 1999, CEDAW was supplemented by an Optional Protocol. The Optional Protocol creates a mechanism allowing individual claims of violations under CEDAW to be made to the CEDAW Committee, and a procedure enabling the committee to initiate inquiries into situations of grave or systematic violations of women's rights. As of 2010, 99 states were party to the Optional Protocol.[13]

As with CEDAW and the *SDA*, there were political difficulties with acceptance of the Optional Protocol as a result of the Howard Government's general disenchantment with the human rights treaty body system. Australia had received heavy criticism over its treatment of Indigenous Australians and asylum-seekers from the Committee for the Elimination of Racial Discrimination in March 2000.[14] In a joint press release in August 2000, key ministers indicated that Australia would not ratify the Optional Protocol as part of this wider dissatisfaction with the UN human rights system.[15] Hilary Charlesworth has

---

11   See Hilary Charlesworth, Inside/Outside: Feminist International Legal Studies and Thirty Years of the CEDAW Convention, Paper delivered at the Asian Society of International Law Conference, Tokyo, August 2009.

12   See further: Andrew Byrnes and Jane Connors, *The International Bill of Rights for Women: The Impact of the CEDAW Convention*, Oxford University Press, UK, (forthcoming).

13   There are also provisions relating to non-discrimination and equality in the other key UN human rights treaties. See further: Alice Edwards, 'Violence against Women as Sex Discrimination: Judging the Jurisprudence of the United Nations Human Rights Treaty Bodies' (2008) 18 *Texas Journal of Women & the Law* 1. Article 6 of the new Convention on the Rights of Persons with Disabilities specifically addresses multidimensional discrimination against women. There are also special protections for women and girls under international humanitarian law (including the Geneva Conventions and the Rome Statute). See further: Judith Gardam and Michelle Jarvis, *Women, Armed Conflict and International Law*, Kluwer Law International, The Hague, 2001.

14   See further: Spencer Zifcak, *Mr Ruddock Goes to Geneva*, UNSW Press, Sydney, 2003.

15   Alexander Downer, Daryl Williams and Phillip Ruddock, Improving the effectiveness of United Nations committees, Joint media release, 29 August 2000, Parliament House, Canberra.

stated that '(t)he thrust of the press release…was that the treaty bodies not only need reform but that they need reform because they are criticizing Australia a bit too much'. [16] Although the government's decision not to sign or ratify the Optional Protocol was opposed by more than 200 women's groups and by a senior Liberal Party member, Dame Beryl Beaurepaire, the government did not change its decision during its following two terms.[17] Australia finally acceded to the Optional Protocol on 24 November 2008 under the Rudd Government, and Australian women could make complaints from March 2009.[18]

There is also increasing 'soft law' in the area of women's rights at the United Nations. The Declaration on the Elimination of All Forms of Violence Against Women was adopted by the UN General Assembly in December 1993. The Beijing Conference for Women in 1995 adopted a Platform for Action, the implementation of which is currently undergoing a 15-year review at the 2010 meeting of the Commission for the Status of Women. The Security Council has also issued a series of resolutions on women, peace and security, including Resolutions 1325 (2000) (peace building), 1820 (2008), 1888 and 1889 (2009) (sexual violence in armed conflict).[19] Women are also increasingly engaging with the international trade and development frameworks.[20]

This is not to say that the United Nations offers a perfect or even an adequate framework for the protection of women's rights. The UN system is a product of elite diplomacy in which women are under-represented[21] and, until very recently, it lacked effective gender architecture.[22] Indeed, as Caroline Lambert states, the UN human rights treaty system 'is a partial site of justice for women and a site of partial justice'.[23] It does, however, offer an international space in which to debate issues of gender equality and a set of standards to which signatory states can be held to account. Australian participation in the development of these standards is illuminating.

---

16   Hilary Charlesworth, 'Australia's Relations with the United Nations in the Post Cold War Environment', *Australian Federal Parliament, Joint Standing Committee on Foreign Affairs, Defence and Trade: Joint Committee Hansard*, 21 March 2001, p. 429.

17   Joanne Kinslor, '"Killing Off" International Human Rights Law: An Exploration of the Australian Government's Relationship with United Nations Human Rights Committees' (2002) 8(2) *Australian Journal of Human Rights* 16, 19.

18   See further: Simone Cusack, 'Discrimination against Women: Combating its Compounded and Systemic Forms' (2009) 34(2) *Alternative Law Journal* 86, 89–91.

19   See further: Dianne Otto, 'A Sign of "Weakness"? Disrupting Gender Certainties in the Implementation of Security Council Resolution 1325' (2006) 13 *Michigan Journal of Gender and Law* 113.

20   See further: Sharon Pickering and Caroline Lambert (eds), *Global Issues, Women and Justice*, Sydney Institute of Criminology Series, NSW, 2004.

21   See further: Hilary Charlesworth and Christine Chinkin, *The Boundaries of International Law*, Manchester University Press, UK, 2000.

22   The UN General Assembly agreed to the establishment of a new gender architecture at its last session of 2009.

23   Caroline Lambert, 'Partial Sites and Partial Sightings: Women and the United Nations Human Rights Treaty System', in Pickering and Lambert, *Global Issues, Women and Justice*, p. 165.

Elizabeth Evatt and CEDAW

Elizabeth Evatt has had a stellar career combining international and domestic work in pursuit of human rights, especially women's rights. Evatt was Deputy President of the Australian Industrial Relations Commission in the 1970s, before becoming the first Chief Justice of the Family Court of Australia. From 1988 to 1993, she was president of the Australian Law Reform Commission and then Chancellor of the University of Newcastle. Notably, she chaired the Royal Commission on Human Relations from 1974 to 1977, which dealt with a wide variety of sensitive social issues, such as abortion, contraception, sex education, family law and violence against women. The royal commission broadened official definitions of domestic violence to include emotional and verbal as well as physical abuse. [24]

In 1984, soon after the *SDA* finally made it through Parliament, Evatt was elected as an expert to the CEDAW Committee. When Anne Summers reportedly called Evatt to ask if she accepted the government's support for her nomination, she was surprised and asked if the CEDAW Committee did anything 'useful'. Summers replied that the government was nominating her precisely because they wanted CEDAW to do something useful.[25] And so it came to pass. Between 1984 and 1992, Evatt was a member of the committee, serving as its chair from 1989 to 1991. She was then elected a member of the UN Human Rights Committee from 1993 to 2000, which she combined with a role as a part-time commissioner of the Australian Human Rights and Equal Opportunity Commission (now the Australian Human Rights Commission) from 1995 to 1998. These simultaneous appointments exemplify Evatt's bond between the international and the domestic spheres.

During her long terms with both the CEDAW and the Human Rights Committees, Evatt embarked on a tireless agenda of procedural reform and succeeded in working with a group of like-minded committee members to improve the quality of analysis of general comments, the structure and length of meetings, the reporting procedures and the breadth of subject matter of the committees.[26] This procedural concern led to many substantive outcomes for women's rights, especially in the General Recommendations on sexual stereotyping, incompatible reservations to the Convention on the grounds of culture and

---

24   See further: Marian Sawer, *Making Women Count: A History of the Women's Electoral Lobby in Australia*, UNSW Press, Sydney, 2008, p. 48.
25   Peter Thomson, Elizabeth Evatt: Integrating Women's Issues in the United Nations Human Rights System, 'Australians at the United Nations', Unpublished ms, 13 August 1996, Department of Foreign Affairs and Trade, Canberra, p. 4 (on file with author).
26   Thomson, Elizabeth Evatt, pp. 8–10.

religion, and female circumcision. The document she is best known for, General Recommendation 19, drafted in 1992, found that violence against women constituted discrimination.[27]

This was important because, notwithstanding the numerous strengths of CEDAW—including its extension to private actors and its aim to eliminate harmful customary practices [28]—one of the most glaring shortcomings of the Convention is the omission of violence from its terms. Under Evatt's direction, the CEDAW Committee endeavoured to rectify this deficiency through Recommendation 19, which specifies gender-based violence as a form of discrimination prohibited by the treaty. [29] The adoption of the Declaration for the Elimination of All Forms of Violence Against Women by the UN General Assembly in 1993 also responded to this gap. [30] This work has been the foundation of many global policies and jurisprudence. Recommendation 19 and the Declaration provide the conceptual basis for and coherency of 'Outcome 4: Responses are just' under the *Time for Action* 2009 report of the National Council to Reduce Violence Against Women and their Children.[31]

Evatt's work with the Human Rights Committee was equally groundbreaking—working again on the compatibility of reservations to the International Covenant on Civil and Political Rights (ICCPR), contributing to drafting the controversial *General Comments on Article 18* (freedom of religion)[32] and drafting Article 25 (free elections and universal suffrage).[33] She worked hard to realise the 'scope and potential' of the ICCPR's emphasis on the right to equality to be a 'powerful tool' to protect the rights of women in all fields, but found it a struggle.[34] Many of her interventions on violence against women, rights in marriage and gendered forms of persecution in asylum claims appear, however, in the revised *General Comment on Article 3* (equal rights of men and women) on which she worked closely with Professor Cecilia Medina of Chile. It was issued in March 2000.[35]

---

27 *CEDAW Committee General Comment 19 on Article 16 (and Article 5), Violence against women*: 29/01/92, A/47/38.

28 See Articles 2 and 5.

29 *CEDAW Committee General Comment 19 on Article 16 (and Article 5), Violence against women*: 29/01/92, A/47/38.

30 General Assembly Resolution 48/104 of 20 December 1993.

31 National Council to Reduce Violence Against Women and their Children, *Time for Action: National Council's Plan for Australia to reduce Violence against Women and Children 2009–2021*, Canberra, 2009.

32 Human Rights Committee, *General Comment 22, Article 18* (Forty-Eighth Session, 1993), UN Doc CCPR/C/21/Rev 1/Add 4 (1993), reprinted in *Compilation of General Comments and General Recommendations Adopted by Human Rights Treaty Bodies*, UN. Doc. HRI/GEN/1/Rev 6, 2003, p. 155.

33 Human Rights Committee, *General Comment 25*. The right to participate in public affairs, voting rights and the right of equal access to public service (Article 25), (Fifty-Seventh Session, 1996), UN Doc CCPR/C/21/Rev 1/Add 7 (1996), reprinted in *Compilation of General Comments and General Recommendations Adopted by Human Rights Treaty Bodies*, UN Doc. HRI/GEN/1/Rev 6, 2003, p. 168.

34 Thomson, Elizabeth Evatt, p. 19.

35 Human Rights Committee, *General Comment 28*, Equality of rights between men and women (Article 3), (Sixty-Eighth Session, 2000), UN Doc CCPR/C/21/Rev 1/Add 10 (2000), reprinted in *Compilation of General Comments and General Recommendations Adopted by Human Rights Treaty Bodies*, UN Doc HRI/GEN/1/Rev

Elizabeth Evatt's vision of human rights is ultimately a unifying one. Her particular genius has been the ability to look beyond artificial legal boundaries and examine legal instruments from the standpoint of the holistic lived experience of an affected person, but then to translate this view into impeccably logical, analytically rigorous and technically accurate legal discourse. She sees life in all its messiness, but renders it in judicial prose. When you read the General Recommendations and comments she drafted, they sound so much like shining good sense, it is hard to remember how groundbreaking and controversial they were at the time, and how much Evatt had to invest in procedural reform for long periods to realise the opportunity to produce the documents.

Evatt's work for human rights certainly did not end with her time at the United Nations,[36] but my argument is that just as her international work was influenced by her domestic experience, so too has that international dimension added richness and weight to domestic advocacy—her own and that of the many of us influenced by her. Her critique of the *SDA*, then, is worth close examination.

CEDAW and the *SDA*

Evatt's central question in 2004 on the twentieth anniversary of the *SDA* was 'how well does the *SDA* fulfil Australia's obligations under the Women's Convention? Her answer: not very well at all. Of course, this is only one indicator of success, as the other contributions to this volume attest.

Evatt's critique of the *SDA* was based on its partial implementation of CEDAW, compared with the *Racial Discrimination Act 1975* (Cth), which tracks closely the provisions of the Convention on the Elimination of All Forms of Racial Discrimination (CERD). While praising the political breakthrough of the *SDA's* passage, Evatt lists criticisms that the Act's 'definitions and restrictions are too narrow to deal with systemic discrimination; it has too many exemptions':

> The SDA annexes the Women's Convention. But it aims to implement only certain provisions of the Convention. Its main aim was to prohibit sex discrimination in certain areas and provide remedies for discrimination. That was a significant innovation at Commonwealth level, one which some thought would bring us to the end of civilization.[37]

6, 2003, p. 179.

36 Evatt was a judge of the World Bank Administrative Tribunal, a Visiting Professor at the University of New South Wales and chair of the Board of the Public Interest Advocacy Centre in Sydney. She has for many years been a member of the Australian section of the International Commission of Jurists and was elected as a commissioner in April 2003. She has made valuable contributions to the public debate in recent years on sedition laws, the treatment of asylum-seekers and the need for an Australian Human Rights Act.

37 Evatt, 'Falling Short', p. 58.

We see in her 2004 speech many of the themes Evatt grappled with at the international level: unfair or illogical exemptions to the Act, often based on religious grounds, which she felt should be challenged; restrictive interpretations of the grounds of discrimination; grounds too bound up in the male comparator;[38] interpretation using a very narrow view of a woman's life and the discrimination she could face over the life cycle.

Evatt's analysis was taken up in the NGO reports to the CEDAW examination of Australia and the concluding observations in 2006 correlate with her views.[39] Her arguments were used or closely mirrored in many of the submissions to the 2008 senate inquiry into the effectiveness of the *SDA*,[40] and were also submitted by many groups in support of the need for a Human Rights Act or Equality Act in the national consultation on human rights led by Frank Brennan in 2009.[41] In my view, Evatt would be quite pleased with the recommendations of the senate inquiry into the *SDA*,[42] especially Recommendations 1–3, which link the *SDA* more closely with CEDAW and other human rights treaties (see Box 12.1). The reforms would also focus on improving the machinery behind the *SDA*, especially the role of the Sex Discrimination Commissioner. The development of domestic machinery will be crucial to the effectiveness of the complaint mechanism under the Optional Protocol to CEDAW for Australian women.

Jane Connors and Andrew Byrnes: The Optional Protocol to CEDAW, 1994–2009

A key achievement since Evatt's speech in 2004 has been the belated accession by Australia to the Optional Protocol to CEDAW in November 2008. The failure

---

38   See further: Thornton's 'benchmark male' (Margaret Thornton, 'Feminism and the Changing State: The Case of Sex Discrimination' (2006) 21(50) *Australian Feminist Studies* 151).

39   Committee on the Elimination of All Forms of Discrimination Against Women, *Concluding Comments of the Committee on the Elimination of All Forms of Discrimination Against Women: Australia*, UN Doc CEDAW/C/AUL/CO/5 (2006). 'Australia's implementation of CEDAW was criticised by the Committee in a number of respects including the lack of adequate structures and mechanisms to ensure effective coordination and consistent application of the Convention in all states and territories, the absence of an entrenched guarantee prohibiting discrimination against women and providing for the principle of equality between women and men, the lack of sufficient statistical data, disaggregated by sex and ethnicity on the practical realization of equality between women and men in all areas covered by the Convention, and information on the impact and results achieved of legal and policy measures taken' (Sara Charlesworth, Submission 39 to Senate Standing Committee on Legal and Constitutional Affairs, *Inquiry into the Effectiveness of the Commonwealth* Sex Discrimination Act 1984 *in Eliminating Discrimination and Promoting Gender Equality*, 8 August 2008). See further: Hilary Charlesworth and Sara Charlesworth, 'The *Sex Discrimination Act* and International Law' (2004) 27 *University of New South Wales Law Journal* 858.

40   On 26 June 2008, the Senate referred to the Legal and Constitutional Affairs Committee the matter of the effectiveness of the *Sex Discrimination Act* 1984 (Cth) in eliminating discrimination and promoting gender equality.

41   Available at <http://www.humanrightsconsultation.gov.au/>

42   See further: Cusack, 'Discrimination Against Women', pp. 87–9.

to ratify under the previous, Howard Government was all the more galling for human rights advocates because three Australians were key players in its conception and drafting phase in 1993–94: Evatt herself and experts Jane Connors and Andrew Byrnes.[43]

Jane Connors has been the Chief of the Special Procedures Branch at the UN Office of the High Commissioner for Human Rights since 2002. She joined the United Nations as the Chief of the Women's Rights Division in the Department of Economic Affairs in 1996. Before that, she taught law at various tertiary institutions, spending 15 years at the School of Oriental and African Studies in London. She has written widely on the human rights of women and the treaty body system. Andrew Byrnes is Professor of International Law in the Faculty of Law at the University of New South Wales. He has published extensively on human rights topics, especially CEDAW and the human rights of women, with Jane Connors. He has been closely involved in the development of the Convention on the Rights of Persons with Disabilities in recent years.

Box 12.1

Recommendation 1

11.9. The committee recommends that the preamble to the Act and subsections 3(b), (ba) and (c) of the Act be amended by deleting the phrase 'so far as is possible'.

Recommendation 2

11.8. The committee recommends that subsection 3(a) of the Act be amended to refer to other international conventions Australia has ratified which create obligations in relation to gender equality.

Recommendation 3

11.10. The committee recommends that the Act be amended by inserting an express requirement that the Act be interpreted in accordance with relevant international conventions Australia has ratified including CEDAW, ICCPR, ICESCR and the ILO conventions which create obligations in relation to gender equality.

Extract from Senate Standing Committee on Legal and Constitutional Affairs 2008, Report on the Effectiveness of the Commonwealth Sex Discrimination Act 1984 in Eliminating Discrimination and Promoting Gender Equality, 12 December 2008, Parliament of Australia, Canberra, p. xiii.

---

43 Andrew Byrnes and Jane Connors, 'Enforcing the Human Rights of Women: A Complaints Procedure for the Women's Convention' (1995–96) 21 *Brooklyn Journal of International Law* 679; Andrew Byrnes, 'Slow and Steady Wins the Race?: The Development of an Optional Protocol to the Women's Convention' (1997) 91 *American Society of International Law and Procedure* 383.

At the Vienna Conference in 1993, there was considerable attention given to the idea of establishing an optional protocol to CEDAW. A group of NGOs, funded by the Dutch Government, met in Maastricht towards the end of 1994. Evatt attended, along with two other members of the Human Rights Committee and three members of the CEDAW Committee. Byrnes and Connors produced an influential background document for this meeting, which after successful negotiation produced a draft protocol that included both a complaints procedure and an inquiry procedure, based on the Optional Protocols to the ICCPR, CERD and the Convention Against Torture (CAT). The Maastricht document was then considered by the CEDAW Committee and a draft adopted in January 1995.

The General Assembly, acting without a vote, adopted the 21-article Optional Protocol to CEDAW on 6 October 1999, and it entered into force on 22 December 2000 after receiving the tenth state signature. While initially supporting the ratification process in the region, the Howard Coalition Government announced in 2000 that it did not intend to sign the Optional Protocol—ostensibly due to continuing concerns about the UN treaty body system.[44]

Despite her personal experience of this rocky road to reform, Jane Connors, in my interview with her, focused on the key advantages of engaging with the UN system.[45] She noted that concluding observations from the UN committees, general comments on the treaty provisions and individual communications were all opportunities to test the Australian Government against an international standard, to add 'oomph' to an argument and to shine a spotlight on a particular domestic practice. In the case of the European Court of Human Rights, this led to binding gender jurisprudence.

Connors noted that NGO reports were a very effective strategy in structuring issues against a set of standards over the passage of time, which could also have domestic impact and act as a 'baseline' of minimum standards. Advocates have to manage their expectations of what the UN system can achieve. The practice of International Women's Rights Action Watch (IWRAW) is an excellent regional and global example of using shadow reporting.[46] Australian NGOs have had a strong history of extensive grassroots community consultations producing high-level analytical reports that have had influence on the committee's concluding observations.[47]

---

44 Hilary Charlesworth, Madeline Chiam, Devika Hovell and George Williams, *No Country is an Island: Australia and International Law*, UNSW Press, Sydney, 2006, p. 88.

45 Interview with Jane Connors, 11 September 2009.

46 For more information on IWRAW, see <http://www1.umn.edu/humanrts/iwraw/>

47 See further: WRANA, *Australian NGO Shadow Report on the Implementation of CEDAW*, 2005; and YWCA Australia and Women's Legal Services Australia, *Australian NGO Shadow Report on the Implementation of CEDAW*, 2009.

Connors also noted that this baseline approach was particularly useful in tracking regressions on particular issues, such as same-sex relationships. A particular challenge for many states in the United Nations was the issue of the rights of Islamic women in secular states. Connors urges patience when engaging in UN processes, observing that the international community is often not good at locating the centrality of gender concerns in issues that do not come obviously labelled as women's issues, including climate change, the global financial crisis and threats against peace and security. As Hilary Charlesworth notes: 'the players in international law crises are almost exclusively male…The lives of women are considered part of a crisis only when they are harmed in a way that is seen to demean the whole of their social group.'[48] Nonetheless, used strategically, the UN system can educate member states on their own achievements and blind spots, and the successes of other states. Connors reflected on the progress she had seen in UN debates over gender equality in the past decades. Her own career is testament to the influence individuals can wield within the international system to advance gender equality, just as Byrnes' work has often provided progressive force for women's rights and the rights of people living with disabilities from outside the system. Their experience teaches current advocates to play the long game, draw on the energy and resources of civil society and to be involved early in drafting processes.

Helen L'Orange: UN Declaration of Violence Against Women, 1993

Helen L'Orange is probably best known as one of Australia's leading public servants who focused on women's policy: the archetypal 'femocrat'. She headed national and State government (NSW) offices for the status of women from 1980 to 1993. During her time in the Women's Coordination Unit (WCU) in the NSW Premier's Department, supported by then Premier Neville Wran, major advances were made in the areas of domestic violence, sexual assault, rape and child protection in terms of law reform and policies and service delivery programs.[49] As Janet Ramsay notes of this period:

> Partly as a result of the skill and energy of L'Orange and her staff, partly through the continuing enthusiasm of Wran and his government for the electoral rewards of the women's project and partly through the growing energy of the NSW women's policy community, L'Orange's term at the WCU saw an explosion of structural and policy achievement. The

---

48 Hilary Charlesworth, 'International Law: A Discipline of Crisis' (2002) 65 *Modern Law Review* 377, 389.
49 The Women's Advisory Council to the Premier of NSW (WAC) played an important role in devising policy and supporting the unit.

'hub/wheel' model of women's machinery expanded and the women's policy issues addressed spread to include non-sexist education, the access of girls to apprenticeships, community based child care, the establishment of women's health centres, women's access to housing, and the dependency of women on minor tranquillisers. Ongoing work on rape, sexual assault, domestic violence and eventually child abuse proceeded in this energetic context.[50]

Marian Sawer states that it is not widely known that, along with Canada, Australia has developed a more comprehensive policy response to violence against women than any other democracy.[51] Sawer attributes the wheel model as an early influence on the 'gender mainstreaming' framework adopted at the Beijing Conference in 1995.[52] She attributes this leadership to some skilful footwork by femocrats during the Whitlam Government for the initiation in 1975 of federal funding for the women's refuges that had started appearing in 1974, and notes that the widespread nature of domestic violence quickly became apparent once refuges were available.[53] Sawer also acknowledges the success of the women's movement both in having the issue recognised within public policy as one of gender inequality and in achieving government funding for refuges run by feminist collectives.[54]

Despite the change of government at the end of 1975, federal funding of refuges continued—albeit with some serious problems caused by the devolution in 1981 of refuge funding to sometimes hostile State governments.[55] There was insider/outsider activism over devolution as refuge workers camped in protest outside Parliament House in Canberra and the National Women's Advisory Council under Dame Beryl Beaurepaire lodged objections. Specific-purpose funding, however, was not reinstated until the Hawke Government was elected in 1983.[56]

In the meantime, some State governments were taking a proactive role. In 1985, the NSW Premier, Neville Wran, declared that his was the first government in the world to proclaim in 10 languages that wife bashing was a crime.[57] This message appeared on billboards at railway stations and on buses and trains.

---

50   Janet Ramsay, The Making of Domestic Violence Policy by the Australian Commonwealth Government and the Government of the State of New South Wales between 1970 and 1985: An Analytical Narrative of Feminist Policy Activism', PhD thesis, 27 March 2006, University of Sydney, NSW, p. 177 (references omitted).
51   Sawer, 'Disappearing Tricks', p. 7. See further: S. Laurel Weldon, Protest, Policy and the Problem of Violence Against Women: A Cross-National Comparison, University of Pittsburgh Press, Pa, 2002.
52   Sawer, Making Women Count, p. 45.
53   Marian Sawer, The Long March Through the Institutions: Women's Affairs Under Fraser and Hawke, Australasian Political Studies Association 28th Annual Conference, Brisbane, 27–29 August 1986, p. 7.
54   See further Marian Sawer, Sisters in Suits, Allen & Unwin, Sydney, 1990.
55   Sawer, The Long March Through the Institutions, p. 15.
56   Sawer, Making Women Count, p. 158.
57   Carmel Niland, 'Women's Policy' in T. Bramston (ed.), The Wran Era, Federation Press, Sydney, 2006, p. 187.

When Helen L'Orange moved from the position of NSW Women's Adviser to that of Commonwealth Women's Adviser, she brought with her a commitment to a national community education program on domestic violence.[58] The 'Break the Silence!' Program launched by Prime Minister Bob Hawke in 1988 was again innovative in its community outreach both to migrant communities and to church and rural communities. [59]

It was in this context of recognised global best practice that L'Orange went to Vienna. My interview with L'Orange focused on this international work, which has received less attention than it should.[60] From 1991 to 1993, she was a key member of the drafting team for the Declaration on the Elimination of All Forms of Violence Against Women adopted by the UN General Assembly in December 1993. The UN web site says that 'until that point, most Governments tended to regard violence against women largely as a private matter between individuals and not as a pervasive human rights problem requiring State intervention'.[61]

The Vienna Conference on Human Rights led to new machinery for gender equality. It called for the adoption of the Declaration, the creation of the mandate of special rapporteur and also urged the Commission for the Status of Women to embark on the elaboration of the Optional Protocol. The next year, the Commission on Human Rights adopted resolution 1994/45 of 4 March 1994, in which it decided to appoint the Special Rapporteur on Violence Against Women, including its causes and consequences. Many of the issues in the Declaration were developed further by the Beijing Platform for Action and the outcome document of its review by the twenty-third special session of the General Assembly in 2000.

In L'Orange's view, the role of international forums such as the United Nations was to serve as an opportunity or even a duty to use domestic learning and progressive policies for the benefit of women in developing or less progressive nations because at that time Australia was 'ahead of the game' in most policy areas. The exceptions in her view were issues faced by Aboriginal and Torres Strait Islander women. When it came to drafting the UN Declaration on Eliminating Violence, women in Canada and Australia took the lead because effective feminist lobbies in Canada and Australia had led to machinery in government for women, a full 15 years earlier than the United Kingdom, for example. L'Orange observes that in the early 1990s, CEDAW reports on Australia's machinery for implementation made other countries 'quite envious'. Germany had only two women's refuges, for example. This would sometimes work in the other

---

58   Sawer, *Making Women Count*, p. 241.

59   Erika Sabine, 'Break the Silence: The State and Violence against Women' (1990) 36 *Refractory Girl* 13.

60   Interview with Helen L'Orange.

61   Office of the High Commissioner for Human Rights, *Women and Violence*, <http://www.un.org/rights/dpi1772e.htm>

direction—L'Orange noting that the Organisation for Economic Cooperation and Devlopment (OECD) data were very influential in the continuing debates on paid maternity leave in Australia.

L'Orange was the Australian delegate sent to drafting sessions in Vienna in 1991 and 1992. She drew on NSW legislation in a 'major' way, believing that violence against women was a matter for state practice and criminal law. She said it took her a while to realise that this Declaration was leading the world towards 'a new perspective on violence against women'. She drew on her experience with the NSW Domestic Violence Task Force[62] and the Supported Accommodation Assistance Program, which included refuges and public housing priority for women and children affected by violence.

Notably, it was the NSW Government report that led to the introduction into NSW law of Apprehended Domestic Violence Orders (ADVOs) in 1982 (South Australia was first). L'Orange asked Pat O'Shane to contribute the chapter on Indigenous violence. Ms O'Shane examined how violence split the Indigenous community in complex and interrelated ways. The ADVO was seen as a method of trying to find a way through these complexities for women, so that women would call the police and then at least the incident would be recorded. The hope was that police would react in a more timely manner when an ADVO had been issued.

In my interview with L'Orange, I saw again an emphasis on creating government machinery that could be responsive to women's needs. For example, she detailed how over eight years, her team 'colonised' other NSW departments, building units in health, education, industrial relations and housing.[63] In UN forums, Australia could then present its views in the following way:

> We would hope that our national experience would be a useful resource for others. This is not to say we would want to be prescriptive in our suggestions. Rather, we would hope that others might feel able to draw on some of our experience, perhaps avoiding some of the difficulties we have encountered.[64]

In terms of her experience with the United Nations, L'Orange has had mixed experiences. Generally she finds CEDAW and the Convention on the Rights of the Child very useful instruments because the reporting mechanism holds

---

62 New South Wales Task Force on Domestic Violence, *Report of New South Wales Task Force on Domestic Violence to Hon N K Wran QC, Premier of New South Wales*, 1981, and follow-up report in 1985.

63 L'Orange said this model was highly influential and when she moved into the federal sphere, she tried to recreate the scheme, but in departments the machinery was mostly limited to Women's Desks, which were not very effective compared with units.

64 Statement of Helen L'Orange, Leader of the Australian delegation to the 33rd session of the Commission for the Status of Women, Vienna, March–April 1989, p. 16.

states accountable. She found aspects of international diplomacy 'heavy going', including, for example, intense negotiations over who would host a particular meeting of the Commission for Status of Women (CSW). She recalls how many issues were off limits. At the 1985 Women's Conference in Nairobi, she followed the drafting of a statement that violence against women was a 'universal' phenomenon around the globe. The USSR objected in the strongest terms, stating that there was no violence against women in Russia, only in capitalist countries, and the Vatican tried to strike the sentence out of the final report.[65] (In fact, there is barely any reference to domestic violence in the Nairobi final report.)

L'Orange is not necessarily an advocate for using human rights principles more broadly as an advocacy strategy. She felt that in the arena of public health, human rights as an advocacy tool was weaker than a focus on good public policy—laudable, but when the goal is to influence the practice of member states, it does not provide great leverage. She added that protection of women from violence has 'a different note' to rights. This could be a matter of style; Janet Ramsay says of L'Orange that she held a 'strategic conviction' that 'the way for feminist policy activism to succeed was through a punctiliously professional observation of bureaucratic forms and processes'.[66] L'Orange advocates generational gender analysis: she urges advocates to look out for emerging issues from grassroots organisations, create policy, get political support, then work to have programs implemented by mainstream agencies.

Where L'Orange would completely agree with Evatt, Byrnes and Connors would be the central role of gender analysis backed by evidence. L'Orange is now involved with developing gender-sensitive health indicators and other measurement tools. She is critical of gender mainstreaming in organisations such as the World Health Organisation, but also domestically. She states that 'gender mainstreaming ought to work but the transition in Australia didn't work because there was not enough training given—the key is gender analysis skills'. She points to the recent National Indigenous Eye Health Survey; there was no reference to gender in the 22 key findings released by the Centre for Eye Research Australia.[67]

---

65 Final report, <http://www.un.org/womenwatch/daw/beijing/otherconferences/Nairobi/Nairobi%20 Full%20Optimized.pdf>
66 Ramsay, The Making of Domestic Violence Policy by the Australian Commonwealth Government and the Government of the State of New South Wales between 1970 and 1985, p. 191.
67 Available at <http://Indigenouspeoplesissues.com/attachments/2143_IHES_SummaryReport.pdf> This contrasts with the work done in several developing countries by Canadian Dr Paul Courtright and his colleagues. Nearly two-thirds of blind people worldwide are women and girls. In many places, men have twice the access to eye care as women. Of the 30 million blind people in China, India and Africa, 20 million are women. Women bear about 75 per cent of trachoma-related blindness. Compared with men, women are 1.8 times more likely to have trichiasis and account for about 70 per cent of all trichiasis cases. In Tanzania, these findings were used to develop gender-sensitive strategies, including transport programs to get women to clinics and village-level activities to counteract the attitude that women's eyesight was not valued. Dr

Asked to reflect on the twenty-fifth anniversary of the *SDA*, L'Orange feels it contains good principles and some useful machinery but does not seem to have the 'teeth' that it once had. In terms of the status of Australian women in 2010, she had mixed feelings. Increased economic independence for women and young feminists made her optimistic about the future but she was nervous about the long-term impact of the very early demarcation of gender roles, especially the increasingly pink/blue dichotomy of consumerism and of 'having rather than doing' associated with modern childhood.[68]

Analysing current debates

It would have to be said that much of the machinery established by L'Orange and others has been dismantled and the sharing of good practice in UN forums such as described by Connors and Byrnes has all but disappeared. Winter reports that from having become known as one of the two countries with the most comprehensive government response to the issue of domestic violence, Australia, in 2003, astonished overseas observers when it 'borrowed' unspent money from its domestic violence and sexual assault programs to pay for anti-terrorism fridge magnets mailed to every Australian household.[69]

In 2004, the federal government attempted to suppress an Access Economics report, commissioned in part by the Office for the Status of Women, which found that the cost to the economy of domestic violence was $8 billion per annum. The report, which was heavily criticised by men's rights groups for describing most perpetrators as male, was released only after a successful freedom-of-information (FOI) application by the FOI Editor of *TheAustralian* newspaper.[70] According to Marian Sawer, another 'low point' was the release by the Australian Bureau of Statistics of an Executive Summary of the findings of the 2005 'Personal Safety Survey', which seemingly confirmed the beliefs of men's rights groups

---

Courtright has also established similar programs in Nepal, India, Guatemala, Tibet, Egypt, Kenya and Malawi. See further: S. Lewallen, A. Mousa, K. Bassett and P. Courtright, 'Global Issues: Cataract Surgical Coverage remains Lower in Women' (2009) 93 *British Journal of Ophthalmology* 295.

68 See further: <http://www.designboom.com/weblog/read.php?TOPIC_PK=2376>

69 On the transfer of domestic violence funds to anti-terrorism fridge magnets, see Bronwyn Winter, 'Preemptive Fridge Magnets and other Weapons of Masculinist Destruction: The Rhetoric and Reality of "Safeguarding Australia"' (2007) 33(1) *Signs* 25.

70 Sawer, 'Disappearing Tricks' 7. See further: Chilla Bulbeck, 'Gender Policies: Hers to His' in Peter Saunders and James Walter (eds), *Ideas and Influence: Social Science and Public Policy in Australia*, UNSW Press, Sydney, 2005, p. 150.

that similar proportions of men and women engaged in domestic violence.[71] In fact, the figures referred only to the proportion of assaults by an opposite-sex perpetrator that were by a partner, and were later corrected. [72]

Under the Rudd Government, there were important policy developments. In 2009, the Prime Minister launched the report *Time for Action: National Council's Plan for Australia to reduce Violence against Women and Children 2009–2021*. The government took the report to the Council of Australian Governments (COAG) and turned it into a Commonwealth plan: Protecting Children is Everyone's Business: National framework for protecting Australia's children 2009–2020. These reports will join *The Road Home: A National Approach to Reducing Homelessness* as part of a social policy reform agenda, with a disability strategy still in progress.

The *Time for Action* report corrected the record on the prevalence and cost of domestic violence. It states that one in three Australian women will report being a victim of physical violence and almost one in five will report being a victim of sexual violence in their lifetime, according to the Australian Bureau of Statistics. Approximately 350 000 women will experience physical violence and 125 000 women will experience sexual violence each year. Violence against women also comes at an enormous economic cost—$13.6 billion a year—but is mostly preventable.[73]

The reports reflect a strong link between these three issues: domestic violence, child abuse and homelessness. What was stark in reading the reports side by side was that the overlapping area between these triangular issues seems to be where the government response is likely to be weakest. Both of the new reports acknowledge that Indigenous women and children are being failed in devastating ways by the current system. Again, there seems to be a lack of strength in the response, reflecting the government struggling with the intersection of race and gender. Despite the launch by the Prime Minister, this response partly reflects the fact that of the responsible ministers—Jenny Macklin and Tanya Plibersek—only one is a cabinet minister and is able to influence the continuing policy process more directly. The Minister for Housing and Women is not a cabinet post, although it should be.[74]

---

71 Sawer, 'Disappearing Tricks' 7.
72 Ibid. See further: Michael Flood, 'Violence against Women and Men in Australia: What the Personal Safety Survey can and can't tell us', *DRCV Newsletter* 4, 2006, 3–10.
73 National Council to Reduce Violence Against Women and their Children, *Time for Action: National Council's plan for Australia to reduce violence against women and children 2009–2021*, Executive Summary, Canberra, 2009, p. 1.
74 See further: Susan Harris Rimmer, 'Grand Plans' in B. Nelson and A. MacIntyre (eds), *Capturing the Year 2009: Writings from the ANU College of Asia and the Pacific*, The Australian National University, Canberra, 2009, p. 74.

The *Time for Action* report showed that strengthening government action to protect Indigenous women and children on the basis of their rights and full citizenship is still a major challenge 25 years after signing CEDAW. 'Healing centres' in remote areas where Indigenous perpetrators can receive culturally appropriate counselling is a good idea, but not at the expense of justice available to other Australian women. The focus must be on access to justice and providing a broader range of choices to women, wherever they live in Australia, and whatever their race. In fact, it could be that the current moves to reform the legal profession and improve access to justice will have the most impact, including calls to provide incentives for lawyers to practise in rural and regional areas and to provide better funding and conditions for Aboriginal and Torres Strait Islander legal centres. Some problems remain unchanged. In other words, Australia has lost its international edge in effective government machinery to prevent violence against women. In 2010, the Australian Law Reform Commission (ALRC) and the NSW Law Reform Commission (NSWLRC) released a consultation paper for a joint inquiry into family violence laws.[75] This inquiry represents an opportunity to engage with these architectural issues.

Conclusion

There are three main themes I gleaned from analysing the experiences of Elizabeth Evatt, Helen L'Orange, Jane Connors and Andrew Byrnes. First, these individuals were willing to work within the system and were supported by the Australian Government at key moments: Evatt's nomination, L'Orange's appointment as head of the Australian CSW delegation in Vienna and government funding for the expert meeting in Maastricht for the Optional Protocol. If Australians are to continue to make an impact on the international system, they need to be supported in key ways to have a presence on the world stage but also to remain independent and respected at home for their expertise. For example, Erika Feller, Assistant High Commissioner in the Office of the UN High Commissioner for Refugees, is the most senior Australian woman in the UN system, lauded globally for her expertise in protection of refugees and asylum-seekers, but she receives very little recognition within Australia (outside her field).[76] The picture is not as rosy if we look at the history of women engaging with CERD,

---

75   Australian Law Reform Commission and New South Wales Law Reform Commission (ALRC/NSWLRC), *Family Violence: Improving Legal Frameworks*, Consultation Paper 1, 2010, <http://www.alrc.gov.au/inquiries/current/family-violence/CP1/index.html>

76   Names of Australian women engaging with the United Nations include: Linda Bartolomei, Margaret Bearlin, Quentin Bryce, Gabrielle Cullen, Megan Davis, Anne-Marie Devereux, Alice Edwards, Louise Hand, Ellen Hansen, Lee Kerr, Caroline Lambert, Eve Lester, Libby Lloyd, Caroline Millar, Robyn Moody, Annie Petit, Margaret Reynolds, Ariane Rummery, Eileen Pittaway, Carole Shaw, Leanne Smith, Rosalind Strong, Irene Watson, Pera Wells, Penny Wensley, Donelle Wheeler, Natasha Yacoub, and many more.

the Declaration on the Rights of Indigenous Peoples or the Migrant Workers Convention, let alone the wider UN system, where progress in integrating women's rights has been much slower and harder.

Second, political leadership combined with adviser and bureaucratic expertise is a winning combination for women's rights at both domestic and international levels, and this is a rare commodity. Helen L'Orange and Neville Wran, Anne Summers, Geoffrey Yeend and Paul Keating, Susan Ryan, Mike Codd, Margaret Reynolds and Bob Hawke, Gough Whitlam and Liz Reid are all good examples of leadership in different roles that respected the expertise involved in good gender analysis.[77] Tanya Plibersek, Liz Broderick and Sally Moyle could draw on these past models of influence.

We need to have this expertise and leadership represented overseas where possible in order to help women in other societies and receive insights that can benefit women in Australia. The biographical lens employed in this chapter underscores that necessity. At the Commission for the Status of Women in 2009, Australia finally sent the first ever delegation of Indigenous women. Australia was successful in nominating lawyer Megan Davis for election to the Permanent Forum of Indigenous Peoples in 2011. Australia did not, however, nominate a candidate in 2010 for the CEDAW Committee, despite the noted international expertise of several Australians, not least Andrew Byrnes, Dianne Otto and Hilary Charlesworth.

Leadership must come from many levels. Government support for Australian NGOs to engage with the UN human rights system is extremely limited and ad hoc. Learning the procedures of the UN system takes training, financial support and patience. Often the rewards come after many years of intricate drafting discussions. Australian NGOs could have that expertise, but usually it resides in one or two individuals, often with little capacity or support for reporting back on international developments. A more systematic and long-term approach for NGO representation would improve the overall quality of Australia's engagement with the United Nations.

Third, procedural reform is important and fundamental to substantive gains. My firm view is that gender-sensitive laws are crucial but the aim is that preventative policies mean that individuals do not have to resort to legal action. Despite a long period of bipartisan support, a government adverse to the women's sector was still able to unravel substantial gains. General human rights machinery is

---

77   Anne Summers notes that the 'femocrats had to fight and wheedle just like any other bureaucrat, even if their political masters were perhaps at times more sympathetic than other political leaders at different times' (Personal communication with author, 24 February 2010).

still not in place, therefore women's rights always require an extra struggle. The uneven history of Australia's ratification of CEDAW and its Optional Protocol, considered alongside the rocky passage of the *SDA*, is testament to this fact.

In 2004, Evatt was extremely pessimistic and ended her speech on a despondent note, situating the failings to secure the rights of Australian women in this broader human rights context, stating that the Australian Government

> has refused to ratify the Optional Protocol to the Women's Convention as well as that to the Torture Convention. It has consistently refused to respect decisions of the treaty bodies relating to the detention and treatment of asylum seekers. This is part of a wider picture in which disregard of human rights by the Government has been manifested in the anti-terrorism laws and in the failure to uphold the human rights of our citizens detained in Guantanamo Bay; it is manifest in neglect of the self-determination rights of Indigenous people, and in the denial of reparations for the stolen generation.[78]

In 2010, the landscape has changed significantly in terms of human rights protections, at least in relation to Australia's more welcoming view of the United Nations. During its first two years, the Rudd Government ratified the Optional Protocol to CEDAW and CAT, ratified the Disability Convention and its Optional Protocol and signalled acceptance of the Declaration on the Rights of Indigenous People. The government has extended an open invitation to the UN special procedures, resulting in the visit of James Anaya and Arnand Grover so far. The Nauru detention centre has been closed, temporary protection visas abolished and detention debt done away with. A National Security Legislation Monitor has been appointed and terror laws were reviewed. The Australian Agency of International Development (AusAID) is bedding down a new gender policy. National plans on social policies—such as public housing, domestic violence, homelessness, mental health and child protection—offer real hope of a rights-based approach to improving the conditions of life fundamental to wellbeing.

Generally, however, Elizabeth Evatt could still say we have much further to travel in making the rights of women part of the central project of protecting human rights in Australia, and simply achieving a Human Rights Act will also not be enough, if her experience with the ICCPR is any guide.[79] Debates over paid maternity leave were framed primarily in terms of economic benefit during the financial crisis. Debates over the Northern Territory intervention use paternalistic and partial tones when it comes to the rights of Indigenous women and girls. There remains parlous representation of women on corporate boards.

---

78   Evatt, 'Falling Short', pp. 77–8.
79   The Rudd Government rejected the recommendation for federal human rights legislation in April 2010 and said the decision would not be reviewed until 2014.

There is continued lack of recognition of gendered persecution in asylum claims. The need for more quality and convenient child care and after-school care was a goal abandoned by the Rudd Government in April 2010. The possible outcomes of the Henry tax review for women have not been fully explored. Many other current issues speak of lack of motivation and commitment, a partial and narrow national imagination and a paucity of use of existing evidence for gender analysis when it comes to really valuing Australian women, recognising their dignity and fulfilling their rights.

The CEDAW Committee in 2006 singled out Australia on the following matters: the low level of participation of women, particularly Indigenous women and women belonging to ethnic minorities, in decision-making bodies; the continuing prevalence of violence against women; the lack of a comprehensive approach to combat trafficking and exploitation resulting from prostitution; the gender-specific impact of law and policy on refugees and asylum-seekers; the lack of uniformity in work-related paid maternity leave schemes; women's ability to access health services; discrimination of immigrant, refugee and minority women and girls; and inequalities suffered by Aboriginal and Torres Strait Islander women.[80] Many of these issues remain unaddressed to the satisfaction of women's NGOs in the 2009 report.[81] The committee is due to conduct hearings on Australia's combined sixth and seventh periodic reports in July 2010.[82]

If we take Evatt's human rights test of whether Australia is committed to 'raise from the lowest level those whose needs are greatest', I am not convinced that Australia's parliamentary legislative process, bureaucratic machinery, political debate or data and evaluation methods are designed with that aim in mind. The experience of our heroes in this story of raising women up shows that progress will be slow, but possible. The fiftieth anniversary of the *SDA* could see the fruits of determination and patience in the current generation of advocates.

Bibliography

Books and articles

Bulbeck, Chilla, 'Gender Policies: Hers to His' in Peter Saunders and James Walter (eds), *Ideas and Influence: Social Science and Public Policy in Australia*, UNSW Press, Sydney, 2005.

---

80 Committee on the Elimination of All Forms of Discrimination Against Women, *Consideration of Australia's Combined 4th and 5th Report*, 30 January 2006.
81 YWCA Australia and Women's Legal Services Australia, *Australian NGO Shadow Report on the Implementation of CEDAW* (2009).
82 CEDAW presented Australia with a 'List of Issues' in September 2009, CEDAW/C/AUL/Q/7 (2009).

Byrnes, Andrew, 'Slow and Steady Wins the Race?: The Development of an Optional Protocol to the Women's Convention' (1997) 91 *American Society of International Law and Procedure* 383.

Byrnes, Andrew and Connors, Jane, 'Enforcing the Human Rights of Women: A Complaints Procedure for the Women's Convention' (1995–96) 21 *Brooklyn Journal of International Law* 679.

Charlesworth, Hilary, 'International Law: A Discipline of Crisis' (2002) 65 *Modern Law Review* 377.

Charlesworth, Hilary, Inside/Outside: Feminist International Legal Studies and Thirty Years of the CEDAW Convention, Paper delivered at the Asian Society of International Law Conference, Tokyo, August 2009.

Charlesworth, Hilary and Charlesworth, Sara, 'The *Sex Discrimination Act* and International Law' (2004) 27 *University of New South Wales Law Journal* 858.

Charlesworth, Hilary and Chinkin, Christine, *The Boundaries of International Law*, Manchester University Press, UK, 2000.

Charlesworth, Hilary, Chiam, Madeline, Hovell, Devika and Williams, George, *No Country is an Island: Australia and International Law*, UNSW Press, Sydney, 2006.

Cusack, Simone, 'Discrimination Against Women: Combating its Compounded and Systemic Forms' (2009) 34(2) *Alternative Law Journal* 86.

Edwards, Alice, 'Violence Against Women as Sex Discrimination: Judging the Jurisprudence of the United Nations Human Rights Treaty Bodies' (2008) 18 *Texas Journal of Women & the Law* 1.

Evatt, Elizabeth, 'Falling short on Women's Rights: Mis-matches between SDA and the International Regime' in Marius Smith (ed.), *Human Rights 2004: The Year in Review*, Castan Centre for Human Rights Law, Monash University, Melbourne, 2005.

Flood, Michael, 'Violence Against Women and Men in Australia: What the Personal Safety Survey can and can't tell us', *DRCV Newsletter* 4, 2006.

Gardam, Judith and Jarvis, Michelle, *Women, Armed Conflict and International Law*, Kluwer Law International, The Hague, 2001.

Harris Rimmer, Susan, 'Grand Plans' in B. Nelson and A. MacIntyre (eds), *Capturing the Year 2009: Writings from the ANU College of Asia and the Pacific*, The Australian National University, Canberra, 2009.

Kinslor, Joanne, '"Killing Off" International Human Rights Law: An Exploration of the Australian Government's Relationship with United Nations Human Rights Committees' (2002) 8(2) *Australian Journal of Human Rights* 16.

Lewallen, S., Mousa, A., Bassett, K. and Courtright, P., 'Global Issues: Cataract Surgical Coverage remains lower in Women' (2009) 93 *British Journal of Ophthalmology* 295.

Niland, Carmel, 'Women's Policy' in T. Bramston (ed.), *The Wran Era*, Federation Press, Sydney, 2006.

Otto, Dianne, 'A Sign of "Weakness"? Disrupting Gender Certainties in the Implementation of Security Council Resolution 1325' (2006) 13 *Michigan Journal of Gender and Law* 113.

Pickering, Sharon and Lambert, Caroline (eds), *Global Issues, Women and Justice*, Sydney Institute of Criminology Series, NSW, 2004.

Ramsay, Janet, The Making of Domestic Violence Policy by the Australian Commonwealth Government and the Government of the State of New South Wales between 1970 and 1985: An Analytical Narrative of Feminist Policy Activism, PhD thesis, 27 March 2006, University of Sydney, NSW.

Sabine, Erika, 'Break the Silence: The State and Violence Against Women' (1990) 36 *Refractory Girl* 13.

Sawer, Marian, The Long March Through the Institutions: Women's Affairs under Fraser and Hawke, Australasian Political Studies Association 28th Annual Conference, Brisbane, 27–29 August 1986.

Sawer, Marian, *Sisters in Suits*, Allen & Unwin, Sydney, 1990.

Sawer, Marian, *Femocrats and Ecorats: Women's Policy Machinery in Australia, Canada and New Zealand*, United Nations Research Institute for Social Development, Geneva, 1996.

Sawer, Marian, 'Disappearing Tricks' (2008) 27(3) *Dialogue: Academy of the Social Sciences in Australia* 4.

Sawer, Marian, *Making Women Count: A History of the Women's Electoral Lobby in Australia*, UNSW Press, Sydney, 2008.

Thomson, Peter, Elizabeth Evatt: Integrating Women's Issues in the United Nations Human Rights System, in 'Australians at the United Nations', 13 August 1996, Unpublished ms, Department of Foreign Affairs and Trade, Canberra [on file with author].

Thornton, Margaret, 'Auditing the *Sex Discrimination Act*' in Marius Smith (ed.), *Human Rights 2004: The Year in Review*, Castan Centre for Human Rights Law, Monash University, Melbourne, 2005.

Thornton, Margaret, 'Feminism and the Changing State: The Case of Sex Discrimination' (2006) 21(50) *Australian Feminist Studies*, <http://www. informaworld.com/smpp/title%7Edb=all%7Econtent=t713402962% 7Etab=issueslist%7Ebranches=21-v21>

Weldon, S. Laurel, *Protest, Policy and the Problem of Violence Against Women: A Cross-National Comparison*, University of Pittsburgh Press, Pa, 2002.

Winter, Bronwyn, 'Preemptive Fridge Magnets and other Weapons of Masculinist Destruction: The Rhetoric and Reality of "Safeguarding Australia"' (2007) 31(1) *Signs* 25.

Zifcak, Spencer, *Mr Ruddock Goes to Geneva*, UNSW Press, Sydney, 2003.

Reports and miscellaneous primary sources

Australian Human Rights Commission and the Australian Government Office for Women, *Women of the World: Know Your International Human Rights*, Australian Government, Canberra, 2008.

CEDAW Committee General Comment 19 on Article 16 (and article 5), Violence against women: 29/01/92, A/47/38.

Charlesworth, Hilary, 'Australia's Relations with the United Nations in the Post Cold War Environment', *Australian Federal Parliament, Joint Standing Committee on Foreign Affairs, Defence and Trade: Joint Committee Hansard*, 21 March 2001, p. 429.

Charlesworth, Sara, Submission 39 to Senate Legal and Constitutional Affairs Committee, Inquiry into the Matter of the Effectiveness of the *Sex Discrimination Act 1984* (Cth) in Eliminating Discrimination and Promoting Gender Equality, 8 August 2008.

Committee on the Elimination of All Forms of Discrimination Against Women, *Consideration of Australia's Combined 4th and 5th Report*, 30 January 2006, United Nations, New York.

Committee on the Elimination of All Forms of Discrimination Against Women, *Consideration of Reports submitted by States Parties under Article 18 of the Convention on the Elimination of All Forms of Discrimination Against Women, Combined sixth and seventh periodic Reports of States Parties: Australia*, CEDAW/C/AUL/7, 9 March 2009, United Nations, New York.

Declaration on the Elimination of All Forms of Violence Against Women, A/RES/48/104, United Nations, New York.

Downer, Alexander, Williams, Daryl and Ruddock, Phillip, Improving the Effectiveness of United Nations Committees, Joint media release, 29 August 2000, Parliament House, Canberra.

Human Rights Committee, *General Comment 22, Article 18 (Forty-eighth session, 1993)*, UN Doc CCPR/C/21/Rev 1/Add 4 (1993), reprinted in *Compilation of General Comments and General Recommendations Adopted by Human Rights Treaty Bodies*, UN Doc HRI/GEN/1/Rev 6 at 155, United Nations, New York, 2003.

Human Rights Committee, *General Comment 25, The right to participate in public affairs, voting rights and the right of equal access to public service (Art 25), (Fifty-seventh session, 1996)*, UN Doc CCPR/C/21/Rev 1/Add 7 (1996), reprinted in *Compilation of General Comments and General Recommendations Adopted by Human Rights Treaty Bodies*, UN Doc HRI/GEN/1/Rev 6 at 168, United Nations, New York, 2003.

Human Rights Committee, *General Comment 28, Equality of rights between men and women (Article 3), (Sixty-eighth session, 2000)*, UN Doc CCPR/C/21/Rev 1/Add 10 (2000), reprinted in *Compilation of General Comments and General Recommendations Adopted by Human Rights Treaty Bodies*, UN Doc HRI/GEN/1/Rev 6 at 179, United Nations, New York, 2003.

L'Orange, Helen, Statement of Helen L'Orange, Leader of the Australian delegation to the 33rd session of the Commission for the Status of Women, Vienna, March–April 1989.

National Council to Reduce Violence Against Women and their Children, *Time for Action: National Council's Plan for Australia to reduce Violence against Women and Children 2009–2021*, Canberra, 2009.

New South Wales Task Force on Domestic Violence, *Report of New South Wales Task Force on Domestic Violence to Hon N K Wran QC, MP Premier of New South Wales*, July 1981, and follow-up report in 1985.

Optional Protocol to the Convention on the Elimination of All Forms of Discrimination Against Women (A/RES/54/4), United Nations, New York, 2000.

Senate Standing Committee on Legal and Constitutional Affairs, *Report on the Effectiveness of the Commonweath* Sex Discrimination Act 1984 *in Eliminating Discrimination and Promoting Gender Equality*, Parliament of Australia, Canberra, 2008.

UN Beijing Conference on Women, *Platform for Action and Final Report*, United Nations, New York, 1995, <http://www.un.org/womenwatch/confer/beijing/reports/>

UN Nairobi Conference on Women, *Final Report*, United Nations, New York, 1985, <http://www.un.org/womenwatch/daw/beijing/otherconferences/Nairobi/Nairobi%20Full%20Optimized.pdf>

United Nations Convention on the Elimination of All Forms of Discrimination Against Women *GA res. 34/180, 34 UN GAOR Supp. (No. 46)* at 193, UN Doc. A/34/46; 1249 UNTS 13; 19 ILM 33, United Nations, New York, 1980.

WRANA, *Australian NGO Shadow Report on the Implementation of CEDAW*, 2005.

YWCA Australia and Women's Legal Services Australia, *Australian NGO Shadow Report on the Implementation of CEDAW*, 2009.

13. Can We Feminise Human Rights?[1]

Margaret Thornton

In view of the malaise besetting the Sex Discrimination Act 1984 *(Cth) (SDA), this chapter considers whether a national charter of human rights might be able to re-energise it. With particular regard to the Brennan proposal, the chapter overviews the foundational UN conventions that underpin this initiative and similar domestic charters. The issues of universalism, equality and intersectionality are examined as possessing particular gendered significance. Attention is drawn to the suspicion and scepticism that tend to affect legally binding human rights instruments in the Australian context, which have resulted in an approach that favours rhetoric over a commitment to substantive equality. It is suggested that the immunity accorded private sector actors is a striking example of an overly cautious approach.*

Introduction

Human rights have become what Costas Douzinas terms 'the lingua franca of the New Times'.[2] Animated by economic globalisation and the 'War on Terror', human rights have made a dramatic return to the world stage. In this chapter, I set out to explore the significance of human rights for Australian women against the backdrop of the *Sex Discrimination Act 1984* (Cth) (*SDA*). The exploration is somewhat tentative because the Commonwealth has neither an entrenched bill of rights nor a statutory charter, although legislation was proposed by the *National Human Rights Consultation Report* (*Brennan Report*) in 2009.[3] In addition to considering this proposal, the discussion will be informed by the conjunction of discrimination and human rights statutes enacted in the Australian Capital Territory,[4] Victoria[5] and the United Kingdom,[6] which espouse a similar dialogic model.

---

1   A version of this chapter was presented at the 2010 Annual Meeting of the Law and Society Association, Chicago, 27–30 May 2010. Thanks to Dr Trish Luker for research assistance.
2   Costas Douzinas, 'The End(s) of Human Rights' (2002) 26 *Melbourne University Law Review* 445, 453.
3   Commonwealth of Australia, *National Human Rights Consultation Report*, Commonwealth of Australia, Canberra, 2009 [*Brennan Report*].
4   *Human Rights Act 2004* (ACT) (*HRA* [ACT]).
5   *Charter of Human Rights and Responsibilities Act 2006* (Vic.) (Victorian Charter).
6   *Human Rights Act 1998* (UK) (*HRA* [UK]).

As ably demonstrated by the contributors to this collection, the *SDA* represents a crucial step in the protracted struggle by Australian women to be accepted as full citizens but it falls well short of securing substantive equality. Most notably, discrimination is proscribed only in certain areas of public life, which means that the private sphere—the source of many gender inequities—remains largely immunised against challenge despite the fact that the Convention on the Elimination of All Forms of Discrimination Against Women (CEDAW) is not so constrained. Even within the public sphere, the *SDA* has been unable to address adequately the intransigent discriminatory structures that lie deep within the social psyche, such as the discomfiting relationship between the feminine and authority. An individualised and ad-hoc, complaint-based anti-discrimination system simply cannot disinter and confront systemic discrimination that is imbricated with power.

Despite the fact that identity is constituted in complex ways in terms of sex, race, sexuality, religion and a range of other characteristics, the approach of the *SDA* and similar Australian anti-discrimination legislation tends to be one-dimensional and essentialist. That is, a complainant is expected to focus on sex *or* race *or* sexuality, or other identifiable characteristics rather than sex *plus* race, or sex *plus* sexuality, or some other combination of grounds.[7] Intersectionality is implicitly discouraged at the federal level because of the separate Acts.[8] Hence, an Indigenous woman who lodges a complaint under the *SDA* is expected to slough off the elements of race that go to shape her identity, regardless of the extent to which it contributed to the harm she endured. Similarly, if she lodges her complaint under the *Racial Discrimination Act 1975* (Cth) (*RDA*), she is expected to present herself as sex-*less*. A similarly vexed choice besets all complaints arising from multiple grounds.[9] I interpolate here that class is completely invisible in anti-discrimination legislation, even though economic status and education are key determinants of autonomy and freedom in our society. The class element in sex *plus* class or sex *plus* race *plus* class is always sloughed off so that it is worth considering whether a national charter of rights might be able to step into the breach.

---

7 'Sex plus' has been recognised in the US jurisprudence of the *Civil Rights Act* for many years, although it is by no means unproblematic. See, for example: Susan J. Best, 'Sexual Favoritism: A Cause of Action Under a "Sex-Plus" Theory' (2009) 30 *Northern Illinois University Law Review* 211; Enrique Schaere, 'Intragroup Discrimination in the Workplace: The Case for "Race Plus"' (2010) 45 *Harvard Civil Rights-Civil Liberties Law Review* 57.

8 *Racial Discrimination Act 1975*; *Sex Discrimination Act 1984*; *Disability Discrimination Act 1992*; *Age Discrimination Act 2004*. The streamlining of these Acts into a single Act has been announced. See Attorney-General Hon. Robert McClelland MP and Minister for Finance and Deregulation Hon. Lindsay Tanner MP, Reform of Anti-discrimination Legislation, Media release, 21 April 2010, Parliament House, Canberra. This will not, however, automatically overcome the uni-dimensionality problem, which is thoroughly entrenched in the discrimination jurisprudence of omnibus State and Territory Acts.

9 Australian Law Reform Commission, *Equality Before the Law: Justice for Women*, Report No. 69, Australian Law Reform Commission, Sydney, 1994, Part I, pp. 63–9.

There is also the *SDA*'s lack of flexibility in being able to respond to changed economic and socio-political circumstances—most notably the passionate embrace of the free market, which has impacted significantly on working women even though female workforce participation has increased.[10] At the turn of the millennium, job tenure became parlous and contingent work expanded, with stable, full-time work becoming a relic of the past for many.[11] Consequently, the movement towards gender equality at work was stymied as women were deployed to legitimise the expansion of global capital.[12] Perversely, the neo-liberal swing and the market embrace caused *in*equality rather than equality to become the dominant social norm.[13] Neo-liberalism also went hand in glove with moral conservatism, which saw women's human rights interests disappear from political and policy agendas in favour of 'gender mainstreaming'.[14] In evidence presented at a recent review of the *SDA*, it is noteworthy that even the federal Sex Discrimination Commissioner, Elizabeth Broderick, considered the progress of the *SDA* to have stalled.[15]

Feminist legal scholarship has devoted surprisingly little attention to the fate of domestic human rights in the face of globalisation, although an astonishing proliferation of literature on gender and international human rights began to emerge in the 1980s[16]—at the same time as the genesis of the *SDA*. Legal feminism has undoubtedly been captivated by the 'endearingly grand' themes of peace and equality in an international frame.[17] Why is this so? According to Thérèse Murphy, more optimism is associated with international law.[18] It could also be that the Australian legal academy has been seduced by 'northern hemispherism', as well as the need to demonstrate the international relevance of its scholarship.[19]

---

10   In 2008, the labour force participation of women was 58 per cent (<http://www.dfat.gov.au/facts/women.html>).

11   For example: Judy Fudge and Rosemary Owens (eds), *Precarious Work, Women and the New Economy: The Challenge to Legal Norms*, Hart Publishing, Oxford, 2006; A. B. Sukert, 'Marionettes of Globalization: A Comparative Analysis of Legal Protections for Contingent Workers in the International Community' (2000) 27 *Syracuse Journal of International Law & Commerce* 431.

12   Hester Eisenstein, 'A Dangerous Liaison? Feminism and Corporate Globalization' (2005) 69 *Science & Society* 487.

13   Margaret Thornton, 'Free Trade and Justice: A Discomfiting Liaison' in Kevin Walton, Helen Irving and Jacqui Mowbray (eds), *Julius Stone: A Study of Influence*, Federation Press, Sydney, 2010.

14   Marian Sawer, 'Disappearing Tricks' (2008) 27(3) *Dialogue: Academy of the Social Sciences in Australia* 4.

15   Evidence presented to Senate Standing Committee on Legal Constitutional Affairs (*Report on the Effectiveness of the Commonwealth* Sex Discrimination Act 1984 *in Eliminating Discrimination and Promoting Gender Equality*, Commonwealth of Australia, Canberra, 2008, p. 47).

16   Karen Engle, 'International Human Rights and Feminisms: When Discourses Keep Meeting' in Doris Buss and Ambreena Manji (eds), *International Law: Feminist Approaches*, Hart, Oxford, 2005, p. 47.

17   Thérèse Murphy, 'Feminism Here and Feminism There: Law, Theory and Choice' in Doris Buss and Ambreena Manji (eds), *International Law: Modern Feminist Approaches*, Hart, Oxford, 2005, p. 77.

18   Ibid.

19   The Excellence in Research for Australia (ERA) emphasises metrics that include international standing and journal rankings (<http://www.arc.gov.au/era/era_2010.htm>).

In light of the contemporary malaise at the domestic level, it is worth considering whether a charter might be able to re-energise the *SDA* or provide an alternative course of action.[20] As human rights instruments have emerged from a neo-liberal climate where the market is the measure of all things, one cannot help but feel just a tad sceptical at the outset. The political backdrop to introducing a domestic charter is also one of suspicion and scepticism.

In weighing up the pros and cons, I review the concept of human rights, a claimed universal but with a masculinist bias, which has had currency in an international rather than a domestic context as far as Australia is concerned; I consider the UN conventions that underpin domestic charters, drawing attention to the preference for form over substance, showing how these values are mirrored in the Brennan proposal; I then consider the pre-eminent values of liberalism—freedom and equality—which are privileged in human rights charters but are in perpetual tension with one another; finally, I look at intersectional discrimination claims as an exemplary site where a charter might be invoked to ameliorate a fundamental weakness of the *SDA* and other anti-discrimination legislation.

Human Rights and the Challenge of Universalism

The universalism of human rights carries a certain appeal as it means that rights apply to everyone regardless of sex or other characteristic of identity. When we look below the surface, however, a paradox quickly manifests itself: 'Human rights must be universal if they are to apply to all people and in all places…And yet, being universal, they must be expressed so as to have a strong resonance for all people, regardless of race, religion, sex or culture.'[21]

We all believe that we have some idea of what it is to be human, but, as soon as we move beyond the material needs of food, water and shelter[22] to rights in the abstract, disagreement surfaces, and cultural and contextual factors insistently disrupt the universal claim.

---

20 The *Fair Work Act 2009* (Cth) (s. 342) provides another option that could prove to be more effective than anti-discrimination law in employment complaints. See: Carol Andrades, *Intersections Between 'General Protections' under the* Fair Work Act 2009 *(Cth) and Anti-Discrimination Law: Questions, Quirks and Quandaries*, Working Paper No. 47, Centre for Employment and Labour Relations Law, University of Melbourne, Vic., 2009.

21 Peter Bailey, *The Human Rights Enterprise in Australia and Internationally*, LexisNexis Butterworths, Chatswood, NSW, 2009, p. 4.

22 Any concept of a 'minimum core' is itself indeterminate, as argued by Katharine G. Young, 'The Minimum Core of Economic and Social Rights: A Concept in Search of Content' (2008) 33 *Yale Journal of International Law* 113.

A definition of rights must also include an agonistic element. To this end, Sjoberg et al. define human rights as 'social claims made by individuals (or groups) upon organized power arrangements for the purpose of enhancing human dignity'.[23] Without avenues for redress, the exploitative and oppressive acts of the powerful remain hidden, and human rights are consigned to a merely rhetorical plane, although the morality of what is right and what is wrong engenders endless contestation. An element of presbyopia, for example, underpins the Eurocentricism of human rights discourse. Indeed, it was long averred that human rights were unproblematic or irrelevant in the Australian domestic context because violations occurred mainly in illiberal regimes, such as South American dictatorships or developing states. This international/domestic dichotomy is also a subtext of women's human rights.

The insistence that women's rights are human rights has become a rallying cry of the international feminist movement,[24] but one that is echoed only faintly at the domestic level where sex discrimination discourse operates in a different register. The idea that there might be a constellation of human rights specific to women was long viewed with incomprehension by the mainstream,[25] and it was suggested that the masculine domination of the United Nations and its agencies contributed to the construction of 'human rights as men's rights'.[26] Such a construction, however, draws on 2000 years of the Western intellectual tradition, during which time 'the human' acquired a totalising meaning, equating it with the masculine and relegating the feminine to the Other.[27] This gendered dualism, which has shaped the entire panoply of liberal rights discourse, has presumed the rights holder to be 'an ontologically autonomous, self-sufficient, unencumbered subject'[28] that has historically excluded women.

Only in recent years have international human rights bodies begun to acknowledge the more extreme violations of women's human rights, such as torture, trafficking, slavery and violence.[29] Metonymically, these embodied acts of violence, often associated with international armed conflict, have come to be

---

23   Gideon Sjoberg, Elizabeth A. Gill and Norma Williams, 'A Sociology of Human Rights' (2001) 48 *Social Problems* 11, 42.

24   Siobhán Mullally, *Gender, Culture and Human Rights: Reclaiming universalism*, Hart, Oxford and Portland, Ore., 2006, p. ix.

25   Charlotte Bunch, 'Transforming Human Rights from a Feminist Perspective' in Julie Peters and Andrea Wolper (eds), *Women's Rights, Human Rights*, Routledge, New York, 1995, p. 12.

26   Hilary Charlesworth, 'Human Rights as Men's Rights' in Julie Peters and Andrea Wolper (eds), *Women's Rights, Human Rights*, Routledge, New York, 1995. Cf. Rebecca Cook, 'Women's International Human Rights Law: The Way Forward' in Rebecca Cook (ed.), *Human Rights of Women: National and International Perspectives*, University of Pennsylvania Press, Philadelphia, 1994, p. 3.

27   The most detailed exposition of this proposition remains that of Simone de Beauvoir (*The Second Sex*, Translated and edited by H. M. Parshley, Four Square, London, 1966).

28   Wendy Brown, 'Suffering Rights as Paradoxes' (2000) 7 *Constellations* 230, 239.

29   Elissavet Stamatopoulon, 'Women's Rights and the United Nations' in Julie Peters and Andrea Wolper (eds), *Women's Rights, Human Rights*, Routledge, New York, 1995, pp. 38–9.

equated with the sum total of women's human rights. The result is that there is a reluctance to view other manifestations of discrimination, such as those that detrimentally affect women economically and socially, as conduct that violates their human rights.[30] As Rachael Johnstone points out, gender discrimination is tolerated in ways that would be viewed as totally unacceptable in the case of race.[31] The individualisation of sex discrimination complaints also serves to construct acts of discrimination as aberrant and ad hoc—in contrast with the supposedly universal or class-wide character of human rights. This is despite years of endeavour by feminist scholars to emphasise the systemic character of sex discrimination.[32]

Universality was initially viewed as a progressive development in the constitution of human rights because it erased differences linked to class. The inclusion of women within the universal category was trenchantly resisted by the gatekeepers from the outset, despite the egalitarian rhetoric. Indeed, the acclaimed (universal) Declaration of the Rights of Man and of the Citizen of 1789 did not in fact include women and Olympe de Gouges was sent to the guillotine soon after writing *The Rights of Woman* in 1791.[33] First-wave feminism nevertheless continued to be drawn to the idea of universalism in the struggle to be 'let in' to the community of equals.

The appeal of universality collapsed as far as second-wave feminism was concerned by the late twentieth century—partly under the weight of postmodernism and partly because feminist scholars became more interested in the particularity of women's experiences. Some were of the view that a (masculinised) universal simply could not accommodate female corporeality and care or the idea that women spoke in a different moral voice.[34] Disillusionment set in because of the way 'the category woman' (also conceived as a universal) occluded the raced, sexualised, able-bodied and aged identity of the female subject.

The prospect of a national charter of rights begs the question: can the universalism of human rights be reclaimed absent its masculinist bias? Siobhán Mullally

---

30   Jill Marshall, *Humanity, Freedom and Feminism*, Ashgate, Aldershot Hants, UK, 2005, pp. 13, 138.

31   Rachael Lorna Johnstone, 'Feminist Influences on the United Nations Human Rights Treaty Bodies' (2006) 28 *Human Rights Quarterly* 148, 151. For a competing point of view, see Fellmeth, who argues that international law is now compatible with feminism because of its emphasis on equality, inclusiveness, cooperation and care (Aaron Xavier Fellmeth, 'Feminism and International Law: Theory, Methodology, and Substantive Reform' (2000) 22 *Human Rights Quarterly* 658, 730–1).

32   For example: Margaret Thornton, *The Liberal Promise: Anti-Discrimination Legislation in Australia*, Oxford University Press, Melbourne, 1990.

33   Olympe de Gouges, *The Rights of Woman*, Translated by Val Stevenson, Pythia Press, London, 1989. De Gouges also wrote anti-slavery tracts and had criticised the leaders of the French Revolution. It is notable that de Gouges' treatise appeared just before Mary Wollstonecraft's famous *A Vindication of the Rights of Woman* (Second edition, Edited by Carol H. Poston, Norton, London, 1988 [1792]).

34   Marshall, *Humanity, Freedom and Feminism*, p. 52. The work of Carol Gilligan has been enormously influential. See Carol Gilligan, *In a Different Voice: Psychological Theory and Women's Development*, Harvard University Press, Cambridge, Mass., 1982.

suggests that feminism cannot afford to turn its back on human rights despite its historical baggage.[35] She suggests that the shift away from universalism is damaging for feminist theory and practice, particularly for an emancipatory agenda.[36] Mullally suggests that putting a positive gloss on universality does not mean gender blindness, but gender and contextual sensitivity.[37] This understanding of the rights-bearing subject emphasises personal identity, personal autonomy, personal development and intersubjectivity. Jill Marshall argues that respect for a person's private life is a central plank of human rights that is a provision of the European Convention for the Protection of Human Rights and Fundamental Freedoms 1950.[38] While Australia does not have access to a supra-national court like members of the European Community to jostle it along, judges can look to the European Court's rulings in interpreting the UN conventions to which it is party, rather than taking refuge in strict legalism and an outdated notion of self-referentialism. The scrutiny of private sphere values—a key concern of second-wave feminism—would be welcome in light of the immunity under anti-discrimination legislation, but would it be feasible under a charter?

UN Conventions

In addition to the foundational UN Declaration of Human Rights, state parties have been most influenced by the International Covenant on Civil and Political Rights (ICCPR) and the International Covenant on Economic, Social and Cultural Rights (ICESCR).[39] The ICCPR encompasses the formal rights associated with citizenship, which are essentially freedoms from state interference, whereas those contained in the ICESCR include material rights to education, housing, employment and wellbeing, although the focus is again directed to state action, albeit in a positive rather than a negative sense. Human rights instruments at the municipal or domestic level tend to oscillate between these two covenants, although procedural rights are invariably privileged over the substantive in accordance with the principles of liberal legalism. This suggests that we have not advanced very far beyond the civil rights associated with the Enlightenment, for there is continuing resistance and suspicion towards substantive rights of the kind associated with the ICESCR. Indeed, it is notable that the *Australian Human Rights Commission Act 1986* (Cth) includes the rights set out in the ICCPR, but not those set out in the ICESCR. The *Brennan Report* also proposed

---

35   Mullally, *Gender, Culture and Human Rights*, pp. xxxi–xxxii.
36   Ibid, p. xxxi.
37   Ibid.
38   Jill Marshall, *Personal Freedom Through Law? Autonomy, Identity and Integrity under the European Convention on Human Rights*, Martinus Nijhoff, Leiden, 2009, pp. 1–3 et passim.
39   Sjoberg et al., 'A Sociology of Human Rights' 13.

that the principles emanating from the two covenants be treated differently within a charter. The report recommended the possibility of initiating proceedings against a public authority in the case of civil and political rights but not in the case of economic, social and cultural rights. The different attitude towards rights claims regarding these two foundational covenants points to the difficulty in engendering new ways of thinking about human rights.

The bias in favour of formal rights associated with the ICCPR might also be linked to the long tradition of civil liberties within the Anglo-Australian legal tradition. Whitty et al., in justifying their study of civil liberties law in an age of human rights in the United Kingdom, refer to the 'somewhat swollen status of "human rights"', which they set out to deflate,[40] although there is no clear line of demarcation between civil rights and human rights, especially when the ICCPR is seen as the backbone of any domestic human rights instrument.

Distributive justice initiatives are highly contentious in a neo-liberal climate where the focus is on individual responsibility for one's life course. In any case, as Judy Fudge points out, courts are not a very good avenue for securing redistributive justice.[41] Formalism is preferred by courts (and governments) because it allows dangerousness to be sloughed off. Not only does formalism preserve the myth of equality by adherence to strict equal treatment, it also limits the ambit of juridification, which is another source of concern with a charter of human rights. Detractors argue that it is for the legislature, not 'unelected judges', to make determinations about the allocation of resources.[42] Formalism, however, means that the intractable issues of gender, race, class and power remain unchallenged.

The Universal Declaration of Human Rights in conjunction with the ICCPR and the ICESCR constitute the International Bill of Rights. The gender specificity of CEDAW has rendered it marginal to this international human rights core. Separatism has 'reinforced the idea that men's rights are universal and women's rights an afterthought'.[43] Thus, CEDAW, the very instrument designed to benefit women, could have the effect of instantiating otherness and marginality.

---

40   Noel Whitty, Thérèse Murphy and Stephen Livingstone, *Civil Liberties Law: The* Human Rights Act *Era*, Oxford University Press, UK, 2005, p. 15. Cf. Chinkin, Wright and Charlesworth's reference to the 'triumphalism' of human rights in the 1990s. See Christine Chinkin, Shelley Wright and Hilary Charlesworth, 'Feminist Approaches to International Law: Reflections from another Century' in Doris Buss and Ambreena Manji (eds), *International Law: Modern Feminist Approaches*, Hart, Oxford, 2005, p. 23.

41   Judy Fudge, 'The Canadian Charter of Rights: Recognition, Redistribution, and the Imperialism of the Courts' in Tom Campbell, K. D. Ewing and Adam Tomkins, *Sceptical Essays on Human Rights*, Oxford University Press, UK, 2001, p. 349.

42   James Allan, 'The Effect of a Statutory Bill of Rights where Parliament is Sovereign: The Lesson from New Zealand', in Campbell et al., *Sceptical Essays on Human Rights*, p. 389.

43   Johnstone, 'Feminist Influences on the United Nations Human Rights Treaty Bodies', p. 151. Even more pointedly, Catharine MacKinnon poses the question, are women human? See Catharine A. MacKinnon, *Are Women Human? And Other International Dialogues*, Belknap, Harvard, Cambridge, Mass., 2006.

Nevertheless, the diligent work of feminist international legal scholars has not been entirely in vain. In 2000, for example, the Convention on the Elimination of All Forms of Racial Discrimination (CERD) developed a specific recommendation regarding the impact on women of the conjunction of race and sex.[44]

Could a charter provide a way of invigorating CEDAW to compensate for its cautious and qualified implementation through the *SDA*? Would it be possible to draw on a range of international instruments, including CERD, the Convention on the Rights of Persons with Disabilities and the International Labour Organisation (ILO) Convention Concerning Discrimination in Employment and Occupation, in order to give effect to the wide-ranging injunctions in favour of women's equality contained in CEDAW?

A National Human Rights Charter

The introduction of human rights instruments with domestic application into Australia has been beset with ambivalence, as illustrated by the numerous abortive attempts to enact a domestic bill of rights.[45] The only current federal human rights legislation, the *Human Rights and Equal Opportunity Commission Act 1986* (Cth) (*HREOCA*), falls well short of a charter of human rights.[46] Furthermore, as Peter Bailey points out, this Act displays a schizophrenia about human rights because it combines a hortatory approach to human rights in general with a framework for enforcement of the federal discrimination statutes (including the *SDA*).[47] Unsurprisingly, in light of the timidity towards human rights, the *HRA* (ACT) and the Victorian Charter—the only Australian human rights charters to date—are also cautious instruments that emphasise the rhetoricity of rights.

The *Brennan Report* similarly proposes that priority be given to the fostering of a human rights culture and conformity with human rights principles in public decision making.[48] This softly-softly approach would undoubtedly make a charter more politically palatable for sceptics concerned about the agonistic

---

44 *General Recommendation No XXV, Gender Related Dimensions of Racial Discrimination, Common the Elimination of Racial Discrimination*, 56th Sess, annex V, 152, UN Doc A/55/18 (2000), <http://www.unhchr.ch/tbs/doc.nsf/(Symbol)/76a293e49a88bd23802568bd00538d83?Opendocument>

45 For an account of these attempts, see: Andrew Byrnes, Hilary Charlesworth and Gabrielle McKinnon, *Bills of Rights in Australia: History, Politics and Law*, UNSW Press, Sydney, 2009, pp. 23–43; Bailey, *The Human Rights Enterprise in Australia and Internationally*, pp. 141–52.

46 For detailed discussion, see: Bailey, *The Human Rights Enterprise in Australia and Internationally*, pp. 327–95.

47 Cf. ibid., p. 608.

48 *Brennan Report*, p. 131 ff.

nature of human rights adjudication.[49] The model proposes that litigation be resorted to as a shield rather than a sword, which is secured via an interpretative obligation imposed on courts and tribunals.[50] That is, the mode does not confer enforceable rights of action against another party, but an obligation to interpret legislation in light of charter principles. While not empowered to invalidate legislation, a court would merely declare it incompatible with human rights; it would then be up to the legislature to act on the recommendation. Deference would allow legislative sovereignty to be upheld so that juridification was minimised.

It is notable that the Brennan model restricts human rights to individuals, thereby precluding their application to corporate entities, as occurred in Canada under the Charter.[51] The downside is that there is no scope for an aggrieved person to call to account either another individual or a private corporation for a breach of human rights; the focus is entirely on public entities, other than if incidentally caught by a focus on adjudication (a public act). The effect of the public focus largely immunises private sector employment and corporate power, even though women generally are more likely to suffer a derogation of human rights at the hands of private rather than public actors.[52]

The way in which the Brennan proposal, the Victorian Charter and the *HRA* (ACT) all focus on public rather than private action supports the thesis of Sjoberg et al. that the human rights movement has emerged out of a context in which the state has weakened.[53] This thesis of state deference to the market is underpinned by the neo-liberal deregulatory imperative, which became pronounced in Australia in the 1990s with the transference of power from government to the corporate sector.[54] The state has not abandoned its regulatory role altogether, but, in effecting a liaison with the market, it has shifted its attention away from civil society. The result is that social justice and egalitarianism are treated as

---

49 Adam Tomkins, 'Introduction: On being Sceptical about Human Rights', in Campbell et al., *Sceptical Essays on Human Rights*, pp. 8–9.

50 For a detailed discussion and critique of the *HRA* (UK) from the perspective of civil liberties, see Whitty et al., *Civil Liberties Law*.

51 This to avoid the expansive interpretation that developed under the Canadian Charter of Rights. For example: Kent Roach, 'Judicial Activism in the Supreme Court of Canada' in Brice Dickson (ed.), *Judicial Activism in Common Law Supreme Courts*, Oxford University Press, UK, 2007, p. 74. For detailed studies of the subversion of international human rights law by corporate power, see: Anna Grear, 'Human Rights – Human Bodies? Reflections on Corporate Human Rights Distortion, the Legal Subject, Embodiment and Human Rights Theory' (2006) 17 *Law Critique* 171; Tony Evans, 'International Human Rights Law as Power/Knowledge' (2005) 27 *Human Rights Quarterly* 1046.

52 Cf. Johnstone, 'Feminist Influences' 152.

53 Sjoberg et al., 'A Sociology of Human Rights'.

54 Mark Western, Janeen Baxter, Jan Pakulski, Bruce Tranter, John Western, Marcel van Egmond, Jenny Chesters, Amanda Hosking, Martin O'Flaherty and Yolanda van Gellecum, 'Neoliberalism, Inequality and Politics: The Changing Face of Australia' (2007) 42(3) *Australian Journal of Social Issues* 401.

passé, while globalisation, free trade and the maximisation of corporate wealth are privileged. This does not bode well for relying on a charter in the interests of women and Others.

In light of the propensity of human rights to marginalise women, it is notable that a mere half-page of 460 pages in the *Brennan Report* is devoted to women.[55] While it is proper to emphasise Indigenous rights, the intersection between race and gender is accorded short shrift, despite the (obvious) fact that at least half of all Indigenous people are female. The inference once again is that violations of women's rights are expendable or more properly conceptualised as aberrant manifestations of discrimination that fall within the rubric of CEDAW and the *SDA*.

A study by Byrnes et al. of the first year of operation of the *HRA* (ACT) found that while the legislation exerted a profound effect on the legislature and the executive, it had little effect on the judiciary.[56] Indeed, there have been few discrimination cases in either the Australian Capital Territory or Victoria where the *HRA* or the Charter has raised significant issues. The most notable involved an application for an exemption from the *EOA* (Vic.) by a company seeking to restrict gated community accommodation to people over fifty.[57] Bell J provides a thoroughgoing analysis of equality in which he identifies it as the primary human right that 'permeates every pore of the Charter'.[58] He makes it clear, furthermore, that equality is understood in substantive, not merely formalistic terms. Bell J is critical of a decision of Peedom P in the Australian Capital Territory,[59] because the latter implied that the presence of a Charter made no difference to the exercise of the discretion.[60]

In a subsequent criminal case in Victoria,[61] the Court of Appeal explored the interpretative role of the Court in light of the Victorian Charter (s. 32[1]): 'So far as it is possible to do so consistently with their purpose, all statutory provisions must be interpreted in a way that is compatible with human rights.'

The Court held that there was nothing in Section 32(1) that required an interpretation that would overrule parliamentary intention.[62] The Court declined to follow *Ghaidan*, the leading case of the House of Lords, in interpreting a similar provision in the *HRA* (UK).[63] In the process, the Court of

---

55 *Brennan Report*, p. 85.
56 Byrnes et al., *Bills of Rights in Australia*, p. 72.
57 *Lifestyle Communities Ltd (No 3) (Anti-Discrimination)* [2009] VCAT 1869.
58 Ibid. [106].
59 *Raytheon Australia P/L & Ors and ACT Human Rights Commission* [2008] ACTAAT 19.
60 *Lifestyle Communities* [103].
61 *R v Momcilovic* [2010] VSCA 50, per Maxwell P, Ashley and Neave JJA (*Momcilovic*).
62 Ibid. [74]. Cf. *R. v Fearnside* [2009] ACTCA 3.
63 *Ghaidan v Godin-Mendoza* [2004] 2 AC 557.

Appeal overruled a decision of Bell J in *Kracke v Mental Health Review Board*,[64] who had sought to interpret the Victorian Charter in accordance with the more expansive interpretation of *Ghaidan*. In support of its minimalist position, the Court of Appeal quoted at length from the parliamentary debates on the Victorian Charter, including the views of opponents of the Bill.[65]

What we see in *Momcilovic* is an attempt to read the dialogic model of human rights as nothing more than a signal from the judicial branch to the legislature that some action needs to be taken—as long as the judiciary itself does not respond by doing anything that might be construed as making law. Of course, it is a myth that judges do not make law, just as legislative intent itself is another myth. Indeed, in the case of the *SDA* and other anti-discrimination texts, parliamentary intent is frequently left uncertain, which could expand the leeway of choice in a charter's encounter with discrimination legislation.

I suggest that it is not just a question of the legislative texts that is important in the novel hermeneutics of a human rights charter. The questions as to who are the judges, how they are appointed and what adjudicative stance they adopt are clearly of great moment.[66] When Australian Acting Prime Minister Tim Fischer announced in 1996 after the trailblazing but contentious native title decisions of *Mabo*[67] and *Wik*[68] that the Howard Government would appoint 'Capital C Conservatives' to the High Court,[69] six new judges were appointed (out of seven), which led to a discernible change in adjudicative style in a remarkably short time.[70] A shift occurred from a purposive approach in anti-discrimination legislation jurisprudence, in which the remedial aims of the legislation were taken seriously, to a technocratic and legalistic approach that sloughed them off.

The exercise of discretion in interpreting human rights in context, as with discrimination and other progressive legislation, is the very point that disturbs human rights sceptics.[71] Nevertheless, judges of all hues are likely to adopt a cautious approach to human rights legislation that is foreign to them or where deference to the legislature is the norm. Not only was this the experience, at least

---

64   [2009] VCAT 646.

65   *Momcilovic* [81]–[96].

66   Mark Tushnet, 'Sceptism about Judicial Review: A Perspective from the United States' in Campbell et al., *Sceptical Essays on Human Rights*, p. 360.

67   *Mabo v Queensland (No. 2) (1992) 175 CLR 1*.

68   *Wik Peoples v Queensland (1996) 187 CLR 1*.

69   Nikki Savva, 'Fischer seeks a more conservative court', *The Age* (Melbourne), 5 March 1997, pp. 1–2.

70   For example: *New South Wales v Amery* (2006) 230 CLR 174. See also: Margaret Thornton, 'Sex Discrimination, Courts and Corporate Power' (2008) 36 *Federal Law Review* 31; Margaret Thornton, 'Disabling Discrimination Legislation: The High Court and Judicial Activism' (2009) 15(1) *Australian Journal of Human Rights* 1.

71   For example: Allan, 'The Effect of a Statutory Bill of Rights Where Parliament is Sovereign', p. 389; Michael Pelly and Natasha Robinson, 'Charter risks clogging courts, says judge', *The Australian*, 12 October 2009.

initially, in regard to the *HRA* (UK),[72] it is also apparent in the early Australian adjudicative experience of anti-discrimination legislation.[73] The danger is that unless they are given very clear guidance, courts will fall back on a formalistic approach in preference to a substantive one. A formalistic approach could do more damage for women by creating unduly narrow precedents at the outset. We should therefore not allow ourselves to feel complacent before the warm, fuzzy glow that a discourse of human rights can engender, but should rigorously interrogate the content. In particular, we should not shrug our shoulders and accept unquestioningly the Brennan proposal that only state and public entities should be bound by a human rights charter.

Freedom and Equality

Freedom and equality—the twin variables of liberalism—are generally regarded as the pre-eminent human rights.[74] They do not sit easily together, however, and their antinomy means that they perennially compete for ascendancy.[75] Women's selfhood has been suppressed by the way freedom and autonomy have been used against them.[76] The dilemma is invariably how to balance the right to freedom with the right to equality, although the idea of effecting a balance assumes that all claims are of comparable value.[77] The invisibility of power within liberal legalism contributes to the myth that a state of equilibrium is attainable.

Philosophically, equality is a notoriously elusive concept despite its status as a—if not *the*—pre-eminent human right. Indeed, it is described by Julius Stone, following Aristotle, as 'the test of justice'.[78] Formal equality, or equality before the law, is a basic principle of liberal legalism and there is a sizeable gap between it and substantive equality, or equality of outcome—a disparity that I have alluded to in the underlying premises of the ICCPR and the ICESCR, respectively. The focus on formalism enhances the freedom of 'Benchmark Men' (those who are Anglo-Celtic, heterosexual, able-bodied and middle class,

---

72   Susan Easton, 'Feminist Perspectives on the *Human Rights Act*: Two Cheers for Incorporation' (2002) 8 *Res Publica* 21, 23.

73   Thornton, *The Liberal Promise*, pp. 198–206.

74   In contrast, Bailey identifies equality and dignity as the meta-principles of human rights. See Bailey, *The Human Rights Enterprise in Australia and Internationally*, p. 397. But see also Réaume, who suggests in her analysis of Canadian Charter jurisprudence that dignity could be used to deny equality claims (Denise G. Réaume, 'Discrimination and Dignity' in Fay Faraday, Margaret Denike and M. Kate Stephenson [eds], *Making Equality Rights Real: Securing Substantive Equality under the Charter*, Irwin Law, Toronto, 2006, pp. 123–77).

75   Wendy Brown, *States of Injury: Power and Freedom in Late Modernity*, Princeton University Press, NJ, 1995, p. 67.

76   Catharine A. MacKinnon, *Toward a Feminist Theory of the State*, Harvard University Press, Cambridge, Mass., 1989, p. 216.

77   For critique of the idea of effecting a 'balance', see: Bailey, *The Human Rights Enterprise in Australia and Internationally*, pp. 104–10.

78   Julius Stone, *Human Law and Human Justice*, Maitland Publications, Sydney, 1968, p. 332.

who favour a right-of-centre politics and who adhere, at least nominally, to a mainstream Christian religion). Provided that there is equality of opportunity at the outset, the law is satisfied; it is not concerned with outcomes, which involve distributive justice. In fact, substantive equality could be no more than a chimera—an ideal end point to which women and Others aspire, since compromise is unavoidable in real life.

All individuals necessarily live lives of interdependency, and the privileging of one person's freedom could cause a diminution of equality for another and vice versa. The introduction of institutional power into the equation skews the imbalance further. Employers, for example, are anxious to maximise their freedom by appointing whoever they wish on whatever terms they wish—a practice that has long contributed to bias towards women and disfavoured Others in the labour market, particularly as far as authoritative positions are concerned. Although state regulation of the terms and conditions of work is widely accepted, the idea that discrimination is unlawful is resisted because regulation is perceived to impede the freedom of the market. As Whitty et al. note, discrimination was a late development in the civil rights trajectory,[79] pithily suggesting that courts were 'equality averse'.[80] Nevertheless, substantive equality, or some semblance of it, is realisable for women and Others only with the support of the state—fickle though it might be. The free market cannot be relied on to achieve equality of outcome when the modus operandi of competition is *in*equality. The neo-liberal state, however, has become increasingly reluctant to delimit market freedom by fostering equality measures, which has exacerbated the malaise surrounding the *SDA*.

The case of religious freedom should also be mentioned because of the deleterious impact of religion on women.[81] As Gila Stopler points out, all mainstream religions are patriarchal, and deference to them operates as a status-enforcing mechanism that perpetuates women's inequality.[82] Religion could also be imbricated with grounds such as race and ethnicity, which render it difficult to untangle issues of freedom and equality. The point is illustrated by the marked tensions arising from prescriptions pertaining to religious clothing, such as headscarves, which disproportionately affect women and girls.[83] Their 'freedom of choice' could in fact be shaped by patriarchal religious leadership, family, community and state.[84]

---

79   Whitty et al., *Civil Liberties Law*, p. 390.
80   Ibid., p. 393.
81   Frances Raday, 'Culture, Religion, and Gender' (2002) 4 *International Journal of Constitutional Law* 663; Aileen McColgan, 'Class Wars Religion and (In)equality in the Workplace' (2009) 38 *Industrial Law Journal* 1, 5–7.
82   Gila Stopler, 'The Liberal Bind: The Conflict between Women's Rights and Patriarchal Religion' (2005) 31 *Social Theory and Practice* 191, 196.
83   For example, *R. (on the application of Begum) v Head Teacher and Governors of Denbigh School* [2006] UKHL 15.
84   Nicky Jones, 'Beneath the Veil: Muslim Girls and Islamic Headscarves in Secular France' (2009) 9 *Macquarie Law Journal* 47, 65.

In omnibus State and Territory anti-discrimination statutes, the outlawing of discrimination on the ground of religious belief is treated as a mirror image of sex, race, sexuality or other ground, which highlights the 'one size fits all' approach to anti-discrimination legislation.[85] Paradoxically, religion also occupies a privileged status in the legislative framework by virtue of the express exemptions that waive the proscription against discrimination for religious organisations. Despite the liberal state's express support for the equality of citizens regardless of belief or non-belief, all Australian anti-discrimination legislation defers to religion.[86]

In the *SDA*, a religious body is exempted from the non-discrimination principle in the case of an act or practice that conforms to the tenets of a particular religion or if it is 'necessary to avoid injury to the religious susceptibilities of adherents of that religion'.[87] This could apply to sex, marital status, pregnancy, potential pregnancy or family responsibilities in all operable areas, other than sexual harassment. There have been repercussions for women employed by religious organisations in respect of issues such as sexual orientation, de facto relationships, single motherhood and a preference for men in positions of authority.[88] The legislative exemptions point to the fact that freedom of religion tends to be valued more highly than either equality or freedom of choice for women.

The point is clearly illustrated in the case of sexual orientation, which can intersect with sex, although not included in either the *SDA* or dedicated federal legislation. At present, gays and lesbians experiencing discrimination have no option at the federal level other than to lodge a complaint for inquiry and recommendation under the *AHREOCA*. Sexual orientation also continues to be a highly contentious ground in the context of human rights, even in those jurisdictions where discrimination is proscribed.[89] While the traditional privileging of religious organisations, together with their relative power in the community, suggests that the scales are likely to continue to be tilted in their favour, decisions from elsewhere suggest that a human rights instrument could

---

85   McColgan, 'Class Wars, Religion and (In)equality in the Workplace' 2.

86   A government review of exceptions to the *EOA* (Vic.) recommended that the religious exceptions be retained on all grounds other than race, impairment, physical features and age. See Scrutiny of Acts and Regulations Committee, *Exceptions and Exemptions to the* Equal Opportunity Act 1995—*Final Report*, Government Printer for the State of Victoria, Melbourne, 2009, Recommendations 48 and 49, pp. 62–4.

87   *SDA*, s. 37(d).

88   Margaret Thornton and Trish Luker, 'The Spectral Ground: Religious Belief Discrimination' (2009) 9 *Macquarie Law Journal* 71, 76-79; Reid Mortensen, 'A Reconstruction of Religious Freedom and Equality: Gay, Lesbian and De Facto Rights and the Religious School in Queensland' (2003) 3 *Queensland University of Technology Law & Justice Journal* 320.

89   In an application for judicial review of a sexual orientation statute by a number of religious bodies in Northern Ireland, the applicants claimed that it was the orthodox belief of Christians that homosexual practices are sinful. See *An Application for Judicial Review by the Christian Institute et al.* [2007] NIQB 66.

make a difference and restrain religious freedom. In *R. (Amicus)*,[90] various institutional claimants sought annulment of the *Employment Equality (Sexual Orientation) Regulations 2003* (UK), arguing that their ability to adhere to their religious beliefs and carry on their teaching would be undermined if they were forced to employ people whose sexual practices were at odds with their own religious beliefs and practices.[91] They failed to demonstrate discrimination.[92] In an application for judicial review of a sexual orientation statute in Northern Ireland, the applicant religious bodies argued unsuccessfully that the right to freedom of thought, conscience and religion contained in Article 9 of the European Convention was absolute.[93] While respectful of religious freedom, courts will not defer to religious freedom if it involves trammelling the self-worth and dignity of gays and lesbians, even when sexual orientation is also a proscribed ground under the legislation. Thus, even if the respondent regards homosexual conduct as sinful, European and Canadian courts bound by human rights principles have endeavoured to find a way to minimise its discriminatory effect in the interests of equality.[94]

In contrast, there is no question of 'balancing' rights in the case of an express exemption for religious bodies within Australian anti-discrimination legislation. The privileging of religion then perpetuates women's inequality in both the public and the private spheres.[95] Perhaps, because of the UK experience, or because of the increasing political power of religion in Australia,[96] both mainstream and fundamentalist religious bodies have expressed strong opposition to a charter of rights in the belief that it will diminish their freedom.[97] Overtures not to proceed with a charter were made to the federal government in 2009 by mainstream religious leaders when the *Brennan Report* was released.[98] Submissions were also made to the Victorian Attorney-General by a range of religious bodies regarding the repeal of wide-ranging exemptions for religion under the *EOA* (Vic.).[99]

Powerful institutional forces therefore shape rights to freedom and equality in very particular ways. The immunity accorded the private corporate sector in

---

90   *R. (Amicus & Ors) v Secretary of State* [2004] EWHC 860 (Admin).

91   Ibid. [30].

92   Ibid. [198]–[199].

93   *An Application for Judicial Review by the Christian Institute et al.* [2007] NIQB 66.

94   For example, *Ontario Human Rights Commission v Brockie* [2002] 22 DLR (4th) 174.

95   Cf. Stopler, 'The Liberal Bind' 194.

96   Marion Maddox, *God Under Howard: The Rise of the Religious Right in Australian Politics*, Allen & Unwin, Sydney, 2005.

97   Patrick Parkinson, Christian Concerns with Charter of Rights, Paper presented at Conference on Cultural and Religious Freedom under a Bill of Rights, Canberra, August 2009. Mullally (*Gender, Culture and Human Rights*, p. 138) notes the occurrence of the same phenomenon in the United States.

98   Nicola Berkovic, 'Clergy unite over charter', *The Australian*, 23 October 2009, p. 1. It was subsequently reported that federal cabinet had rejected a national charter of rights. See Chris Merritt, 'State charter sets lawyers on path to isolation', *The Australian*, 19 February 2010, p. 29.

99   Scrutiny of Acts and Regulations (SARC) Committee, *Exceptions and Exemptions to the* Equal Opportunity Act 1995.

the proposed charter, together with the privileged status accorded mainstream religions in anti-discrimination legislation, reveals once again that the imperative in favour of equality for women and Others is invariably trumped by power.

Human Rights and Intersectionality

As mentioned at the outset, Australian anti-discrimination legislation has been characterised by a one-dimensional and essentialist approach to grounds that has inhibited the ability to address multiple and intersecting strands of inequality. There is a substantial literature from the United States that shows how a unitary consciousness deleteriously affects Afro-American women for whom sex and race cannot be easily disaggregated.[100] I suggest that invoking the equality prescript of a national charter could be a way of placing intersectionality on the agenda, although conceptualising gender equality merely as non-discrimination is clearly a problem in the present framework.[101]

Dao v Australian Postal Commission[102] is a paradigm of intersectionality arising from the dual grounds of sex and race in the Australian context. It involved two female Vietnamese postal workers who were precluded from obtaining permanency because they failed to satisfy the minimum body weight according to a scale based on height and sex. Because of the slighter body mass of Vietnamese women, the issues of race and sex could not be disaggregated, although intersectionality was not pursued, as the case foundered on constitutional grounds.[103]

The typical approach to multiple grounds in Australia is to address two or more grounds simultaneously rather than intersectionally. In *Wiggins*,[104] the complainant alleged sex, sexual harassment and disability discrimination. Only the ground of disability was upheld, it being the view of McInnis FM that the serious depressive illness of the complainant affected her memory of the other two grounds. That is, the grounds were treated as discrete, although an intersectional approach might have considered whether the sexual harassment and the sex discrimination contributed to the mental illness.

---

100   Leading articles include: Kimberle Crenshaw, 'Demarginalizing the Intersection of Race and Sex: A Black Feminist Critique of Anti-Discrimination Doctrine, Feminist Theory and Antiracist Politics' (1989) *University of Chicago Legal Forum* 139; Angela P Harris, 'Race and Essentialism in Feminist Legal Theory' (1990) 42 *Stanford Law Review* 581.
101   Cf. Judith Squires, 'Intersecting Inequalities' (2009) 11 *International Feminist Journal of Politics* 496, 506.
102   *Dao v Australian Postal Commission* (1987) 162 CLR 317.
103   For discussion, see: Hilary Astor, 'A Question of Identity: The Intersection of Race and Other Grounds of Discrimination' in Race Discrimination Commissioner, *The Racial Discrimination Act: A Review*, AGPS, Canberra, 1995; Australian Law Reform Commission, *Equality Before the Law*, Pt I, pp. 63–9.
104   *Wiggins v Department of Defence—Navy* [2006] FMCA 800.

These cases were determined without the benefit of a charter and might be considered alongside *Pearce*[105]—a case decided in the United Kingdom soon after the introduction of the *HRA*. The case involved a lesbian teacher who had been subjected to harassment at her school. The grounds arose from sexual orientation as well as sex. At that stage, there was no legislation outlawing discrimination on the ground of sexual orientation, so the complainant lodged a complaint on the ground of sex. Some of the harassing terms used by pupils, such as 'lezzie' and 'dyke', were clearly gendered, but the complaint was dismissed by the lower tribunals on the ground that there was no evidence that the pupils would have treated a male homosexual teacher more favourably than they treated the complainant. The gravamen of the appeal related to the *HRA* (UK) (s. 3[1]), which requires a court to give effect to the European Convention on Human Rights 'so far as it is possible to do so'.[106] While Baroness Hale stated that the significance of the *HRA* is that it enables courts to give legislation a different meaning to that previously held,[107] sexuality was nevertheless found to be an irrelevant circumstance for the purpose of the comparison required by the *Sex Discrimination Act 1975* (*SDA* [UK]) (s 5[3]): 'sex' in the Act meant gender, not 'sexuality'. It is conceivable that the outcome might have been different had the focus been directed to the gendered words alone but, by defining the relevant ground as sexual orientation rather than sex, the complainant was precluded from being able to succeed. In fact, as with *Wiggins*, the intersection of sex and sexuality was not addressed at all.

Despite the opportunity that the *HRA* (UK) theoretically offered novel ways of thinking about intersectionality, the prevailing values of discrimination jurisprudence were not jettisoned in favour of equality. As Douzinas observes, the universal becomes the handmaiden of the particular at the hands of a legal system.[108] Thus, 'human rights' can be just as restrictive as discrimination jurisprudence if the values of a charter are treated as subordinate to the statute under consideration, as suggested in the case of *Momcilovic*. Precedents, the norms of the relevant hermeneutic community, the subjectivity of individual judges and the spectre of religion are all going to play a role in shaping human rights in ways that comport with the status quo. The complainant in *Pearce* was harassed and denigrated by virtue of the twin signifiers of sex and sexuality. She was denied the right to a discrimination-free workplace as well as a right to equality. The primary focus of the decision was technocratic, privileging the specification of comparability under the *SDA* (UK) rather than equality under the *HRA* (UK).

105 *Pearce v Governing Body of Mayfield School* [2001] EWCA Civ 1347.
106 Cf. *HRA* (ACT) s. 30.
107 Ibid. [14], per Lady Hale. A more robust approach to the question of the *HRA* (UK) effecting a change to an earlier ruling on the facts was adopted by the House of Lords a few years later. See *Ghaidan v Godin-Mendoza* [2004] 2 AC 557. Legislation proscribing discrimination on the ground of sexual orientation had nevertheless been enacted by that time. See Employment Equality (Sexual Orientation) Regulations 2003 (UK).
108 Douzinas, 'The End(s) of Human Rights' 459.

Even though there is no proviso in the *HRA* (UK) limiting the meaning of discrimination to that contained in the *SDA* (UK), as with the Victorian Charter, *Pearce* was dealt with as though the tacit understanding of equality for women was the equivalent of non-discrimination under the relevant statute. The case shows how the potential for a charter to address intersectional dilemmas in new ways can be frustrated by a conventional and conservative approach by judges towards interpretation. The focus on comparability in the *SDA* (UK) caused the court to lose sight of equality as the telos of the human rights statute, although the marshmallow wording favoured by the legislature—'so far as it is possible to do so'—did not help. Reliance on an ostensibly depoliticised interpretative methodology of literalism allows courts to claim fidelity to parliamentary intention, even though this means privileging one constellation of moral values over another.

Australia, like the United Kingdom, favours a weak form of judicial review, as opposed to the strong form associated with the United States.[109] That is, the weak form defers to parliamentary sovereignty, whereas the strong accords greater latitude to the judiciary to strike down legislation. The difficulty with anti-discrimination legislative texts is that they tend to be couched at a high level of abstraction so that legislative intention vis-a-vis intersectionality, for example, is unclear. Just because the issue has not been addressed in the past does not mean that an injunction in favour of equality in a charter can be accorded short shrift. The interpretative mandate requires judges to reconcile both texts, which provides scope for the creativity I am exhorting.

Conclusion

The warning of Whitty et al. that the passage of human rights legislation can induce a sense of euphoria in the belief that it will provide an instantaneous panacea for multiple shortcomings is salutary as Australia hesitantly acknowledges the possibility of a domestic culture of human rights. While human rights were initially greeted enthusiastically in jurisdictions such as Canada, successes led to a backlash against juridically enforced rights.[110] Fudge links this backlash particularly to the success of gays and lesbians before the courts.[111] UK legal feminists have not necessarily regarded the *HRA* (UK) euphorically either,[112] although some see it as contributing to a new and evolving rights

---

109 Mark Tushnet, The Rise of Weak-Form Judicial Review, Paper presented to ANU College of Law, The Australian National University, Canberra, May 2010.
110 Fudge, 'The Canadian Charter of Rights', pp. 337–8.
111 Ibid., p. 340.
112 Aileen McColgan, 'Women and the *Human Rights Act*' (2000) 51 *Northern Ireland Legal Quarterly* 417; Easton, 'Feminist Perspectives on the *Human Rights Act*'.

jurisprudence.[113] While the discourse of human rights does not carry the seeds of invidiousness and victimhood that discrimination discourse has acquired, I do not think that feminists in Australia can place their faith in a national charter of rights either.

I have shown that the ambit of the proposed legislation is limited and confined largely to the formal rights of the ICCPR, with the ICESCR and substantive equality carefully circumscribed.[114] In addition, the immunity accorded corporations and the private sector, together with the privileging of powerful institutional interests, such as patriarchal religions, does not look as though it could revive an ailing *SDA*. The normative understanding of equality as non-discrimination also constitutes a barrier to novel ways of thinking about intersectionality because it falls back on conventional assumptions within discrimination jurisprudence, such as that of comparability. Of course, judges who are prepared to take a robust approach to interpreting indeterminate charter language can make a difference, but the hermeneutic pressure is invariably to opt for the safe course of action and privilege stare decisis and the status quo.

The ultimate paradox of a charter is that it is a creature of the state yet focuses solely on ills caused by state action. Inevitably, according to the norms of Westminster constitutionalism, the state is anxious to restrict the extent of judicial discretion and ensure deference to the legislature. The eighteenth-century declarations of human rights were regarded as natural rights that were inalienable and independent of government.[115] The twenty-first century incarnation is contingent on the state—a neo-liberal state where loyalties are more likely to be directed towards fostering entrepreneurialism and free trade in global markets than effecting substantive equality between all citizens in accordance with social-liberal ideals.

Nevertheless, as rights are the familiar language of progressive politics, which provide an avenue for redress, their rejection is just not a viable option. As Wendy Brown points out, feminists are compelled to accept the paradoxical nature of rights because they '*appear* as that which we cannot not want'.[116] That is, we want the right to be free from exploitation, the right to autonomy, the right to be treated with dignity and the right to equality. We therefore cannot turn our backs on a federal charter—if, perchance, one should materialise—despite its likely defects and the vagaries of judicial interpretation, nor can

---

113   Joanne Conaghan and Susan Millns, 'Special Issue: Gender, Sexuality and Human Rights' (2005) 13 *Feminist Legal Studies* 1, 4.
114   This position contrasts with the *Constitution of South Africa*, which has been described as the most far-reaching example of the entrenchment of economic and social rights. See Katharine G. Young, 'Freedom, Want, and Economic and Social Rights: Frame and Law' (2009) 24 *Maryland Journal of International Law* 182, 202.
115   Douzinas, 'The End(s) of Human Rights' 448.
116   Brown, 'Suffering Rights as Paradoxes' 23.

we allow ourselves to be seduced by the siren call of the global at the expense of the local. It is up to us to engage with the mainstream and ensure that new meanings of equality are developed and that rights are not deployed against women and Others in the name of freedom for the powerful—especially private corporations and mainstream religions.

Bibliography

Books and articles

Allan, James, 'The Effect of a Statutory Bill of Rights where Parliament is Sovereign: The Lesson from New Zealand' in Tom Campbell, K. D. Ewing and Adam Tomkins, *Sceptical Essays on Human Rights*, Oxford University Press, UK, 2001.

Andrades, Carol, *Intersections between 'General Protections' under the Fair Work Act 2009 (Cth) and Anti-Discrimination Law: Questions, Quirks and Quandaries*, Working Paper No. 47, Centre for Employment and Labour Relations Law, University of Melbourne, Vic., 2009.

Astor, Hilary, 'A Question of Identity: The Intersection of Race and Other Grounds of Discrimination' in Race Discrimination Commissioner, *The* Racial Discrimination Act: *A Review*, AGPS, Canberra, 1995.

Attorney-General Hon. Robert McClelland MP and Minister for Finance and Deregulation Hon. Lindsay Tanner MP, Reform of Anti-discrimination Legislation, Media release, 21 April 2010, Parliament House, Canberra.

Bailey, Peter, *The Human Rights Enterprise in Australia and Internationally*, LexisNexis Butterworths, Chatswood, NSW, 2009.

Berkovic, Nicola, 'Clergy unite over charter', *The Australian*, 23 October 2009, p. 1.

Best, Susan J., 'Sexual Favoritism: A Cause of Action Under a "Sex-Plus" Theory' (2009) 30 *Northern Illinois University Law Review* 211.

Brown, Wendy, *States of Injury: Power and Freedom in Late Modernity*, Princeton University Press, NJ, 1995.

Brown, Wendy, 'Suffering Rights as Paradoxes' (2000) 7 *Constellations* 230.

Bunch, Charlotte, 'Transforming Human Rights from a Feminist Perspective' in Julie Peters and Andrea Wolper (eds), *Women's Rights, Human Rights*, Routledge, New York, 1995.

Byrnes, Andrew, Charlesworth, Hilary and McKinnon, Gabrielle, *Bills of Rights in Australia: History, Politics and Law*, UNSW Press, Sydney, 2009.

Charlesworth, Hilary, 'Human Rights as Men's Rights' in Julie Peters and Andrea Wolper (eds), *Women's Rights, Human Rights*, Routledge, New York, 1995.

Chinkin, Christine, Wright, Shelley and Charlesworth, Hilary, 'Feminist Approaches to International Law: Reflections from another Century' in Doris Buss and Ambreena Manji (eds), *International Law: Modern Feminist Approaches*, Hart, Oxford, 2005.

Conaghan, Joanne and Millns, Susan, 'Special Issue: Gender, Sexuality and Human Rights' (2005) 13 *Feminist Legal Studies* 1.

Cook, Rebecca, 'Women's International Human Rights Law: The Way Forward' in Rebecca Cook (ed.), *Human Rights of Women: National and International Perspectives*, University of Pennsylvania Press, Philadelphia, 1994.

Crenshaw, Kimberle, 'Demarginalizing the Intersection of Race and Sex: A Black Feminist Critique of Anti-Discrimination Doctrine, Feminist Theory and Antiracist Politics' (1989) *University of Chicago Legal Forum* 139.

de Beauvoir, Simone, *The Second Sex*, Translated and edited by H. M. Parshley, Four Square, London, 1966.

de Gouges, Olympe, *The Rights of Woman*, Translated by Val Stevenson, Pythia Press, London, 1989.

Douzinas, Costas, 'The End(s) of Human Rights' (2002) 26 *Melbourne University Law Review* 445.

Easton, Susan, 'Feminist Perspectives on the *Human Rights Act*: Two Cheers for Incorporation' (2002) 8 *Res Publica* 21.

Eisenstein, Hester, 'A Dangerous Liaison? Feminism and Corporate Globalization' (2005) 69 *Science & Society* 487.

Engle, Karen, 'International Human Rights and Feminisms: When Discourses keep meeting' in Doris Buss and Ambreena Manji (eds), *International Law: Feminist Approaches*, Hart, Oxford, 2005.

Evans, Tony, 'International Human Rights Law as Power/Knowledge' (2005) 27 *Human Rights Quarterly* 1046.

Fellmeth, Aaron Xavier, 'Feminism and International Law: Theory, Methodology, and Substantive Reform' (2000) 22 *Human Rights Quarterly* 658.

Fudge, Judy, 'The Canadian Charter of Rights: Recognition, Redistribution, and the Imperialism of the Courts' in Tom Campbell, K. D. Ewing and Adam Tomkins, *Sceptical Essays on Human Rights*, Oxford University Press, UK, 2001.

Fudge, Judy and Owens, Rosemary (eds), *Precarious Work, Women and the New Economy: The Challenge to Legal Norms*, Hart Publishing, Oxford, 2006.

Gilligan, Carol, *In a Different Voice: Psychological Theory and Women's Development*, Harvard University Press, Cambridge, Mass., 1982.

Grear, Anna, 'Human Rights—Human Bodies? Reflections on Corporate Human Rights Distortion, the Legal Subject, Embodiment and Human Rights Theory' (2006) 17 *Law Critique* 171.

Harris, Angela P., 'Race and Essentialism in Feminist Legal Theory' (1990) 42 *Stanford Law Review* 581.

Hulls, Rob, Religious Freedom to be protected under Equal Opportunity Changes, Media release by the Victorian Attorney-General, 27 September 2009, Parliament House, Melbourne.

Johnstone, Rachael Lorna, 'Feminist Influences on the United Nations Human Rights Treaty Bodies' (2006) 28 *Human Rights Quarterly* 148.

Jones, Nicky, 'Beneath the Veil: Muslim Girls and Islamic Headscarves in Secular France' (2009) 9 *Macquarie Law Journal* 47.

McColgan, Aileen, 'Women and the *Human Rights Act*' (2000) 51 *Northern Ireland Legal Quarterly* 417.

McColgan, Aileen, 'Class Wars Religion and (In)equality in the Workplace' (2009) 38 *Industrial Law Journal* 1.

MacKinnon, Catharine A., *Toward a Feminist Theory of the State*, Harvard University Press, Cambridge, Mass., 1989.

MacKinnon, Catharine A., *Are Women Human? And Other International Dialogues*, Belknap, Harvard, Cambridge, Mass., 2006.

Maddox, Marion, *God Under Howard: The Rise of the Religious Right in Australian Politics*, Allen & Unwin, Sydney, 2005.

Marshall, Jill, *Humanity, Freedom and Feminism*, Ashgate, Aldershot Hants, UK, 2005.

Marshall, Jill, *Personal Freedom Through Law? Autonomy, Identity and Integrity under the European Convention on Human Rights*, Martinus Nijhoff, Leiden, 2009.

Merritt, Chris, 'State charter sets lawyers on path to isolation', *The Australian*, 19 February 2010, p. 29.

Mortensen, Reid, 'A Reconstruction of Religious Freedom and Equality: Gay, Lesbian and De Facto Rights and the Religious School in Queensland' (2003) 3 *Queensland University of Technology Law & Justice Journal* 320.

Mullally, Siobhán, *Gender, Culture and Human Rights: Reclaiming Universalism*, Hart, Oxford and Portland, Ore., 2006.

Murphy, Thérèse, 'Feminism Here and Feminism There: Law, Theory and Choice' in Doris Buss and Ambreena Manji (eds), *International Law: Modern Feminist Approaches*, Hart, Oxford, 2005.

Parkinson, Patrick, Christian Concerns with Charter of Rights, Paper presented at Conference on Cultural and Religious Freedom Under a Bill of Rights, Canberra, August 2009.

Pelly, Michael and Robinson, Natasha, 'Charter risks clogging Courts, says Judge', *The Australian*, 12 October 2009.

Raday, Frances, 'Culture, Religion, and Gender' (2002) 4 *International Journal of Constitutional Law* 663.

Réaume, Denise G., 'Discrimination and Dignity' in Fay Faraday, Margaret Denike and M. Kate Stephenson (eds), *Making Equality Rights Real: Securing Substantive Equality under the Charter*, Irwin Law, Toronto, 2006.

Roach, Kent, 'Judicial Activism in the Supreme Court of Canada' in Brice Dickson (ed.), *Judicial Activism in Common Law Supreme Courts*, Oxford University Press, UK, 2007.

Savva, Nikki, 'Fischer seeks a more conservative court', *The Age* (Melbourne), 5 March 1997.

Sawer, Marian, 'Disappearing Tricks' (2008) 27(3) *Dialogue: Academy of the Social Sciences in Australia* 4.

Schaere, Enrique, 'Intragroup Discrimination in the Workplace: The Case for "Race Plus"' (2010) 45 *Harvard Civil Rights-Civil Liberties Law Review* 57.

Sjoberg, Gideon, Gill, Elizabeth A. and Williams, Norma, 'A Sociology of Human Rights' (2001) 48 *Social Problems* 11.

Squires, Judith, 'Intersecting Inequalities' (2009) 11 *International Feminist Journal of Politics* 496.

Stamatopoulon, Elissavet, 'Women's Rights and the United Nations' in Julie Peters and Andrea Wolper (eds), *Women's Rights, Human Rights*, Routledge, New York, 1995.

Stone, Julius, *Human Law and Human Justice*, Maitland Publications, Sydney, 1968.

Stopler, Gila, 'The Liberal Bind: The Conflict between Women's Rights and Patriarchal Religion' (2005) 31 *Social Theory and Practice* 191.

Sukert, A. B., 'Marionettes of Globalization: A Comparative Analysis of Legal Protections for Contingent Workers in the International Community' (2000) 27 *Syracuse J International Law & Com* 431.

Thornton, Margaret, *The Liberal Promise: Anti-Discrimination Legislation in Australia*, Oxford University Press, Melbourne, 1990.

Thornton, Margaret, 'Sex Discrimination, Courts and Corporate Power' (2008) 36(1) *Federal Law Review* 31.

Thornton, Margaret, 'Disabling Discrimination Legislation: The High Court and Judicial Activism' (2009) 15(1) *Australian Journal of Human Rights* 1.

Thornton, Margaret, 'Free Trade and Justice: A Discomfiting Liaison' in Kevin Walton, Helen Irving and Jacqui Mowbray (eds), *Julius Stone: A Study of Influence*, Federation Press, Sydney, (forthcoming).

Thornton, Margaret and Luker, Trish, 'The Spectral Ground: Religious Belief Discrimination' (2009) 9 *Macquarie Law Journal* 71.

Tomkins, Adam, 'Introduction: On being Sceptical about Human Rights' in Tom Campbell, K. D. Ewing and Adam Tomkins, *Sceptical Essays on Human Rights*, Oxford University Press, UK, 2001.

Tushnet, Mark, 'Sceptism About Judicial Review: A Perspective from the United States' in Tom Campbell, K. D. Ewing and Adam Tomkins, *Sceptical Essays on Human Rights*, Oxford University Press, UK, 2001.

Tushnet, Mark, The Rise of Weak-Form Judicial Review, Paper presented to ANU College of Law, The Australian National University, Canberra, May 2010.

Western, Mark, Baxter, Janeen, Pakulski, Jan, Tranter, Bruce, Western, John, van Egmond, Marcel, Chesters, Jenny, Hosking, Amanda, O'Flaherty, Martin and van Gellecum, Yolanda, 'Neoliberalism, Inequality and Politics: The Changing Face of Australia' (2007) 42(3) *Australian Journal of Social Issues* 401.

Whitty, Noel, Murphy, Thérèse and Livingstone, Stephen, *Civil Liberties Law: The* Human Rights Act *Era*, Oxford University Press, UK, 2005.

Wollstonecraft, Mary, *A Vindication of the Rights of Woman*, Second edition, Edited by Carol H. Poston, Norton, London, 1988 [1792].

Young, Katharine G., 'The Minimum Core of Economic and Social Rights: A Concept in Search of Content' (2008) 33 *Yale Journal of International Law* 113.

Young, Katharine G., 'Freedom, Want, and Economic and Social Rights: Frame and Law' (2009) 24 *Maryland Journal of International Law* 182.

Legislation

Age Discrimination Act 2004 (Cth)

Charter of Human Rights and Responsibilities Act 2006 (Vic.)

Disability Discrimination Act 1992 (Cth)

Employment Equality (Sexual Orientation) Regulations 2003 (UK)

Fair Work Act 2009 (Cth)

Human Rights Act 1998 (UK)

Human Rights Act 2004 (ACT)

Racial Discrimination Act 1975 (Cth)

Sex Discrimination Act 1984 (Cth)

Cases

An Application for Judicial Review by the Christian Institute et al. [2007] NIQB 66

Dao v Australian Postal Commission (1987) 162 CLR 317

Ghaidan v Godin-Mendoza [2004] 2 AC 557

Kracke v Mental Health Review Board [2009] VCAT 646

Lifestyle Communities Ltd (No. 3) (Anti-Discrimination) [2009] VCAT 1869

Mabo v Queensland (No. 2) (1992) 175 CLR 1

New South Wales v Amery (2006) 230 CLR 174

Ontario Human Rights Commission v Brockie [2002] 22 DLR (4th) 174

Pearce v Governing Body of Mayfield School [2001] EWCA Civ 1347

R. (Amicus & Ors) v Secretary of State [2004] EWHC 860 (Admin)

R. (on the application of Begum) v Head Teacher and Governors of Denbigh School [2006] UKHL 15

R. v Fearnside [2009] ACTCA 3

R. v Momcilovic [2010] VSCA 50

Raytheon Australia P/L & Ors and ACT Human Rights Commission [2008] ACTAAT 19

Re McBain: Ex parte Australian Catholic Bishops Conference (2002) 188 ALR 1

Wiggins v Department of Defence—Navy [2006] FMCA 800

Wik Peoples v Queensland (1996) 187 CLR 1

Reports and miscellaneous primary sources

Attorney-General Hon. Robert McClelland MP and Minister for Finance and Deregulation Hon. Lindsay Tanner MP, Reform of Anti-discrimination Legislation, Media release, 21 April 2010, Parliament House, Canberra.

Australian Law Reform Commission, *Equality Before the Law: Justice for Women*, Report No. 69, Australian Law Reform Commission, Sydney, 1994.

Commonwealth of Australia, *National Human Rights Consultation Report*, Commonwealth of Australia, Canberra, 2009 [*Brennan Report*].

European Convention on Human Rights

Scrutiny of Acts and Regulations Committee, *Exceptions and Exemptions to the Equal Opportunity Act 1995—Final Report*, Government Printer for the State of Victoria, Melbourne, 2009.

Senate Standing Committee on Legal and Constitutional Affairs, *Report on the Effectiveness of the Commonwealth Sex Discrimination Act 1984 in Eliminating Discrimination and Promoting Gender Equality*, Parliament of Australia, Canberra, 2008.

United Nations Convention on the Elimination of All Forms of Discrimination Against Women, United Nations, New York.

14. Sex, Race and Questions of Aboriginality

Irene Watson and Sharon Venne

Human rights jurisprudence would have us believe that all people are accorded the same rights: not to be discriminated against on the grounds of sex. This 'right' is, however, experienced differently by different people. This chapter considers how that difference could be measured and scaled according to how close one is located to the centre of white privilege. Similarly, questions of race and the experience of race discrimination could also be measured against one's proximity to the centre of white privilege. My inquiry here is to consider where Indigenous identity situates in terms of discrimination experiences and how we might measure Indigenous life stories of discrimination. How do these stories situate with the Sex Discrimination Act 1984 *(Cth) (SDA) and to what extent might the UN Declaration on the Rights of Indigenous Peoples create a space within which we can not only hear those stories but also effect change?*

Introduction

Indigenous women of Australia suffer from multiple disadvantages linked to race and gender.[1] Indigenous identity also brings to the mix of disadvantage the experiences of a historic and continuing colonialism. Thornton's chapter raises issues about the capacity of human rights laws and in particular the *SDA* to address the imbalance between the 'feminine and authority'; in part, Thornton argues this imbalance is a result of the law's individualised and ad-hoc complaint-based approach to anti-discrimination, which is also interdependent with the

---

1   Australian Law Reform Commission (*Equality Before the Law: Justice for Women*, Report 69, Australian Law Reform Commission, Sydney, 1994, pp. 119–20, 123–4, 126), in which high levels of violence perpetrated against Indigenous women by Indigenous males were recorded. Critique of more recent Indigenous community violence is drawn from Northern Territory intervention records and the federal government response in the *Northern Territory National Emergency Response Act 2007* (Cth). For a critical analysis of the representation of Indigenous violence, see: Irene Watson, 'Indigenous Women's Laws and Lives How Might We Keep the Law Growing?' (2007) 26 *Australian Feminist Law Journal* 95; Irene Watson, 'In the Northern Territory Intervention, What is Saved or Rescued and at What Cost?' (2009) 15(2) *Cultural Studies Review* 45; Aileen Moreton-Robinson, 'Imagining the Good Indigenous Citizen: Race War and the Pathology of Patriarchal White Sovereignty' (2009) 15(2) *Cultural Studies Review* 61.

same authority that it is authorised by. The approach of Australian human rights laws is one-dimensional and incapable of addressing the multiple identities of a complainant, in particular the diverse identities of Indigenous women.

Gender Equity and Self-Determination

The subjugation of Indigenous women within colonial states is continuing and, for this reason, as well as the ones above, the Indigenous women who attended the Fourth World Conference of Women in Beijing in 1995 produced a paper titled, 'Gender Equity vs Self-Determination',[2] in which they argued that a global strategy of the women's movement should be in terms of self-determination for women, in preference to gender equity. Self-determination is an inclusive concept, which incorporates the right of women to determine their political status and economic and social development. Gender equity, on the other hand, is a narrow concept, focused on sex-based discrimination, which is manipulated by nation-states and avoids issues of racial, environmental, civil, political and cultural inequities, and also the injustices resulting from historical and continuing colonialism. The few cases in which Indigenous women have engaged with Australian sex-discrimination complaints-based processes that do exist illustrate the gap or the exclusion of Indigenous knowledge and how that gap or exclusion works to dispossess Indigenous peoples of even the possibility of a fair hearing of race and sex discrimination complaints.[3] We might then ask: what is the point of pursuing a sex discrimination complaint by Indigenous women, particularly when the benchmark measure of equality is a white man, when the path always leads to the same one option—that is, to assimilate? The pressure for Indigenous peoples to assimilate with the dominant settler culture just goes on and on even while the possibility of another future continues to be talked up and struggled for by Indigenous women. It is the same for all women, however; they are all expected to assimilate.[4] In earlier work, Thornton identified the problem of the state being positioned as the final fixer of inequities, particularly when the complaints of inequities are directed to the 'same masculinist state that legitimated the injustices in the first place'.[5] And the state has no will to fix inequities that are the same inequities that hold

---

2   Hardcopy held by the authors.

3   Hannah McGlade, 'Reviewing Racism: HREOC and the *Racial Discrimination Act 1975* (Cth)' (1997) 4(4) *Indigenous Law Bulletin* 12; Rosemary Hunter and Alice Leonard, *The Outcomes of Conciliation in Sex Discrimination Cases*, Working Paper No. 8, Centre for Employment and Labour Relations, University of Melbourne, Vic., 1995. In their study, they identified that three complaints out of a total of 238 were made by Aboriginal people and they were all from South Australia; one of them was by a male complainant.

4   For an earlier discussion, see: Irene Watson, 'The Power of Muldarbi and the Road to its Demise' (1998) 11 *Australian Feminist Law Journal* 28; and for a more recent discussion, see: Regina Graycar and Jenny Morgan, 'Thinking about Equality' (2004) 27 *University of New South Wales Law Journal* 833, 838.

5   Margaret Thornton, 'Feminism and the Changing State' (2006) 21 *Australian Feminist Studies* 150.

its foundations together.[6] While there is an idea that 'feminism has no theory of the state',[7] Indigenous women's activism has historically centred claims in respect of our rights as peoples in international law, and challenged the settler states to decolonise.

At the Beijing conference, Indigenous women argued that the empowerment of women could be realised only within the context of self-determination, but that the struggle for 'gender equity' occurs outside the context of decolonisation, resulting in the preclusion of Indigenous women. They concluded that gender equity for Indigenous women could be achieved only within an anti-colonial and anti-imperialist framework.

In this chapter, I review initiatives taken by Indigenous women to gain a space free from the terror and the colonialist policies of the state, which would enable our survival. As it is, the historical and contemporary policies of state assimilation agendas are against us. In the late 1970s, Indigenous women and men became globally engaged in the drafting of minimum international standards intended to safeguard and ensure the survival of Indigenous peoples. That process was taken up by the United Nations in the 1980s and culminated in the Declaration on the Rights of Indigenous Peoples. The Declaration has been celebrated as setting 'an important standard for the treatment of Indigenous peoples that will undoubtedly be a significant tool towards eliminating human rights violations against the planet's 370 million Indigenous people and assisting them in combating discrimination and marginalisation'.[8]

The following is a critical review of the Declaration and an analysis of the extent to which it is likely to advance the position of Indigenous women and their communities. While the question of sex discrimination is important, the following critique considers the larger political questions that are impacting on Indigenous life across Australia and that have an equal impact on the position of Indigenous women and the possibility of their freedom from sex discrimination. We will argue that during its drafting and passage through the United Nations, the Declaration moved away from the original intent of the Indigenous drafters and now represents a shift in focus to the illusive concept: human rights of Indigenous peoples. The original intent was to re-establish the rights of peoples to be self-determining, while also initiating a process of decolonisation for those Indigenous peoples who have survived.

---

6   Ibid. 155. Thornton argues that the state is unable to fulfil its promise under sex discrimination legislation for the equality of women because the social norm is *inequality*.
7   Ibid. 153, citing Catharine MacKinnon, *Towards a Feminist Theory of the State*, Harvard University Press, Cambridge, Mass., 1989, p. 157.
8   *Frequently Asked Questions: Declaration on the Rights of Indigenous Peoples*, United Nations Permanent Forum on Indigenous Issues, <http://www.un.org/esa/socdev/unpfii/documents/FAQsIndigenousdeclaration.pdf>

The UN Declaration on the Rights of Indigenous Peoples

In its final version, the Declaration raised the following important question: does the Declaration have the capacity to deliver on its original intention, to eradicate the continuing discrimination faced by Indigenous peoples and to promote Indigenous self-determination and survival of genocide? In this chapter, I will critique the capacity of the Declaration to recognise the rights of Indigenous peoples as peoples. A UN declaration is not a legally binding instrument under international law. Its status, at the most, is inspirational and persuasive, providing a model for the development of international law in the form of future conventions. It is important to note that Australia maintained its opposition to the Declaration until April 2009, and New Zealand until April 2010, while Canada and the United States remain, at the time of writing, opposed to its adoption.

The Australian state has never explored the option of Indigenous self-determination in any truthful way. The term 'self-determination' has been appropriated by the Australian federal government in the enactment of various initiatives since the 1970s, but a quick examination of each of those acts and polices reveals their continuing colonial nature and intent.[9] It is clear that to simply gain control of state institutions is not enough to enable decolonisation and, as Taiaiake Alfred suggests, 'without a cultural grounding, self-government becomes a kind of Trojan horse for capitalism, consumerism, and selfish individualism'.[10] The simplistic project of gaining political space without Indigenous content is as meaningless as replacing the white mission managers with our own mob, while continuing mission policies. The interpretation of decolonisation as an act of populating white political space with Indigenous people as managers of that white political space is not an act of decolonisation; it is rather a turn in the colonial project that enables Indigenous management of the colonial project.

It is my argument that this is what the Declaration became, that it is not an act of decolonisation. It is instead an instrument that ensures the continuation of the colonial project and is intent on the assimilation of Indigenous peoples.

---

9   The Australian Government established the Aboriginal and Torres Strait Islander Commission (ATSIC) and promoted it as an initiative in self-determination. For a while, it did provide an element of independence, although this was more in the form of Indigenous management of the colonial state's policies than real autonomy. As a statutory body of the Australian Government, ATSIC was tied to its purse strings and was rendered ineffective due to the limited powers allowed it. Further, its role and authority were progressively restricted by the conservative Howard Government, which for more than a decade ignored numerous reports highlighting a neglect of essential services to Indigenous communities and a growing crisis across Australia. The government allowed and fomented reporting of a series of scandals involving ATSIC leadership and eventually dismantled it, citing it a failure of an Indigenous self-determination policy.

10   Gerald Taiaiake Alfred, *Peace, Power, Righteousness, An Indigenous Manifesto*, Oxford University Press, New York, 2009, p. 3.

For a real act of decolonisation to occur, we need to regain an Indigenous centre—that is, an Indigenous centre that engages in its own decolonisation and repairs the damage of the effects of colonialism—and to enable that centre to occupy the spaces of political power, rather than let it become assimilated into colonial processes of power sharing. To decolonise, the process needs to assimilate the colonisers into Indigenous processes of power sharing. It is clear that the UN declaration is light years away from undertaking that turn in power-sharing arrangements. It is also clear the Declaration will not enable Indigenous women to become more self-determining.

The Passage of the Declaration

The Declaration was adopted by the UN General Assembly in New York in September 2007. It was a shadow of the Indigenous Declaration that had been initially developed by the UN Working Group in Geneva. In the final UN General Assembly Declaration, a number of articles essential to the recognition of self-determination had been expunged. Indigenous peoples' rights to exercise their free, prior and informed consent were violated in 2007 when the United Nations voted on the passage of the Declaration. At that time, Indigenous peoples were given only three days' notice of the document coming before the General Assembly for the final vote, and it was impossible in that time for their representatives to examine it and to act to remedy any deficiencies or betrayals within it. It therefore should not be construed that Indigenous peoples had fair and constructive notice of its passage. As it happened, the UN Declaration on the Rights of Indigenous Peoples was adopted by the General Assembly. Some 143 countries voted in its favour, 11 abstained and four voted against. Australia, Canada, New Zealand and the United States were the four countries that voted against the Declaration. On 3 April 2009, however, the Australian Government changed its position and formally supported the Declaration.[11] Evidently, the Australian Government came to realise that the Declaration posed no threat or risk to the state's hegemony. The likelihood of the Declaration enabling the rights of Indigenous peoples to self-determination was nil and, by 2009, the Australian Government had become confident enough that it provided no risk to its paramountcy and continuity.[12] It was clear that the colonial project would emerge intact, indeed virtually undisturbed, with the Declaration upheld as a major initiative in the recognition of Indigenous rights.

---

11 Jenny Macklin MP, Minister for Families, Housing, Community Services and Indigenous Affairs, Statement on the United Nations Declaration on the Rights of Indigenous Peoples, 3 April 2009, Speech delivered at Parliament House, Canberra, <http://www.un.org/esa/socdev/unpfii/documents/Australia_official_statement_endorsement_UNDRIP.pdf>
12 In 2007, the newly elected Rudd Labor Government was also likely to have influenced the federal government's endorsement in 2009 of the UN Declaration on the Rights of Indigenous Peoples.

Human Rights or Rights of Peoples? A History of the Declaration

Indigenous peoples initiated the drafting of the Declaration and at the beginning the drafting process was Indigenous business. In the beginning, the process had no relationship to the UN system but this was to change in 1981 when it was taken up by the United Nations and vested with the Working Group on Indigenous Populations (WGIP) in Geneva. Notably, the drafting being taken up by the WGIP took place without the consent of Indigenous peoples. Nevertheless, the WGIP went ahead with a mandate to draft standards and also to review recent developments. The drafting of the Declaration did fulfil these two objectives and, while the WGIP sessions during the 1980s and 1990s involved Indigenous peoples, the same sessions also included state governments, including those of Canada, New Zealand, Australia and the United States. Once the drafting had become incorporated into the UN system, states began their own manipulations, principally lobbying Indigenous groups to surrender inherent rights as peoples.

In 2006, the drafting of the Declaration moved from Geneva to New York where Indigenous people working close to governments participated in its final drafting. It was at this stage that it was expunged of articles that referred to the UN Charter and rights to self-determination. The Declaration does refer to 'internal rights' to self-determination; these are rights that are determined by the various colonial states that occupy Indigenous peoples' lands. References to international standards in the Declaration are now redundant and the focus has shifted from the rights of peoples to self-determination under international law to Indigenous peoples' rights as human rights issues within their respective colonial states. Thus, Indigenous peoples are further encumbered; rather than retaining the rights of peoples as enshrined in the UN Charter, we have become objects of local human rights issues. The UN Declaration that was ratified by the General Assembly has been stripped back to a human rights instrument rather than an instrument that would provide a mechanism for advancing Indigenous peoples as peoples. The Declaration enables recognition of a range of human rights but fails to progress in any meaningful manner the Indigenous right of peoples to self-determination as recognised under the UN Charter. Until the drafting was shifted from Geneva to New York, Indigenous peoples held the line on the international-law recognition of our status as peoples. With the dismantling of the Commission on Human Rights and the Inter-Sessional Working Group, a new UN body—the Human Rights Council—decided to move the Declaration along to the UN General Assembly in New York.

When the Declaration did move to the General Assembly, there was no presentation made that described the historical process and how the Declaration had evolved. This was important; the historical context of the Indigenous struggle for self-determination was not given the context it should have been. Instead, indigenes and others who participated in this final process appear to have looked at it as simply a process of getting the Declaration through. There should have been a further critical analysis of its final content with final submissions made by Indigenous peoples as to its inadequacies or otherwise as a statement on Indigenous peoples' rights in international law. The following discussion refers to articles—part of the Geneva draft of the Declaration— which were removed from the final document, accepted and passed by General Assembly in 2007.

The Geneva Draft: Colonisation

The Geneva draft of the Declaration referred to colonialism in reference to Martinez Cobo's definition of Indigenous peoples; this had developed from Cobo's UN study on discrimination practised against the world's Indigenous peoples. In his study, Cobo had worked towards the development of a universal definition of 'Indigenous people':

> Indigenous communities, peoples and nations are those which, having a historical continuity with pre-invasion and pre-colonial societies that developed on their territories, consider themselves distinct from other sectors of the societies now prevailing in those territories, or parts of them. They form at present non-dominant sectors of society and are determined to preserve, develop and transmit to future generations their ancestral territories, and their ethnic identity, as the basis of their continued existence as peoples, in accordance with their own cultural patterns, social institutions and legal systems.[13]

Cobo discussed the process he had adopted in coming to a definition of Indigenous peoples in these terms:

(a) Indigenous peoples must be recognised according to their own perceptions and conception of themselves in relation to other groups co-existing with them in the fabric of the same society;

(b) There must be no attempt to define them according to the perception of others through the values of foreign societies or of the dominant sections in such societies;

(c) The right of Indigenous peoples to define what and who is Indigenous, and the correlative, the right to determine what and who is not, must be recognised;

---

13 Jose Martinez Cobo, *Study of the Problem of Discrimination Against Indigenous Populations. Volume 5, Conclusions, Proposals and Recommendations*, UN Doc E/CN 4/Sub 2/1986/7 Add 4, paras 379 and 381.

(d) The power of Indigenous peoples to determine who are their members must not be interfered with by the state concerned, through legislation, regulations or any other means; artificial, arbitrary or manipulatory definitions must be rejected. The special position of Indigenous peoples within the society of nation-states existing today derives from their historical rights to their lands and from their right to be different and to be considered as different.

The Cobo definition highlights that in many cases Indigenous peoples have been dispossessed by the processes of colonisation and have not been able to decolonise due to political circumstances. This definition applied to Indigenous peoples of the Americas, Canada, Australia, New Zealand and parts of the Pacific. It was very clear who was being embraced by the Declaration. There is a link between colonisation, territories, lands and resources, but these references were removed from the final UN General Assembly Declaration in 2007. Moreover, the Declaration broadens the concept of 'Indigenous' and, as a result, it is no longer clear to whom it applies. This is particularly problematic for Indigenous peoples who have not had the opportunity to deal with the key issues of colonialism and the power to develop decolonisation processes.

The New York Declaration and Individual/Collective Rights of People

The UN Declaration added reference in the preamble to individuals; previously the draft had referred to collective rights of Indigenous peoples. The following is taken from the draft:

> *Recognizing* and *reaffirming* that Indigenous *individuals* are entitled without discrimination to all human rights recognised in international law, and that Indigenous peoples possess collective rights which are indispensable for their existence, well-being and integral development as peoples. (Emphasis added)

The following is taken from the Declaration; in addition to the preamble, Article 1 was added:

> Indigenous peoples have the right to the full enjoyment, as a collective or as individuals, of all human rights and fundamental freedoms as recognised in the Charter of the United Nations, the Universal Declaration of Human Rights and international human rights law.

It is difficult to imagine how the choice between being a member of a collective or an individual within a nation-state might work. In the early days of drafting the Declaration, Indigenous peoples were not thinking about individual human rights but rather the inherent rights of peoples to their lands and the right of the group to be self-determining. The tension between individual and collective rights is manifest in the 2007 Declaration, which further provides no guidance as to how collective rights might be attained and recognised by the state. What impact does this dual position then have on the idea of a collective right of Indigenous peoples? For example, are you an individual citizen of the state or a member of an Indigenous nation, and does the individual identity position work to erode that of the collective?

Exercising in Conformity with International Law

Indigenous peoples originally began working on a declaration because the existing international legal norms did not protect them. The work was supported by the Cobo report, which reported on the high levels of discrimination Indigenous peoples experienced. Instead of referring to international legal norms and guaranteeing the same standards to Indigenous peoples, the 2007 UN Declaration ensured that legal matters were internalised and that international legal norms were absent: '*Convinced* that the recognition of the rights of Indigenous peoples in this Declaration will enhance harmonious and cooperative relations between the state and Indigenous peoples, based on principles of justice, democracy, respect for human rights, non-discrimination and good faith.'

So does the above leave anything that might compel the Australian state to desist from further breaches of Indigenous rights? Rhetoric concerning principles of justice, democracy, respect and good faith is beguiling, but unlikely to shift the genocide process in Australia or that suffered by any first nations peoples.

When Indigenous peoples initiated the Declaration's drafting, we were lobbying not for human rights but for recognition of our rights as peoples. Why would we develop a separate and distinct set of human rights standards? It is the recognition of the right to self- determination that was claimed, the logic being that if the right to self-determination was realised, so would basic human rights, including the right of women not to be discriminated against.[14] The process of recognition should have been in reference to international legal norms as expressed in the UN Charter and intended to apply to all peoples.

---

14   The Declaration concept is layered with allusions to recognition—allusions that are impossible to realise due to tensions with the state. Consider Justice Brennan in *Mabo v The State of Queensland* (1992) 175 CLR 1 30, in which he declared that any rupture within the foundation of the Australian state would disrupt founding principles of law. In *Mabo*, that rupture would have been a claim to sovereignty made by Indigenous

So what was the intent of developing a distinct standard of human rights for Indigenous peoples, particularly when Indigenous peoples live within democracies such as Australia, Canada, the United States and New Zealand, which are deemed to uphold justice and human rights? The problem is that when it comes to recognition of Indigenous peoples, the human rights track record of these states is poor, and all of them have breached international norms regarding Indigenous peoples. So how might they give recognition when the UN Declaration does not call these states to comply with international legal norms when dealing with Indigenous peoples?

Indigenous peoples lobbied for recognition as peoples and as members of the international community at the United Nations for more than three decades. The quest was for recognition of our rights as sovereign peoples, not just human rights. In an important way, human rights diminish the collective rights of Indigenous peoples because they concern individuals within the paradigm of a particular state. Just as we do not talk about the human rights of the state, we talk about the territory and the sovereignty of the state.

Human rights, applied universally, also have the capacity to negate the Indigenous world view, in which we have both obligations and rights. The individual rights angle is a Western notion and has never been a good fit for Indigenous peoples. The right of individuals is often at odds with those of the collective and the collective relationship to the lands and territories and the natural environment of each people. While also within the collective, Indigenous women hold women's laws and gendered spaces. The agents of *terra nullius* ignored this fact as they also ignored the existence of Aboriginal laws in general.

Genocide and the Declaration

Article 6 of the original Draft Declaration, read as follows:

> Indigenous peoples have the collective right to live in freedom, peace and security as distinct peoples and to full guarantees against genocide or any other act of violence including the removal of Indigenous children from their families and communities under any pretext. In addition, they have the individual rights to life, physical and mental integrity, liberty and security of person.[15]

The above clause was removed and replaced with Article 7, which again elevates the rights of the individual over the collective:

---

peoples. For further discussion on human rights and state tensions, see: Wendy Brown, 'The Most We Can Hope For: Human Rights and the Politics of Fatalism' (2004) 103(2/3) *South Atlantic Quarterly* 451; Jacques Ranciere, 'Who is the Subject of the Rights of Man?' (2004) 103(2/3) *South Atlantic Quarterly* 307.

15   UN Doc E/CN 4/Sub 2/1994/2Add 1, Draft Declaration on the Rights of Indigenous Populations.

Article 7

1.   Indigenous individuals have the right to life, physical and mental integrity, liberty and security of person.

2.   Indigenous peoples have the collective right to live in freedom, peace and security as distinct peoples and shall not be subjected to any act of genocide or any other act of violence, including forcibly removing children of the group to another group.[16]

The gutting of the original is of particular concern especially when we are reminded that the prime reason for the Declaration was to provide minimum standards that would prevent the continuing genocide of Indigenous peoples.

Self-Determination

The possibility of addressing the power differentials that exist between Indigenous peoples and states was seen to require the most significant intentions of the Draft Declaration on the Rights of Indigenous Peoples. It was Article 3 that referenced the right to self-determination: 'Indigenous peoples have the right of self-determination. By virtue of this right, they freely determine their political status and freely pursue their economic, social and cultural development.'[17]

More importantly, Article 3 was reinforced by Paragraph 14 in the preamble:

Acknowledging that the Charter of the United Nations, the International Covenant on Economic, Social and Cultural Rights and the International Covenant on Civil and Political Rights affirm the fundamental importance of the right of self-determination of all peoples, by virtue of which they freely determine their political status and freely pursue their economic, social and cultural development.

Any reference or nexus to the UN Charter so as to affirm the significance or possibility of a core or solid recognition of self-determination was, however, removed from the Declaration. As a result, the final version of the Declaration was reduced in its capacity and potential to provide for the recognition of the right to self-determination and as a result Indigenous peoples will remain captives of the colonial state, contained by its internal rights discourse or 'domestic paradigm', which Schulte-Tenckoff argues is the regime Indigenous

---

16   The Declaration on the Rights of Indigenous Peoples is available online (<http://www.iwgia.org/sw248. asp>).
17   UN Doc E/CN 4/Sub 2/1994/2Add 1.

peoples continue to live under.[18] In limiting the right to self-determination, the Declaration has no external or international law meaning and is without capacity to effectively negotiate a true Indigenous space and in particular a space for Indigenous women. Article 5 provides for a superficial recognition of self-determination—Indigenous development will be enabled within the confines of the state: 'Indigenous peoples have the right to maintain and strengthen their distinct political, legal, economic, social and cultural institutions, while retaining their right to participate fully, if they so choose, in the political, economic, social and cultural life of the State.'

Without a nexus to the UN Charter, Indigenous peoples are, however, reduced in our capacity to participate more fully within the UN system. It will continue to remain the position that whenever Indigenous ways of knowing the world collide with the agenda of the state, the state will take over and determine the outcome. For example, where Indigenous peoples are opposed to development that is in conflict with their political, legal, social and cultural values but is sanctioned by the state, there will remain no mechanism, in spite of the existence of the Declaration, which will assist in determining pathways to coexistence. Instead, the state's perspective will overtake and determine the development, or otherwise. As we know, much of the history of colonial contact with Indigenous peoples has been a long process of genocide. The Declaration will not perform against that historical and continuing trend.

The 2007 UN Declaration ensures that the principle of self-determination as it is applied to Indigenous peoples is limited and this is noted in its preamble in the following: 'Solemnly proclaims the following United Nations Declaration on the Rights of Indigenous Peoples as a standard of achievement to be pursued in a spirit of partnership and mutual respect.'

These are fine words, but the truth of respect and partnership can be realised only where the differentials of power are balanced and this will not occur while the position of Indigenous peoples is determined by the state. It will not occur while international legal norms are disabled from applying to the Declaration and this is evident in the preamble, which has no relevance to them. You cannot have partnership where an imbalance of power works against the possibility of that partnership being realised. This position will not correct itself unless international legal remedies are able to compel states to comply. The state remains the final determiner of all things within the life of the state, including the lives of Indigenous peoples. This has been the way since the advent of colonisation and nothing in this Declaration is likely to shift power imbalances that exist and that continue to determine the future of Indigenous peoples.

---

18   Isabelle Schulte-Tenckhoff, 'Re-assessing the Paradigm of Domestication: The Problematic of Indigenous Treaties' (1998) 4 *Review of Constitutional Studies* 239.

Article 9 of the Declaration is rendered ineffective in a similar way: 'Indigenous peoples and individuals have the right to belong to an Indigenous community or nation, in accordance with the traditions and customs of the community or nation concerned. No discrimination of any kind may arise from the exercise of such a right.'

Again, the above clause stands able to be interpreted by nation-states that the right to perform as communities or nations as might be determined or permitted by them. Therefore core concepts of Indigenous obligations to care for country will be determined by the state. The same will go for the keeping of Indigenous women's laws. It is also clear that the state will not permit the return of Indigenous lands or prevent their development where any developments are in conflict with state agenda.

Throughout the Declaration, changes have occurred and reduced the capacity of Indigenous peoples to determine our futures. For example, Articles 12, 13, 14 and 15 of the Draft Declaration have been changed and now pose a limit to the possibility for the development and continuing sustainability of Indigenous cultures. The UN Declaration focuses on the present and has no commitment to revitalising past practices or to providing for the restitution of a stolen past. Without such recognition, Indigenous peoples engaged in rebuilding their communities stand without a remedy or assistance to regenerate their communities.

The Territorial Integrity of States is what Matters

In addition to the many alterations made to the draft, the UN Declaration added Article 46, which reads:

1. Nothing in this Declaration may be interpreted as implying for any State, people, group or person any right to engage in any activity or to perform any act contrary to the Charter of the United Nations or construed as authorizing or encouraging any action which would *dismember or impair, totally or in part, the territorial integrity or political unity of sovereign and independent States* [emphasis added].

2. In the exercise of the rights enunciated in the present Declaration, human rights and fundamental freedoms of all shall be respected. The exercise of the rights set forth in this Declaration shall be subject only to such limitations as are determined by law, and in accordance with international human rights obligations. Any such limitations shall be non-discriminatory and strictly necessary solely for the purpose of

securing due recognition and respect for the rights and freedoms of others and for meeting the just and most compelling requirements of a democratic society.

3.   The provisions set forth in this Declaration shall be interpreted in accordance with the principles of justice, democracy, respect for human rights, equality, non-discrimination, good governance and good faith.

The fears that the Australian and other governments had of the Declaration—that it might threaten their hegemony—were without foundation. Article 46 makes clear that continuing subjugation could continue while also rendering it impossible that Indigenous peoples would be able to develop and articulate a decolonised Indigenous space.

The Draft Declaration, created by Indigenous representatives, ended with Article 45: 'Nothing in this Declaration may be interpreted as implying for any State or group or person any right to engage in any act or activity or to perform any act contrary to the Charter of the United Nations.'

This draft provided the nexus to the Charter of the United Nations and the intention was that it be interpreted in accord with the legal norms of international law. At last, however, Article 45 reads: 'Nothing in this Declaration may be constituted as diminishing or extinguishing the rights…Indigenous peoples have or may now acquire in the future.'

Again, we have been cut away from international legal standards and as Indigenous peoples deemed to sit outside (or perhaps inside) international law, wherever the states determine our existence or otherwise. As a result of the limitations the UN Declaration places on the position of Indigenous peoples, our rights in international law have in fact been diminished rather than affirmed. The link to the UN Charter was critical to the survival of Indigenous peoples up against the genocidal practices of states and without that link the Indigenous future remains a question as unresolved as it was when Indigenous peoples negotiated their entry to the United Nations in the early 1970s. The Charter is supposed to uphold peoples' rights. It was important to link the Declaration on Indigenous Peoples back to the Charter, because of the reference to nations and peoples. The Charter does not say anything about states having rights to self-determination. It refers to peoples and nations, and that is why the original Indigenous draft Declaration was linked to the Charter. The Indigenous people who were involved in the final ratification of the UN Declaration were not the same and did not have the same historical background as those who had begun the process three decades earlier; they also had limited knowledge of international law. Knowledge of international law was critical to the process ensuring Indigenous peoples were favourably treated. As a result, we have ended up with a UN Declaration that is largely rhetorical and full of hollow statements without power to provide a remedy, and with a document that is far less significant to Indigenous peoples than the draft Indigenous declaration we began with. The ratified UN Declaration does still promise some advantages. In the following, I briefly analyse some of its possibilities, remaining clear, however, that the disadvantages outweigh any perceived advantages.

Advantages

It is possible that the UN Declaration will be used as an international standard to negotiate domestic reform and frameworks for engagement with Indigenous peoples. There is, however, no mechanism to enforce any of those reform measures or frameworks for engagement. The Declaration resides purely in the realm of the goodwill of the state and the more powerful economic interests that limit or conflict with Indigenous peoples' interests. A further advantage could be that the Declaration is used as a tool by the judiciary to assist in the interpretation of the terms used under human rights legislation.

Disadvantages

The biggest problem with the Declaration is that it is not clear to whom it applies. The definition developed by Cobo clearly applied to Indigenous peoples living in colonial states and territories, included Indigenous resources controlled by the colonial state and also applied to Indigenous peoples who did not have the opportunity to be listed and considered by the UN decolonisation committee. This definition applied to Indigenous peoples of Australia, Canada, the Americas, parts of the Pacific and New Zealand. The ratified UN Declaration is broad in its definition of Indigenous peoples and as a result it is unlikely to assist Indigenous peoples who were included in the Cobo definition of Indigenous peoples.

Indigenous peoples sought out UN fora in the 1970s to secure land rights and self-determination, and Indigenous women supported this process as a means of attaining self-determination so as to position the rights of women. This aim remains unfinished business between states and Indigenous peoples and is now further limited and marginalised by the UN Declaration. There are currently no effective UN mechanisms to promote Indigenous peoples' concerns. The UN Indigenous structures that do exist include the Indigenous Permanent Forum and the Indigenous Expert Mechanism; however, both these fora are controlled by the states; the state governments make decisions about what these mechanisms can or cannot do in the setting of agenda. The Permanent Forum, for example, hears presentations from Indigenous peoples, the body then reports on those sessions and those reports are sent off to the Economic and Social Council (ECOSOC). The Permanent Forum is one of a number of bodies that feeds into the ECOSOC agenda. Documents that might be forwarded and reviewed will not, however, be progressed through the UN system, as there are no mechanisms to further advance them. The Permanent Forum cannot draft standards or hear complaints.

The standard-setting and complaints procedures that existed while the UN Working Group on Indigenous Populations was at work in Geneva no longer exist and, as a result, the studies that were developed by the WGIP, such as the Study on Treaties and other Constructive Arrangements between States and Indigenous Populations,[19] remain in a state of limbo, shelved and gathering dust. Without mechanisms that could bring those studies before UN bodies, they are likely to disappear within the UN system. Indigenous peoples now have nowhere to present general complaints and report recent developments occurring on our territories. Under the now disbanded WGIP, Indigenous peoples were able to participate in the forum and to provide information about recent developments. If there was a major event occurring then that information could be moved up through the system, to the sub-commission and then to the Human Rights Commission. The event could also engage the Human Rights Centre and the possibility for the involvement of the High Commissioner for Human Rights. With the advent of the Declaration, the recently created UN Indigenous Expert Mechanism agenda is set by the states. For example, the agenda set for 2008 proposed to meet for three days and discuss Indigenous education. In 2009, the agenda set by the states proposed discussions on housing issues. This forum commits each calendar year as a particular 'policy year' (where a 'special theme' is discussed) and each odd calendar year as a 'review year' (where the implementation of the forum's past recommendations on specific themes is reviewed).[20]

Since the disbanding of the WGIP there are no UN fora or mechanisms by which Indigenous peoples can raise general complaints affecting them; instead, the Indigenous Expert Mechanism reports to the Human Rights Council, and this is considered within the context of all other priorities that come before the Human Rights Council. In the past those priorities have prompted focus on Palestine, Darfur and Afghanistan. It is clear within this context that a report on the lack of education of Indigenous peoples would not be considered a priority.

---

19   Miguel Alfonso Martínez, *Human Rights of Indigenous Peoples: Study on Treaties and other Constructive Arrangements between States and Indigenous Populations*, Commission on Human Rights, Sub-Commission on Prevention of Discrimination and Protection of Minorities, Fifty-First Session, Item 7 of provisional agenda, E/CN.4/Sub.2/1999/20 22 June 1999, United Nations, New York, <http://www.unhchr.ch/huridocda/huridoca.nsf/0/696c51cf6f20b8bc802567c4003793ec?opendocument>

20   International Service for Human Rights, *Permanent Forum on Indigenous Issues: 7th Session*, Human Rights Monitor Series, International Service for Human Rights, <http://olddoc.ishr.ch/hrm/nymonitor/new_york_updates/permanent_forum/nyu_perm_forum_7session_a_fresh_approach.pdf>

The Human Rights Centre provided support for Indigenous peoples in the past, but this is no longer available, and the Indigenous experts who have been appointed are not engaged full-time. The Indigenous Rapporteur is a UN position, but it is a voluntary and unpaid appointment. Therefore the capacity of Indigenous people to act internationally has been substantially reduced as the resources are limited and those used in the past to bring the Declaration into existence no longer exist.

In the past, UN studies would be recommended by the working group and passed on to the sub-commission, or a body of UN experts would approve or otherwise and make their recommendation to the Human Rights Commission. The commission would make a resolution, which, when passed, would have attached to that resolution its financial implications. Funding would be sourced for the study by the secretariat from the Human Rights Centre, which would also provide a warm-body technical support person to assist it. This process ensured that there was institutional support for any studies that were proposed. The Indigenous Expert Mechanism is, however, not part of the new Human Rights Council Advisory Body of Experts, and as they have no relationship to the secretariat, they cannot initiate studies.

At a time when Indigenous peoples have more reason than ever to appeal to the United Nations, the means to argue the importance of our issues are reduced. We have to compete with the large number of issues that comes before the Human Rights Council; we are prioritised. This brings into question the future of both the UN Indigenous Permanent Forum and the Indigenous Expert Mechanism and what they might be able to achieve within the current shifts and the illusionary space the passage of the Declaration has created. Having taken control of the drafting process in its final stages, the state governments crafted the Indigenous Permanent Forum and the Indigenous Expert Mechanism to ensure they are now unable to effectively draft standards and report on and advance complaints that reflect on the current position of Indigenous peoples across the globe. For example, in 2008, a number of Indigenous peoples attending the Expert Mechanism Forum came to speak on recent developments in their territories; one group reported on the massacre of a number of Indigenous people in South America. A widow who came to speak was shut down by the chairperson and advised that unless she was able to speak to the agenda item (at the time it was education) then she could not speak.

The shifts that took place and the current UN responses to Indigenous peoples no longer enable a space for the complaints of Indigenous peoples, which address issues of survival and genocide, to be heard. It is clear today, after more than three decades of Indigenous work within the UN system to develop humane standards for the states and the international community to engage and create coexistence, that we are no more advanced than when the process first began. It is clear that we must return to the main body of the United Nations, as we are finding the UN Indigenous Mechanisms are disabled from hearing our issues. The issue of colonialism has not been addressed and we must continue to argue that the colonial processes remain alive and continue to threaten the survival of Indigenous peoples. We need to ensure that the states of Australia, Canada, New Zealand, the United States and those of South and Central America are not let off the hook for their continuing role as colonialist states, and we must continue to argue the possibilities of decolonisation. For those Indigenous peoples whose lands and lives are controlled by those states, we remain without any effective mechanism to deal with the many issues of our survival and futures.

What is There for Us to Do?

There is a need to return to the main game inside the UN fora; we have to go back to those spaces, out of the side alleys and UN ghetto spaces that we have been herded into. We are peoples and we belong in the main game—that is, to humanise the world and its treatment of all peoples.

In reclaiming our spaces within the main game, we also note that for Indigenous peoples colonialism remains the main object. The colonial states continue to offer assimilation as the only solution. The promise of strong international human rights standards and the Australian Government's acceptance of the Declaration are unlikely to shift the position of Indigenous people here. The assimilation agenda of colonial states continues the reductionist approach to Indigenous rights, the states seizing and setting policies for Indigenous survival and development.

We need to hold the line and our right to conceptualise the Indigenous position. Why should we hand over our right to name who we are to the states—at either a domestic or the international level? The work continues and, as Indigenous people, we have an obligation not to trade off our inherent rights in the form of any agreement, compact or partnership that falls short of recognition in accord with the norms of international law, and our right to determine the future of our lands and lives.

Conclusion

The Australian Government's acceptance of the Declaration is unlikely to shift the continuing regression of Indigenous policy and the position of Aboriginal women in Australia. The assimilation agenda of Australia, which we are witnessing in the Northern Territory intervention, continues as ever, since 1788. We live in a moment when Indigenous law and self-determination as forms of social control are referred to by Peter Sutton as follows:

> The ancient social order, while resting on a mixture of internal and external constraints like any other, depended very highly on external mechanisms of control. This meant fear of consequences more than anything else, including fear of ostracism, exclusion, and humanly imposed physical or supernatural harm or death. In this sense the authoritarian and patriarchal regimes of most of the early Christian missions were, bizarre as this might sound, 'culturally appropriate' in a way that the liberalised and more chaotic regimes of recent times have not been. This is not, of course, to suggest that this particular clock can or should be turned back.[21]

Sutton's suggestion is not that we turn the clock back, but he nevertheless refers to the successes of a patriarchal regime that he saw as having the capacity to pull everyone into gear. This is the Northern Territory intervention model: the state has asserted its power to intervene and elevate its policies of assimilation, with the corollary of the eventual erasure of Indigenous peoples in Australia. We might encourage white women to ask the Angela Davis question: who might the state come for next?

The question of where Indigenous peoples sit in the context of sex discrimination is an important one, but in the light of recent developments and the evident policy shift back to assimilation, those questions need to be measured against the larger political questions that are impacting on Indigenous life across Australia.

Bibliography

Books and articles

Australian Law Reform Commission, *Equality Before the Law: Justice for Women*, Report No. 69, Australian Law Reform Commission, Sydney, 1994.

Brown, Wendy, 'The Most We Can Hope For: Human Rights and the Politics of Fatalism' (2004) 103(2/3) *South Atlantic Quarterly* 451.

Cobo, Jose Martinez, *Study of the Problem of Discrimination Against Indigenous Populations. Volume 5, Conclusions, Proposals and Recommendations*, UN Doc E/CN 4/Sub 2/1986/7 Add 4, United Nations, New York, 1986.

---

21 Peter Sutton, *The Politics of Suffering, Indigenous Australia and the End of the Liberal Consensus*, Melbourne University Press, Carlton, 2009, p. 109.

Graycar, Regina and Morgan, Jenny, 'Thinking About Equality' (2004) 27 *University of New South Wales Law Journal* 833.

Hunter, Rosemary and Leonard, Alice, *The Outcomes of Conciliation in Sex Discrimination Cases*, Working Paper No. 8, Centre for Employment and Labour Relations, University of Melbourne, Vic., 1995.

McGlade, Hannah, 'Reviewing Racism: HREOC and the *Racial Discrimination Act 1975* (Cth)' (1997) 4(4) *Indigenous Law Bulletin* 12.

Macklin, Jenny, Statement on the United Nations Declaration on the Rights of Indigenous Peoples by the Minister for Families, Housing, Community Services and Indigenous Affairs, 3 April 2009, Speech delivered at Parliament House, Canberra, <http://www.un.org/esa/socdev/unpfii/documents/Australia_official_statement_endorsement_UNDRIP.pdf>

Moreton-Robinson, Aileen, 'Imagining the Good Indigenous Citizen: Race War and the Pathology of Patriarchal White Sovereignty' (2009) 15(2) *Cultural Studies Review* 61.

Ranciere, Jacques, 'Who is the Subject of the Rights of Man?' (2004) 103(2/3) *South Atlantic Quarterly* 307.

Schulte-Tenckhoff, Isabelle, 'Re-assessing the Paradigm of Domestication: The Problematic of Indigenous Treaties' (1998) 4 *Review of Constitutional Studies*, 239.

Sutton, Peter, *The Politics of Suffering, Indigenous Australia and the End of the Liberal Consensus*, Melbourne University Press, Carlton, 2009.

Taiaiake Alfred, Gerald, *Peace, Power, Righteousness, An Indigenous Manifesto*, Oxford University Press, New York, 2009.

Thornton, Margaret, 'Feminism and the Changing State' (2006) 21 *Australian Feminist Studies* 150.

Watson, Irene, 'The Power of Muldarbi and the Road to its Demise' (1998) 11 *Australian Feminist Law Journal* 28.

Watson, Irene, 'Indigenous Women's Laws and Lives: How Might we Keep the Law Growing?' (2007) 26 *Australian Feminist Law Journal* 95.

Watson, Irene, 'In the Northern Territory Intervention, What is Saved or Rescued and at What Cost?' (2009) 15(2) *Cultural Studies Review* 45.

Case

Mabo v The State of Queensland (1992) 175 CLR 1

Reports and miscellaneous primary sources

Draft Declaration on the Rights of Indigenous Populations, UN Doc E/CN 4/Sub 2/1994/2Add 1, United Nations, New York.

International Service for Human Rights, *Permanent Forum on Indigenous Issues: 7th Session*, Human Rights Monitor Series, International Service for Human Rights, <http://olddoc.ishr.ch/hrm/nymonitor/new_york_updates/permanent_forum/nyu_perm_forum_7session_a_fresh_approach.pdf>

Martínez, Miguel Alfonso, *Human Rights of Indigenous Peoples: Study on Treaties and other Constructive Arrangements between States and Indigenous Populations*, June 1999, Commission on Human Rights, Sub-Commission on Prevention of Discrimination and Protection of Minorities, Fifty-First Session, Item 7 of provisional agenda, UN Doc E/CN.4/Sub.2/1999/20 22, United Nations, New York, <http://www.unhchr.ch/huridocda/huridoca.nsf/0/696c51cf6f20b8bc802567c4003793ec?opendocument>

United Nations Declaration on the Rights of Indigenous Peoples

United Nations, *Frequently Asked Questions: Declaration on the Rights of Indigenous Peoples*, United Nations Permanent Forum on Indigenous Issues, United Nations, New York, <http://www.un.org/esa/socdev/unpfii/documents/FAQsIndigenousdeclaration.pdf>

Acronyms and abbreviations

AAA	*Affirmative Action (Equal Opportunity for Women) Act 1986* (Cth)
AC	Companion of the Order of Australia
ACT	Australian Capital Territory
ADVO	Apprehended Domestic Violence Order
AHRC	Australian Human Rights Commission
AIAL	Australian Institute of Administrative Law
AIRC	Australian Industrial Relations Commission
AIRCFB	Australian Industrial Relations Commission Full Bench
ALR	Australian Law Reports
ALRC	Australian Law Reform Commission
ALP	Australian Labor Party
AO	Officer of the Order of Australia
AM	Member of the Order of Australia
CAT	Convention Against Torture
CEDAW	Convention on the Elimination of All Forms of Discrimination Against Women
CERD	Convention on the Elimination of All Forms of Racial Discrimination
COAG	Council of Australian Governments
CSW	Commission for Status of Women
Cth	Commonwealth
CLR	Commonwealth Law Reports
DDA	*Disability Discrimination Act*
EA	*Equality Act*
EC	European Commission

ECOSOC	Economic and Social Council (United Nations)
EOC	Equal Opportunity Cases
EEO	equal employment opportunity
EOWWA	*Equal Opportunity for Women in the Workplace Act 1999* (Cth)
ERA	*Equal Rights Amendment* (US)
ERA	Excellence in Research for Australia
EU	European Union
EWCA	England and Wales Court of Appeal
EWHC	High Court of England and Wales
FaHCSIA	Department of Families, Housing, Community Services and Indigenous Affairs
FCA	Federal Court of Australia
FCR	Federal Court Reports
FOI	freedom of information
FLAG	Feminist Legal Action Group
FMCA	Federal Magistrate's Court of Australia
GAOR	General Assembly Official Records (United Nations)
GOQ	genuine occupational qualification
HCA	High Court of Australia
HRA	*Human Rights Act*
HRC	Human Rights Commission
HREOC	Human Rights and Equal Opportunity Commission
HREOCA	*Human Rights and Equal Opportunity Commission Act*
HRM	human resource management
ICCPR	International Covenant on Civil and Political Rights
ICESCR	International Covenant on Economic, Social and Cultural Rights
ILM	International Legal Materials

ILO	International Labour Organisation
IWRAW	International Women's Rights Action Watch
LEAF	Legal Education and Action Fund (Canada)
LP	Liberal Party
MIT	Massachusetts Institute of Technology
MBD	maternity-based discrimination
MP	Member of Parliament
NGO	non-governmental organisation
NHRC	National Human Rights Consultation
NP	National Party
NSP	Needle and Syringe Program
NSW	New South Wales
NSWADTAP	New South Wales Administrative Decisions Tribunal Appeal Panel
NSWLRC	New South Wales Law Reform Commission
NT	Northern Territory
OECD	Organisation for Economic Cooperation and Development
OfW	Office for Women (Australia)
OHCHR	Office of the High Commissioner for Human Rights
OPC	Office of Parliamentary Counsel
OSCE	Organisation for Security and Cooperation in Europe
PAG	Prisoners' Action Group
PBD	pregnancy-based discrimination
QC	Queen's Counsel
RDA	*Racial Discrimination Act*
RLC	Redfern Legal Centre
RSBC	Revised Statutes of British Columbia (Canada)

SC	Senior Counsel
SCC	Supreme Court of Canada
SCR	Supreme Court Reports (Canada)
SDA	*Sex Discrimination Act*
SER	standard employment relationship
UD	Universal Declaration (of Human Rights)
UN	United Nations
UNAIDS	Joint United Nations Programme on HIV/AIDS
UNDP	United Nations Development Programme
UNSW	University of New South Wales
WA	Western Australia
WAC	Women's Advisory Council
WBB	Women Behind Bars
WCU	Women's Coordination Unit
WEL	Women's Electoral Lobby
WGIP	Working Group on Indigenous Populations (United Nations)
WHO	World Health Organisation
WLM	women's liberation movement
WRA	*Workplace Relations Act 1996* (Cth)
WWWW	Women Who Want to be Women
YWCA	Young Women's Christian Association

Index

www.ingramcontent.com/pod-product-compliance
Lightning Source LLC
Chambersburg PA
CBHW061237270326
41928CB00033B/3350